RUTH MANTHEI WILKEY

Ted & Ernie's EXCELLENT ADVENTURES

UNABRIDGED FAMILY EDITION

Copyright © Ruth Manthei Wilkey
All rights reserved.

Published 2023, Sonflower Press, LLC
ISBN 978-1-7338043-4-9

Book cover by TeaBerry Creative

CONTENTS

PART ONE: Our German Roots (1800-1904) 1

Chapter 1   1900s: Coming to America 9

PART TWO: Our Excellent Adventures 14

Chapter 2   1900s: Entering the World 15

Chapter 3   1910s: Growing Up in the Olden Days 23

Chapter 4   1920s: Finding Our Way in the World 53

Chapter 5   1930s: Farming Our Own Land 77

Chapter 6   1940s: From Agriculture to Industry 101

Chapter 7   1950s: Growing Families and Enterprises 169

Chapter 8   1960s: Land, Logging, and Loss 205

Chapter 9   1970s: Retirement Projects 219

Chapter 10   1980s: The Last Days 235

Chapter 11   1990s: Ted's Journey Home to Heaven 275

PART THREE: Legacy of Our Ladies 279

PART FOUR: Our Families Remember 313

Ted's Family Remembers 315

Ernie's Family Remembers 345

PART FIVE: Four Lives Well Lived 359

APPENDIX: Timelines and Family Trees 370

Dedication

Dedicated to the great men and women who lived these stories!

- ∂ Ernie's stories were recorded in 1984 and 1985.
- ∂ Ted's stories were recorded in 1986 and 1987.
- ∂ Christel and Darwin added details in 1990.
- ∂ Reflections by Ernie's children were written in 1997.
- ∂ Cora's stories were recorded in 2018.
- ∂ Mary's stories were compiled from documents and a journal.
- ∂ Photos and archives were collected by Cora and Mary over a lifetime.
- ∂ Photos and archives were lovingly scanned by Judy and Pam with Ruth in 2022.
- ∂ Stories were added by Dan, Garrett and John's girls in 2022.
- ∂ Maps were created by Behling-cousin Carol Johnson.
- ∂ Newspapers came from *Front Page, Los Angeles Times over 100 Years*.
- ∂ Financial contributions came from numerous members of Gen 2 and Gen 3.
- ∂ This book was created by Ruth in 2023.

You are holding a legacy of love… Enjoy!

Preface

Dear loved ones, September 7, 2022

"Give me just one generation of youth, and I'll transform the whole world."
Vladimir Ilyich Lenin

The moment I heard that quote, I thought, *if you can separate one generation from their heritage, you can influence them in any way you wish!* I purposed in my heart to become a strong link in our family chain, connecting future generations with those in the past who gave us life. They provided a firm foundation upon which we can stand through the storms of life. We're reaching back with one hand to grasp onto our heritage, while reaching forward with the other hand to pass it on to you. May you not become "influenced" by the culture around you but hold fast to the faith of your fathers. May you become a strong link in your own family chain—grasping onto God with one hand and passing Him on to your children with the other. May you build up a legacy of God-stories to share with those in your life!

I used to sing a song based on Psalm 112 when I was a child. I can't even remember who wrote the song, but the lyrics sum up the amazing adventures of Ted and Ernie perfectly:

> Happy is the man of God who delights in His commands.
> His children will be happy too, and mighty in the land.
> For he who lends or gives away, the future will be bright,
> For even in darkness the light dawns for the gracious and the upright.

Ted and Ernie delighted in God's commands, endeavoring to "teach them to your children when you rise up and when you sit down and when you walk with them by the way." They were givers. They married wise godly women. I thank God for being raised in such a home.

> Lord, You caused me to trust while upon my mother's breast.
> From birth I was cast upon You;
> From my mother's womb You have been my God (Psalm 22:9-10).

O Lord, You have been good, You have been faithful through all generations! How wonderful to be born into a family where we were baptized and nurtured in God's loving ways. To contemporize 2 Timothy 1:5, "I am persuaded that the faith which first lived in our great-grandmother Christiana and in our grandmother Constance and in our fathers, Ted and Ernie, now also lives in us." I echo the words of Grandma Constance on her deathbed: "When we have our ultimate family reunion in heaven, may "no one be missing, no not one!"

With love and joy,
Ruth

Disclaimer

As I (Ruth) interviewed family members over the years from different generations, I discovered a fascinating truth. Each individual has his own perspective, and those perspectives may not match! Initially, I felt challenged to find the unifying thread that bound them all together. In the end, I decided to let each one tell their own story in their own voice. From time to time, I'll insert some supplemental details for clarity.

Memories are so personal. We tend to remember the things that impact us deeply and forget the things that don't… or that impacted someone else. Two people traveling in the same car may remember totally different parts of the journey. A lighthearted fun-loving person may remember the funny stories, while a serious sensitive soul may remember the hurts and hardships. A cute little girl with curls may remember her father's adoring eyes, while her opinionated brother may remember the spankings he received for talking back. An angry outburst may be forgotten immediately by the aggressor, while the other person may feel injured for years by those hateful words and actions. Knowing about different personality types and how they handle stress can also empower us to understand why a person might get angry or "excited" when facing a challenging situation.

Keeping this in mind, these stories are told through the eyes of very different individuals. That's what makes them so interesting, and sometimes controversial!

Language is a living thing. Spellings changed through time, circumstance, and documents. Here are pertinent family examples:
- Roots within the German Empire are now in Poland
- Schlesien became Silesia
- Manthey became Manthei
- Constanza became Constantia and then Constance
- Emelie became Amelia

Just before sending this to print, I listened to a podcast entitled, "Glory and Horror in the Church: Living in the Mix." This book provides plenty of examples of the glory and horror of living in the mix. Ted and Ernie were not perfect, but they received the baton of faith and passed it on. They believed in God and loved Him and lived for Him. Now they are living *with* Him. I believe nothing would bring them more joy than to see us follow in their footsteps! This is their life…their destiny…their legacy!

Foreword

A Letter from Cora   Christmas, 1997

To my dear Children and Grandchildren,

This includes all of you who were born, adopted, joined, or grafted into our family through marriage. The book you are holding is a labor of love, put together by Ruthie and me, to remind us of the Christian heritage passed down to our family by the faithfulness of God through the last six generations.

What started out as a simple transcription of Father's taped stories, as told to Ruth, has grown to include many more interesting pieces of our history, as we sorted through the memorabilia which I had collected over forty-nine years. We thought all of you would enjoy this history of events in pictures, stories, letters, newspaper, and magazine articles.

But the **real** purpose of this book is to encourage each of you to follow the example of your father Ernie; to do justly and to love mercy and to walk humbly with your God. We are not to become pride-filled over our exceptional Christian heritage, but to be thankful always to our God who has created, redeemed, and sanctified us as a peculiar people, to carry out His work here on earth while we are living.

And to my many precious grandchildren: Remember, God has no Grandchildren. You are either His own child, or you are outside of His Kingdom. It was your grandfather's prayer, and it is mine also, that each of you receive Jesus as your personal Savior, that we all be together in heaven, and that none of you is missing—no, not one! You have a precious legacy to treasure as you look back over the years and remember Grandpa Ernie. He is your link to the past generations and your launch into future ones.

All of you grandchildren have good parents who are rooted and grounded in the true Christian faith, and I admonish you to take to heart the advice, counsel, and wisdom of those who have lived many years longer than you. They have learned many lessons from experience and wish to protect you from the evil influences of this world and the heartache that comes from making wrong choices. I pray for you daily, that you will not forget your Christ-centered heritage and that you will be good witnesses in all you say and do to those around you. Keep the faith!

Our God will not abandon those who are faithful to Him and who strive to do His will. He promises us each a crown of life in **heaven**—our ultimate goal.

"God's Word" tells us in I Peter 1: 4-5: "We have been born into a new life which has an inheritance that can't be destroyed or corrupted and can't fade away. That inheritance is kept in heaven for you, since you are guarded by God's power through faith for a salvation that is ready to be revealed at the end of time."

And now may the Lord bless you and keep you. May He make His face to shine upon you and be gracious unto you. May the Lord lift up His countenance upon you and give you His peace.

Your loving Mom, Grandma, Aunt and Friend

The German Empire—Now Poland

PART ONE

*For we know that God is able to work all things together for good
to those who love Him and are called
according to His purpose.
Romans 8:28*

Our German Roots in the German Empire
(1800-1904)

1878	April 17	Ferdinand Manthei is born	(Oblatzkowo, Posen)
1884	May 21	Constance Menzel is born	(Oblatzkowo, Posen)
1890	Jul 14	Mama Christiana Menzel dies	(Oblatzkowo, Posen)
1892		Oswald remarries and moves	(Wotostwo, Posen)
1893	Dec	Fred Menzel comes to America	(Petersburg, MI)
1895	Feb	Ferdinand comes to America	(Palatine, IL)
1898		Oswald returns to homeland	(Frieburg, Schlesien)
1899	Apr 17	Ferdinand is granted Naturalization	(Joliet, IL)

Ferdinand Manthei

Great-grandfather Manthey was a tall German man with a nice-sized farm. Sadly, he took up drinking and met a petite Polish girl who liked to "kick up her heels on the dance floor." They married and spent most of their time in the "Biergarten" (outdoor pub or beer garden), where they reportedly "drank away the estate" and became dirt poor. Sadly, we don't even know their full names. That upbringing was probably why Ferdinand never let his children go near a beer garden or a dance floor.

When their daughter, Emelie, was born, they laid their baby on the cold ground while they worked in the field. An infection settled into her ears resulting in deafness. In those days, they had no schools for the deaf, so she never learned to speak. Thus, Emelie grew up as a deaf-mute. She learned to work at an early age, gathering brush in the woods for winter fuel. She also gleaned the wheat left behind by the harvesters and, in the evening, she rubbed it in her hands to make flour for her destitute family. When she came of age in her teens, she was "forced" by a Jewish man who sent her home pregnant. The Jewish man sent Emelie's parents two hundred thaler (Prussian currency) to use in raising the child. She was an unwed mother, and her parents were furious with her for shaming them.

> **In today's world, Emelie could have chosen to end the pregnancy with a quick trip to the clinic, and this amazing story would have ended here! This book would not exist. The Manthei family would not exist, nor the businesses that have provided employment to thousands over the past 140 years. Not until heaven will we know how many lives have been touched or blessed because Ferdinand lived.**

Ferdinand was born in 1876 and had a rough childhood. He was the illegitimate son of a single mom who was a deaf-mute. His grandparents were alcoholic and harsh. We can only imagine the abuse he suffered.

As a neglected toddler, he was found wandering in the village of Oblaczcowo by a boy named Fritz Menzel, who brought him home. When Frau Menzel found worms in his diapers, she tracked down his mother, Emelie, and hired her as a milk maid to help with chores. The Menzels provided the first example of one family lifting up another.

The villagers gave Ferdinand a hard time and called him nasty names because he had no father. He was so happy when he learned the Lord's Prayer in the Evangelical School… *Our Father who art in Heaven.* The next time the kids harassed him, he said, "I do have a father. My Father is in heaven!"

In 1897, Ferdinand came to America with Walter Menzel at age seventeen. He changed the spelling of his name from **_Manthey_** to **_Manthei_**. He wanted to leave his past behind. He was a very imperfect man struggling under a shadow of shame.

That's why keeping a good name was so important in our family. This book reveals how any name can become a great redemption story. Even Manthei!

Ferdinand's first job was with a Prussian farmer in Arenzeville, IL. He moved to Chicago to help build the Cortland Street Bridge with the American Bridge Company. That's when Constance Menzel joined his story.

> **Any name can become a great Redemption Story.**

Constance Menzel Manthei

Quite the opposite of Ferdinand, Constance (aka Constanza, Constantia) was born on May 21, 1884 into an idyllic home in Oblatzkowo, Provinz Posen. They never lacked for food, love, or laughter. She found joy and beauty everywhere she looked.

Her grandparents, Carl and Susanna Püschel, were grossgutzbezitzers (respected landowners) in Dittersbach, Provinz Schlesien (aka Silesia). Her relatives included a ship designer, a border inspector, a doctor, two engineers and successful farmers. The youngest of many Püschel children, Constance's mother, Christiana, grew up in this Evangelical-Lutheran family of intelligent and ambitious people. Christiana was devout in her love for the Lord and her family. From this root sprang a legacy of hard work, love of family, and devotion to God.

> **From this root sprang a legacy of hard work, love of family and devotion to God.**

Christiana Püschel married Oswald Menzel, who had been a cook in the German army under Bismark during the war that unified the German Empire. Oswald, who had been an altar boy in the Catholic church, became an Evangelical to win Christiana's hand in marriage. They settled on a farm in Oblacscowo, Prussia, where Oswald was the master blacksmith. Oswald Menzel taught his three sons his trade and infused his family with a fun-loving creative spirit. He built arched entry gates and gazebos and beautiful wooden headboards for his two precious girls. Christiana taught them hospitality, hymns, and prayers. Sadly, Christiana died in childbirth when Constance was just six years old.

That's when Constance began to learn the meaning of hardship. Oswald remarried to "give the little girls a mother." They moved to Wotostwo, and for the next ten years, Constance suffered terribly under the hands of a hateful stepmother. The hymns and prayers of her mother, Christiana, sustained her and trained her to be strong and resilient. When Oswald had his fill of the abuse, he left the woman and took his girls to his homeland in Silesia, where Constance enjoyed two of the most fun-filled years of her life as a lovely young lady.

Home of Carl Gottfried Püschel

Parents
Oswald & Christiana
Menzel

Grandparents
Carl & Susanna
Püschel

Constanza with
Mama Christiana

Edmund, Christel, Fred, Oswald, Constance

Emilie Manthey Family

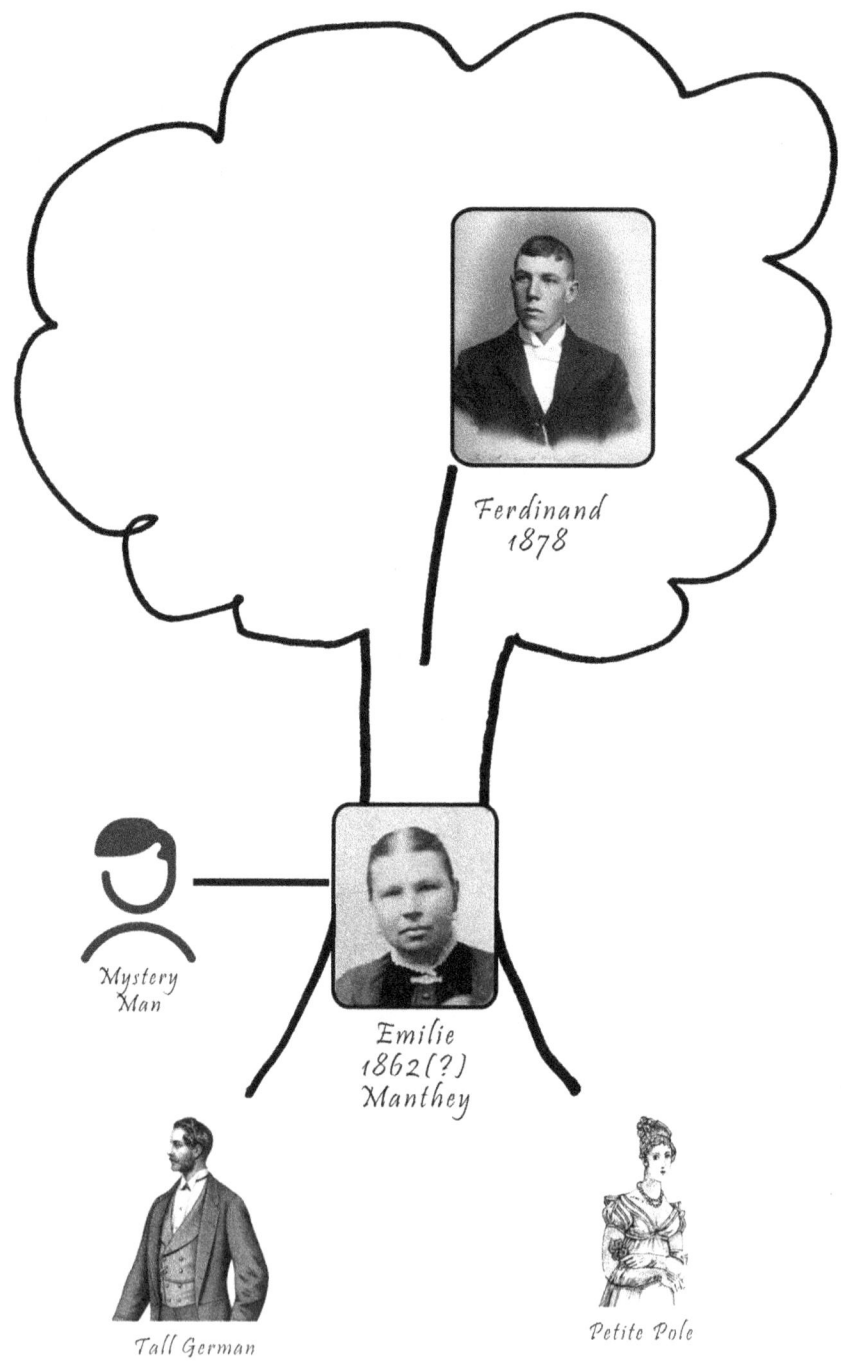

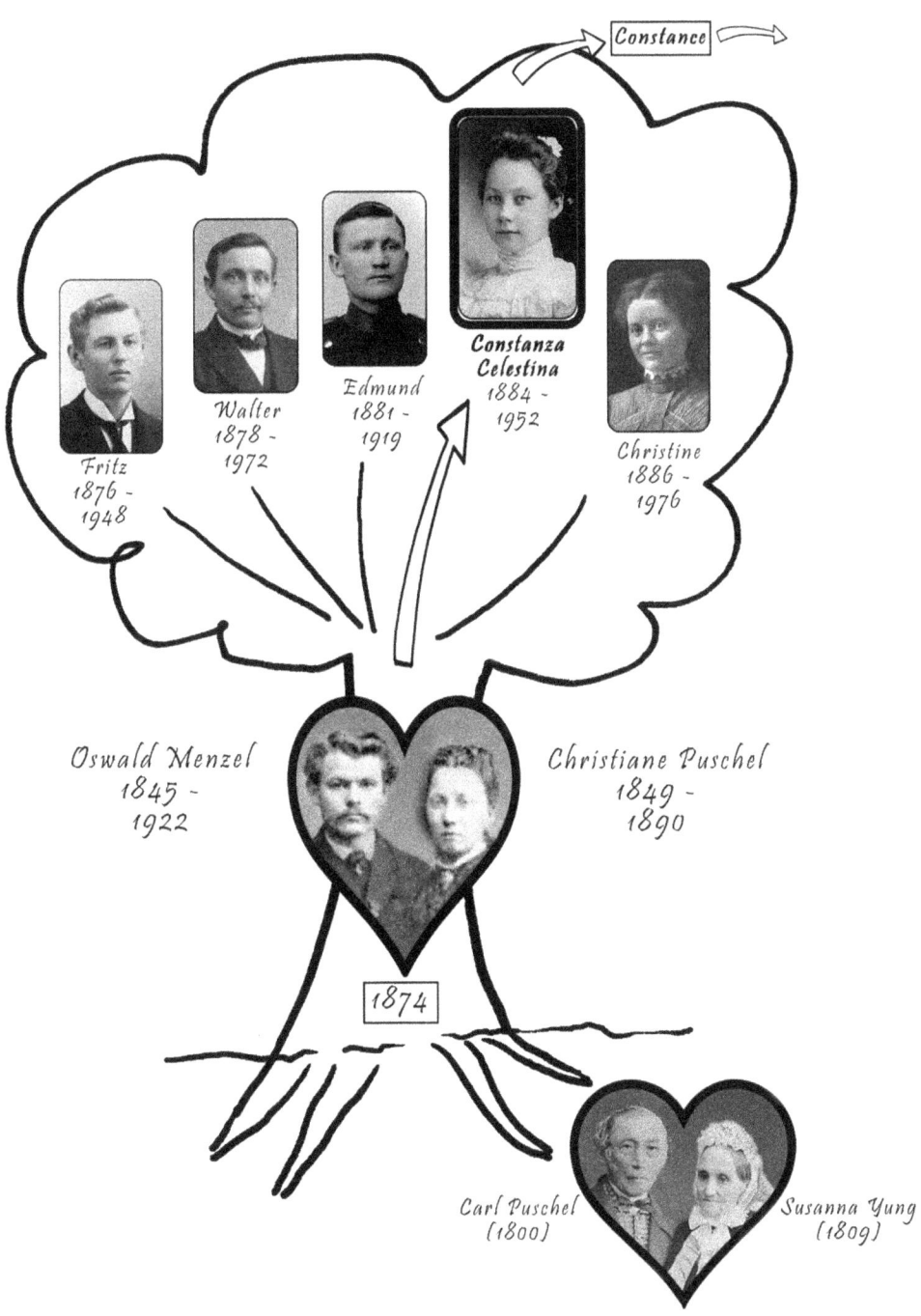

Chapter 1
1900s: Coming to America!

1900	Sep 17	Ferdinand begins working for American Bridge Co, (Chicago)
1901	Jan-Oct	Ferdinand works for American Bridge Co.
	Feb 18	Ferdinand loans Fred Menzel $150 for "trip to Germany" (to pay passage for bringing Constance back?)
	Mar 24	Constance boards SS Pretoria in Hamburg, Germany
	Apr 6	Constance arrives in New York City, USA
		Constance nannies for a professor in Chicago
		Ferdinand's journal, "A Declaration of Love at First Sight"
	Oct-Dec	Ferdinand works for A.I. Bragg in Petersburg, MI
1902	Jan-Nov	Ferdinand works all year for A.I. Bragg in Petersburg, MI
	Aug 8	Ferdinand and Constance wed in Petersburg, MI
1903	Jan 12	Ferdinand and Constance move to Tigerton, WI
	Feb 26	Ferdinand works for Tigerton/Badger Lumber Companies
	Summer	Ferdinand works for G.N.W. Railway Co and Schwanke
	Fall	Ferdinand works for Brockmann Lumber, Arndt Lumber
	Nov 15	Herbert Oswald (Herbie) Manthei is born
	Dec 6	Herbie is baptized
1904	Jan-Apr	Ferdinand works for Tigerton & Badger Lumber Co, Am Bridge
	Feb	Edmund Menzel comes to America (Petersburg, Petoskey)
	Apr	Oswald and Christine (Christel) Menzel come to America
	Jun 4	Ferdinand withdraws savings, Tigerton, WI $253.22
	Jun 6	Ferdinand starts savings account in Petoskey, MI $253.22
	Jun 7	Ferdinand starts working in Petoskey for P.M. Railway, G.R&I. Railway

Constance Comes to America

When Constance was seventeen, her brother Fritz came home from America and invited her to go back with him to the USA. She was a courageous young lady ready for adventure so, of course, she said yes! Little did she know that Fritz was playing matchmaker. In fact, Ferdinand had sent the money to pay for her ferry passage! Constance worked as a nanny in Chicago for a year and Ferdinand visited her on Sundays, walking her to church and showing her the city. An entry in Ferdinand's journal reads; "A Declaration of Love at First Sight."

Constance was surprised when Ferdinand asked for her hand in marriage. She sought the counsel of Fritz, who Papa Oswald had commissioned to be her guardian in America. Fritz tricked her into a loveless marriage by saying, "You led him on by accepting his invitations so now you have to marry him." Had she asked her papa, he would never have allowed the marriage because Ferdinand was from a lower-class family with a dubious upbringing. That's how two people cut from very different cloth were joined in marriage in 1902!

Wedding Day, August 8, 1902

Ferdinand and Constance were wed in Petersburg, Michigan, where Ferdinand worked for a farmer and Fritz was a master blacksmith. Fritz and his wife, Minnie, were their attendants.

Constance and Ferdinand spent their first years of marriage in Tigerton, Wisconsin, where Ferdinand worked in the lumber mills and Constance gave birth to Herbie.

Hause in Tigerton, Wisconsin where Herbie was born

Constance was especially impressed to discover that the Constitution of America was based on Biblical principles and that The Ten Commandments hung on the walls of every courthouse. She felt that as long as she raised her children to follow the laws of God, they would be safe living in this land.

> **Constance felt that as long as she raised her children to follow the laws of God, they would be safe living in this land.**

Tigerton Lumber Company where Ferdinand worked

June 5, 1904
Ferdinand and Constance Arrive in Petoskey, Michigan

November 9, 1904

Having grown up in the German Empire under Kaiser Wilhelm II of Prussia, Ferdinand and Constance were fascinated to learn how the American government worked. What exactly was a Democratic Republic? The church was abuzz with heated conversations about candidates and laws. They hoped that Roosevelt would be a good president.

PART TWO

Ted and Ernie's Excellent Adventures Begin!

Chapter 2:

1900s: Entering the World

1905	May 2	Theodore (Ted) Manthei is born
	June 19	Ferdinand purchases a farm on Townsend Road
1909	July 10	Ernst (Ernie) Manthei is born

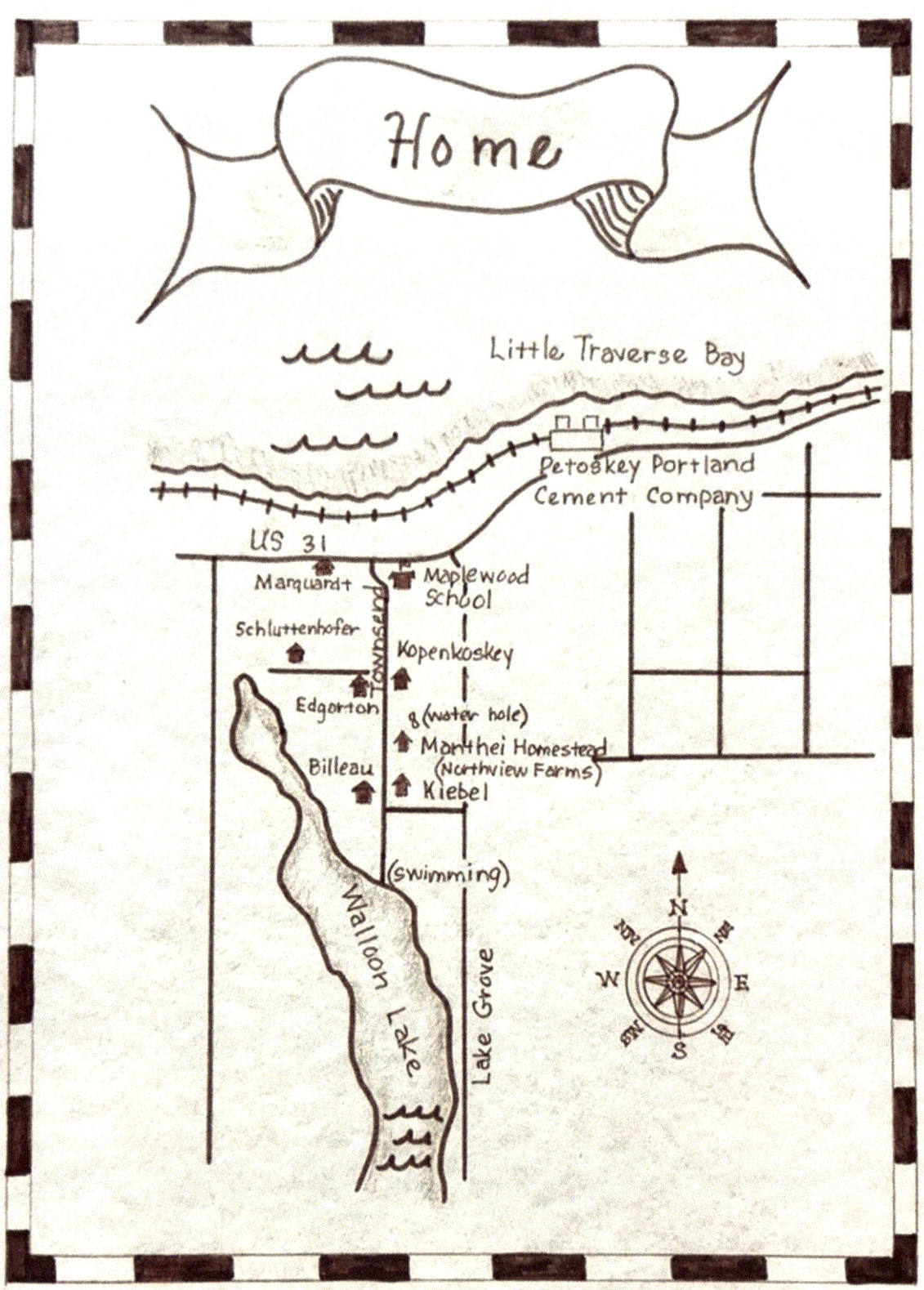

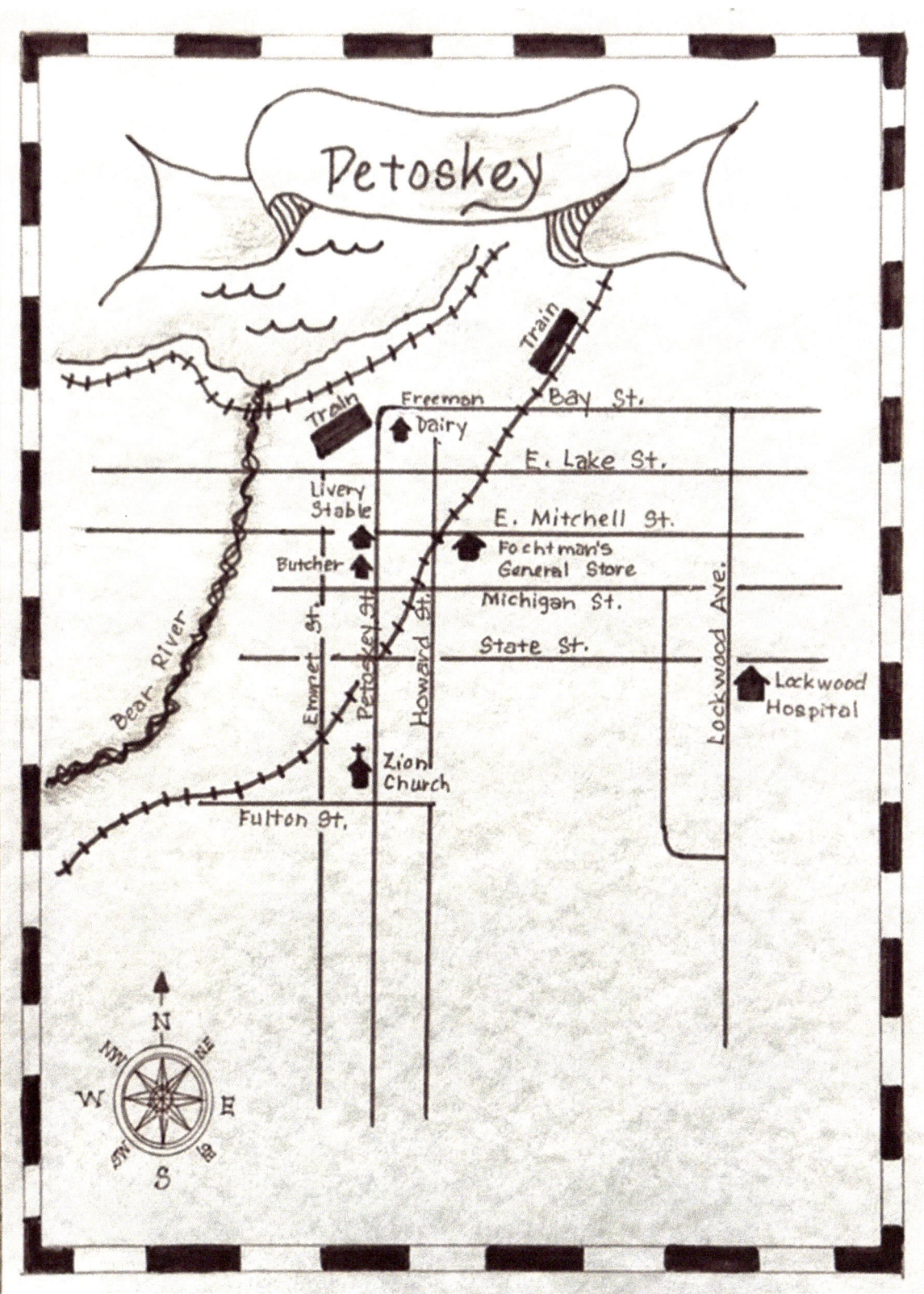

Ted: Born May 2, 1905

Herbie & Ted

Ernie: Born July 10, 1909

Ted's Adventures Begin (1900s)

The World That I Was Born Into

Ted

My brother Ernie used to brag about being born in the same house where he raised his own family. I said, "I wouldn't be born in a shack like that!" The truth is, I was born in Petoskey just after my folks moved here and they were renting a house in town. Then they found the farm.

In the sitting room, we had a stove that would take big chunks of wood and it would heat pretty good. But the wind blew right through that shack. There was no insulation. The curtains would blow right out into the middle of the room through the walls. It was very, very cold. Anybody who lived through it was just tough, that's all.

You had to go outdoors to get to the outhouse and sometimes it filled up with snow. You had to go out there and sit in that snow like an Eskimo! Rough life! It was a two-seater. And then if you were sick with a fever and had to go out there, you'd catch yourself a worse cold! That was hard on us. No inside plumbing at all. None! We'd carry the water in and out. But most of the houses were that way them days.

We only had a bath every two weeks and you took that whether you needed it or not. We didn't change our clothes every day. We had one set of clothes for work and another for Sunday. You didn't have to hunt long to find what to wear.

The kitchen had a wood cook stove. No linoleum—just rough pine floors, tongue-and-groove, worn through pretty much from scrubbing. The roof over the kitchen was just one story but there was an upstairs on the rest of the house. Later they rebuilt the house and raised the kitchen roof so it was level with the other part. My parents' bedroom was on the first floor and there was a little pantry along the wall that led to the stairs to the basement. To get upstairs, there were stairs above the pantry.

We had chickens and eggs and meat. We always had chickens. We didn't buy them. We'd just put eggs under the chickens and hatch them out. Then the chicks would follow the hen around and she'd find 'em a little food some place. They grew up running loose. Then we'd add some grain, a little wheat and corn and they'd sleep in the chicken coop. All of us helped take care of the chickens. Mother would remind us. "It's time to feed the chickens." We knew what to do. We'd feed them clabbard (thick, sour milk) that came from the cows and was left over. That feed made really good-tasting chicken meat! That's still the way Mary raises good chickens today. When we'd have a pig, we'd feed it clabbard milk too.

Boy, I tell you, life on the farm was hard! We raised the cows. We'd buy a little heifer for a dollar and raise her up. Feed her hay and a little grain. Take her to meet the neighbor's bull and pretty soon you had a calf and some good milk.

We never killed no cows. Just ate pork mostly. Once in a while we'd buy a quarter of a steer from somebody and mother would "can" it in jars. That way we'd have meat to eat. We always had quite a few vegetables in the basement... like "beggies" (rutabagas), apples and potatoes, and a lot of carrots. They'd keep pretty good in the basement where it was cool.

Farming wasn't easy when we were young. You see, that area of northern Michigan was originally all forest. The lumber industry had cut down most of the trees already. I think there were 5-6 of those virgin trees left in our place that they couldn't get out when the snow broke up in the spring. They were great big things—four-foot-wide maples! Our field on top of the hill that's a garden now used to be all stumps. We had to clear that. Grub the stumps out and burn them. We used a little dynamite sparingly but most of them was gotten out by muscle. At first, we'd farm around the stumps if they were too big, too strong, or not rotten enough. We just worked around the stumps. You couldn't use a binder (harvesting) machine in a place like that because there were too many stumps in the way. So, you farmed in amongst the stumps. That's the way you raised your hay and grain. Everything was harvested by hand, with a cradle and handrake. It was about 15 miles over there with a horse and wagon. We had a buggy too, which stayed in the barn.

Handrake

The sleigh sat outside. There wasn't much to a sleigh, you know. All you got is a runner made out of wood with a shoe of iron bolted to the underside that would slide along the ice and snow. Instead of wheels we had runners—like a bobsled that would slide on snow, about 3½ feet wide. A lot of that stuff was made by hand. The bunks and side rails were made out of wood. We'd go out to the woods and knock a tree down and fit it in there. Everything was built that way them days. You'd just make it yourself. We made most of the things we needed. They would haul heavy loads of logs to the mills with those sleighs.

Sleigh

Then they had light sleighs too—a cutter they'd call them. They were real light with narrow tracks. They all had wood with iron under it that was braced up. I liked those two-seated cutters where you sit and drive a horse and go to town that way. They were kind of nice. We didn't have a cutter that I remember. We had a two-runner box. Not everybody could afford a cutter.

We never had a good team of horses. When I got enough money from working hard one year, I wanted my dad and mother to buy a good team, which they could have done. But what did they do instead? They let someone talk them into buying a piano! Christel needed to have music. My parents liked having music in the house. My mother was very musical. So was my dad. I played the piano by ear, Ernst played the piano and fiddle. Mother and dad sang.

Mother sewed clothes for us when we were little. She'd also make over a hand-me-down coat or something like that to fit us. She was a good seamstress. She could help herself with anything. We didn't have a lot, but we learned to be grateful for what we had.

> **We didn't have a lot, but we learned to be grateful for what we had.**

November 4, 1908

Could an election really bring prosperity to those who were struggling to survive? Living in America was truly a unique experience with the exchange of political powers and philosophies. This was a fascinating topic for the family to discuss throughout the coming years.

Chapter 3

1910s: Growin' Up in the Olden Days

1910	Aug	Ferdinand shingled the granary, bought a buggy
	Sep	Ted starts school
1912	Apr 16	Sinking of the Titanic
	Jun 13	Christel is born
1914		Ernie starts school Ted starts trap line Billeau barn goes up
1915		Constance becomes an entrepreneur: • Hosting chicken dinners at Northview Farm • Shipping asters to Chicago First telephone and car Sport dies
1917	Apr 6	America goes to war with the German Empire German-Americans are rendered "undesirable" Ferdinand is warned to "Stay out of town!"
1918		Herbie and Ted profess their faith and received Confirmation at Zion Lutheran Church
1919	Jan	Scarlet Fever! Ernie nearly dies—miracle story Ferdinand drills for water
	Sep 28	Uncle Edmond Menzel dies in a cement plant accident

Ernie's Adventures Begin!

Ernie: Home Life

Our original house was very primitive with just the bare necessities of life. The house was built like a barn, with open eaves upstairs. The wind blew in snow under the eaves! We children had two beds upstairs, and in the winter, we would wake up with snow covering our beds. Our parents slept downstairs.

One winter, Christel got sick and needed to sleep downstairs with mother. I drew the bad lot of having Father sleep in my bed. Herbie and Ted slept together. Father had the habit of rolling over and taking the covers with him, and there I'd be, all uncovered. He was a huge man and I was just a little feller! While I was sleeping, the cold would overcome me, and I wet the bed. The pee went right up Father's back. I never woke up 'til the stick was on my rear. That's how I was brought back to life and kept from freezing to death! I was afraid to fall asleep after a while for fear the blanket would come off, exposing me, and I'd be in trouble again. I complained to Mother, who got after Father as best she could. It was difficult to get across to him, so Mother let me sleep downstairs 'til Christel was better.

Over the kitchen was a lean-to roof, like a woodshed. In the winter, the cats would honeymoon on the roof and wet on the snow. Then, in the spring, that stuff would melt and drip into our bean soup. Many times, that water dripped onto our table. Mother got very upset about it! It smelled something terrible because those cats kept celebrating up there all the time.

*Ferdinand and Constance
Ted, Ernie and Herbie*

Lively Dinnertable Conversation: Ernie and Christel Reminisce with Family

Ted, Ernie, Christel, Herbie

Christel was born on June 13, 1912, and joined the family adventures.

Christel: There used to be a pantry in the dining room where the buffet is now. The pantry wasn't too big because in this room there was a bedroom, bathroom, stairway, and a pantry with shelves on both sides. The stairway went up over the pantry. Another stairway went below the pantry into the cellar. The stairway going up was very steep and had a bend in it with about three steps going up from there. Over the pantry was a plank for a walkway. We'd go and play in the room over the bedroom. But there was a gap between the stairway and that room where we'd play.

Ernie put a board over the gap to carry toys over. He used to have me try to walk across on a plank and I would fall down and go "Boom, boom, boom" down the steps. He used to say: "Come on Sis, let's go upstairs and play." Then he'd say, "Come on, let's go over there and play." I'd say, "No, I'm afraid." I was just a small wobbler then. He'd say, "Oh, come on. There are a lot of nice toys over here." He'd get me to come over and I'd come just wobbling over and I'd look down and I'd fall. Here I go! Boompety, boompety, boom! I'd fall all the way down until I'd hit the door right close to the steps with a BANG! And then I'd cry, "WAAH!! And Mama would come running. She'd open the door and pick me up and hug me (that felt so good) and kiss me and everything was real good. Well, that happened a couple of times. Each time he'd have a better sales talk to get me over there and then each time I fell.

Ernie: She was a dumb one!

Christel: No, I trusted him because he was just three years older. That makes a big difference when you're only three!

Ernie: Get a *good* story! Don't make me look bad. That reveals your true character!

Christel: Well, the last time, he carried a *lot* of toys over there and he really had to put on a sales pitch because it was about the third time. There was company downstairs at the time—one of the big girls in the neighborhood I really admired. My mother opened the door and this time she paddled me!

Ruth: Paddled you??

Ernie: She had it coming, didn't she?

Christel: Oh, was I hurt! And embarrassed!! That big girl saw my mother spank me! She didn't spank hard. Well, that was the last time I listened to *him*.

Ernie: Seems you would have learned your lesson long before that!

Christel: Well, big brothers are pretty persuasive, and I admired him to no end. *My big brother*, and he was *smart*.

Ernie: You got in more trouble than it was worth!

Christel: But then there's the story of the Ben Davie tree. We were playing under that tree, and we'd put our feet in the sand and pour water over and build houses. We'd pull our feet out and there was a house! He had built some kind of a city, and I was building a city. Well, every time before I could get it finished, a big wind would come along. *He* was the wind! And he'd *blow* my city down!! Not once, but several times! Finally, I got enough of it. I got all set that I was going to finish this city. I built some big ones and got a lot of sand piled on with holes in it where my foot was and here came that hurricane and blew it down! Well, that was enough! I couldn't take any more of that, so I picked up that kettle with a long handle on it and swung it back. I had to get up enough momentum 'cuz I was just little. He didn't notice 'cuz he was playing.

Ernie: I probably was praying, not playing—don't you think so?

Christel: I went back and forth 'til I got enough momentum and then I hit him on the head!! And boy, did he cry. He ran inside to Mom and said, "Christel hit me!" My mother was watching the whole thing through the window, and we didn't know it. She had wondered how long I would take it. She knew he was teasing me awful hard. She told him, "Ach, that little thing couldn't hurt *you*. Not a big boy like you!!" Ernie said, "She did! She hit me with ein *topf* (a kettle)!"

Ernie: You'll have to admit. Christel wasn't acting very much like a Christian, was she?

Cora: Did your mother spank him for it?

Christel: No, *I* did that!

Ernie: She told me I had it coming. Look at what kind of mother I had!

Christel: She just said, "Now, that little thing couldn't hurt you. A *big* boy like you and a *little* girl like that!" She thought he should have some punishment and I gave it to him!

Ernie: And all I was doing was acting out real life! Life is hard.

Ruth: And you made it harder for some people, huh?

Ernie: Well, I played my part!

Christel: And so he got his part!

> **I was teaching her that real life is hard!**

****

Ernie: When we were young children, maybe eight or nine years old, Mother and Father would go to the Medicine Show, and they would be real excited because that guy would tell some really good stories. Here's one story I remember…

This fellow was walking along after drinking too much, and he fell down on the road and into the ditch and rolled alongside an old sow. And there he lay! Along came this fine lady and when she saw that old drunk lying alongside that old sow she said, "You can always tell a man by the company he keeps." Well, that old sow immediately got up and walked away! And that's the end of that story.

Ruth: Since you two are here together, tell us more stories about when you were young.

Ernie

Ernie: The members in our family were Herbie (who died at fifteen), Ted, me, a stillborn baby girl, then Christel, and Mathilda.

Ted and I inherited some of Mother's qualities. She brought us up Christian, had a lot of energy, and was an optimist. She saw things on the bright side rather than the sour side. She was very friendly. The neighbor ladies thought a lot of Mother. They would come and visit. She was a good conversationalist. She was well-educated. She was cheerful and helped us kids wherever she could. Mother was the type of person who always got a kick out of life. That's the reason her story is so nice. She always saw things on the funny side. In that respect, I take after my mother.

Ferdinand, Herbie, Ted, Ernie, Constance and Christel

Ted was very serious and very smart. Ted looks like Mother's grandfather by the name of Püschel. He owned big coal mines in Silesia, Germany, and was quite a wealthy man. Ted is the spittin' image of him. Ted is a very smart businessman and made good moves in life. He probably took after some of the other relatives in Mother's family. They had engineers. If you listened to Ted and worked with him, you could go places in life. He didn't take the Bible lightly. I might have taken the Bible more lightly had I not had a stable brother like Ted. That's a good point to thank the Lord for, and I do thank Him for it!

> **Mother was the type of person who always got a kick out of life. She always saw things on the funny side. In that respect, I take after my mother.**

Christel inherited more of Father. He had Polish in him and was suspicious of people. I felt more that you could trust people. They'd have to prove that they were shady characters. It didn't always work out that way, so I had some problems, but I more or less let a person prove himself.

Mathilda was a year or so older than Cora. We called her Babe because she was the youngest, ten years younger than Christel. When she was thirty-four or five, she had a stroke which completely paralyzed her right side. The doctor said she would probably never walk or talk again. She was unconscious for several days and they thought she would die.

> **I might have taken the Bible more lightly had I not had a stable brother like Ted. That's a good point to thank the Lord for, and I do thank Him for it!**

They called all the family together. She told us later that they thought she couldn't hear anything, but she could hear them talking. She'd just go in and out of consciousness.

Cora: Not only did she learn to walk but she even sewed her own clothes. She talked haltingly. If she had a story to tell, you'd have to play twenty questions. Ernie wasn't very good at it, but I could figure it out pretty well. She would always start at the end and work backwards until you finally got the whole story.

Ernie: It was like Joseph telling his brothers the dreams in the Old Testament. Everything she said was like a riddle you'd have to figure out.

Cora: Then she'd answer, "That's right. That's right!" Or she'd exclaim, "Boy, oh boy, oh boy!"

She died of a heart attack when she was fifty-nine. The week before, Babe had called me wanting to know about Ernie's heart problem because her heart was making funny noises, going "Gurgle, gurgle, gurgle." I said, "Babe, you better go to the doctor!" She scheduled an appointment for the next Monday. Meanwhile Ernie had bought an old piano for Gwen and had arranged for a man from our church to fix the keys. Ed Henning was a good friend of Babe's and brought her along when he came to Mark and Gwen's house to look at the piano. While they were there, Ernie took Ed to see some of the jobs the boys were working on in town and they left Babe with Gwen and me. Little Elizabeth was just 1½ years old and I was reading to her. We were sitting on the couch and Babe was in the chair, listening and laughing. Gwen was on the phone and all of the sudden she said, "Mom, Mom, look at Aunt Babe." I looked up and Babe was slumped over. We ran and got the nurse who was living in the townhouse next door, and she said, "Call the ambulance. Quick!" The medics worked and worked on Babe. They couldn't get her heart going so they loaded her up quick and took her to the hospital, where they worked another 45 minutes to get her heart going again. She lived one day after that, but she never regained consciousness. Babe's son, Bert, said CPR wouldn't have helped because she was gone. Her heart had stopped. Perhaps the gurgling was fluid in the heart cavity and the heart just gave out all at once.

> **We never know how much time we have to love the people we love, so I want to love people well while I can.**

Ruth: Every time I go to a funeral I think, "We never know how much time we have to love the people we love, so I want to love people well while I can."

Swapping Horse Stories

Ernie: *(Passing gas)* Sometimes it's healthy to let off a little gas! When our horse got sick, we'd take him out in the yard and chase him around and pretty soon he'd put his tail up in the air and let it go. Then he'd feel better. Only I don't have a tail!

> **Sometimes it's healthy to gas off a little!**

Christel: One day my calf, Dolly, got sick. We took her out and I chased her around and around. I had to keep her up. She wanted to lay down so bad. They said, "Keep her going. Keep her going. The minute she lays down, she'll die!" So, I had to keep that poor calf running around. That's the way we'd cure them when they had *hoven* and were bloated. They'd have to run the gas off.

Ernie: Sure! Then there was the story of Roy Stanton, a good friend of Ted's. They used to go to California together. I got a kick out of Roy.

He told me he bought a horse one time, a nice fat horse. He got on the horse and started riding it home to his barn. Well, he noticed the horse kept getting thinner and thinner and he wondered what in all the world was the matter. By the time he got to the barn, it was just skin and bones. They had pumped air under the hide and as they rode along, the air leaked out and the horse kept disappearing under him! That's a true story! Those old-timers had a lot of tricks! That's why I've got a lot of respect for Roy Stanton. He was a real honest hard-buying horse buyer. He's had gray hair since he was eighteen years old.

> When a son takes over a farm, he doesn't want to use his father's old tools. He needs something more modern. I went from better to worse.

Father had a good team to start with. Prince was a good faithful horse. Billy was a bit mischievous. When we'd try to put on his collar, he'd step on our feet. Then, he'd stand on the foot and not get off. He knew as long as he stood on your foot, you couldn't put the harness on him. I'd get mad at him and hit him. You'd have to really get under him and push him off your foot. He did that to me quite a few times! Prince would never do that. They were good honest horses and worked well together, so we thought that all horses were that way.

But Prince and Billy were getting old so we figured we had to make a change. I should have kept them and worked with them. But Father wanted me to farm and, when a son takes over a farm, he doesn't want to use his father's old tools. He needs something more modern. I had that feeling too. So, I sold Father's old horses and bought another team, older than the ones I'd sold! I went from better to worse.

My brother and I bought a horse one time. We didn't have no tractors. In those days, we had to buy horses. They say you're supposed to open the mouth and look at the teeth. Well, we didn't know how to do that. So, what I'd do is look under the tail and if there was any rust on the exhaust pipe, I figured he'd had it!

So anyway, my brother and I bought a horse from this fellow by the name of Burnett. The horse was nice and fat and looked like it was in good shape. We needed a horse awful bad for cultivating and plowing.

I asked, "How much do you want for him?"

He said, "Thirty dollars."

Ted and I thought, "That's cheap. Sure, we'll buy that horse! He's in good shape."

So, we got him home, hooked him up, and found that he was honest and faithful. He pulled the plow nice. Then we put him in the barn and gave him some nice alfalfa hay. He was chewing and chewing and it would go in one side of the mouth and out the other side of his mouth.

I said, "Now what in all the world is the matter with that horse?"

Horses are supposed to be hay eaters, you know, but he couldn't eat hay. So we opened up his mouth and his teeth were worn right down to the gums. He had no teeth! We found out they'd been feeding him ground oats and middlings, stuff he could eat. No hay! We said, "What'll we do now? We've got him bought and we have to work!"

So, we taught that horse to eat beans! We had old beans we had culled out from the good seed beans. We dumped them in the pot and put some grain in and mixed it up. Then we cooked it up and fed that horse pork and beans! No, really, it was oats and beans, but we called him "Pork & Beans."

We fed him that stuff all summer and he learned to eat it. He could digest it and he'd plow good for us. He was an honest, hard-working horse, but he couldn't eat! We got by with that horse all summer. He worked on our farm and then we put him in the pasture, and he'd eat green grass. He could chew that.

Then we needed a mate for him so we found a dandy, lively, willing little horse. Only it was a racehorse! Whenever we plowed, it would be one length ahead of the other horse. Then, old "Pork & Beans" would get mad and bite him on the rear. Then the pacer would go faster! Oh, it was a terrible team to plow with!! That's how I plowed the field and got the food in that year.

In the fall, we put "Pork & Beans" in the pasture and he kept getting thinner and thinner and finally we gave him to Johnny Kopenkosky, and he sold him to the fox farm. There was a man up here who raised fox for the hides, just like my cousin Rudy who owned a mink farm.

The next year, we got rid of the pacer and bought a good, young team of Westerners. Say, there was a nice-looking horse! One was a bucker, but I got him broke. To break him, I hooked him onto a sleigh and he took the harness so nice. But when I said, "Getty-up," he suddenly got a stubborn streak and wouldn't move.

"Well," I said, "I'll fix you!" So, I hooked him onto the sleigh, got some straw, and built a fire under him. I thought I'd fix that bugger. By golly, he moved off the fire just far enough so that the *sleigh* was over the fire and that's how I nearly burnt up my sleigh! That was a fright.

They have a way to fix those horses now-a-days. They've got a stick with a spike on the end and a battery in it. You can give 'em a real shock in the hind end. You can break a horse pretty good these days. If you say "Getty-up" and he won't go, you just make a loud clicking noise like "ppkk," and let me tell you, boy, he goes! It works much better than in the olden days. But I finally broke him and made those Westerners into a decent team.

I could never trust them though. One time, we were raking hay and I needed a drink, so I parked them by a hay shock and said, "You fellas eat here while I go and get a drink." They looked real peaceful.

My mother's cousin was visiting, sitting in the house and reading a book. We all called him Uncle Veynor. He said, "My, this is a beautiful place. So quiet."

He barely finished saying that and here come the horses, running for all they were worth! They turned into the driveway so fast that they wrapped the hay rake around the maple tree, bending it all to pieces. Then they ran out of the harness and down to the barn and there they stood together, trying to get through the barn door at the same time. They got stuck in the barn door and couldn't go in or out!

That was some excitement! Uncle Veynor was used to the hustle and bustle of New York city. Those horses made this peaceful place become very exciting!

Ruth: Besides horses, I know you had a special dog. Tell us about him.

Christel: I was just a little girl. I wasn't going to school or anything. My mother would let me go into the woods if I'd take Sport along, because Sport would kill snakes and take care of me. He was the best dog we ever had.

Ernie: Our dog, Sport

We had a dog to herd the cattle by the name of Sport. He was a Shepherd/Collie mix. He was a very intelligent dog. Never again in my life have I seen a dog that intelligent. You could tell Sport to go down into the pasture and get the white cow. By golly, he'd come home with the white cow! You'd tell him to go after the bull, and he'd bring back the bull!

The funny thing was the odd way that dog came to us. My father was in town one day with the horses and sleigh. He and Mother went to town to buy groceries. That dog came to my father while he was sitting on the sleigh, waiting for Mother to come out of the grocery store.

Father said, "Go home. Go away."

The dog left, but he always came back right away. Father couldn't figure that out. He didn't know where the dog came from. Must have gotten lost and he thought Father looked like his owner. When they finished shopping, they rode home in the sleigh and that dog followed them all the way home.

Father noticed him as they drove into the yard and didn't know what to do with him. He finally said, "Well, he's here now!" He fed him some bread and milk. Then he thought he'd see if the dog was any good. He took him to the barn and said, "Sic 'em." The dog grabbed that cow right quick.

Ferdinand with Sport

Father knew someone had trained that dog well. He was a shepherd. Whoever trained and lost him must have felt terrible. But we didn't know where he came from or who he belonged to. He just stayed here and never did leave our place. That's how we got that wonderful dog.

Later on, a man told us there was an ad in the paper looking for a dog similar to Sport and they offered a reward for his return, but he didn't know who it was. By that time, he had lost the address. So, Sport never went back to his original owner.

That dog was a real blessing to our family. He helped us in so many ways. He was a very smart dog. Sport was not afraid to handle anything he was told to do. He obeyed my father perfectly. He thought the world of my father.

Father would say, "Go get that calf." He'd go, but he would never bite the calf. He knew it was helpless. If you told him to go after a cow, though, he'd bite it low in the heel, real hard. Those cows were so scared of Sport, they still remembered him three months after he died. We could say, "Sport, go get 'em!" and those cattle would take off running to beat the band! So much respect they had for that dog.

One day, Father was visiting his neighbor, Paul Marquardt. Paul had a very vicious bull that would paw the ground and snort.

Paul said, "I've got a bull that your dog won't tackle."

My father said, "My dog is not afraid of any bull!"

So, Paul said, "Send him after that one!"

Father said, "Sport, go get that bull!"

When the dog came close, the bull pawed and snorted and put on quite an act. Sport just kept circling around him.

Paul said, "See, he's afraid."

But Sport was watching for his chance. When the bull was in the right position, Sport jumped up and clamped onto his tail right under the rear and hung on for dear life! You should have seen that bull take off. He ran down that pasture bellowing and yelling. The dog hung on the whole way. It must have hurt the bull pretty hard. Finally, Sport let go. That bull kept running with his tail between his legs, turning around and looking behind him because he was really scared of that dog.

Paul Marquardt offered Father one hundred dollars to buy that dog. We kids immediately started crying when he said that because we thought so much of Sport. We needed the money bad. One hundred dollars in those days would have meant a lot to us because we were so poor.

Father said, "I could never do that. In the first place, I don't think that dog would ever stay with you. In the second place, he's part of our family and I don't think I could ever sell him."

Sport lived with us quite a while, but one time Father put some rat poison in the basement on bread. We had just installed our first telephone and, of course, that was a big deal for us boys. We had to show our neighbors what a wonderful thing we had! We opened the cellar door and showed them how everything was installed. They all admired it, because that was a big thing in those days. Meanwhile, Sport went around sniffing out the bread and ate it up. Then he got very sick.

He disappeared and, for four days, we couldn't find him. We cried and hollered for him. What he did was went down into our swamp and drank water. Finally, he came back and we were so happy! We loved him up and everyone was so thankful that Sport came home. He went around and looked at each of us as if to say goodbye. Then he crawled under the granary and died!

We cried for days. We loved him so much. He used to play with us. When we went sledding down the hill, he'd jump on our backs and ride. When the sleigh sunk into the crust of the snow and hit a soft spot, we'd slide right over the top of the snow. Then Sport would lick our faces and help us up. Of course, he was always riding on top, so he was the first one off.

Sport was an outstanding dog. He was practically human. Rarely do you find an animal that smart. Never have we thought so much of a dog as we did of Sport!

> **Never have we thought so much of a dog as we did of Sport!**

Ted: Harsh Discipline

Ted

There was one time when I was watching Ernst. He was a baby—maybe 2 years old—and I was just a little kid myself, about 6 years old. Well, the cow got out and she got into the corn crib. A cow won't stop eatin' til she kills herself from overeating. A mule will stop eating and a horse will too, but not a cow. And just because that cow got out and I didn't catch her out there, my father beat me up so my ears hung down. I was all swollen around the head and everywhere. He thought it was my fault that the cow got that corn, even though she survived it. Whether she would have died or not was just as much his fault as it was mine, and probably more because he was a man, and I was just a small child! God only knows where he was at the time. He was around someplace. But I had the obligation to watch Ernst and I was doing it very faithfully. I didn't see the cow out there. I don't know if I'd have known what to do if I did see her. I wasn't milking yet at that age. Mother was in town. She went to do some shopping and came back about dark. When she seen me all beat up, boy, she really lit into the old man. She gave him an awful tongue-lashing. She didn't leave us alone with Dad after that. She'd take us into town with her. Later, she would take our dad and leave us at home.

A dad should have a reason when he hits a kid with a stick. The kid's got to have done something really naughty. But our dad would hit us for no reason. Sometimes Dad was real nice. But it wouldn't take long and he'd get a spell. It came out of the blue moon. You could never tell where it would come, when it would come, or how it would come. When he got that way, you didn't know what to do. After I got older, I'd just walk away and wait for him to cool down. I'd leave him out there. If he was cuttin' wood, I'd just go fishin'.

> **Sometimes our dad would get angry and yell at us and hit us for no reason. When I got older, I'd just walk away and wait for him to cool down.**

But he tackled me a few times after that. When I was 23 years old, he almost killed me. He had me by the throat in the kitchen. If my mother hadn't come behind him with that fryin' pan and hit him over the head, I believe he'd have gotten me. That temper was terrible! He didn't have to have a reason, you know. He could do it without a reason just as good. When he got that way, he wasn't reasonable. You could be working and doing your best to please him and all at once, you could see it in his eyes. I think Satan got a hold of him. Then he'd tie into you. First, he'd start with words and after that with a stick. I seen him just about kill a horse one time with a club. A grown horse. He had a terrible temper!

There were times when he was really good. Yah! But you couldn't tell when he would take off.

Ernie: Money for Food

Ernie

When I was very young, Father worked on a railroad section, driving in spikes and putting ties down for the track. Father earned low wages and gave Mother a few dollars a week to run the household. With that she bought our groceries, clothes, and everything. She kept house on nearly nothing!

One time, Father got a job at the cement plant and Mother was so happy. She sat down and started figuring how she could whittle down the debts they owed. She had her budget all figured out and was so happy that Father was working. He rode to work with Albert Billeau, who owned a little old car.

After about three weeks, Father came home and said, "I've quit my job!"

That ruined all Mother's intentions of paying off the bills. I remember her feeling so bad because she wanted to pay the bills off and get on her feet. She was real disappointed. Father would say he couldn't get along with this one or that person at his job and then he'd quit or get fired and come back home. He was not a very stable person.

Mother would buy dog bones for ten cents a box. The butcher stripped the meat off and then threw the bones away into a big box for dogs. But they weren't for our dog—Mother bought those bones for our dinner! She would bring them home and saw them into three-inch lengths with her meat saw. Here and there would be just a bit of meat, but those big bones had a lot of marrow in them. Then she'd use them to cook up vegetable soup with carrots, potatoes, onions, celery, beans, sometimes bacon, and that would make marvelous soup! She'd throw the bones in there and the marrow would cook out, making delicious soup. I wished I had some right now! Sometimes, she'd make bean soup with ham bones. We lived on the "high end of the hog" that way. We grew up healthy on that. I never went to the doctor, except when I had Scarlet Fever and the doctor came to the house.

When Father was out of work, Mother would save the butter from the cows to make grocery money. She sold the butter and bought cotesuet (cottonseed oil mixed with beef suet) which was terrible stuff! She would buy that for cooking purposes, and maybe a little oleo in place of butter. She was paid enough difference from her butter to buy our groceries for the week.

We were very poor in those days. We always owed money to somebody, but Mother was honest and always paid them back. She scraped and scratched to pay the interest.

April 16, 1912—The Sinking of the Titanic

Klas Alvin Klasen deserves to be remembered!

The sinking of the Titanic was big news! Everyone talked about it at church and in school. Nearly everyone knew immigrants who had come to America on ships from Europe, like the Mantheis. Little did Ernie know that his son, Jim, would marry Marlys, the great-niece of a Swedish immigrant who perished in this disaster. Seventeen-year-old Klas Alvin Klasen was enroute to Illinois to visit his beloved sister Frieda (Marlys' grandma) for her birthday. Traveling with Klas was his sister-in-law and a toddler and an infant headed for Los Angeles to reunite with his brother. Four lives lost!

Ted

Ted: School Days—Learning was Serious Business

We went to Maplewood School, which was a one-room schoolhouse. The farmers would bring wood to stock the woodshed, but some days it was so cold. The wind blew off Little Traverse Bay and oh, how we froze! The teacher took care of the fire, along with forty kids in that one room. Girls sat on one side and boys on the other. They were kept apart. They were seated so those in the first grade were in the front and older ones in the back. We faced the north, toward the bay.

The cars went by right close to the school. The old road was just a few feet away. We played across the road from the school. Yeah, if anybody made it in them days, they were just tough, you know.

We walked a mile to school. I'd walk alone most of the time. Sometimes I'd walk with whoever was walking at the same time.

There were always two at a desk, side by side on one bench. Georgie Kopenkosky and I always sat together. The teacher would put people together. If you couldn't get along with that one, then she'd have to find you someone else you could get along with. I got along with Georgie pretty good. I pushed him out of the seat a time or two but not very often. That was not a popular thing to do! The teacher would want to know why he was down on the floor. He'd say, "Ted pushed me." I'd say, "He pushed me." I was definitely stronger and pushed him out. Then the teacher would find out and there'd be the stick. Teachers were strict in them days.

The first teacher I remember when I was real young was Miss Margaret Hegel. She was about eighteen years old when she started teaching, and I really liked her. She was a real good person and did a good job of teaching. Marvelous gal. She took it seriously and was an excellent teacher. Forty kids and a young teacher. She was an accomplished teacher and knew how to get those kids to do what she wanted. I don't know if she quit teaching or went to a different school. But when she was past 60, she finally got married. I went to see her and took her some strawberries when she was about 75.

> **If a person knows history, they just about know what's going to happen in the future, because human beings are predictable.**

We learned reading, writing and arithmetic. We learned some history too but not when I was young. That came later. If a person knows history, they just about know what's going to happen in the future, because human beings are predictable. We used to say, "Their arms have to go through the sleeves, not around them," meaning you all have to put on your shirt the same way.

Ted: Trapping (1914)

Ted

I was a very ambitious youngster. When I was about nine years old, I needed a hunting trap and couldn't get one. The parents wouldn't buy me any. Somehow or other I just wanted to get one lousy trap, you see. I don't know how it wiggled its way around, but I got myself one trap. And with that one trap I started my trap line. Once I got a good pelt, then I could buy myself more traps! The traps were 25-30 cents apiece, so if I got a pelt worth $2-3, then I was in business. By the time I got going good, I had 10-15 traps. Twenty traps! I got to be rich!! That was really somethin'! I made $16-17 one year. That bought the shoes for Ernst and for me.

We got coon, muskrat, and skunk. Just because a skunk smelled bad, that didn't stop me any. There was always a few bucks at the end of that ordeal. (laughing)

One night I got seven skunks out of one hole. I went after supper and dug 'em out with a shovel. They live like a woodchuck in the ground. In fact, the woodchuck generally digs the hole and then the skunk moves in when they move out. You look around the woods and you can see these holes... you can tell if there's something in there. I always stunk like heck when I went skunkin' but that didn't stop me. We'd just dig 'em out of the hole. Take a shovel. And ax. Get the roots out. Dig 'em right out of there. Lots of hard work. At first we didn't own a gun and I had to club 'em any way we could, with a stick or whatever we had. We got musked up with those skunks. It didn't seem to bother us any.

I probably got 30-40 skunks in my lifetime. We trapped a lot of skunk. They were alive in the trap, and it wasn't too bad getting it out after I had a rifle. I'd take it home and skin it. Stretch it out so it cured nice and hang it on the wall to dry. We stunk to high heaven, that's for sure! The neighbors put up with us. They had to. Everybody was skunkin' there. We started it and everyone caught on that there was money to be made that way. When I found a skunk that weighed 5-6 pounds, why, everyone heard and it was hard to make it as a skunk in them days. We'd get 50 cents to five dollars per pelt. That was quite a bit of money. If you had a good black skunk you could get five bucks. Didn't get a black one very often cuz they usually have a stripe across the back. The broader the stripe the less they'd pay you for it. The narrower the stripes, the more they'd pay. Some skunks just had a little white spot on the head and the rest was black. Oh, they'd pay you good for that! The price depended on the grade of the fur. You could get 15 cents to a dollar. Good black skunk with no stripe might go for five dollars. Those were hard dollars to raise. Of course, dollars in those days were quite valuable—$17 would have bought eight (100 pound) kegs of nails and I'd still have a dollar left. So, you can see there was quite a bit of value there.

When it was cured out, you'd send it to the fur company in St. Louis. There were a lot of fur companies in St. Louis but we sent ours to a fellow by the name of Taylor. FC Taylor Company. You'd ship your hides down there. They'd send you materials of what they were paying and how to grade the pelts. Then they'd send the check. You had to depend on their grades. They could cheat you and there was nothing you could do. What are you going to do about it? I don't know if they ever cheated us, but there would be no reason why they couldn't. As long as there was nobody policing it. And how are you going to police it? Couldn't do it. But they had furriers down there and I imagine they made coats and stuff out of those pelts. They'd pay us whatever they thought they were worth. We probably got beat bad but what the heck. A buck was a buck them days.

We trapped pretty heavy every winter. I'd always make a few bucks. Not very much. Maybe $15-20. But that came in pretty handy. It could buy shoes for the whole family. I always took my money home. They needed it so I'd give it to them. I never used it. I wouldn't buy a bicycle, even though I needed one. I had quite a bit of trap line on Walloon Lake, that was about five miles to walk. I tried to check my traps every day. I'd get up at 3:30 in the morning to run my trap line before school. I was ambitious. Nobody had to get me up. I seen that I'd get me out there and do it. Most of the time I'd get nothing. Once in a while you'd have a muskrat or mink or coon. It was a hard life. We lived quite a bit off the land. Wherever we could pick up a buck, we'd do it.

Now mink, they brought in pretty good money—ten or twelve bucks for a pelt. They're hard to catch though. They're pretty shy. They're a suspicious animal. One week I got two nice mink out on the point where you go out into the bigger lake. You know how I got 'em?

> **It was hard work, but the money meant I could buy shoes for the whole family.**

The lake was just starting to freeze over... the ice was real thin and I saw that some fish had come up to sun themselves under that ice. Nice little perch. I took my club and I hit that ice with all my might, and I stunned those fish! Now I had bait. Mink like those fish. I arranged them nice and camouflaged my trap so that when the mink came up for the fish, I caught the mink!

Mink live off of fish and anything they can catch in the water. They like the water and they go right into it. I remember one time, I walked past Lake Grove to where a small stream ran off the shore into the lake. I dug a hole into the bank and made a little tiny pond there. Then I set a trap right into the entrance of that hole I dug. Mink are very curious. When they see something that's disturbed like that they come and take a look. And I got that mink!

I didn't get a lot of mink, but they were expensive pelts. One time I caught one right close to this place (the lodge) where the creek goes into the lake. It made an awful fuss and tore stuff up around there. But somebody stole it right out of my trap. We had a neighbor who used to walk around the woods, and I know he was a thief. He admitted that he was a thief. He stole the oars out of my boat a few times. I'd just go up to his place and find 'em behind his door. (laughing) Got my oars back! We didn't have much thievery around there, but we had some.

Ernie: Tough Stuff and Shenanigans (1914)

The first day I went to school, I could speak only good German like my parents spoke at home. Fortunately, our teacher was also German, and she spoke to me in my own language.

I thought, "Great, I've got it made. This will be easy. I'll talk German and live this thing out very gracefully."

Ernie

But the next time she spoke, it was in English, and I thought she was getting mean. Now I was in trouble! She said, "From here on, I'm going to talk only English to you! You need to learn English. That's why you're coming to school."

I thought she was really going to harass me, so I had to buckle down and learn. It wasn't long before I could get along pretty good in English. Young children learn languages fast. For older people, it comes slower.

My folks were very poor. They had bought me some shoes, but we had a very cold, wooden floor at school. I always had poor circulation in my feet. I had no rubbers and, one day, it was very cold and my toes froze. I still suffer from chilblain (swelling and itching from frostbite) up to this day. Those were some of the joys of my youth.

Billy Kiebel and I sat at the same desk at school to do our work together. I was always more mischievous than Billy. I would look over and he would be working away real serious on a project. But it was just too quiet and boring for me. So, I braced myself on the other end of the seat and pushed hard and "BINGO!" there went Billy, out the other side and onto the floor.

The teacher said, "William, can't you sit in your seat?"

He just said, "Hwmf, Hwmf."

He didn't give me away. He just got back into his seat. Things quieted down and he got busy studying again, and it was too quiet for me. I couldn't get anything out of my lesson, and thought Billy was overdoing it a little studying so serious like that. So, the first thing you know, "BINGO!" and he's out on the floor again.

I think it was a girl who finally gave me away. I was severely reprimanded and warned not to do that again or I'd get a lickin'!

****

One time, I said to Billy, "Come on over to my place and help me clean my stables. You know, my place comes first and then comes your place. We'll clean out my stables first, then I'll come down and help you clean out yours." He had more work than I did because they had more animals. So, we made that agreement and he stopped by our place to help me.

He was very industrious and ambitious. He got right behind the horse and started scraping the floor to clean the stall out good. I stood by watching the operation. Pretty soon, the horse's tail went higher and higher, and I knew just what was coming. He was under the tail raking away and it wasn't long before the noodles started falling on his head. That was amusing to me, of course, and I started laughing. Billy threw down his shovel and that was the end of our deal. He walked away and that was it! I shouldn't have laughed, but it was funny! It was just one of those things. I was mischievous, like kicking poor Billy out of his seat.

Another time, I was down at the lake and we were swimming. One of the older boys was standing there, dressed real nice. We farmboys were lumpich (frumpy) looking. He stood there at the end of the dock and I figured the only thing to do was to push that guy in the lake. Sure enough, I pushed and into the water he went! That was dynamite!! When he came out, he gave me a real lickin'! He was a lot older than I was. I couldn't run away because I was enjoying a good laugh.

****

When I was young, I was quite mischievous, probably because I was healthy and energetic. Sometimes, it did not bring a good reward and I was punished. But I thank the Lord for that because it straightened me out. I'd do foolish things and Father whipped me pretty hard.

Mother was easier. She said that was just life. Besides, she herself at times enjoyed doing a little mischief. Mother was a very sensible Christian person. I'm looking forward to seeing her in heaven.

One time, Ted and I did something very naughty.

My folks had a carbide gas light contraption. We made our own gas for lights and also cooked on it. That was quite an improvement over the old wood stove. We thought we were getting very modern. We learned that we could put this carbide gas into a can to form tremendous pressure, which is how they ran the gas plant. Then we could light a match to it and make an awful big noise. We used to have a lot of fun doing that. We'd put the carbide in a baking powder can, make a hole in the end, and light a match to it. The cover would blow off and we'd produce a tremendous BANG! To us kids, that was a big deal!!

Well, they used to have a preacher come to our area and use the schoolhouse to preach the Word of God. My brother and I were brought up in the Lutheran Church and we had more or less the feeling that anyone who was not in the Lutheran Church could not enter into the Kingdom of God. We know now that we were wrong, but that's the feeling we had back then.

One day when the preacher was talking in the schoolhouse, we got the idea that we would shoo all the people out because that man couldn't possibly be preaching the true Word of the Lord.

It was a terrible thing to do, but we took the carbide and can and got together with six or seven neighbor boys. The air vent for the furnace came to the outside of the building. When they got the program going in the school, we lit off the carbide in the air vent and made that terrible BANG!

Indoors, through the pipes, it must have made a tremendous noise! Some of the women fainted. The minister jumped four feet straight in the air.

He said, "There must be some naughty boys out there doing the devil's work!"

I was really only an "innocent bystander." My brother and another boy lit the bomb. We ran home and, the next morning, the minister came up for a visit. He must have stopped all the way along the road and found out that the Manthei boys were the instigators who had the carbide.

I remember that day because we got a terrible thrashing from Father. We never wanted to be the servants of Satan again. Never! That was a wicked thing we'd done. I'm glad Father took things into his hands to correct us because we needed correction. Like Ted said, sometimes Father would be too severe in punishing us but that time we surely deserved it. That's what good parents do. When a child is naughty, it's a blessing to correct him so he doesn't, later on in life, get into worse problems. Although I don't condone anything violent or abusive, to this day, I thank the Lord that Father disciplined us so we learned our lesson.

> **When a child is naughty, it's a blessing to correct him so he doesn't get into worse problems later on in life. To this day, I thank the Lord that Father gave us the discipline that we deserved.**

Interesting Instructions to the parents and the pupils!

TO THE TEACHER:
This folder contains all the reports necessary regarding the deportment, attendance and progress of the pupil. At the close of each month, fill the blanks neatly and accurately. Send the folder to parents regularly and see that it is returned promptly, bearing the proper signature.

Make all entries with pen and ink, carefully avoiding all erasures. The manner in which these reports are made will indicate the general character of your work.

The monthly grades should be the average of the pupil's class work and such oral or written examination test as you may have. Be just in your markings.

MARKINGS—For exact grading, use figures; for approximate grading use the following letters: E (EXCELLENT), 95 to 100; G (GOOD), 85 to 95; F (FAIR), 75 to 85; U (UNSATISFACTORY), 70 to 75; P (POOR), below 70.

TO THE PARENTS or GUARDIAN:
That the objects for which our public schools were established may be realized, the teacher and parent must co-operate with each other in securing the interest, regular attendance, excellent deportment and proper effort of the pupil. The necessary results are rarely secured if this co-operation does not exist.

These reports should be carefully considered, as they show a complete summary of the pupil's work. Should you at any time observe anything of an unsatisfactory character in these reports or elsewhere, please call upon and consult with the teacher at once. You will thus aid in removing all cause of every difficulty, and the pupil's welfare will be promoted.

Signature of Parents:
1. Mrs. F. Manthei
2. Mrs. F. Manthei
3. Ferd. Manthei
4. Ferd. Manthei
5. Ferd. Manthei
6. Mrs. F. Manthei

Write it on your heart that every day is the best day in the year.
—EMERSON

Public School Report
EMMET COUNTY, MICHIGAN

Name: Ernst Manthei
District: No. 4
Township: Resort

Promoted to _____ Year

TO THE PUPIL:
1. Be clean in person, dress, habit, thought and speech.
2. Be dutiful, polite and respectful to parents, teachers and all whom you may meet.
3. Strive to build up a good character, and your reputation will take care of itself.
4. Be earnest in play in the time for play, and equally earnest in work in the time for work.
5. Cultivate promptness, energy and patient industry. They are worth more to you than money or influence in securing success in life.
6. Finally be courteous, obedient, thoughtful, earnest, attentive, studious and industrious, if you would win the highest esteem of your teachers, schoolmates, parents and the general public.

Please keep this report neat and clean. When you enter school next term, please present it to the teacher for inspection.

A. H. WASHBURN,
County Comm'r. of Schools.

Ted: Those Bloomin' Asters (1915)

Ted

When Mother started growing flowers, my dad wasn't too good to her. We tried to help her, but he would take us and make us grub thistles out of the oat field or something, so she had to work alone. Mother was a courageous person. When she first started, the flowers were way down in the woods where it's all growing up down there. That's where she started, at the end of the pasture. It was pretty nice ground. She had to walkway down there to the bottom of the hill.

I was probably about 10 years old when Mother started the flowers. She got the information from a neighbor lady, Mrs. Ashenbrenner. Mother would help her sometimes down on her farm (currently the Equestrian Center property). She was a small woman. Later, the father got both of their daughters pregnant and wound up in prison for life. Sadly, Mrs. Ashenbrenner couldn't live with the shame, so she hung herself.

Another farmer in the neighborhood knew all about raising asters but he wouldn't give Mother any information whatsoever! He had a whole field of asters but wouldn't give her a bit of information. Oh no! They were cruel.

I give all the credit to Mother for those asters. After she started making money, our dad was the first one to pick up the check. He started helping her after the flowers started bringing in some checks like he'd never seen before. Them days you wouldn't see a check like $50 or $75. That was out of this world!

The businesses down in Chicago could use no end of flowers because that's a big city. We grew really nice asters up here in Petoskey and they matured at a time when they didn't have too many of those growing in Chicago. And, of course, they could use a lot of flowers. Amling Brothers was one of the main companies Mother dealt with. They were Christians. They belonged to our church, the Missouri Synod Lutheran Church. They had quite a business running in Chicago and also in California. I met them in California after I grew up and got married. They were millionaires, but they treated Mother real nice. They gave her a nice check. The short-stemmed flowers didn't bring as much money as the longer ones, you know. They went by the length, not by the flower. Mother would make a wooden crate and lay wrinkled paper across it soaked in water.

> **I give all the credit to Mother for those asters. He helped her good after they started bringing in some checks like he'd never seen before.**

The bouquet could lay on the ruffled-up paper that was nice and moist and it wouldn't squeeze them. The asters would arrive down in Chicago in perfect shape overnight.

They'd hit the train about 10:00 in the morning. The trains would run into town. There was a train going there about every 15 minutes! By the next morning, the flowers would be in Amling's shop in Chicago. Amling paid 1-2 cents per flower. We'd have them all put up in bouquets—some with shorter stems and some longer.

Eventually a disease came in and ruined the flowers. But Mother raised those asters for many years and it got to be a mainstay for the family income. I think she made up to $500-600. That helped pay the mortgage and the interest. We always had to think about how to pay the mortgage and feed the family.

Life was tough and I did everything I could to help Mother. She was heavy and her legs often hurt, so I would rub her feet at night and try to make her life easier. But she always favored Ernie a little. He liked to laugh and kinch around, and she got a kick out of him.

We learned from Mother very early that when the going gets tough, the tough get going!

When I was old enough to drive, we bought our first car. That must have been around 1920 and I was 15 years old by then. I was one of the first drivers.

Our upbringing was not easy. It was very hard. But we learned from Mother very early that when the going gets tough, the tough get going!

Ernie: Mother Runs a Business

Ernie

Father was not a good provider. On farming, they made a very meager living, so Mother had to take things into her own hands. She decided to grow asters.

Someone gave Mother a magazine about flowers. She studied that and learned that you could raise asters and ship them to Chicago. There were several flower companies, but Amling was the name of the company she went with. They were Lutheran. They encouraged people to raise asters and ship them to Chicago; explained just how to do it. They said if you followed their plan, they would buy the flowers.

So, Mother decided we were going to raise asters. Father couldn't see the sense in it. He wasn't with the program at all, but Mother finally convinced him to plow up some ground for her to grow asters. Then she made the connections with Amling so they would buy the flowers she planted. We boys and Mother cultivated and hoed them. Father helped very little.

When fall came, Mother had some beautiful flower—a wonderful crop of red, white and blue asters!

Then Mother studied over the plan from Amling's to learn just how to ship them.

The kids all helped. We'd go out into the field to cut those that had blooms of a certain size. We'd put them in the basement where it was cool. Mother would strip the stems and put them in bunches by size. We kept the flowers in water, wrapped in wet paper. Then we would lay them nicely in big crates about six feet long and four feet wide. Father made the crates out of lath (thin flat strips of wood). Mother probably built the first one and then Father said, "I can do better than that!" He built them after that. They lined the crates with newspaper and wrapped up the flowers some way to keep the moisture in. Then she packed them carefully and Father nailed them shut.

They put the crates on the Express train in the evening and the next morning, the train would be in Chicago. They said the flowers arrived in perfect condition! They bragged her up.

Father thought it wouldn't amount to anything, but Mother took the initiative and after the checks started coming in, then Father became very interested. He helped pick, strip, and pack the flowers. But Mother really got the thing going.

> **Father was not an aggressive starter. He was always afraid. Mother was the courageous one.**

That first year, Mother took in about $300. With that, she bought a brand-new Ford Touring Car for $275. Money went a long way in those days. She sold quite a few flowers that way, year after year, and made enough money to pay off some of our debts. That was our source of income, our money crop.

At the end, they got a disease and turned yellow, so she had to quit raising asters. By that time, we boys were older and had started working. Then we helped her with money.

Father was not an aggressive starter. He was always afraid. Mother was the one who had the ideas and would initiate action. She was the courageous one. Nowadays we'd say she was an entrepreneur.

Ernie: Northview Farm (1915)

Ernie

We thought a lot of our mother because of her gifts. Mother was a marvelous cook. A man once said she could take a beet and make it taste like the nicest beef you ever ate! So, you know what she did? Mother decided to offer dinners at our farm. Father built her a gazebo with a nice sign on it that said "Northview Farm." They advertised "Chicken Dinners at Northview Farm" on the Charlevoix-Petoskey Road.

Dr. Reycraft brought his nurses out once or twice a year for chicken dinners in our home, and Mother would entertain his nurses. Dr. Reycraft used to love Mother's cooking. Finally, one day, he said, "I've got a hotel, (the Reycraft Hotel in Petoskey). I'd like you to come down and be the hostess over my kitchen and show my people how to cook like you do. I'll pay you good money."

She turned down that good job in order to raise us in the nurture and admonition of the Lord.

She told Dr. Reycraft, "That is a very tempting offer. I would love to take that job, but I can't."

He said, "Why not? Why can't you take the job? I'll pay you well!"

She said, "I know you would. If I were gone working all day, my children would grow up on the street and be good for nothing. I have to stay home and bring up my children. Even if I have to raise them in poverty, I want to teach them the Christian way of life, to work and to pray. I'm sorry, but I cannot take that job!"

Northview Farm
Chicken Dinners at Northview Farm were hosted by Constance Manthei. Little did she know that in 2023, the Manthei Family Office would be housed at Northview Plaza!

She turned down that good job in order to raise us in the nurture and admonition of the Lord. She had exceptional understanding and was an outstanding mother. How many mothers would do that today? Even though Mother turned down the job, it hurt Father's pride and he sent Dr. Reycraft away, telling Mother she could never use him as a doctor again.

April 6, 1917

The declaration of war with Germany was very sad news for the Manthei family. Constance was so grateful to be in America, but she was concerned for her relatives who remained in the German Empire. Ferdinand was warned to "stay out of town if he valued his life." German-Americans were now "undesirables," and with his explosive personality, who knew what might happen!

Ernie: Shoes and Water (Fall 1918)

Ernie

Sometimes, my shoes wore out on the farm. I used to herd the cattle for my father. We were poor, so in the summer we never had shoes. Shoes were also being rationed because of the war, so we ran barefooted. If we did get a pair of shoes that fit, by fall we had outgrown them anyway, so Father would wait until the first frost before we got new shoes.

I'd walk on that cold ground with my bare feet. Sometimes, they'd get so-o cold that when the cow lifted its tail, I'd quick run over and stand in the fresh hot cow pie to warm my feet. That was a heavenly feeling!

I remember when I'd get my new pair of shoes and socks for winter, what a wonderful feeling that was! But when I stood in those cow pies, my feet were warm even though the ground was cold, and I thought for sure that I was the winner over Mother Nature—I wasn't going to give in to the cold ground!

Our well was 1/8-mile away, down by the basswood tree in the pasture. At first, we carried the water up from the well with a yoke over our shoulders and a pail hanging on each side. Walking one-quarter mile with that wooden yoke makes the shoulders sore, so we developed a new method. We put a big barrel on a heavy stone sled and used the horses to drag it up and down the hill. Then we'd have enough water for one or two days of cooking and scrubbing. That was our only source of water.

In the spring, the snow would melt off the manure pile by the barn and trickle down the hill into that water hole. It got so bad that the water looked yellow. We had to drink that stuff! We had no other source of water. We had to continue using that polluted water even after we got Scarlet Fever because we had no other source. We lived in a primitive world in those days without purification systems like today. Our folks moved out here to the farm around 1905. We used that water until 1940 when we finally dug the new well here by the house. All those years, we carried water up from that well.

November 11, 1918

Thank God! The war was finally over!!
Now life could go back to normal, right?

Ernie: Scarlet Fever (March 1919)

When I was about nine, I came down with Scarlet Fever. I thought maybe we got that from drinking polluted water. Herbie and I got it real bad. We learned later that it's a highly contagious virus, and Ted thought we caught it from playing cards at Kopenkosky's, because some of their kids came down with it the day after the card game. Herbie got it the worst. Father made him go out and work in the cold even after he was sick, which weakened his immune system. Herbie's Scarlet Fever turned into Bright's Disease, a disease of the kidneys. Everything went bad: kidneys, liver, and finally his heart. He died from that.

Ernie

Mother put all our beds in the living room because she couldn't run upstairs all the time to take care of us. She was our nurse, the cook, and everything. When Herbie died, I watched him. He was lying there very, very sick.

All at once, Herbie said, "Mother, come quick! Come quick!!"

She figured he needed help, so she ran to his side and said, "What is it?"

He pointed up to the corner of the room and said, "Look right up there! I see the Lord Jesus and the angels. They're singing and playing the harp. Oh, it's beautiful music!" He was seeing into heaven!

Mother said, "Where?"

"Come close," he said. "Look right up there."

She came real close and, of course, she couldn't see anything. Then she remembered, from Germany, that whenever people saw into heaven, they died. They were meant for heaven, not earth. So, she shook Herbie!

> **Mother remembered from Germany, that whenever people saw into heaven, they died. They were meant for heaven, not earth.**

He said, "Mother, why did you do that? It was so beautiful." Six hours later, the angels carried Herbie to heaven to be with the Lord.

It happened in the corner of the music room. Ben will inherit this place and I always told the boys and Ben, "Never sell this house! As long as the Lord lets you stay here, keep it, because the angels of the Lord have been in this house!" This all happened right here and, to me, that's real! No guesswork.

It's a marvelous thing that the Lord sent Herbie a vision like that to show us that there is indeed a heaven. There is a hereafter, and the Bible is the true Word of God. I've heard other people tell the same thing. Wally Schultz's friend also saw into heaven before he died. This is one way the Lord has assured us that there is a heaven, angels, and the Lord Jesus, just like the Lord says in His Holy Word. That's what Herbie saw and related to us. It's still vivid in my mind at seventy-five years old, just like I heard it yesterday.

I read in the Bible the other day that we should recognize the day of the Lord's visitation. The Lord visited us that day and we need to recognize that and thank Him for it. The angels visited Herbie here in this house, and six hours later he was in heaven.

After Herbie died, Mother saw Herbie in a dream and asked him if he was in heaven. He said, "Don't worry about me. I'm very happy here in heaven." Then she asked which was the right religion, Catholic, or Lutheran. He said, "You just keep on believing in the Lord Jesus Christ and you will be here with me."

I had to stay here and battle it out! I was so sick that I was in bed for three months! Mother grew weary from caring for us and jumping up every time we called. One night, she had a dream that the angel of death was slinking around the house, looking in the windows. He was real humped up, laughing, and he said, "I'll get another one!" Mother quick hung blankets over the door and windows so that the death angel couldn't get in. She fought to keep him outside. He was looking at me! She would go to the window where he was and hang a blanket up so he couldn't see me. Finally, "Death" slunk away. After that, she was quite confident she had won the victory.

Then I got worse and was about to die. We'd been to a doctor who'd mix up a little medicine for me each day, but I just kept getting sicker and sicker. He was a very poor doctor. That's probably why Herbie died.

Finally, against Father's wishes, Mother went to another well-known doctor in town by the name of Dr. George Reycraft. Father didn't like him and had kicked him out of the house once, telling him he never wanted to see him in our house again. Mother thought he was a good doctor and that Father had made a mistake, so she went and got him herself.

Dr. Reycraft came out and examined me. He said, "That child is very, very sick. I have one medicine I'm going to try. If that doesn't take hold, I'm afraid there's nothing else I can do. He'll be gone." He also put me on a special diet. I could eat no eggs. My kidneys were so bad already. Mother put me on a strict diet of milk and water. I took the medicine like he said and, by the grace of God, I started coming out of it. Mother prayed real hard and I got well. She figured she had really won the victory over death.

Then, while I was recovering, I developed an abscess in the ear. It gave me terrible headaches! The doctor said that if the abscess burst to the inside, it would go to my brain and I would die. In order to prevent that, they'd have to take me into town and operate.

Mother said, "Now they'll kill my other boy. This is sure death!" So, she threw herself onto the bed and prayer that the Lord would save my life. While she was laying there, awake and praying, a voice came to her and said, "Go and steep up Camilentea (Chamomile Tea) in a four-quart pail and let it steam into his ear."

She jumped up quick from her bed and did exactly as she was told! She happened to have chamomile tea in the house, so she put it in a 4-quart pail and got it good and hot on the wood stove. Father had some old leather gloves, so she used them to funnel the steam into my ear. In an hour's time, that abscess burst and a whole lot of matter went down into that four-quart pail!

See how the Lord worked? He answered her prayer, right quick! They probably would have operated and made a real poyotz (dummkopf or a stupid person) out of me! My brains would have gone into the pail!! But see how the Lord operates? A whole lot of pus came out and I lived! For a long time, I couldn't hear well at all in that ear. I finally gained back about half of my hearing in that ear. But it impressed me how the Lord spoke and told Mother what to do. To give the glory to God is a beautiful thing! When I got out of bed after three months, Mother and Ted walked me around the yard for an hour or two until I got brave enough to walk by myself. Imagine that. I forgot how to walk! I turned ten that summer.

Ted: Losing Herbie

My older brother Herbie and I were pretty close. I looked up to him. Herbie liked fires and he always carried matches in his pocket. One day we just happened to be walking down on the neighbor's land and he lit quite a fire. I was right there with him when he did it. Then he just jumped for joy. It was a thrill to him. He always did that anyway when he was awful excited. He would just shake. When he seen that the fire was getting out of hand, then it was no thrill to him anymore. He knew what the end of that could be! We didn't have no water to put on it. But we had enough presence about ourselves to quickly tramp it out. If that would have got real bad, we would have never been able to trample it out. We knew it was a very hazardous and dangerous thing to happen in a forest like that. No fire department or nothing around there to put a fire out. It could have burnt through the whole forest! That would have been really something. Yeah, Herbie was the guy that did that. He was the offender.

When Herbie got sick, our dad made him keep working until he was just about on his deathbed.

It was hard on my mother when Herbie died. She couldn't get over it for a long time. It hurt her. Herbie was pretty close to her and that was hard on her. Herbie would comfort her before he died. He seemed to have a premonition and told her she shouldn't worry or pine after him. That when a person died, it was just like taking off an old coat. You put that into the grave and the soul would go to the Lord. Like an old coat. I remember him sayin' that. He would comfort her that way.

Confirmation Day
Herbie & Ted

Herbie died very shortly after we professed our faith and were confirmed at church. Think of that! The Bible says, "If you confess Me before men, I will confess you before My Father who is in heaven." And that's exactly what happened to Herbie. He died on April 2nd and that year he spent his first Easter in heaven.

Ernie: Uncle Edmund and Cousin Irv Menzel

Ernie

Herbie died in April of 1919. Five months later, Uncle Edmund died in a cement plant accident on September 28, leaving behind a newly pregnant wife, a daughter and a son, who was my Cousin Irv. Uncle Edmund was buried very near to Herbie in Greenwood Cemetery. Our poor mother had lost two people she loved dearly, and she had nearly lost me! Eight months later, we were at the cemetery again… burying the still-born baby daughter of Uncle Edmund and Aunt Anna.

Cousin Irv and I were close in age. He lived in town, but we saw each other at church every week. We were around nine when I had lost my brother and he lost his dad and baby sister. We forged a friendship through those tough times that lasted our entire lives.

Edmund Alexander Reinhold Menzel

Herbert Oswald Manthei
(Incorrect stone inscription;
Herbie died April 2, 1919.)

> **To find the family graves, Ernie would say: "Go straight to the big stone cross, turn right, and look to the right. *You always want to stay on the right side of the cross!*"**

Chapter 4
1920s: Finding Our Way in the World

1920	Oct 13	Manthei family receives USA Certificate of Naturalization
	Winter	Ferdinand remodels the house
1921	Apr 27	Mathilda (Babe) Manthei is born
		Ted and Ernie start building a motorboat, first creative enterprise
		Ted works at Petoskey Portland Cement Company
1922		Ted partners with John Kopenkoskey
		Ted and John buy 80 acres from Frank X Schluttenhofer
	Aug 9	Grandpa Oswald Menzel dies downstate
1923	Summer	Ted & John cut 355 cords of firewood in 55 days
	Fall	Ted and John trap near Wilderness State Park
1924	Spring	Ted picks rocks off land
	Summer	Ted starts farming with counsel from MSU
	Sep 28	Ernie is confirmed at Zion Lutheran Church
		First family car
1925	January	Deed recorded in John Kopenkoskey's name in the morning. (Half to Ted in afternoon. Paid $1500)
	Jun 15	Ernie receives his 8th grade diploma from Maplewood School
		Ernie's works as water boy at Petoskey Portland Cement Co.
1926		The flowers fade (asters develop sickness)
		Ted pays off his farm from sale of bean crop
1927		Ted and Ernie finish building their speedboat
		Christel graduates and wins canning competition
		Ernie cuts ice in Gladwin to avoid landing in jail
1928	Oct/Nov	Ted and Ernie sell Super Maid Cookware, Ted lands in jail
1929	Winter	No jobs in Petoskey or Chicago.
		Ted and Ernie work for Oldsmobile in Lansing, MI.
		Stock Market crash!

Ernie

Ernie: Home Improvements (1920)

After Herbie died, Father did a lot of work on this place. He fixed the roof and put on shingles. He dug a well and made sure we had clean water.

Our barn he built new. Uncle Walter came up from Gladwin and helped Father build it. Then, when Walter built his barn, Father went down and helped him for two or three weeks.

Father built the chicken coop too. He hauled those cedar logs out of the woods to build the chicken coop. I added on the cement blocks and camouflaged it with white boards.

Then he built the greenhouse. The folks raised tomato plants there in the spring. Father built the granary too. Later we converted it into a little house.

Ernie: The Fortune Teller

Ernie

We were, by far, the poorest people financially on our road. Most of them arrived ahead of us and were better established. My father was not a good provider. The result was that we were always about as low on the totem pole as you can get.

My mother once went to a party and met a lady who had the gift of telling fortunes. I don't know if she was a Christian or not. My mother called her, "Schwartze (Black) Bogrum." Her last name was Bogrum, but people were suspicious of her because she could tell how things were going to go in your life, so Mother called her the "Black Bogrum".

To make a little fun at the party, this Schwartze Bogrum called Mother over and said, "I want to tell you your fortune."

Mother said, "Oh, no, I don't believe in telling fortunes."

"Oh, come on!" she says, "it's all in fun! Why don't you just sit down, and I'll tell you what's going to happen to you."

Now why she did that, I don't know. But Mother sat down and this lady looked at her hand and said, "I see that, someday, you're going to be a wealthy woman."

"Ach," Mother said, "you sure are crazy!"

She told us later, "That Schwartze Bogrum is a witch! No way am I going to believe her. I don't care much for that lady."

Mother never liked her after that, but maybe the woman saw something that wasn't so funny. I don't know if she got that gift from the devil or from the Lord, but that woman did know something about the future on people.

I don't believe, when we were young, that there was anyone in our community poorer than we were. Again, that was a blessing. Later, the Lord allowed us to be, maybe, some of the wealthiest in our neighborhood by the grace of God. Isn't that an odd thing?

The more I think about it, the more I believe that people are gifted with different gifts. She, no doubt, had a gift. She said, "Your family is going to be well-off. They're going to run businesses." Her name was Bogrum, but Mother added that "Schwartz" (black) to her name. She thought she was a witch.

That's the way we grew up. I knew there must be something better in life. From there on, everything got easier and easier.

> **Those hardships were a real blessing in disguise because we continually thanked the Lord as life got easier.**

Those hardships were a real blessing in disguise because we continually thanked the Lord as life got easier. If it had started out easy and nice, we wouldn't have thought to thank the Lord for all the nice things when they came. We'd take them for granted. That's a sad state of affairs. It's much better when the Lord takes us through training periods. That's Biblical.

Ernie: Joy Ride Gone Wrong

Ernie

I think I deserved every spanking I ever got, but I think maybe Ted got a few that were overly harsh.

One time, when I was twelve and Ted was sixteen, we went swimming down at the lake. One of the older boys there had a motorboats and offered to take us all for a ride. There was a dance hall down the lake a ways and they wanted to watch the people dance. Ted and I weren't interested in that. In fact, my father was strictly against dancing. If he heard we even went near a dance hall, we'd get a good lickin' already, but we went for the boat ride.

No one really noticed us. It was a beautiful experience out there on the lake! When we got to the dance hall, they tied the boat up, and the older boys went up to the dance hall. Ted and I stayed around the boat.

We stayed and stayed and stayed. It finally got to be late at night and we knew we were in serious trouble. Boy, were we nervous. We knew we'd get a lickin' for sure when we got home! But what could we do? We were stuck. Finally, those boys came back and by the time we got home, it was maybe 2:00 in the morning.

Ted said, "We can't go in the front door."

I said, "What will we do?"

He said, "We'll climb up the cedar tree in the back side over the porch and sneak into the bedroom. Father will never know when we came home."

"Oh," I said, "that's a good idea."

So that's exactly what we did. He said to me, "You go first."

I went up the cedar tree in front of the bedroom window. We had a nice porch roof where you could walk up real easy. I got up in front of the window, and here stood a pair of underwear! Old-fashioned long underwear. I knew who was inside those underwear! Boy, I never stopped to climb down the tree. I jumped off that porch! I took off round one side of the house and my brother took off around the other side.

My father never asked any questions. He never asked what went on or what was the problem. Oh, no! He was prepared, right now, to settle it with no questions asked!

My brother took the wrong way around the house! Dad caught him and gave him a good lickin' with the stick. My brother was getting to the age where he shouldn't have gotten that kind of treatment. That's one reason why my brother never felt very warm toward my father. He got an awful spanking.

While my brother was getting it, I sneaked around the other side of the house, went upstairs quick, and climbed into bed. When my father came up to the bedroom, I was snoring away! He didn't know what to make of that. Was I along with Ted or not? I got out of that without a lickin' but my brother caught it good!

Father treated the older children very harshly and, probably, often unjustly. I don't know up to this day if my brother ever forgave Father fully for all those things. I hope he did. I never held anything against my father because I was more mischievously inclined.

One thing I give my father credit for is that he always saw that we got to church! Even on a cold day, he would hook up the horses and take us to worship. He also was in favor, and saw to it, that we took catechism instruction. He saw that we got our lessons. Those are very valuable things, and I give my father a lot of credit for that. He was very instrumental, along with mother, in making sure we got our Christian education.

Father made it very clear that he better **never** catch us in a dance hall or in a beer garden. He had such a hard bringing-up from his grandmother. She was a Polish girl who liked to "kick up her heels on the dance floor" and led his grandfather down the wrong path so that they drank away the family estate. Father felt that going to those places meant going right into the devil's den. I think he had a good point there, and I thank him for bringing us up that way.

We never went to the dance hall and I'm thankful for that. I got a good wife without going to a dance hall! I didn't need to go to the beer garden to make friends. I had better friends outside the beer garden!

There was a blessing on all of this and I look at the blessings more than the other things. Man thinks and the Lord leads. The Lord's ways are good ways and to Him be the glory!

> **Father felt that going to those places (where there was drinking and dancing) meant going right into the devil's den.**
>
> **I got a good wife without going to a dance hall! I didn't need to go to the beer garden to make friends. There was a blessing on all of this, and I look at the blessings more than the other things.**

Ted: Petoskey Portland Cement Company (1921)

I helped build the cement plant. I bet I worked on every foundation in that plant when I was 16-17 years old. I helped on those big foundations where the giant kilns rested and where the boilers sat. Those big boilers had a couple thousand horsepower! They paid me good—25 cents an hour—and believe me, they kept you going. You really worked for that! A day's labor was cheap. They could never have built that plant if it weren't for cheap wages.

Ted

I did quite a bit of work loading the boats too. Sometimes you'd get a chunk of dust in your nose and when you blew it out, it'd cut your nose so that it bled. That's hard on the lungs too, you know. Some of the guys did wear masks but when you're young and strong, you don't mind that. There were a couple of Indians that did the packing. And the dust, oh my! I was right under the big packing machine. They'd pull a lever and the whole thing was weighed right there. When it would come up to 100 pounds, they'd pull the lever to stop it, then grab another sack from a pile of sacks, shove it under, pull the valve and blow that sack full of cement. Then they'd pull the sack off and it would slide down onto the belt.

My job was to straighten those sacks out so they didn't plug the belt up and do damage. I did quite a bit of work on the belt—a long conveyor belt that was maybe 200 yards. The sacks would ride on the conveyor, and they'd pull 'em off on the boat. Sometimes, I worked right on the boat stacking those sacks.

Ernst did some work there too. He was quite a bit younger, so they probably didn't put him on a job like that. If I was 16; he was only around 12. I think he was a water boy for a while.

Ted: Partnering with John Kopenkosky (1922)

Ted

The farm was bought when I was about eighteen years old. The farm was forty acres. Ernst was still in school.

I decided to go into partnership with Johnny Kopenkosky. We decided to buy the land together from Frank Schluttenhofer. Dad wouldn't co-sign for me at the bank, and I was too young to get credit myself, so Mother went down with me and convinced the banker to let her sign, even though it was not proper for a woman to sign for a loan in them days. Later, the banker told me in private that he knew we would pay it off come hell or high water, so he co-signed for me himself. He was a good man! That's how I was able to buy that farm.

We built a little shack and cut wood in the woods with a cross-cut saw. We cut 355 cords in 55 days! One cord is equal to about two pickup trucks' full of wood. That's a lot of wood! We got our first few bucks that way too.

Old Man Kopenkosky (Johnny's dad) was a fair man. He was Polish, you know. He was fair and he was also honest. He showed us how to sharpen the saw. He was an expert filer. He showed us how to do it and I filed the saw. If I hadn't become a good filer, it wouldn't have worked. When you cut those chunks, it has to be a sharp saw and it has to be balanced right on the set. It has to be about perfect otherwise you're just wasting your time. It gets stuck in the tree.

That first year we didn't farm. We just summer-fallowed and prepared the fields for planting. It was all quack grass. We picked off the stones and hauled onto piles—10-15 stone piles! All those big stones that we discovered when we plowed it the first time had to be dug out, you know. Johnny was a good worker. We dug 'em all out so that became a nice piece of field there.

The end of October, we went up to Carp Lake to trap for the winter. Each of us bought ourselves a .22 rifle. One of the neighbor kids had a very old Model T car and drove us up there to the woods and dropped us off. We didn't know where we were going to sleep. We just brought sleeping bags and I think we slept right out in the open that night. In the morning we went down to the lakeshore and found some driftwood from an old craft (boat). It was about 8' x 8', made out of logs and had a roof on it. We took those old boards and logs out of the water, picked 'em up and carried 'em to our spot. Then we scrounged burnt nails from an old lumber shack that had burned down. And we had hardwood lumber. That was quite a combination... hardwood and burnt nails. We put a roof on there and bought a roll of tar paper, and that's where we slept 'til the middle of January.

We got some coon, mink, quite a few muskrats. We built a little lean-to on the side of that shack about eight feet wide, and that's where we put our pelts.

We lived off rabbits we'd get in the woods, and partridges, and there was an apple orchard right close by where we ate quite a few apples. That's the way we lived. Right out there in the woods. We'd cut wood from dead trees and build a fire and keep the place warm. When you're out in the woods there's not so much wind blowing around. It was quiet. Easier to heat. There was a stream, and we'd go out and get ourselves some trout. We just lived off the land. We could walk about three miles to a store and buy a little bread. Maybe some salt and bacon, baking powder. We had a little oven made out of tin and I'd make baking powder biscuits. We'd catch a lot of rabbits in those box traps. They were no good for pelts, so we ate a lot of rabbit stew.

Johnny was very frugal. He used both sides of the toilet paper. He had two pairs of underwear. He would wear one and hang the other on the line to air out. Then he'd turn that one inside out and wear it again, hanging his second pair on the line to air out. He didn't want to waste any water on washing.

In the spring, we planted beans and oats. We did okay. I started talking with Michigan State University Agricultural Extension program, and they put us on a crop rotation.

Ernie: Learning from Ted (1923)

Ernie

When my brother started coming into his own, Ted trapped fur, mink, and weasels. He'd sell them and make enough money to buy himself and me a suit or some clothes. Then, he'd go fishing on the lake and bring home fish for Mother. He helped in many ways. Ted was always a hard worker and a good provider.

I learned a lot from Ted in that respect. He was very aggressive. I don't think he ever shut his mind off. I think he kept it running day and night. When he'd sleep, he'd be thinking about what he'd do the next day, or even what he could do while he was sleeping. He had a very active mind, and he was a promoter. He could promote something out of a pile of manure! You can see from his life that he's a very successful man and came a long way in this world.

Another thing about Ted. I could never hold money like he could. I was more easygoing with spending it. But whenever I needed money, I knew that Ted would always have a little in his pocket! He was savvy. He would not spend anything unless it was absolutely necessary, but you could always borrow from him.

One time, my brother wanted to buy a farm and Father wouldn't co-sign for his loan at the bank. So, Mother said, "I'll sign!

She went down and the banker said, "This is not the right way to do it. You and your husband are both supposed to sign. But since your husband is so stubborn, I'll take just your signature." The banker was very kind that way. It was not legal. Mother didn't know that her signature without Father's didn't amount to much, but the banker knew mother was a good solid woman and took her signature. It all worked out well.

When Ted bought his farm, there was a lot of dead wood lying around from fallen trees. It was a beautiful virgin forest, which still hasn't been touched. But the fallen trees, he and his partner, Johnny Kopenkosky, collected and sold to the lime kiln as kiln wood to melt the lime. Ted cut up that dead wood and, with the money from the lime kiln, he paid off the loan for his farm and still saved his timber. Ted was a hard worker, and I learned a lot from him.

> **I learned a lot from Ted in that respect. He was very aggressive. I don't think he ever shut his mind off. I think he kept it running day and night.**

Ernie: Three years in the 8th Grade

Ted and I trapped when we were young. We'd get up at 5:00 in the morning to run our trap lines. Then we'd rush home and do chores: milking the cows and cleaning the barn and throwing out the manure before breakfast. We didn't have a bus to catch. We had to walk to school! In fact, we'd run to school and try to make it in time to avoid a lickin'. Them days, they'd use a stick on you if you were late!

I was out of school early because I never went to school very long. I only had eight grades of education, and it took me three years to finish the 8th grade!

I was a mediocre student. I loved machinery and was not so interested in modifying predicates and adjectives. If they'd had a course in engines, I would have been a top scholar. I did do well in History because I loved history. I did okay in Arithmetic and Agriculture. I loved Agriculture! Those three subjects got me through school.

I spent, nonetheless, three years in the eighth grade!

The first year, I was busy cutting wood with Father and helping out on the farm. Then I got very sick with Scarlet Fever, so that year was lost. The next year, we went for three months, and they fired the teacher for some reason and never replaced her, so I lost that year too. The third year, we had a very good teacher. That year, I got solid A's!

I always told my children I was three years in the eighth grade and then they found my report card one day. They said, "Father, you must have been telling us stories because you had solid A's!"

I said, "After three years, I should have had solid A's!"

It probably wasn't all my fault that I spent three years in the eighth grade. We had some problems, and in those days, they weren't worked out as seriously as they would be today. People didn't consider them so important. We just did the best we could, by the grace of God, to make it through. Most of the time, it was survival of the fittest anyway.

Ted: Florida, Toledo, Lansing, Chicago (1927)

Ted

We couldn't farm during the winter, so we found other ways to earn money. I worked in the cement plant out of Toledo Ohio. I was about 17-18 when we worked down there. A penny saved is a penny earned, you know, and I saved every penny I could save. Didn't waste any money on living. Never went to a show. Never went anywhere or bought any new clothes. I wore what I had. My folks used the money to buy that piano that we have down there in the lodge. I paid at least half of that brand new.

Other times we'd go down to Florida to pick oranges in the winter to make a little money. We did that for three different years. I paid my farm off doing that.

One winter, we were working in the Oldsmobile factory in Lansing. I was on the loading dock, loading these automobiles into box cars and Ernst was working there too. We had to cross a big bridge over the river to get where we were staying.

We were just approaching the bridge when a guy came off it and said, "Don't cross the bridge. There's a hold-up man in the middle out there!"

> **A penny saved is a penny earned, you know, and I saved every penny I could save. Didn't waste any money on living.**

That gave me needles! I don't think he'd have made it even if he had a gun. When you're young, you're fast and there were three of us. We were daring. Oh heck. We walked right out there and, sure enough, he held us up.

Ernst grabbed him like lightning (laughs). I never seen anybody move so fast! Ernst had that guy hanging over the bridge (laughs) and the robber was crying for help. Ernst hung his whole body right over the bridge. It was a long way down there, you know. We were about 200 feet above the water. It was a high bridge!

Ernst was strong, you know. We had fun with that guy all right. He was awful tickled just to get off that bridge alive. We should have dragged him to shore and took him to jail. That's what we should have done.

Another time we were riding in a streetcar in Chicago in the evening. We were trying to look up a certain place and didn't know where it was, so we asked the conductor. He was a little shrimper, I remember. Boy he was cocky.

I said, "Do you know anything about how we could find this place here?"

He looked at us and said, "Do you think I'm a walking directory?"

We didn't know whether he was or not and we went back and sat back down to talk it over. We said, "That's a public servant there. He should at least be civil." He could have said, "I don't know where that is. I'm green on the job..." or something like that. But what he said was kind of a dirty way to treat a stranger.

So, we went back up to him a short time later, about fifteen minutes, and asked him again and he answered the same way.

Ernst grabbed hold of him and said, "Now listen fella. We're not foolin'. You're going to tell us where we are and where we're supposed to go and we're gonna find out right now!" He shook him a little, you know. Suddenly that shrimper knew exactly where we were! He directed us to the right car and we got where we needed to go. I'll never forget that.

Ernst shook him a little and said, "You're a public servant and you're going to be civil. We're going to get down to business now. You know where you're at in Chicago and we don't know. So, let's see what we can find out, now!"

That was what he needed. He got us to the right streetcar and we landed where we were supposed to land. Chicago is not a small place. There's a lot of city there. You take a couple of farm kids, and you can get lost pretty quick. But we were tough enough to get the information we needed to succeed.

> **That's one thing about Ernie and me. We were young, fast, and daring. We weren't afraid of anything. We were tough enough to get the information we needed to succeed.**

Ernst also did some trucking for the county. When they repaired the roads, they'd hire guys like him to do a little work. It would last only a few days and you'd get a few bucks, but not very much. I think he bought his truck before we went into Super Maid cookware.

The Prohibition

The Prohibition era lasted from 1920 to 1933, but Uncle Walter would not be stopped! He continued brewing for family and friends until the day he was told that the Feds were on their way to arrest him. Walter quickly dumped his mash in the pig pen and cleaned out his still. When the Feds arrived, all they found were a bunch of squealing pigs happily rooting around in the mud!

Ernie: Me? A Jailbird? (1927)

The Bible says in Proverbs 22 that "A good name is rather to be chosen than great riches."

When I was eighteen years old, I had to work very hard one winter to save our good family name.

Mother suggested that I go down during the winter to visit Uncle Walter. He liked to visit with me. So, I rode down with someone going that way and I planned to stay a week to play with "Cousin Fritz" in Midland.

> "A good name is rather to be chosen than great riches."

Uncle said, "I just bought a new five-shot repeating shotgun and I've got a good hunting dog. Why don't you go hunting?"

"I'm not much of a hunter, and I don't care much about hunting," I said.

"Manthei," he said, "You've got to do something while you're here. Now you go out there and hunt!"

He practically forced me out the door. He put his nice new gun in my hands and said, "Here, now you go hunting."

While he went to the barn to feed the sheep and horses, I took that good gun back, hung it up, and to make him happy, I took his single-barrel shotgun with me.

He had told me, "All you do is follow the dog," so I followed the dog right across the frozen river and up the other side to a road. I wasn't out there fifteen minutes when we came to the road.

Uncle Walter makes Ernie go hunting

Here came a car. I had a funny feeling about it and turned to go back into the woods. The car stopped and the driver motioned me to come out. He saw me in the woods. There were no leaves to hide me and just snow, so I came out.

He said, "Hey you! Come on over here." I went to the car. "Show me your license!"

"I don't have any license. I'm Uncle Walter's nephew and he insisted I go hunting. I never thought about a license. In fact, I didn't even intend to hunt!"

"Well, you've got a gun and no license, so I'll have to arrest you!" he said. Think of it! Uncle pushed me to go hunting and I'm out there not even fifteen minutes when a sheriff spots me. "You must come with me!" he says, so I got in the car. I don't know where the dog went.

"Boy, I don't know," I said. "Before we do that, we better go tell Uncle Walter where I am so he's not worried." The sheriff knew Uncle Walter.

Walter came out, heard the story, and said, "Roy, you can take the boy, but please leave my gun."

"What do you want the gun for?" he asked.

"I just bought that repeating shotgun. It's a good gun!"

The sheriff said, "I don't have no repeating shotgun."

Uncle Walter says, "Let me see that gun!" The sheriff showed him the gun and Walter said, "That's a smart boy! Okay, you can go!" There was no sympathy. It was like playing dominoes; it's not a sympathy game!

The sheriff took me in before the judge. The judge said, "You've been caught for hunting without a license."

"Yes," I confessed. I told him the story and how Uncle insisted I go hunting and never mentioned a license.

He says, "You're in trouble. I'll have to fine you." He was a real stinker. He gave some exorbitant fine, like a hundred dollars.

I had no money to pay the fine, being a young kid! Uncle Walter wasn't about to bail me out. I could have called home and asked my parents to send me the money, if it were possible, but they were poor and I wasn't about to do that.

I said, "Look, I'm from the north. I don't know anything about hunting." I tried to explain the situation, but he just said I was under arrest. Then he gave me two choices.

"You can either go to jail or put up ice (carve ice blocks) for the City of Gladwin for two weeks!"

I thought, *Boy, I got into this mess and now I'll have to work myself out!*

"I cannot get a bad name," I told the officer. "My mother would be sick about it, and I don't want jail time on my name. I can't go to jail. I'll have to put up ice!"

So, I went to work right away, then called Uncle Walter and explained my situation. He had friends by the name of Schantzes, four miles out of Gladwin, who were much closer to the city than Uncle. He was out about twelve miles.

He said, "I'll make arrangements for you to stay with Schantzes at night while you're putting up ice during the day."

I had to get up at 5:00 a.m. and walk four miles to put up ice for ten hours at the lake near Gladwin. We cut the ice into twenty-inch square cakes with a cross-cut saw. Sometimes, the ice was twenty-four inches thick!

The other workers were getting paid, but I was a jailbird, working for nothing. They treated me bad! All this was because Uncle wanted me to go hunting when I didn't even want to hunt! Uncle Walter insisted, put the gun in my hand, and sent me out to get a rabbit. He told me, "Follow the dog!" So, I followed that dog right over the river and down the road. Think of it! I wasn't out there fifteen minutes!

I was so bushed at night. Then, I had to walk four miles back to the house for supper.

Mrs. Schantz wanted me to get acquainted with a nice young lady staying there by the name of Bertha, but I ate supper and went right to bed so I could get up at 4:00 the next morning to put up ice.

> **I felt I'd really accomplished something when I finished that job. I kept my good name!**

I did that for over two weeks, and I felt I'd really accomplished something when I finished that job. I kept my good name!

Later, I went back to Gladwin to sell Super Maid Cookware with my brother. I made pretty good money selling in that area. I went back to that judge and said, "Do you remember me?" We talked and I told him I thought he went overboard on his sentence.

"But you were a good man," he said. "A good man!"

Ted

Ted: Super Maid Cookware (1928)

One year, Ernie and I sold Super Maid cookware. We got into Super Maid when a fella by the name of Round came to demonstrate, and Mother bought some cookware from him. He was a round guy who looked round too. He inspired Ernst to sell, which he did. We wanted Ernst to sell Super Maid and Ernst was very much in favor of it. But to tell you the truth about it, every time Ernst did something when he was young, he was always afraid. He would always back up. And I was always dumb enough that I wanted to see if we could make a go of it. I thought if I could go along with him down there a little while, then he could go on his own and I could go back home again. It was in the fall, and we were done with our work around the farm and there was no reason why we couldn't stick together a while and sell pots and pans. We were the best salesmen they had in that area! We got a nice grip (briefcase) out of it as a reward for high sales. We were ranked right at the top. Yeah, Ernst turned out to be a real good salesman. He persuaded them real good and sold a lot of stuff. He never felt good about charging so much money though, and I didn't either. I think the Lord didn't want us in that. We were hayseeds by trade. That's when we got in trouble with a car wreck in Grand Rapids and all that stuff.

Ernie

Ernie: The Real Jailbird was Ted!

While we were selling Super Maid cookware in Grand Rapids, we had an accident. Ted was driving. He went through an intersection where the traffic light wasn't working and banged right into the side of another car. It was slippery and we couldn't stop on a dime. Thankfully, no one was hurt. Ted gave him an awful bang, but the other driver wasn't hurt. He said his head bumped the top hard, but that was all. It smashed up our car, so we had to borrow Mr. Round's car to get to where we were staying. It was an old Rio.

There were no police at the site. We stayed overnight, went to church the next morning, and then reported the accident to the office in Grand Rapids. We went to the station and reported it to the police ourselves.

Mr. Round advised us on how to handle the situation. "You did everything you could possibly do. Just go down to the courthouse and tell them you'd like to go before the judge and get this over with."

Mr. Round had told us, "Just plead guilty, pay the ten-dollar fine, and then come back here and go to work." So, we went before the judge. I think his son or someone had gotten caught for drunk driving and got a good rap, so this judge was mad!

He said, "Guilty or not guilty?"

If we said, "Not guilty," we'd have to hire an attorney and take it to court. We just wanted to pay our fine and get out of there.

Ted said, "I don't feel I'm guilty. What do you think I should do?"

"Well," I said, "Mr. Round said to plead guilty, pay the fine, and get out of here." So, we did what he said we should do.

The judge said, "So you're guilty!"

Ted said, "Not really, but I did hit him."

"You're guilty. Okay," he says, "forty-five days in jail and $105 in court costs." Boy, now that was a really rough rap! "Take him away!" he says to the guard.

So, they handcuffed Ted and took him off and threw him in jail.

I went back to the office, and everyone thought that was a terrible thing, but they didn't know what to do. He was in jail under sentence.

I decided the only thing to do was to go home and tell Mother, so I jumped in the Rio and drove home. When I told Mother what had happened, she said, "They threw Ted in jail amongst those robbers?"

I said, "I don't know about robbers, but they handcuffed him and threw him in jail."

"Oh, my golly," she says. "We've got to do something right away!"

I said, "What are we going to do?"

She says, "We're going down to see Governor Green!"

Mother had a tremendous amount of initiative. This was a mother defending her son. Mother was a real strong-willed woman!

I said, "Maybe I can rest a little and we'll go in the morning."

Mother said, "Oh no, we can't wait!" She got dressed up, took her coat, and said, "Let's go!"

I got back in that car, and we drove all night to Lansing. We got there in the morning. Ted was sentenced Monday. I left that afternoon and drove home. Then I drove back to Lansing, so this must have been Tuesday morning since the accident happened Sunday morning.

We sat all day Tuesday, waiting to see Governor Green. His secretary (Arlin Lay) kept coming out and saying, "Please don't wait. You cannot see the governor. He's busy today."

Mother would say, "I'm staying right here until I see the Governor!"

"Okay," he'd say. So, she sat there, and the secretary kept coming out to try to get us to leave.

Finally, in the afternoon, he says, "I'll tell you what. You give me that message you want to give to the Governor. Write it down on paper, give it to me, and I'll see that he gets it. Tell me just what happened." So, he sat down with us and Mother told him the whole story.

He said, "That does sound ridiculous! I'll give it to the Governor, and you trust me that this case is going to be handled. We'll look into this!"

He took the message to the Governor, who turned it over to Mr. Nichols. He was the head of the Department of Welfare. He went right to Grand Rapids to investigate.

He checked everything out and said, "This is ridiculous! First offense. The boy's a farm boy from Northern Michigan and knows nothing about laws. They weren't drunk! This is a terrible sentence!"

He talked to the judge, then talked with Ted and told him, "You'll be out of here within hours."

Mr. Nichols was very provoked! He went back to the judge and really bawled him out. Then, he went back and told Ted, "You're going to be pardoned out of this prison within so many hours. When you get out, you can sue the City of Grand Rapids for putting you in jail and defaming your name."

> **"If I get out of jail, I'll be very thankful. I don't want to sue nobody."**

Ted said, "If I get out of here, I'll be very thankful. I don't want to sue nobody."

"Well," he said, "I just want to tell you that you got a rotten deal."

By that time, Ted had been in jail four or five days. That was an awful thing, and I did all I could to get him out of there. Mother and I did a lot of running around.

Ernie: Cousin Irv

Ernie

As we were out there peddling cookware and making a name for ourselves as expert salesmen while trying to stay out of trouble, our cousin Irv Menzel was busy making a name for himself as a popular athlete. When his mother remarried and moved away, he chose to stay in Petoskey to finish his high school career. He lived with friends and set some football records that have never been broken.

Irv and I thought a lot of each other and always enjoyed our times together. Later, he got a job in Traverse City as the high school football coach.

Popularity Section

Heading the popularity list for this year are Margaret Bain and Irvin Menzel. We think that we have made a good choice, too. These two are not only popular in their own groups but are well known and liked throughout the whole school. In the Senior class Margaret is everybody's friend, and Irvin's popularity cannot be denied.

Margaret has made herself very well known and liked by her classmates because of her enthusiastic support of the worthwhile activities of our class. "Bain," with her views and suggestions, is a familiar figure at all class meetings. She is one who is always ready to help her friends and her class in any way that she is able. She is a prominent figure at all social functions.

"Irv" is one of whom our class may be justly proud. As all Northern Michigan knows, he is a prominent athlete as well as a leader in social life. His pleasing personality is shown by the host of lasting friends he has acquired during his scholastic career at Petoskey High. He is a most reliable member of our class and can be counted upon to perform his part in all class activities.

CAPTAIN MENZEL

Ernie

Ernie: Our Speedboat (1928)

Ted and I once bought an old boat and rebuilt it.

We put in new wood strips for ribs, put in planking, and we worked together hard on the boat for a few years.

The only thing we needed to buy were screws. Father was never in favor of the project, but Mother saved a little out of her butter money to buy us screws and we fixed that boat up.

Then we needed to buy an engine. I'm not sure where we got the money, but maybe Mother scraped it out of her butter money and gave us three dollars. With that, we bought a Continental engine from a car that had been in an accident.

Ted and I would earn a little money picking strawberries for a neighbor and we'd buy a piece of this or that to work on our boat. We worked three or four years and finally got that boat running beautifully. We put a steering wheel in it from a car, had that engine, and made a nice-looking boat.

Aldie Ganshaw bought a DeWitt speedboat and paid a lot of money for it. We had built ours up ourselves, and I could pass Aldie! My boat was faster. That was quite a feat! He had put a lot of money into his.

We would entertain the young people with our boat; take them across the lake for marshmallow roasts and take them for rides on the lake. We tried our best to divide up the joys with all the Lutheran Walther League Young Adult group. We'd load that boat down until the water almost came over the rail. Everyone wanted a ride.

Father was never really sold on it, even then. He was a pessimist and looked at the sour side. But Mother was always very encouraging and wanted to help us. Mother would say, "As long as you boys are working on your boat, I know you're not getting into mischief. You're doing something worthwhile."

Mother did all she could to help us. She was an outstanding mother. She was like an angel, a very special mother. She never *discouraged* us, but always *encouraged* us.

****

Mother used to read to us about the problems that went on between the Catholics and Lutherans in Germany. The stories were so well-written, you could almost smell the flowers. She was such a good reader that you could picture everything in your mind, and it was better than a movie. Some nights, Ted and I would be ready to go out with the boys and Mother would say, "Tonight, I'm going to read a story." We would close the door and sit right back down to listen. Her stories were that good!

Father was just the opposite. When he would read, we wanted to fall asleep. But we didn't dare! If we had a blizzard and couldn't get to church, Father would read one of Luther's sermons, which were about 1½ hours long. We had to sit through that, and believe me, we much preferred going to church!

****

Now it was time to grow up and get serious about life. We were in our twenties, and it was time to act like adults. On top of our normal struggles for survival, we were now entering the Great Depression.

74

October 30, 1929

Stock Market Crash

Ernie never forgot the newspaper pictures of people jumping out of skyscrapers in New York when the stock market crashed. He advised the family to avoid investing in the stock market and put their money into land instead.

When asked how the Great Depression affected the family, Ted said: "The Great Depression? We never had nothin' anyway, so we just had a little less of nothing."

Chapter 5

1930s: Farming Our Own Land

1930	Winter	Constance and Ted go to a clinic in Missouri for health issues
1931	Winter	Ernie attends Michigan State College, Ice Cream Makers Course
		Ernie works at Freeman Dairy
		Christel meets Chet
1932		Ernie buys a truck and hauls gravel for Emmet County
		Ferdinand develops a heart disease
		Ernie takes over farming at the homestead
	Winter	Ernie works in Belding, MI.
		Christel gets engaged
1933	June	Ted and John buy south half of farm from Frank B Schluttenhofer
		Ernie farms with Ted and John
1934	Spring	Ted and John pay off mortgage and split property
	Jun 13	Christel marries Chet
	Summer	Ted and Ernie partner and start farming certified seed beans
	Sep 1	Death of Ferdinand, age 56, from chronic myocarditis
1936		First indoor bathroom
	Winter	Ted and Ernie pick oranges in Florida
1937		Ted takes Bible seriously and teaches Ernie in the fields
		Ted sees future office in a dream
		Ted experiments with strawberries
		Ted and Ernie buy a Maytag washing machine for Constance
		Ernie gives Christel land to build a home
		Ted experiments with strawberries, winters in FL with Goebel
1938		Dave Fero helps Ernie on the farm
		Bad bean year! Electricity comes to Resort Twp, radio story
		Hitler invasions begin in Europe
1939		Big bean year! Dave Fero leaves in August
		Ernie researches irrigation with Michigan Dept of Agriculture

Ernie: Moving to Nebraska? (1930)

At one time, Father wanted to sell the farm and move to Nebraska where he could farm in a big way and make money. Some of the farmers around here tried that, like the Schwartzfishers. The two brothers had a nice farm here, which they sold and bought a big farm in Nebraska. Then they had a bad dry spell, the Dust Bowl, and lost everything. They came back and had to start all over again.

When Father suggested selling our farm, Mother said, "Oh, no. I like this place and I'm staying right here. If you go, you're going by yourself!"

There had to be one boss, and, in our family, Mother wore the pants. It was a good thing that she did!

The Dust Bowl

Ernie: Freeman Dairy (1931)

I was the head ice cream maker at the Freeman Dairy for about three years, starting when I was about nineteen.

Bud Schultz went to our church. His father was the minister so I knew him well and used to invite him out to the farm. We were good friends. Bud said, "Why don't you come and work for the dairy with me. You can help me, and we'll work together."

Ernie

I got thinking and talking it over and said, "Alright."

It was just a small plant, but they sent me to Michigan State College for three months and paid all my expenses. Two companies checked my efforts and offered me year-round work. One was Sanders Ice Cream Company from Detroit. But Freeman Dairy had sent me down there and paid all my expenses. I couldn't take another job. It wouldn't have been fair to them. So, I came back.

Bud was the butter maker and I became the ice cream maker. I liked my work because I could sample the ice cream.

Every morning, the truck came from their headquarters in Flint with the refrigerated ice cream mix. All I had to do was put it in pans and mix in the flavorings for all the different ice creams: chocolate, sherbet, and all the flavors. Then I'd put them in the old-time freezer.

> **I may have become a permanent ice cream maker! But man thinks and the Lord leads.**

My wages in those days, (if I remember right) were $22.50 per week. With that income, I helped Mother. I also saved money and bought myself a truck.

The only problem was that ice cream, in those days, was only a summer job. I worked from May through September, and then they'd send me home. $22.50 a week wasn't enough where you make a good living working only four or five months out of the summer. Otherwise, I may have become a permanent ice cream maker! But man thinks and the Lord leads.

Ernie: Hauling Gravel (1932)

When I quit the dairy, I went into hauling gravel for Emmet County. I hauled a lot of gravel for them. I bought a brand-new Chevy truck. I saved very carefully, helped at home, maybe borrowed some to boot and bought that brand new truck. I put an old dump body on it. Couldn't afford to buy a new one. I hauled for the county by the load. They paid so much per load. I'd run fast and make a little money. They had their own gravel and hired us to haul it.

During the winters, we milked the cow and did chores and took the butter into town at the end of the week to buy Cotesuet. That's what we lived on during the winter. Then I'd put up ice, cut wood, pick up a job whenever I could do an odd job. We weren't lazy. Wherever we could get a job to pick up a nickel or dime, we'd do it. I also helped Ted during the summers on his farm.

Ted: Ending My Partnership with Johnny (1934)

Eventually, my farming partner, Johnny Kopenkosky, wasn't interested in beans anymore. It was hard work with low prices. We decided to split up the land and go our separate ways.

I gave Johnny the right to choose which land he wanted, the upper or lower half. I wanted the lower lakefront land 'cause I loved to go fishing, even though some of it was worthless swamp. Our shack was on the upper land. I prayed hard that Johnny would choose the upper part, remembering how Abraham let Lot choose his portion first and how God blessed Abraham for it. It happened to be the rotation year to plant beans on the lower land, so sure enough, Johnny chose the upper part and that's how I ended up with this nice lakefront property.

Abraham let Lot choose his portion first and God blessed him for it. I believed God would do the same for me.

By that time, Ernst had finished school, and we decided to be partners.

> **Abraham let Lot choose his portion first and God blessed him for it. I believed God would do the same for me.**

MANTHEI BROTHERS PARTNERSHIP

Ernie: Partnering with Ted

Ernie

During the time I was hauling gravel for the county, Ted was working with Johnny Kopenkosky.

Once Ted and Johnny got everything paid off, Ted decided to get married and establish a home of his own. Johnny stayed single all his life. Ted prayed when they split up because he wanted the lower part of the farm by the lake. They had built a shack on the upper end and Ted figured that, since Johnny was not a builder, he would probably take the upper half where he could live in the shack.

Ted told Johnny, "I'll let you decide which part you want." But he prayed hard that the Lord would put it into Johnny's heart to take the upper end.

Sure enough, Johnny chose the upper half and Ted got all the lake frontage.

One day, he came to me and said, "Ernie, you'll never get anywhere working for the county with a truck. You better come and work with me. We'll raise beans together. We'll farm my land and raise crops. We'll do all right."

That was when Ted and I decided to become partners and that's how he and I got into the "oats and beans" business.

> **"Ernie, you'll never get anywhere working for the county with a truck. You better come and work with me. We'll raise beans together. We'll do all right."**

Partners Ernie & Ted

Threshing

Hired man Dave Fero → on left

53-B

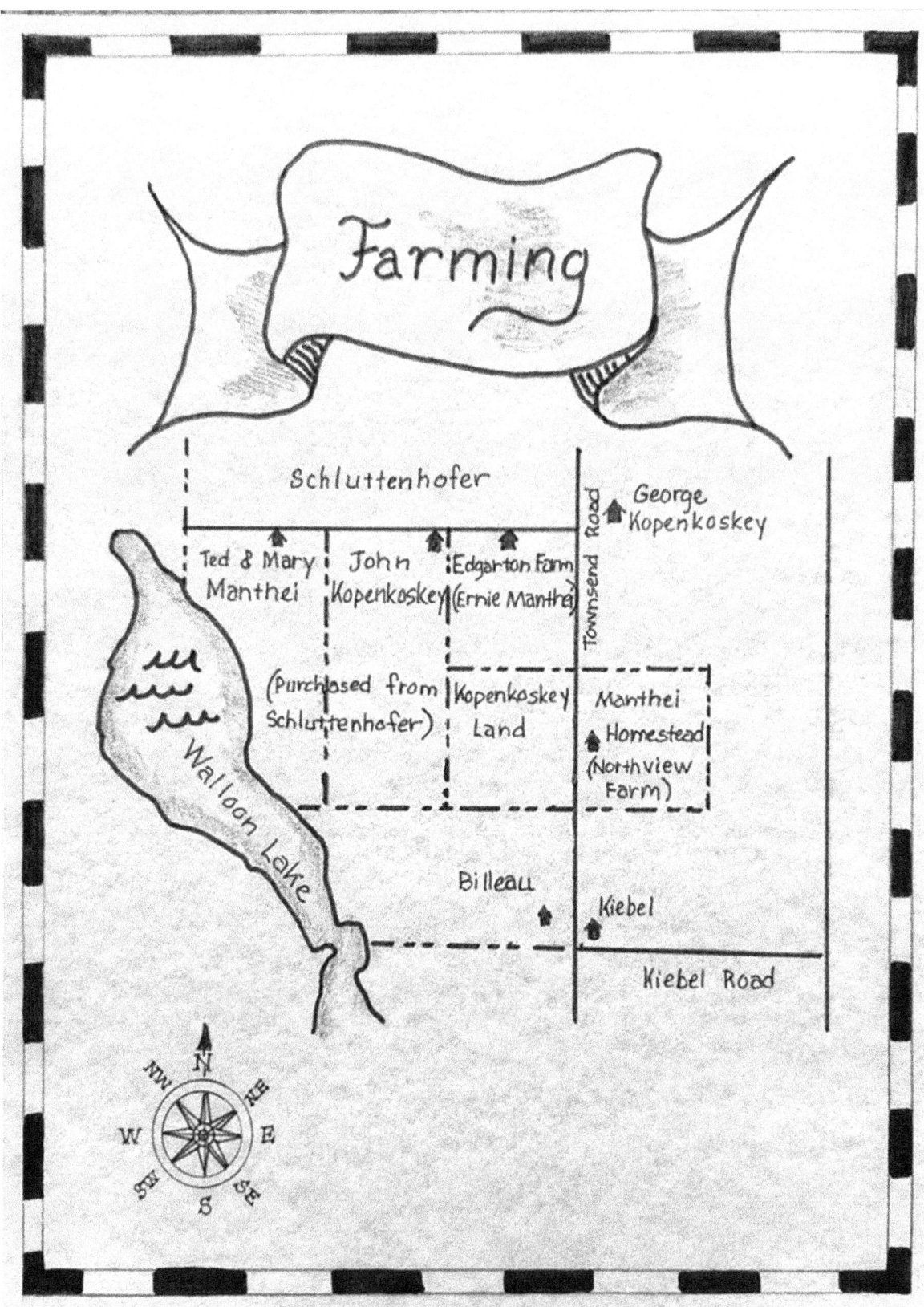

Ted: The Inheritance

Ted

When I was farming beans with Ernie and had no house and just nothing, I had a marvelous dream or vision. The Bible says without a vision the people perish (Proverbs 29:18). This vision ended up guiding my life.

In this vision, the setting was a great big ranch. It was a tremendous establishment. Ernst, me, and a friend were working for an old widow, and she had a lot of real estate. It reached as far as the eye could see. And the weeds were bad! I was a farmer and that was a good way to approach a guy like me because I knew what had to be done with those weeds. We really worked at taking out those weeds!

> **The Bible says that without a vision, the people perish. This vision ended up guiding my life.**

The thing that struck me so hard in the vision was this... How could anyone get me to work so hard not even knowing if I was going to get paid? Not that I was worried about not getting paid, but I was wondering to myself how could anyone motivate me like that. We worked there from early dawn until dusk when we couldn't see no more. As the light faded, we all walked down this lane that ran across the estate. I picked up the wire so Ernst and our friend could crawl through, and then we stood in line, the three of us all in a row. I looked to the north and, down the cattle lane, here came a big, beautiful limousine. In it was the poor widow we were working for! She had us all fooled. She stopped her car right where we were standing and said, "I've come to give you your pay." This was the answer to my thought!

She handed our friend a *check*, and all his life he received a paycheck for what he did. Isn't that interesting?

She pointed to Ernst and said, "You are going to get a *reward*." That was way above a check because you don't know what it is. It's more alluring, you know. More attractive.

And then to me, an *inheritance*... (laughing) ...which is above a reward. I just felt wonderful! I had no inheritance coming from my folks. But I was going to get an inheritance from the Lord!

Then I woke up. That was quite a vision I had there!

And it was given to me to know that this poor old widow was the church. We were serving the Lord there, you see. We three always worked together in the church for the Lord. We were the officials. And when you're working for the Lord, you don't get paid, do you? Not physically. The Lord blesses but you don't get a payroll. He makes provision for a blessing, you see.

That big estate was the world that needs dressing (being tended or taken care of). The Lord told Adam, "I made this world and now you dress it." Take care of it and make it fruitful and multiply it. And woe to anyone that doesn't dress it. He's in trouble. He gets down in the slop barrel. He's gotta get out there and help dress that earth. Even if he's doing it under someone else's tutorship, he should be out there dressing the earth!

A lot of people don't want to do that, you know. They'll steal and do anything else, but they don't want to dress that earth. And that means not to hurt the earth but to dress it. Clear out the stumps and the stones and plant the crops and mine the minerals out of the ground and make the thing produce. That's the way the Lord laid the thing out. Exactly like that! You dress it. And I understood that real well. I was a dresser of the earth.

> **That big estate was the world that needs to be taken care of. The Lord told Adam, "I made this world and now you dress it and keep it" (Genesis 2:15). Take care of it and make it fruitful and multiply it.**

Ernie

Ernie: Hard Work

Our fields were mostly down by the lake. When Ted and Johnny split up, we farmed Ted's property. Whatever we raised, we divided up. Later, I bought the Edgerton farm and when we put crops in there, we always divided up the harvest.

Ted and Johnny bought our first tractor. They bought an old 10-20 International. It had iron lugs and when it would get into the field, those lugs would plug up with dirt and be just one big ball of dirt all around. Especially if the ground was sticky. Then it wouldn't pull nothing!

I think Ted let Johnny keep the tractor. We didn't have much tractor business. We worked with horses until, one time, after we raised beans for about ten years, we sold one crop for good money. Until then, we sold them for very little money. Low wages every year. Hardly even paid for our fertilizer!

Ted and I both learned to be aggressors from our mother. We were inventive and inherited her tendency to actively go ahead and do things.

Ted and I cut wood with a cross-cut saw for a neighbor, Roland Risk. We had to cut it in sixteen-inch lengths, split it, and pile it so they could measure it. All that work for 65 cents a cord!

Ted and I worked hard at that all winter. We worked so hard that we could hardly eat enough to keep meat on our bones. We were working in the woods on the other side of Kiebel's. We'd walk home for dinner, and Mother would feed us good. She'd make us a nice warm dinner. Then we'd walk back and cut again all afternoon, steady and hard. About four cord of hardwood is all we could cut in a day. That was our budget. At night, I would do the chores and Ted would file the saw so the next morning, we could cut again. We did that all winter long.

Ernie: Partnering with the Lord

Ernie

My brother once said, when we were working in the woods together, "Unless we take the Lord into business with us, it will not work. If we will take the Lord into business in whatever we do, and give the Lord His portion of ten percent, the Lord will bless the effort of our hands."

I said, "How do you know that?"

He said, "I've been reading the Bible."

Ted was always very attentive and active at reading the Bible. We would be hoeing and then he would tell me some of the stories he read in the Bible. Actually, I learned a lot right from Ted hoeing in the field.

> **Ted said: "Unless we take the Lord into business with us, it will not work. If we will take the Lord into business in whatever we do, and give the Lord His portion of ten percent, the Lord will bless the effort of our hands."**

The Lord tells us we are to do that with our children. We are to talk of the Lord when they sit at the table with you, when you work in the fields, and when you walk on the way. We are to tell them of the glories of the Lord and of the Holy Word of God.

Ted used to read the Bible and then tell me the story he read. He read a lot more than I did because he was older. He'd tell me Bible stories while we were hoeing or whatever we were doing. I'd think, *I wonder if Ted really got that story right. He could be wrong.*

I'd ask him, "Where is that written?"

He would tell me and then he'd say, "Now, if you don't believe me, you go and read it yourself." That's how he got me reading the Bible! Then I'd go and read it. I'd find that he was right on the ball. Once we had both read it and agreed, then we could discuss it together.

We started tithing and the Lord blessed us in many ways to make it possible to give money to His work. We tithed for many years out of our veneer mills. The Lord's portion was always sent in. The Lord says, "Without Me, you can do nothing." So, by the grace and with the help of God, we were able to accomplish what we did in this life. The glory goes to God!

It was the "hungry thirties," and people couldn't raise the money to pay the minister, so one time my brother and I turned all our earnings for one week over to the minister so he could buy groceries, too!

We always helped Mother with our earnings. We never figured that Mother should feed us for free. We did all we could to help at home, my brother and I.

Ted and I bought Mother her first gasoline washing machine, a Maytag, so she no longer had to do the laundry by hand. Were we ever proud! Ted and I did some odd jobs and pooled our resources. Before that, she washed all our family's clothes by hand with a scrub board and tub. Mother didn't have electric mixers, wash machines, dryers, gas stoves, automatic furnaces, and all that. She had to do everything by hand, as well as helping Father haul hay. Then she'd come in and make lunch. I don't know how those women in her generation ever stood that. They were outstanding women! How they ever were able to accomplish all that is beyond me. But the Lord gave her strength, and she was able to do it.

Ernie: Registered Certified Robust Beans (1934)

Ernie

We raised Registered Certified Robust Beans for ten years. Those beans were very popular in those days. They were little white ones, a special variety of bean. They were called "Robust" because they produced well, but it was very hard labor!

We kept raising those beans year after year after year. We always pulled them by hand. Thirty acres! You know what that's like to pull thirty acres all by hand? Maybe that's why my back still hurts a little today. It's a reminder of pulling those beans. That was hard work!

> **I never played tricks on Ted. No. He was not mischievous like I was. He was a hard worker—not much for fooling around or playing.**

Then we'd put them up on stakes. They call that the "McNaughton Plan", which was a good name, but there was a lot of work to it! We stacked them all up to shed water and ours didn't spoil.

Ted was pretty strict, a hard worker—not much for fooling around or playing. Didn't appreciate a joke too much. Ted was not much for monkeying around and playing. He *would* go swimming. I never played tricks on Ted. No. You'd get the wrong end of it with Ted. He was not mischievous like I was. He was older and very serious. You didn't fool around and kid much with him. He was very sincere.

McNaughton Method—
pulling & stacking beans
so they can dry.

Old Man Edgerton
with his dog.

MANTHEI BROTHERS
SEED GROWERS
PETOSKEY, MICHIGAN

April 11, 1934.

Farm Bureau Services Inc.
Lansing, Michigan.

Dear Mr. Bennett:

In reply to your valued favor of April 6, will state that our Cert. Robust Seed Beans have been sold for $4.00 per cwt. f.o.b. Petoskey without complaint, however most of these went out of the State. We have only a small amount left on hand and can place without difficult.

In regard to the clause on our stationary we wish to express our sincere appreciation for calling our attention to the existing mistake in connection with Cert. Seed, as we also grow and sell common seed we had this clause put on without even giving it another thought. For this valued favor we are sending you a gal. of our maple syrup.

Thanking you we remain,

Yours very truly,
MANTHEI BROTHERS

(Growers)
B. Manthei- T. Manthei- J. Kopenkosky.

Ted: Preparing Dad to Die (1934)

Ted

Mother was always very helpful. But them days you didn't show much affection. Life was too hard. Dad wasn't much good at affection. And he wasn't a steady worker. He never could work too long because he'd get in a fight with somebody or somethin' would happen. He was never on the job long enough to make a good wage and pay things off.

A father like my dad was a dangerous man! My dad admitted that he was awful fortunate in his life not to kill somebody with his temper. There were a lot of people that were badly hurt by him. He would tackle 'em.

But he did go to church. He did bring us up in the nurture and admonition of the Lord, even though he himself, I don't believe, was completely converted 'till on his deathbed. Towards the end of his life, he was sick and helpless. That's when I could really plow with him. I was the guy who would talk to him every night. He was very cutting, you know. He could really cut you down! Then I would go back to the

Ferdinand's final days, suffering with dropsy.

forest, and the Spirit of the Lord was working on me. I'd come back the next night charged up just like I was the night before. I was ready to tackle the tiger, you know. And I would study the Scriptures, you see. He didn't know the Scriptures as good as I did, and I finally could whittle him down when he got to the point where he got to be helpless and couldn't fight back.

When he died, he called on the name of the Lord, and that's all you can do. I didn't shed a tear when he died. We were tickled he was gone. We didn't have much love for him. He never sowed any love, you know. He sowed all his stuff with a stick.

> **When he died, he called on the name of the Lord, and that's all you can do.**

Ernie: The Death of our Father

The doctor told Dad that, if he didn't get his anger under control, some day it would kill him. Sure enough, his heart gave out. He couldn't lie down because he had dropsy, a heart disease that results in poor circulation. The legs would swell up and get big; the blood didn't circulate, and his legs started to deteriorate. They start rotting right on the bones. He smelled to high heavens from gangrene! It was like having a carcass in the house. He was rotting from the bottom up.

Mother had to wrap him every day with rags where the water would seep out. She'd wash those rags and finally they'd get so bad that I'd have to go and bury them. I buried them right under the cedar hedge by the barn. She'd use them for 3-4 days, then beg and borrow for more rags. The hospital wouldn't take him at all. And furthermore, we were poor and wouldn't have been able to pay.

That went on for nigh unto a year. Every day, she would change his dressings. Twice a day at the end! And the odor was terrible! You could smell him from down the road. He couldn't walk. He just sat there, but his mind was still good.

Ted did a lot to help Father accept Christ as his Savior. My dad would read the Bible, but some people can be ministers, reading the Bible, and somehow it never goes down into their hearts. That is something you need to pray for, that the Holy Spirit works faith in your heart to accept Christ as your true Savior, who died in your stead on that cross for your sins and mine. The Bible says the Holy Spirit works faith in our hearts to believe. I think that even ministers can preach the Word without truly believing it all the way.

Father would say, "I don't know if the Lord could ever forgive my sins. I'm a big sinner. How could the Lord ever forgive *my* sins?" Then Ted would tell him about Abraham and Joseph and the disciples. Ted knew Scripture and he told Father that when the Lord says He died on the cross to pay for our sins, you need to believe that! He'd get right after Dad. Ted did a lot of good witnessing.

The last 2-3 weeks of his life, Father became very humble. Finally, he said, "I know that *my* Redeemer lives." You can't say that unless you really believe it, see?

Shortly after that, he died. He was ready to go home. It's a special blessing when the Lord lets you live long enough to really accept His Word.

Father died in this house, sitting in the piano room. I was around twenty-five when Father died.

> **Father became very humble. Finally, he said, "I know that *my* Redeemer lives."**

At that time, there was a debt on the house of $600-700 and I had no money to speak of. We needed shingles for our roof and tin for the barn roof. I bought it on credit and worked it all off at the Petoskey Ice Company that winter and picked up jobs whenever I could. I paid everything off and took care of Mother.

Ernie: Mischief (1939)

I was mischievous and used to get a lot of spankings as a kid. When I got older, I played a few tricks on Mother. She was happy and enjoyed playing tricks. I played them on her and she played them on me. She was a little mischievous herself!

Dave Fero worked for us one summer while we were raising oats and beans. Dave was from Pellston. He was younger than me. He was a good worker, and I liked him. We got along exceptionally good. He was a good fisherman and a very accomplished young guy. He was a good boy, but mischievous, like I was.

Dave and I worked hard all day, shocking grain and got tired. Ted ran the binder and cut the grain, then Dave and I had to shock it up.

One night, it got to be 7:00 and the field wasn't all set up yet.

Ted said, "I'm taking Mother to the show tonight, but you two didn't work hard enough." He always had an excuse that we didn't work hard, but we worked as hard as we could. They were going to see *Gone with the Wind*. We wanted to go to the movie too, but Ted said, "No, you didn't work hard enough today. You're going to stay and finish shocking that grain. You can't go."

So, we had to go down and shock that grain. Then Dave and I came home, hungry and tired. We ate some supper and, while scrounging around, we found some champagne. You see, Mother had some sparkling wine given to her by a friend, Chimmy Curtis, and she always marked the bottle to know exactly how much was left. It was high-quality champagne. The bottle was about half-full yet.

Dave liked to drink a little, so he said, "Let's hit that bottle!"

"Oh," I said, "that's Mother's."

"Yes, I know," he said. "What we'll do is, we'll drink it down and then we'll fill it back up to the mark with water and that gargling stuff." We had some gargling stuff the same color as that wine. "That way we'll celebrate, too!"

"By golly," I said, "that's not a bad idea.

So, we drank that half bottle right down to practically nothing. Then we put in that gargling stuff and water right up to the mark where we started.

The next morning was Sunday. After church, I said, "Mother, are you going to give us a little drink of your wine?"

"Oh, no," she said, "that's mine! That was my present. I treat you fellers pretty nice, but I'm going to drink that myself."

"Okay," we said, "you drink it then."

She took down the bottle. We watched as she poured herself a small glass and started drinking. "Oy," she said, "that's terrible tasting stuff! I know it's wine, but why should it taste like that?" She drank another six, seven, eight swallows. Finally, she said, "Oh my, that's terrible stuff! What happened to this?"

We said, "We don't know. It's your stuff." Finally, we had to fess up to what happened.

Dave and I got into some awful tricks. Mother didn't get mad though.

She said, "You kids. You're always into some mischief!" But she thought it was pretty good mischief, because when she was young, she liked to pull a few tricks herself.

She laughed and said, "I don't know what I'm going to do with you guys. You sure put one over on me."

That was a dirty trick. That was after Father was gone. But if you dig a grave for someone else to fall into, you often fall into it yourself.

> **I was mischievous, I played a few tricks on Mother. She was happy and enjoyed playing tricks. She was a little mischievous herself!**

Sometime later, my brother and Teddy Lou took out a couple girls for a picnic down by Walloon where his lodge is now. For some reason, they left in a hurry and left a nice bottle of root beer, along with some other things. We were hoeing beans down there, so Dave Fero and I found that. Of course, we drank out the root beer and filled it with lake water, leaving in just enough root beer to give it some color. We put the cork on and put it back where we found it. Later, Ted remembered that he left it there and, since it was still full, he brought it home and put it in the refrigerator for later.

Well, Dave and I came home, looked in the refrigerator, and there we saw the root beer. Boy, that looked good to us and, since no one was home, we hit her and ended up drinking that lousy lake water ourselves!

I said to Dave, "That's terrible tasting stuff!"

He said, "It sure is!!"

Then we found out that Ted had brought it home from the lake!

Ernie: Broadcasting over the Radio (1939)

Another trick came about when Ted and Mother were on a trip down to Saginaw. Ted had a scrimmage with a car.

Dave was a sharp boy and, by that time, we'd made a few dollars; enough to buy a cabinet radio. Dave and I were hauling hay. Ted always said he worked harder than I did so I had to work longer to catch up. Dave and I had to stay home to do the work.

Well, Dave knew how to hook on the power tube of that radio so that we could broadcast over the radio from the basement. He was clever! He rigged up the broadcasting system in the basement while they were gone, using a microphone from the telephone. Then he ran a wire to the radio. All we had to do was turn on the radio, flip a switch in the basement, and we could talk over our radio. We practiced and played and had a lot of fun.

When they came home, Mother had the Ladies Aid over. She liked to listen to "Heiney and the Grenadiers." She got real excited when they played German music. We had not told anyone about the radio. Mother told the ladies, "Heiney and his Grenadiers are on the radio. We all have to listen."

"Oh," the ladies said, "we would like to hear that." She turned on the radio and Heiney was really going at it.

I told Dave. "Now's the time!" We went through the outside door down into the basement. Heiney was singing and playing and then we flipped the switch and I said, "This is Heiney and I want to tell you a story." (*Ich wille euch eine geshickte ersahlen*.) Of course, I had to tell the story in German. About half-way through, I forgot the story, so I said, "Shucks, this whole thing is bull**** anyway!"

Mother was so embarrassed in front of all those women. They said, "What kind of a program are you listening to?"

She got so upset! She said, "I'm going to write a letter to the station immediately and tell them what a terrible thing that man did!"

The ladies all agreed that it was *bad*.

Dave and I were in the basement laughing and we flipped it back over and Heiney came on again.

"My, that was terrible!' Mother said. "He must have been drunk and now he's straightened up again."

We quickly slipped out of the basement and went about our work outdoors.

That night, Mother was determined to write Heiney about that terrible thing he did. We could not dissuade her, and we didn't want her to write in and make a fool of herself.

I knew I had to stop her, but we didn't want to give up our secret too easy.

Just before that, Mother had sent Dave and I out of the house for gassing off after our bean soup supper. We were stinking up the house, so Mother said, "Get out of here!" It was all in fun, of course.

We went into the basement and started broadcasting. Since Ted had just had that accident in Saginaw, I came over the radio and said, "There's a guy by the name of Ted Manthei who had an accident in Saginaw. The police are after him to put him under arrest. His license number is…"

Ted sat there listening and getting worried. Finally, we said, "Mother, if you wouldn't feed us so many beans, we wouldn't gas off like that!"

She said, "That came right over the radio. Did you hear that? What's going on here?"

> **That's how we let her in on our secret about the radio and, oh, did she laugh!**

That's how we let her in on our secret about the radio and, oh, did she laugh! She said, "Do that again!" We went down and broadcasted. Who would have thought we could do that?

****

Another time, a neighbor boy came over who chewed Copenhagen tobacco. We were playing cards when Dave winked at me and excused himself. I knew he was up to mischief. Of course, he slipped down into the basement.

This boy had just taken a good fresh chew of Copenhagen and was chewing away.

Dave started broadcasting over the radio. "We have a new report on Copenhagen chewing tobacco. We found some terrible things in there; chicken feet, chicken heads, and even some chicken manure!"

Bill got red in the face, went outside, and spit out his chewing tobacco. First thing you know, Dave was back up, playing cards as nonchalant as ever.

Dave said, "Bill, wasn't that awful?"

Bill quit playing cards and went home. We never told him what we'd done. We played some dirty tricks.

****

Dave lived here for a while. He was engaged to Babe. For some reason, they broke up. Ted didn't get along too good with Dave. We were raising beans and oats at that time, and Dave also helped haul in hay. I was gone for an operation on my varicose veins in Grand Rapids. While I was gone, Dave disappeared. I figured Ted must have fired him. I always felt bad about that because Dave was a good buddy of mine.

Dave went to Detroit, bought a truck, and drove for Algers for a long time. When he retired, he moved back to Pellston.

Note: It turned out he and Babe were never engaged. It was a rumor cooked up by Mother and Babe and he pulled out when he learned that it was circulating around the neighborhood! He felt bad that he never told Ernie the truth.

Ernie: The Bad Year & The Good Year (1939)

The next year, we had all our beans sacked up nice, hand-picked, and ready to ship. But on the market, they were paying only $1.95 per 100 pounds of beans. We put in so many hours to pick them all by hand and then they didn't even want them! Couldn't sell them.

Ernie

I said, "Ted, what'll we do?"

He said, "Dump them all back into the storage bin."

I said, "Oh, my goodness. After all that work, dump all those beans back into the bin?" We had half-a-car load all sacked and ready to go and had to dump them all back in the bins.

Then I said to Ted, "Now what are we going to do?"

He says, "Next year, we'll plant thirty acres more!"

I said, "We can't even sell what we've got! Plant thirty acres more? Doesn't that sound a little ridiculous?"

But Ted said, "That's just what all the rest of the farmers will say! We'll plant just as many as always."

Ted was a very smart man! He had a lot of sense. He was four years older than I was and he was smart.

Look how the Lord leads! We dumped all those beans back in the bin. In the spring, we got the ground ready and planted thirty acres more, then worked and cared for them all summer. We cultivated, hoed, and pulled them all by hand in the fall. Then, we piled stones on the bottom, and put the beans up on stakes to shed the water if it rained.

That year, it turned out real wet in the state of Michigan. It rained and it rained and it rained. The big bean growers around Saginaw had all their beans spoil on the ground. That's because they harvested with machinery and left the beans on the ground to dry. That year the beans couldn't dry with all the rain and they turned brown, which made them unfit to sell. But ours dried perfectly because they were up off the ground on stakes. We thrashed ours and added them to the ones from the year before, and we had a whole carload of beans!

We didn't know the result until a man came up from Michigan State Agricultural College one or two months later and told us that nearly all the seed beans in the state of Michigan had spoiled because of the weather. But ours he registered! That year, a farmer from Manitou Island and we Manthei's had the only Registered Certified Robust Beans in the state of Michigan. We felt pretty good about that. The McNaughton Plan had finally paid off!

People started writing to us for seed beans. The college had certified us as the only ones who had Registered Certified Seed Beans. One big farmer came up from Saginaw and thought he was going to make a killing on beans the next year so he said, "I'll take *all* your beans. The whole car load!"

We settled on eleven dollars per hundred weight. (Up from $1.95 the year before!) That was a lot of money in those days for a whole carload. We got a pocket full of money, around twelve thousand dollars, all in one pile. In those days, you could buy a lot of stuff for that!

Twelve thousand dollars in those days bought as much as one-hundred-twenty thousand dollars today! We paid off all our debts and bought us each a brand-new Oliver tractor on rubber wheels for the farm and bought us each a car. Ted bought a new car and I bought his, which was about one year old.

Now we were in good shape! We had all our debts paid off and were in the clear. We both had good cars, good tractors, and we were in business!

Look how the Lord leads! Pulling them all by hand, dumping them back. Through hardships He blessed.

This is how the Lord blesses. He wants you to have patience. He wants you to hang in there. We always gave to the church. We always prayed. We didn't complain to the Lord. We just kept right on working and that's what the Lord wants us to do! Then all at once, when the time was right and the Lord felt that we could handle it, then he gave us great results for working steady. We knew it was a blessing from the Lord!

I like a verse in a devotion booklet about the way that God gives—sometimes the greatest blessings are through hardship and suffering. It says, "The choicest delicacies in the pantry of heaven are reserved for the suffering."

After that, I told Ted we better keep some seed back to plant some for next year. But Ted said, "No, next fall you'll buy your seed for peanuts. All the farmers will plant all the seeds in the world because they'll think there's big money in it."

Sure enough, the next fall they had so many beans that you couldn't give them away! They were real cheap again.

Well, we quit the beans right there and went into raising strawberries!

> **This is how the Lord blesses. He wants you to have patience. He wants you to hang in there. We always gave to the church. We always prayed. We didn't complain to the Lord. We just kept right on working and that's what the Lord wants us to do! Then all at once, when the time was right and the Lord felt that we could handle it, then He gave us great results for working steady. We knew it was a blessing from the Lord!**

1938/1939: A World at War

September 30, 1938

It was happening again… Another war!
We were glad Father wasn't here to see what Hitler was doing in his homeland. Mother had been keeping her eye on the news as Hitler moved into the Sudetenland, just across the mountain from her beloved Silesia.

September 1, 1939

When Hitler invaded Poland, Mother thanked the Lord again for His protection in not letting her go back to the German Empire, where she and Father had grown up.

FANCY
DORSETTS
MANTHEI BROS.
PETOSKEY, MICH.

Strawberries ready for market

Chapter 6
1940s: From Agriculture to Industry

1940		Babe marries Bob Notestine
		Ted gets quit claim deed from investors in his farm, including Constance
		Ted and Ernie develop irrigation system with oil lines and boiler flues
		Big berry year! Water cannon
	Sep	Manthei Brothers buy a "crate factory"
	Fall	Ted and Mary get engaged; Ted builds home on edge of strawberry field
1941	Jan 25	Ted and Mary get married, honeymoon to Mexico and California
		Failed attempts at building crates
		Herb Trier moves to Petoskey, helps with berries and crates
	Dec 7	Americans join WWII after bombing of Pearl Harbor, Dave Fero drafted
1942	Feb 12	Dave born to Ted and Mary
	Summer	Ernie meets Margaret
	Fall	Ernie and Margaret get engaged
1943	Jan 31	Ernie marries Margaret in Grand Rapids, MI. No honeymoon (WWII)
	Oct 23	John born to Ted and Mary
1944	Jan 22	Herb is born to Ernie and Margaret
1945	Jan 19	Paul is born to Ernie and Margaret
	March	Ted starts wintering in CA, builds home at 3310 Alma St, Lynwood
		Manthei Bros Veneer Mill is launched! (Lloyd Dorenberg)
	May 8	WWII ends in Europe
	Jun 20	Dan is born to Ted and Mary
	Summer	Manthei Bros ship berries to Mackinaw Island for Governor's Convention
	Sep 2	WWII ends in Japan
1947	Feb 26	Judy is born to Ernie and Margaret
		Veneer mill turns a profit! Shingles go up, Ted's dream fulfilled
	Sep 9	Tim is born to Ted and Mary
	Nov	Ted buys 20 acres in Huntington Beach, CA
	Nov 27	Margaret dies at age 37, leaving behind Ernie, Herb, Paul, and Judy
1948	Summer	Ernie begins oil venture in Blackfoot, Alberta
	Jul 21	Ernie marries Cora Behling in Orange, CA
		Problems with union, Al Behling hired to run the veneer mill
1949	June	Ernie returns to Canada; oil comes in! Problem with Chester
	Dec 3	Tom is born to Ted and Mary

Fancy Fairfax and Dorsett Strawberries (1940)

Editorial Comment: Historic documents about these berries help us understand this story. M.S. Pryor in Salisbury, Maryland, promoted different varieties of strawberries that they supplied in 1933. Here are a few excerpts...

*The **Dorsett** was introduced by the US Dept. of Agriculture in 1933. It promised outstanding flavor that projected it to become "the leading" variety with BIG BERRIES—BIG CROPS—BIG PRICES. "But the thing that impressed me most was the flavor; both Fairfax and Dorsett are outstanding in this respect, being different from other strawberries." Their large size and attractive shape "should attract many buyers and when tested, the flavor will make them buy again and again." Pryor concludes, "I believe... Dorsett is destined to become one of the leading commercial varieties as it has all the points of excellence to make it become a leader." The prices of all Pryor's other strawberry varieties were $.25, whereas the prices of both the Dorsett and Fairfax were $.40.*

> Ernie called them the "Fancy Fairfax and Dorsett." Edgerton and his son tried growing these berries year after year, until they finally went bankrupt and lost their farm.
> After enough farmers failed and the promises were deemed empty, the Dept. of Agriculture listed them as "Unsuitable for Commercial Production." This is where this amazing story begins...

Ernie: Edgerton and His Tasty Berries

We got into strawberries because our neighbor, Edgerton, had a berry called the "Fairfax and Dorsett." They were developed in England. It was a new variety and was an exceptionally sweet, delicious strawberry.

Ernie

Edgerton was half-Indian, and he was a good gardener. He irrigated and raised some beautiful berries.

We used to go down and help him pick berries to make a few pennies. Then, at night, we'd go down and pick some for ourselves for the belly. In the dark! We liked those lovely, sweet strawberries!

Well, we got so taken up with that berry that my brother said, "That's something that we're going to have to raise!"

> **We got so taken up with that berry that my brother said, "That's something that we're going to have to raise!"**

Ted: Too Good to Resist

Old Edgerton, our neighbor, well it just got the best of him when he tasted that berry. He wanted to try growing that berry and he wound up behind the same kind of eight-ball as the rest of them. But there were a few plants here and there that had something to eat. As I walked across his field to go home to eat dinner, I'd walk by his berry patch and that's how I tasted it too. And I finally got to the point where I just couldn't resist them. I'd get to stealing! It was such a good berry, you see.

Ted

I asked Edgerton, and he let me buy the patch from him. The amount of stuff on there wasn't worth taking to market but it was really good. I picked all those berries off and ate 'em!

Then I wanted some of those plants to see if I could produce that berry. I read books about them. Edgerton read the books too. All the farmers read those books. And they all ended up losing money—every one of them.

That first year I did just like the books said. It wrung our financial necks. No berries. Just a few nubby little scrubby things. But they'd buy 'em anyway! We kept raising beans until we could get a good berry patch going. There was no time between beans and berries. We planted both and always had a good crop running.

Ernie: How I Bought the Edgerton Farm

Ernie

It just so happened, about that time, Edgerton wanted to sell his farm, so I bought it. He sold the whole farm, with strawberries on it, for two thousand dollars. I borrowed all the money to buy that from a fellow named Brill.

Brill was a miser in our county, quite wealthy but he lived a poor life. His house was papered with newspaper. He gave his wife $1.50 per year to buy cloth for two new cheap gingham dresses. That's all the dresses she dared to buy. The old overcoat he wore had turned green already from age. It must have been forty years old. I can see it yet today in my mind's eye. He made quite a bit of money. He loaned it out on interest to those of us who needed to borrow money. So, he loaned me the money and I bought the Edgerton place.

I must have bought it a few years earlier because we still didn't have money, and we paid off all our debts with that last year's bean sale. That's probably when I paid off the Edgerton place. Before that, I only made enough money to pay the interest.

The way I bought the farm was a funny deal, too. Edgerton would raise the berries and his single son, Harris, would work for him in the summer. When fall came, his father couldn't pay him, so he'd say, "I can't pay you Harris. I'll write you over the farm." So, he'd give him the farm and Harris was paid. No money involved. Then, they would skip through the winter somehow.

In the spring, Harris would say, "Well, Dad, now you help me raise berries on the farm." So, the father worked for Harris all summer. Come fall, he couldn't pay him, so Harris wrote the farm back over to his father.

This went on for two, three, four years! Every year, they'd write the farm over and pay each other that way. Never any money involved.

The last time it got into Harris' hands, he'd had enough! He said, "I'm fed up with this. I'm not doing it anymore." So, he pulled a fast one on his father. Harris came to me one day and said, "You want to buy my farm?"

I said, "Harris, you don't want to sell that farm. It'll kill your father!"

He said, "I'm going to sell that farm. If you don't want to buy it, I'll offer it to somebody else. I just thought I'd give you the first chance."

We had a reputation for being hard workers and could raise the money. We had a good name, and he wanted the money.

"Well," I said, "if you're going to sell it anyway to somebody, I'll talk it over and see what I can do to raise the money."

He told me, "Let me know in a few days."

"Okay," I said.

I talked it over with Mother and she said, "Maybe you ought to buy that. We'll go to Brill and see if we can borrow the money." They had borrowed from Brill before and paid him off, so we had a good reputation with him. I went to Brill and he said, "Yeah, Manthei, I'll loan you $2,000.00 at 7% interest."

So, I said, "Okay," and he gave me the $2,000.00. I didn't have to pay any interest 'til the end of the first year.

I said, "Okay, Harris. Here's $2,000.00." We went to an attorney, drew up the papers, he signed them, and I signed them. He was feeling good. I don't know if he paid his father for the summer's work, but I bought the farm and let his father live there for a while.

> **Ted was a very good farmer—probably one of the best! I was better with machinery, but Ted liked the soil. Together, it worked out pretty good.**

Edgerton stayed on his farm until, after a while, he somehow ended up in an old folk's home. In no time, he was dead. He was getting old and couldn't run the farm anyway, but it probably bothered him a lot. Harris went to the city and got a job. I think Harris was getting married and needed the money. Now Harris has been dead a long time too. I've still got the farm. The boys own it, and Jim has the farmhouse. I divided it among them. I gave Herb some, Paul, Mark, Jim, and Christel. I didn't give Ben an interest because he was going to inherit our farm.

Edgerton had his strawberries in the woods. Those berries aren't known for producing abundantly, but he irrigated. He still didn't produce as much as we did.

My brother was a very good farmer—probably one of the best! It was just natural for him. He was so interested in the ground and loved it so much that he'd carry it around in his pocket to be sure he had it with him all the time. He was exceptionally good at farming. He knew how to balance the ground. I was better with machinery, but Ted liked the soil. Together, it worked out pretty good.

Ted: Healing the Plant

Ted

It was a very unusual thing that happened with our strawberries. Manthei Brothers were the first to perfect that berry! We were the first to make such a terrific production out of it. It baffled the officials because it went against their writings. It went against the brochures that were turned out by the University of Michigan and the United States Dept of Agriculture. I read all that stuff, you know. They said the Fancy Fairfax and Dorsett variety was "unsuitable for commercial production."

> **The Manthei Brothers were the first to perfect that berry!**

But I figured I was a good farmer, and I could outwit them, you see. How conceited I was! It wasn't me at all. It all tied in with that vision for my inheritance and dressing the earth. Here's how that went...

In the early years we had to take Christel down for a course in Home Economics at the University, and we weren't afraid to get acquainted with those professors and ask questions. I was also a member of the Crop Improvement Association. I had some dog-gone good tutoring, let me tell you. Those professors came up and toured our place and checked the fields where we were growing seed for the beans. We got acquainted and they taught me about *marl*. I didn't know what marl was, but I learned that marl is a highly saturated mineral body. It goes back to the flood. The floodwaters deposited those minerals in the lake. And I understood that pretty well.

> **The success wasn't me at all. It all tied in with that vision for my inheritance and dressing the earth.**

The 100% soluble stuff is like water. It floats in the water. It will never settle to the bottom. It stays in the water and floats out to the sea. That's why the ocean is full of minerals. But the ones that weren't 100% soluble were heavy enough so they would sink. It's kind of a secondary recovery deal.

That marl is worth billions. Especially for your health. According to Dr. Albright from the University of Missouri, man is not capable of making a mineral body like that artificially. Nature has to do that. You get it into the body through the plants.

The University of Michigan helped us get started digging that stuff out! They had quite a few inventors in the university. Fellow by the name of Mussleman invented a cheap contraption out of a few pulleys to dredge marl out of the lakes. They helped us get one and we dredged out about a thousand tons. They knew it was good to put on the ground. That's about all they knew.

After we dredged it up to sell it, nobody would buy it. So, we spread it out on our own fields.

I knew that the mineral was a fantastic fertilizer because the sweet clover grew to be eight feet tall, like up to the ceiling. Most of that body is lime, and the sweet clover just loves lime. It flourishes on that. I didn't know what it was except that we sold some kiln wood and dragged some trees out of the lake, and wherever one of those trees lay the grass grew sky high. Way up above the other grass. You could see it was a valuable fertilizer. I didn't understand it at the time, but the mineral from the marl (mud) had been put on the ground before we planted the beans. When the beans were planted in the ground with those minerals, we raised a superior germ in the seed. We made our first fortune and paid off our farms, bought tractors, and new cars![1]

A lot of time passed between when we first dug out the marl and when we planted the berries. When I got those strawberry plants from Edgerton, the roots were sick. But the crown would send out new roots. I spaded up a bit of virgin soil that had no disease in it. And I raised a pretty good batch of plants there. Then I planted them into a bigger nursery... big enough to plant that four-acre chunk. That took about a half-acre of nursery stock. It took about four years before we got into really producing berries. I had been experimenting while we were raising beans.

That was a fabulous plant. Big beautiful plants. I was so curious. These plants were so big you couldn't cover them with a wash tub. That's a big strawberry plant! We cultured them. We didn't allow them to grow in a matted row. We plucked off the runners so they'd grow bigger and bigger. They'd shoot out these fruiting sprouts and there'd be a blossom on them and then there'd be a nurly little scrubby nubby berry on the end. I knew there was something wrong—vitally wrong—in the feeding of that plant. Otherwise, everything was there, but something was lacking not to make that big berry, you see. I had to do something to find out what that was. But I was just like the rest of the guys. That berry had never been fruited, as far as I know, anywhere in the world. And it had traveled all over the earth. It was crossed in England and then it spread all over... Australia and India and Africa. It was everywhere. And they could not commercially sell that berry.

I know that berry really well. If that berry could talk, I'd say to her, "Your sister (another variety) is producing a beautiful row of berries over here. Why aren't you producing any berries?" And that berry would talk back and say, "You're starving me to death! I only produce good fine berries and that plant over there is cheatin' ya. Those other plants producing berries under those poor conditions are producing an inferior berry. I only produce really good berries!"

I knew that berry was lacking something it needed to thrive. That fall we tested our ground. We found it was completely void of phosphate. And that's how we treated them. They were sickly. The disease was in 'em. Even if they grew pretty good, they were diseased. Root rot.

> **I knew that berry was lacking something it needed to thrive.**

---

[1] Ted: Years later I had the soil analyzed. There was more than just lime. My oldest son, David, helped me get those samples out. I had an extensive sampling system. I made myself a core barrel and went down through the layers. That's 25 feet deep down there. There are millions of tons of precious fertilizer in the lake. John dug some marl again and we found from digging it the second time that you can't preserve it for very long. You need to put it on the ground fresh from the lake, either by pumping or by digging it out and putting it right on the ground—so the gasses in there are preserved. We found out that the life-giving gasses pass off and you lose them. There's a lot of iodine in that lake—tons of it.

I did my experimental work on small plots down by the lodge. We had just cleared it from the timber. Beautiful virgin soil. I went through the same cycle twice. The first cycle, I didn't know what I was doing. The second cycle, I was experimenting and knew what I was doing. We used some phosphate and potash to balance out the soil and a fair amount of nitrates to help them through the winter because the nitrates promote growth. But if you use only nitrates, that don't save the plant. It attracts bugs. A little fertilizer is good. I'm not against that. But it wasn't just the fertilizer that they needed.

When we put on that warm lake water with the extra floating minerals, that added strength to that plant. We spent a lot of money sampling that water. There was no guesswork there. About 13% of it is in flotation. 13 parts per million. When you're pumping hundreds of thousands of gallons of water out of there, this stuff floats down with it. I found out from Dr. Albright that it just takes a little tiny trickle to change the chemical balance. This was a piece of ground that didn't have any prior treatment on it. And the water we pumped onto it had these minerals in it.

Then we planted them out into the four acres on the hill. When the berries finally got onto that field where we had spread out the marl, that mineral was still strong enough to fruit that berry. And we had a crop that equaled, in today's prices, a quarter of a million bucks.

The strawberry root weevil was pretty active there. That was one of the things we overcame completely with that mineral. This branches off into the entomology department. That taught me a real lesson. If you feed the plants, even trees, the insects won't eat them. Most of the insects live off of dead or sick things on the earth. The insects are scavengers. The root weevil is a prime scavenger. When it's not healthy, they are attracted to it. When it's healthy and vibrant, they have no interest in it. I tried it on the apple tree against the worms and I had tremendous success. You would be surprised. It baffled me.

That's why I liked Dr. Albright. He helped me to understand things. After I did my experimental work, I called him up and I asked him, "What happened to the root weevil?"

He said, "The root weevil is a scavenger. He only works on sick plants. The berries you were raising before were sick. It was better to let the root weevil have them because they weren't doing you much good. If you can heal that plant, you've become a doctor. You should have a Doctorate for that."

I was overwhelmed by what he was saying because I knew I had healed that patch. We normally only fruited them once where they did really good, and the next year there were just a few scattered berries here and there and then you had to plow 'em under. But when I put that mineral on that experimental spot, that bed lasted for six years and was still going. Nice, healthy, rich. They had a root system going so strong I took pictures of 'em. Just out of this world! It just baffled me, those roots. They were so white and nice. I knew I had done something.

Then I tried planting a diseased plant in there to see what would happen to it. I was working with diseased plants too. I wanted to know if it would spread. In the other patch, the disease spread like fire over the field. But in that patch, you could plant the diseased one in there and it wouldn't touch the other plants. I healed that plant. And it was the way I was feeding it. I had caught on and this berry patch was just a fabulous thing. I had never seen anything like it before!

Ernie: Fertilizer and Irrigation

The first year we raised those berries, we didn't have much of a crop. The bushes were beautiful, but the fruit all came off in small nubbins. So, we took some of the ground down to the County agent here in town. He tested the soil and told us there was a lot of nitrogen in it. It was good ground, but lacked phosphate and potash, which are fruit-forming nutrients.

So that fall we spread by hand 1000 pounds per acre of that fertilizer. We got a little machine that would go "click, click, click, click, click" and every time it clicked, it would drop some fertilizer. We would go right alongside the berries, up one side and down the other. We'd push it by hand. We had four acres of ground and that's the way we put 1000 pounds on every acre. It was like a cultivator: it made a rut, dropped the fertilizer, and then had a thing coming along behind to cover it up. The mixture of phosphate and potash was called 20-0-20. We put that on and the next year, we had one of the most beautiful crops of strawberries that you ever saw.

Then we'd irrigate. We rigged us up an irrigation outfit, my brother and I. We bought an old pump company from the City of Gladwin. It was the city waterworks. They were putting in a new waterworks and we bought all their old pumps. Then we sold off enough motors and pumps so that we got all of our own equipment free! We pumped water out of Walloon Lake. We brought that pump up and bought a Chevy engine out of a junkyard. We rigged that up and hooked it onto one of those big Fairbanks-Moore centrifugal pumps.

Then we got an oil line from Lima, Ohio. Old dilapidated oil lines. We screwed them together and got so we could irrigate sixty acres of ground by putting all that stuff together. We bought that all for little or nothing and put it together ourselves.

Then we found old boilers around the country: maybe eighteen feet long with as many as 48 flues in them. Four-inch flues. We took a chisel and a hammer, and we chiseled them out by hand which was hard work with the hot summer sun beaming down on that old boiler. These boilers were left over from the logging days. We brought those old boilers home with the flues, cut the ends off, and then welded about three sections together, about 45 feet. Then we'd get a Dayton joint, which was four bolts with neoprene washers that slipped over the ends where they came together. Then we'd tighten up those bolts and make them watertight. But they also allowed for expansion and contraction. When the sun hit them, it would expand and later contract. We had to have a little expansion every so many feet. Those were our transport lines.

Irrigation Project

Pump down on Walloon Lake

Irrigation lines in berry field on Ernie's/Edgerton farm. House is where Jim & Marlys lived when first married- before it burned

Water Cannon used to irrigate berry fields
69-A

With that, we were able to transport water from Walloon Lake all the way up to our field. After we got the water to our field, we went to Michigan State College and they built us a water cannon on four wheels, with a big engine in it. Again, we picked that engine up from a junkyard. They rigged it up for us at Michigan State College. Professor Roby saw that mechanism work over in Germany where they were irrigating golf courses, so he built us a water cannon that could irrigate 2 ½ acres from one setting.

We had a powerful three-stage centrifugal pump sitting in a portable truck. We pumped the water from the lake to the cannon through the boiler flues. That pump could pick up the water and put out 180 gallons per minute against 200 pounds of pressure. The water would peel right off. It was designed so the water would fall real graceful like rain, all the way out for 250-300 feet. Then it would circulate around slowly all the time. In about an hour-and-a-half, we could put an inch of water on those berries.

We raised some of the biggest, finest strawberries you ever saw with that water from the lake. That was good rich water. It had minerals in it that those berries needed, and we raised berries second-to-none in the country. They were so big that you couldn't drop one into a wide-mouth Mason quart fruit jar. They were so big and sweet and luscious. You could can them, freeze them, anything. We had sometimes as few as eleven berries to the quart. They were that big!

I think that marl also gave the ground something it needed. My brother took a sample of that marl to the county agent, who said it was very rich in minerals. Marl is formed by rain, washing the topsoil down into the lowest parts of the lakes and rivers. Through many years, that topsoil keeps washing into the lake. Marl is a *very* rich composition of deteriorated animal life, plant life, and topsoil. If you can get that marl into your ground, the plants eat it up and you can get some beautiful fruit. That, I think, is why our strawberries did so well. We were irrigating with lake water and also putting marl on the ground.

We dug the marl out of the lake with a crane. The county agent told us how rich it was and gave us various systems for using it. That's how Ted learned about it. We wanted to dig marl out and sell it to people and make an operation out of it, which never went over. So we ended up putting the marl on our own ground and that's how we raised those big strawberries. I believe it helped.

> **We got those "unproductive" berries to produce around fourteen-hundred quarts per acre.**

All that, (balancing the soil, irrigating, and using marl), contributed toward our raising some of the finest Fairfax & Dorsett berries ever seen. Michigan State College had them listed as "Unproductive," but also as some of the most delicious berries known to mankind. We got those "unproductive" berries to produce around fourteen-hundred quarts per acre. They couldn't believe it!

Ted: From Marl to Money

Ted

Ernst and I had different gifts. It was my idea to get the water out of the lake. Ernst was a good mechanic. He knew how to build the irrigation system, but I was good on the agricultural end of it. The Michigan State University built the water cannon, but we had to get all the tubing and pipes and put them in place. That was quite an accomplishment. We were putting 500 gallons a minute onto the land. Every other day we'd put an inch of water on those berries and, of course, that contributed to that huge production. Otherwise, they'd just dry up. It was a good investment. Boy, I tell you, we made money with that irrigation outfit. We knew we had to have water. Those strawberries are a marsh berry. They just love to stand in water when they're fruiting. Pumping that water from the lake onto these plants is what made that big crop.

We used oat straw to preserve the roots from the frost and also to keep the berries clean. We didn't have to wash them that way. Down in Florida, they raised the berries right in the dirt and then washed the berries. That water helps destroy them. They put water on them and then put them in the refrigerator and shipped them up to market. But our berries were kept on straw, nice and clean. We had a nice unique system of running that berry patch. We had the berries right up against the woods. It was good ground there. We had the nicest patch of berries you ever seen.

> **Ernst and I had different gifts. Ernst was a good mechanic. I was good on the agricultural end of it.**

Ernie: Berries, Berries, Berries!

Ernie

We raised the berries on Ted's farm by the lake and, later, all around his house up on the hill. Planted them all by hand, hoed them, and cultivated them. We worked at them day in and day out.

Ernie: Pleasant Pickers

Ernie

We made a lot of money that year. Then, we planted four more acres the next year, and ended up with sixteen acres of strawberries at the end. That took a lot of pickers. We hired 125 pickers! It was a big operation, with sixteen acres of berries. Herb Trier helped us a lot on our berries. Herb was a good worker. I think a lot of him.

Herb had hay fever and couldn't breathe down in Fort Wayne, so he moved up here. We met Herb in church; he was a nice-looking young fellow. I liked Herb right from the start. We got visiting and he told us he was here because of hay fever. We invited him out to the house for dinner and told him we had strawberries. He wanted to know if he could help with the berries. We got him a little trailer and he lived behind my chicken coop for a while. He started feeling good right away, so he knew he had to stay up here. We gave him a job and kept him here. He stayed with us and never did go back.

He got married soon after that. Then he lived in the Edgerton place for a number of years. His wife was from Minnesota, I think. She was a parochial schoolteacher and he met her in school. She was a minister's daughter. Martha was a good Christian woman. She didn't hit it off too good with Ted, though. He was quite aggressive in getting his point across, and Martha couldn't take that. She was a mild-mannered lady, but she'd sass Ted once in a while, and that made him mad. I got along good with her. We didn't have any trouble like that.

> **We hired 125 pickers! It was a big operation, with sixteen acres of berries. Herb Trier helped us a lot on our berries.**

Herb and I got along good too, but he and Ted didn't always get along so good. Herb was very kind-hearted, probably a lot like my oldest brother, Herbie. He was always a meek-tempered, good Christian boy. Ted was very aggressive. He could come down on Herb Trier pretty hard, but Herb always took it. I always felt sorry for Herb. We saw things alike.

Once, there were Strokaupft girls who came up to help with the strawberries. This Strokaupft girl was a minister's daughter from Sebawing. She was a nice-looking girl with big eyes. Her name was Margaret—not to be confused with another Margaret you'll meet later on! We met her somehow through church, and she was a very friendly girl.

I liked Margaret. I would have taken her out, but Ted said, "I saw her first. She's *my* girl."

She would shine up to me and I didn't dare to be too friendly to her 'cuz I'd get Ted on my neck. It was a fright. But it was also a blessing from the Lord because we weren't supposed to get married anyway.

Margaret asked me several times if I'd take her out. Ted would always be after her and she'd go out with him, but then she'd say, "I'd like to go out with Ernie." That would make Ted mad. Then he'd say to me, "She's *my* girl and, until I'm through with her, you leave her alone!"

Herb said, "Ted, you're not doing it right. You're not courting her right. That's not the way to go. Women have to make up their minds, too. You're not doing that right." That made Ted mad! Herb expressed his opinion and Ted never liked Herb for that.

I never dared to go out with her. It would have made a rift between Ted and me. I wasn't ready to get married anyway, so why go out with her and cause problems? But she came right out and asked me!

When I was young, I didn't have any trouble meeting girls and getting a date. When they came around, it seemed they always picked me rather than Ted. That irked Ted, and it bothered me too. I didn't like it.

> **I never dared to go out with her. It would have made a rift between my brother and me.**

Margaret also had a sister by the name of Florence, so I thought maybe I'd ask Florence for a date to keep Margaret off my neck. But I couldn't hit it off at all with Florence. She was a different kind of girl. She was tall and not as friendly as Margaret. I think, though, that Florence would have even been hard to get along with.

One year, Mary came up from Boyne City to help us pick. She and Ted took a shine to each other and, before long, they were engaged. That solved all those problems.

Mrs. Skully from Skully Oil Company would come up to our place from her cottage on Walloon Lake and, every other day, she would buy a crate of those nice big berries. That's how we got some of those nice pictures of those big berries. She took those.

My brother always wore an old straw hat and looked older than his age. One day Mrs. Skully came and asked me, "Where is your father?"

I said, "My father is dead."

"Oh, no", she said, "I just talked to him yesterday."

"Oh," I said laughing, "that was my brother!"

Later, when Ted's son Danny was little, a woman came up to Ted and said, "I bet that's your first grandson!" Ted looked like a grandfather for a long time. He was the spittin' image of our Great Grandpa Puschel.

Babe and Constance packing berries

Look how many crates of berries in one day! And they tasted good too!

Ernie: This Big Berry Went to Market

Ernie

We hauled those berries to Detroit every single day. I don't know how we ever stood that. I'd run that truck one week steady to Detroit, and the next week, Ted would take them. They would run for about three weeks, because we were irrigating.

We took the berries to Detroit in an old Chevrolet flat rack. Bought it second-hand for $350.00 We'd leave here with the truck between 6:30 and 7:30 p.m. In those days, we had no freeways. Just had to pick our way down through Saginaw and Bay City. I'd always stop in Standish for a cup of coffee. Driving at night was hard work. I'd think and pray and sing hymns while I drove. It wasn't very fun.

Sometimes the battery would go dead. It stopped on me one time, one or two blocks from the Eastern Market and they had to tow me in. The battery went dead. The lights ran off the battery. Every time there was no car coming at

that hour of the morning, I'd put the light out and drive by moonlight. When I'd see a car coming, I'd turn the lights on. I'd get her down there that way, but within three blocks, that time, they had to tow me in. Ted had some troubles, too.

We ran that way every day and got to the Eastern Market every morning around 3:00 a.m. with a big load of strawberries. The people would be waiting for us when we got there. There was a broker by the name of Coe, who would intercept our truck in Detroit and sell our berries to all his customers there. He'd divide them between the different store and deli owners.

Gerhardt's father, in Wolverine, still remembers those berries in Detroit. When we met this summer, he said, "Are you the one that sold those huge berries at the Eastern Market? I remember those berries!"

Ted: The Best Picker Ever!

Ted

Around 1940, we had one of our biggest crops and needed to hire extra pickers. We hired some Walther League young people from our churches in Petoskey and Boyne City. That's when Mary and I got acquainted in the berry field. She was home from teaching for the summer.

I invited her to join me one night when I was delivering the berries to Detroit and I was very impressed with her character. We got engaged at the end of the season and I started building our house. We were married in January 1941 and went to Mexico and California on our honeymoon. Then we came back and tended another marvelous berry crop.

Ted

Ted: Bumper Crops (1941)

Pretty soon we had so many berries that it was hard getting enough crates to get all our berries to market, so we bought some equipment from someone going out of business. We planned to make our own crates, but we didn't know what we were doing, so that was a bust.

Shortly after I got married, we had that berry crop that made a fortune. It was the equivalent in our money today of a quarter of a million dollars. Can you visualize that? One crop! And most of it was off those four acres right behind our house where Philip is living. It was a four-acre chunk, and it was fabulous!

The Michigan State officials from the college came up and they were planning to make a world premiere documentary on our story. People from the University of Michigan looked at it and asked me questions. Later a second batch of professors came up who were protégées of Decker and Sheldon and Rove. The others had retired but they had briefed the young professors about me and told them that, when it came to strawberries, Manthei was the only guy in Michigan that knew anything.

That was the berry that made us a fortune. The guys at the fruit market in Detroit tasted that berry and they were just overwhelmed with it. They'd pay anything just to get it. They didn't care what the price was!

My, we did well! We made a lot of money. Off that berry field, we would harvest anywhere from $16,000 to $18,000 a year, which is equivalent to a farm today making about $200,000 in buying power. In those days, you could buy a good new tractor with rubber wheels for $1,100. Today, you'd pay, for that same tractor, probably $12,000-15,000. Maybe even $20,000-30,000! So, you see, in buying power, we were actually doing very, very well on this farm raising berries!

Inheritance Vision Fulfilled

We raised those berries for 8-10 years, but that strawberry root weevil was still active and the amount of minerals in the soil was not enough to save the plant indefinitely from the root weevil. The first year would be pretty nice, and the second year, it would wipe 'em out. But by that time, we had the veneer mill going, so you see how God provides from one thing to the next?

> **So, you see how God leads from one thing to the next? That's how our inheritance got started. We were dressing the earth and the Lord seen that we got paid faithfully for it.**

My life has been very colorful (interesting) with these intricacies. I never had schooling to speak of, but I always loved the soil. I just *loved* the soil! I was a natural farmer. I liked the ground. I liked the smell of it and I liked to work on it. And, of course, I liked these plants too. That was a very colorful thing in my life. I could have earned a Doctorate for healing that berry. They were all set to film that for a World Premiere and then the war broke out. It was WWII in 1941.

So that's how our inheritance got started. That was my vision. We were dressing the earth and the Lord seen that we got paid faithfully for it.

This is probably the packing shed area, where Jim & Marlys' new house now stands.

Neat pickup truck hauling crates to the berry fields

Robert Cone - Son of Christel & Chet →

"Whopper" berries like this are common in the Manthei fields. Rubert Marx finds it a mouthful.

Ernie: The Beginning of the End

It's much easier to hire people and train them to work year-round than to hire strawberry pickers. Then, that new method of *striking* came in.

One time I came home from Detroit and the pickers were on strike. They said, "We'll work for Mr. Ernie, but we won't work for Mr. Ted." I guess maybe he was hard on them. I was more easy-going and understanding. I felt bad for Ted. He had to do all the driving after that, and it was not an easy job.

You can't have a field full of ripe strawberries and have the kids say they won't pick unless we give them two-thirds of the crop. That became very unpopular in our kind of work. We decided it was best to discontinue that business.

We don't raise strawberries anymore because berry-raising is very, very hard work. It's a lot of handwork, not machinery work. You've got to hoe them. Then, you've got to spend a lot of time on your knees. You're on your knees pulling off the runners, setting the runners, and picking them. You're down on your knees so much that you become a real prayer-minded person! When you get older with rheumatism and arthritis, you can't take that kind of life anymore. But really, when we got going in the veneer business, that became the dog that wiggled the tail!

> **When we got going in the veneer business, that became the dog that wiggled the tail!**

Ted: Vision of the Veneer Mill

During the time we were farming, I had another prophetic dream. I dreamed we had a white factory down by the lake. It looked just like the original mill with white shingles on it. That was an odd dream. I don't have this quite as clear in my mind anymore like I should. But we were somehow starting out with a poor operation. There were other people involved. They had an office building on the hill and they were giving a tour. They led us to a real nice office and the guy said,

"This is your office."

I said, "How come we would have such a nice office?"

He said, "You pray a lot, don't you?"

I said, "Yah."

And he said, "That makes the difference!"

Ernst thought I was crazy when I told him about my dream. You know how Joseph's brothers laughed when he would tell them his dreams.

Ernie

Ernie: Transition Time

We ran into problems with the berries because we couldn't get enough berry crates, so we decided to make our own crates and bought some equipment. But after we brought it home, we discovered that we couldn't use it to make crates. It was made to cut ply-veneer, not crates! It requires special veneer lathes and clippers to make crates. Our lathe and clippers were designed for plywood veneer. So now we had the wrong equipment. I tried to buy a clipper that would make crates, but it never worked out. So we just let it sit and continued buying our crates.

We let that "wrong" crating equipment sit for a while. In fact, we felt a little sheepish and hid it in a barn. One day, a man named Metzelburg came along. He looked over our equipment and said, "You've got some of the best veneering equipment in the industry! I've got a friend in Wisconsin who is a retired veneer lathe operator. He's a good friend of mine. If I call him, he'll come up here and show you how to run this." (We should visit that man and thank him sometime because he did us a good turn!)

Metzelburg became our mentor. He got his friend, Simon, to come up here. He said, "You board him and pay him a salary and he'll show you how to run the lathe." That man came and in half-an-hour, he had that machine adjusted and had beautiful veneer flowing off that lathe. Our buyer said, "You run like that, and I'll buy all the veneer you can produce." He became our first customer.

Just like that, we were in the veneer business!

> **What's a Veneer Mill?**
>
> **It's a factory that makes beautiful thin wood called veneer. The veneer is used to cover cheap wood to create quality products, like furniture and paneling. Imagine pulling a sheet of paper towel off the roll. The log is the solid roll. As the log turns, the huge lathe cuts it into long thin sheets of wood that roll out and run down a conveyor to a clipper that cuts them into proper sizes. Then it goes through a dryer, gets graded, stacked, and shipped to companies that create the final quality wood products.**

Ted

Ted: Building the Mill (1941)

We started the veneer mill in the fall of 1941 after I got married. We did that so we could employ more family year-round. I had a lot to do with building that mill. I sawed the timbers and cut them up. Ernst would help in between his farming. We were busy people. We had a lot of crops to take care of. We had the strawberries and we still had beans and oats. Ernst was also raising pigs for the war effort, so he helped build the mill in between his other chores, like nights before it got dark in the summer. Once in a while we'd hire a guy for a few bucks. Everything came the hard way. It was a miracle we didn't kill ourselves building that thing.

We cut and shipped parts for making crates, and even though we had the machinery to make the whole crate, we never made any. We just cut the parts and shipped them to a crating factory. They nailed them together. Then we didn't need them anymore because we gradually worked our way out of the berries. We had half-acre fields and made good money off of them, but we didn't have big acres anymore. With the labor situation during the war, it wasn't the best. While we were doing it, that was a wonderful time. We could get all the help we needed. We had 125 pickers in 1940.

When we bought that veneer equipment, we were thinking only of crates. Then Metzelburg came up from Cadillac looking for someone to make panels. We were so impoverished. We didn't know what we were doing. But Metzelburg knew we had equipment that could make a guy smack his lips. He also knew a man in Wisconsin that could help us set the thing up to make good veneer. Metzelburg needed center stock. He couldn't run without it, but it was war time and he couldn't get any. He needed a mill that could at least cut the green stuff for him and then they could dry it down in Cadillac. He sent the guy from Wisconsin, who was a retired veneer lathe operator, and he put that machine into shape right now! We began cutting and we sold a lot of veneer to Metzelburg.

Later, when I moved to California, I'd always come home in the spring and, if there was any building going on, like the new vats, I'd help work on that and anything that was being done. That's the way we gradually built this mill up. That old mill was the starter of everything. That was the mill that really counted.

A Dream Comes True

One year I came back from California and stood at the top of the hill and there it was, just like I seen in my dream, with white shingles on it. Ernst had put on those white shingles in the winter to fix up the building after he made a little money. The office was there by the building, and I knew this was what I seen in my dream—after the white shingles were on it.

Ernie: Mixing Wisdom with Humor

Ernie

We got the mill set up, but then couldn't make grades (quality). We had our customer and got the lathe producing, but then we had trouble drying it. We had sand and everything on it from laying it out on the ground to dry in the sun. Finally, up in Escanaba, I found a dryer. We brought that down, rebuilt it, and set it up. Then we could dry veneer.

With that old machinery, we produced enough money to buy new modern machinery. From there on, the Mantheis were in the veneer business, and have been in it for over forty years. Now, in 1985, we probably have one of the most modern veneer mills in the industry. Much of the credit goes to our sons and nephews who stuck with it and who, today, are considered successful veneer men.

That's basically how we got into the veneer business and then other businesses. It was not smart-ness at all. Actually, man thinks and the Lord leads. It was by the grace of God that we got into all of these things. None of it was smarts. Neither one of us had much education. I like to give the glory to God because I can see where wisdom is a gift of God. The Bible taught me that wisdom rules over knowledge. Wisdom is the lever which controls knowledge and education. If the Lord doesn't bless the efforts of your hands, no matter how much education you've got, it doesn't do you any good. "The fear of the Lord is the beginning of wisdom" (Proverbs 9:10).

> **Wisdom is a gift of God. The Bible taught me that wisdom rules over knowledge. Wisdom is the lever which controls knowledge and education. If the Lord doesn't bless the efforts of your hands, no matter how much education you've got, it doesn't do you any good. "The fear of the Lord is the beginning of wisdom" (Proverbs 9:10).**

For example, Professor Roby down at Michigan State, who built that very water cannon we used in our berry business, was a very smart man. I was surprised at his knowledge! He wanted to go into business, so he started his own little factory building machinery. He lost everything he had and died a poor man. He knew how to tell other people how to do things. But to run a business himself, he didn't have that gift. I felt sorry for the man. But you see, those are all gifts from God. Many people have great knowledge but don't know how to make it work.

One time, I had to go to Lockport, New York, to pick up a new veneer lathe for our plant. I was going empty through Canada to New York, but when they gave me my manifest papers at the border of Canada, they forgot to put the seal of inspection on the trailer door, which I didn't even know I needed. When I got to the border on the American side, I was in real trouble because the seal wasn't there.

"How do we know that you didn't haul a lot of stuff into Canada to sell and are coming out without a seal? You are in real trouble!" they said.

And then I remembered something…

I used to belong to a Kiwanis Club in Sault Ste. Marie for about a year. We were in Canada for a big dinner and one of the men from the club got up and told this story. At that time, the money in Canada was 12% higher than American currency. The exchange was 12% in their favor.

He was bragging and asked, "Do you know why our money is worth more than your money?" At that time, Truman was our president and there were always jokes about him. He was outspoken and came out with odd remarks. So when this guy asked why their money was worth more than ours, we all guessed. You have uranium mines and a big silver mine in Sudbury and oil in the west.

"Oh," he says, "those are all good reasons, but they're not the real reason." So we mentioned the new developments in their country, like new coal resources and such.

Finally, we gave up and said, "What is the *real* reason? Well, we sit here with three queens and you're stuck with the joker!"

They had three queens: the grandmother, the mother, and the daughter. All were queens in England over Canada. Well, that story got to be a real joke.

> **God has a sense of humor, and He gave me the wisdom to tell that joke at just the right moment!**

So now I was sitting at the border, in bad shape, with an unsealed truck and the border patrol says, "We'll have to arrest you. You're in real trouble." I was innocent, but I knew I was in trouble, and I happened to remember that joke. Then I said, "I heard a real interesting joke that I'd like to tell you."

"Oh," he says, "tell me." So, I told him this joke and he got such a kick out of it that he says, "Get going! Get out of here." He let me go with no more problems.

I was innocent anyway, but that was a serious offense to have no seal on my trailer. Somebody slipped up on the other side, but I was in trouble. They could have arrested me and I had no defense. That joke got me out of all that trouble. He laughed, and since he was a Canadian, he thought that was really a good one.

God has a sense of humor, and He gave me the wisdom to tell that joke at just the right moment!

Ernie: Battling It Out for the Best

Ernie

Ted and I fought and had our battles because we were both stubborn. Our peculiarities didn't always mesh. They often clashed.

Once in a while, Ted would talk about different dreams he had, and I'd get peeved at him. Ted dreamt that he was standing at the top of the hill and looked down and saw a big white factory by the lake and it was *ours!* When you're so poor and have no money, and he tells you about a dream where we had a big building and hired men working for us, I thought he was crazy!

I said, "Boy, that's fantastic stuff! Why bother telling me about this?" After all, it sounded so ridiculous! I thought Ted was just a dreamer. In fact, I made sport of his dreams because they seemed so impossible.

Then we built the first veneer mill. Ted was in California while I finished up the siding and started cutting veneer and making money. When he came home, he said, "That is the building I saw in my dream! There it is, just like that one!!"

> **Sometimes the Lord gives a vision ahead of time about what's going to happen.**

That was impressive to me when he said it because I remembered those dreams. It's odd, but sometimes the Lord gives a vision ahead of time about what's going to happen. I've had dreams where I was married, had a nice wife and car, and now, when I look back, I see that I have those things just like the dreams. Some dreams are visions. We don't know exactly how to apply them. Some are not good and I sure hope they never happen. I never put much stock in them. Yet I've had some marvelous dreams.

Well, Ted and I worked together and stayed together. We farmed together, built businesses together, and the Lord blessed the efforts of our hands.

Manthei Brothers Veneer Mill

The beginning

Phase II

Phase III of Mill

Phase IV
This is how the mill looked before it burned in 1967

December 7, 1941

December 11, 1941

Now the war was raging, and America was forced to join the battle. Mary's brother, Herman Behling, was called up to serve as a mechanic for tanks and trucks in North Africa, where Hitler was seeking to dominate the Mediterranean by tying up the Suez Canal and the oil industry. Mary's brother, Bob Behling, dropped out of high school at age seventeen to join the navy, where he was fighting the Japanese in the Pacific. We were trying to raise pigs for the war effort too.

Ernie: Margaret Schillinger (Summer 1942)

I had always prayed for a devout Christian wife. I always figured I would marry a girl with blond hair and blue eyes who could play the piano. She would be a nice, well-built girl.

When I married Margaret, she was just the opposite. She had dark eyes, black hair, and she was a bow-legged nurse! I never figured I would marry a bow-legged girl. But when I prayed for a devout Christian wife, I never asked for blue eyes and blond hair. I just asked for a devout Christian wife. I knew better than to ask for the other things. The Lord gave me the wife that I prayed for, exactly! She was a very devout Christian wife. But He wrapped her in a different package. I recognized that she was the exact answer to my prayer because she had all the qualities that I prayed for. I knew that she was a gift from God.

I met Margaret at a Walther League Camp at Arcadia, near Ludington. It was a nice Christian camp. I got up and talked about the Word of the Lord. It didn't go over too good with the young people because I was quoting some of those old prophecies. They didn't think it fit in with their program. But Margaret was very attentive.

There was another girl there who I liked pretty good too. She was quite vivacious, from out east near Boston or Buffalo, New York. She was smart. She could talk five different languages. I thought, "Now there's a girl I could like!"

> **The Lord gave me the wife that I prayed for, exactly! She was a very devout Christian wife. But He wrapped her in a different package.**

At that time, my varicose veins were giving me a lot of trouble and I spent three days or so relaxing at the camp. Then Margaret had to go back to Grand Rapids. She was a nurse there.

She said, "Can I ride back with you and bring another young lady?"

I said, "Sure, I'm all alone. There's plenty of room."

I had a Ford coupe, so we piled her stuff in the trunk. Margaret sat in the middle, and the other girl sat beside her. She told me some of her experiences as a nurse.

Then I asked, "Do you know all those doctors there in the hospital?"
She said, "Oh, yes."

I asked, "Who would be a good doctor to work on my varicose veins?"

"Oh," she said, "I'll take you down and introduce you to one. He's a good doctor and if he does the work, you can trust him."

That made me feel good. We went right to the hospital, and he operated on my veins. I had to stay there a day or two and Margaret came and visited me. She worked there in that hospital and was very friendly.

As for looks, she didn't match up to that other girl. I didn't think she was quite as smart either because she couldn't talk five different languages. But she was a very nice young lady.

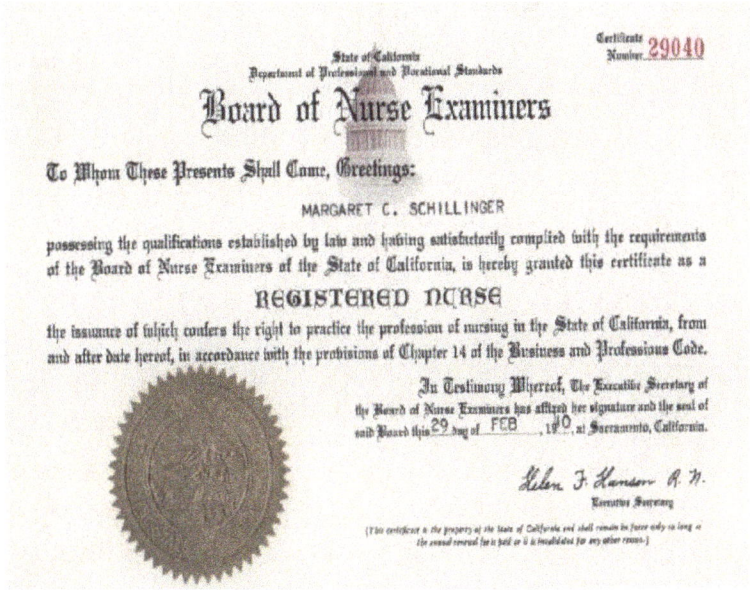

When I got out of the hospital, I came home with the addresses of both girls. I told Mother when I came home, "One of those two girls would make a good wife, but I don't know how to attack this." We talked a little and I decided I would write both of those girls the same letter and see how they would answer."

My letter went this way: I told them I was a pig raiser. (I wanted to throw them off a little.) If I raised pigs, would they be content to be the wife of a farmer who raised pigs?

It wasn't exactly a lie because I was raising a few pigs for the war effort. We did something wrong, with inbreeding, and they turned out to be two-legged pigs! So I really wasn't that much of a pig farmer, but I wanted to see how those two girls would answer.

The girl from Buffalo wrote back, saying that would be the last thing she wanted to do, to be the wife of a farmer who raised stinky pigs!

I said, "That cuts that one out!"

Margaret wrote back and said, "If I loved a man and married him, I would be thankful to do whatever he does and be a good mate and serve the Lord."

I said, "Now, there's a good answer!"

Mother also said, "Yah, there's a girl who would adjust herself to whatever living her husband made and be a faithful wife."

So, I started writing to Margaret. I wasn't raising pigs, just testing to see how they would answer, and I liked her for that nice answer.

> **Mother said that Margaret is a girl who would adjust herself to whatever living her husband made and be a faithful wife.**

I invited Margaret up for Christmas. She came and spent Christmas with us and Mother liked her. I think that's when we got engaged.

While we were engaged, I said to her one day, "Margaret, do you think we're doing the right thing by getting married?"

She said, "I've wondered that, too. But I've prayed to the Lord to guide me and help me not to be concerned that way, because we can have doubts about everything we do in this world. Yes, I have thought about that, too, but I trust in the Lord. The Lord says, '*All things work together for good to those who trust in God*'." She gave me good Christian answers that straightened me up. I said, "I don't question now anymore either."

I met her sometime in June or July, we wrote, and in January, we got married. She adjusted herself well. Margaret was a good woman.

When we got married, I didn't know what women looked like naked. That first night, I asked her, "Are you maybe misformed?"

"No," she said, "I'm a very normal woman."

I said, "I don't know. That isn't the way I had thought it out."

> **When I asked, "Margaret, do you think we're doing the right thing by getting married?" She said, "I've wondered that, too. But I've prayed to the Lord to guide me and help me not to be concerned that way, because we can have doubts about everything we do in this world. The Lord says, '*All things work together for good to those who trust in God*' and I trust in Him."**

She was a nurse and she said, "No, I can assure you that I'm a very normal girl." Then she laughed.

I said, "Why are you laughing?"

She said, "You know, that's a compliment. It shows that you're a clean man."

I said, "I'm glad you look at it that way."

She said, "Yes, that's the way that I look at it."

The point is, I didn't know how the Lord had made the opposite sex. Then, at first, I thought maybe the Lord had made a mistake. It wasn't the way I had it engineered in my mind. She always laughed about that. I thought it was a dumb thing, but she said, "No, I think it's nice!" She was a nurse and knew how to take that.

We didn't take a nice honeymoon because the Japanese had just bombed Pearl Harbor. We were gearing up for war and gas was being rationed. I was very lucky that I didn't get called away to the war. I got out of that because I was a farmer raising pigs for the war effort.

Ernie Manthei marries Margaret Schillinger
January 31, 1943

Ted: 1943 Heading West

Ted

After I had my house built, things were not going good for me in Petoskey, and I was getting these awful attacks of bronchial pneumonia.

Ernst and I didn't always get along. There were times when, seemingly unprovoked, he would mock me and belittle me. I think he would feel sorry after he did that, because in the long run he always wanted me with him. But I couldn't take it and finally there came a time when we had to separate partnership for the simple reason that we just didn't see eye to eye.

Mary and I decided, with all the controversy, it wasn't a good thing for me to be there in Michigan, so we'd better pull out. The feeling around there was very high. Just too much conflict! I felt so bad that I was willing to leave everything behind just to get out of there. Of course, the Lord used that. You've got to look at everything from the Lord's viewpoint. Sometimes it takes quite a bit of physical hurt to make a man move. I should have been out of there. I can see that. It wasn't my place to be there. That was for Ernst to run. Not me.

> **You've got to look at everything from the Lord's viewpoint. Sometimes it takes quite a bit of physical hurt to make a man move. I told Mary, "We're going to go and pick up our inheritance."**

That was quite a big thing to leave our home. We had a new house. It was the first time I had a bathtub in the house. We had hot water running and I had a nice place. I left that nice house and rented it to Mary's brother, Al Behling, for $25 a month, just to show that I was in favor of trying to help all that I could. The mill was young, and Al seemed to be working pretty good. He was a good man. He had flaws too, but he was a real good guy. He was honest and I liked him for that. I moved out of my house, and they all used it. Herb Treir used it. Al used it. I built the home, but I never really lived in it much.

We decided to pull out right in the winter, with that old used trailer and a used Chevy car. We were headed nowhere. I told Mary, "We're going to go and pick up our inheritance."

We headed west and didn't stop 'til we hit the ocean. When we got down to Long Beach, California, we thought we'd go into the trailer business. We had bought a trailer and sold it and made $1000! But the Lord didn't want me in the trailer business. I could see that. Boy, He knocked me out of that in a hurry. I put a small down payment on a lot up in Lynwood and bought it. Then I got another guy to sell trailers and I got a commission. That's how I made my living for a while.

Ted

Tithing

We learned about tithing when we read Malachi. It's very stirring. The Lord says, "TRY ME. Try me and serve me and see if I don't open up the windows of heaven and pour you out a blessing." And the original Hebrew says, "so much that it will smother you." A blessing so great that it will smother you. You can't get away from it.

That's exactly the way it went. That was a terrific step that we took when we started tithing. The banker was against it and my mother thought that it wouldn't work. The church thought that it wouldn't work. Everybody was against it except the Scripture, you see. But I said, "We'll try it. We'll give it a run. We're gonna serve the Lord if it kills us."

So, Mary and I started tithing when we left MI and moved to California.

Ernst was left with the production of the mill. At that point, the mill was running about three years. I talked to him about it when we came back to Michigan for the summer. Ernst didn't want to start tithing. He didn't think we could afford it.

I said, "We've got to start right now!" We had a heck of a fight. We weren't even talking to each other for years. But we did a lot of work for the Gospel after that. He got converted to tithing and it became very important to Him.

****

Overcoming Challenges

Ernst contributed an awful lot to getting the veneer mill going. He wasn't just the manager, but he ran it. He did the work too. He worked with his hands. That was a great accomplishment. Of course, I helped too. He used my money as well as he used his. Ernst was an honest man and he always split everything half and half. He didn't crook anybody.

We were against anybody cheating anybody, even with our help. When a person unloaded the logs, if anybody complained, we'd go right out there and check it out. We didn't take our scalers' word for it. We'd check 'em out and see that nobody was getting hurt.

One fellow had cut a bunch of basswood logs and left them laying in the woods for a whole year. He brought them to us and said they were still good. But the way they looked... my, oh my! Well, what are you going to do? I said, "We're running basswood now. Why don't we try a few and see if they're any good?" They turned out just wonderful! Laid there a whole year and yet they were just as nice as could be! We paid him full price and it tickled him to death.

We always treated our log-sellers fair. If we had a log that telescoped with one end wider than the other, we'd measure both ends and divide up the difference. We didn't cheat. One time John Kopp's father sold us logs and, weeks later, we discovered that we hadn't paid them for two of the logs, so we sent him another check. Their family remembered that for years and years. I didn't want to cheat those farmers. I knew they worked hard for a living.

All kinds of things happen to you when you're running a mill like that. We built that mill because we wanted to provide employment for more of the family. Our sisters had husbands and our wives had brothers.

We hired a relative by marriage and Ernst made him a manager. Robert was an innocent babe in the woods. Didn't know anything about running an operation like that. Very proud. Cocky. He bought all kinds of junk. He ran it about three months and that old mill was going $30,000-a-month in the hole. He was running it to the dogs! Ernst didn't want to fire him and get in a fight with the guy's wife, who was family. She was our bookkeeper taking care of the books at the mill. I went down and wanted to study those books so I could start to straighten things up. But she did a naughty thing. She took the books home so I couldn't see them. I was called some pretty bad names. Eventually I finally got my hands on the books and got everything straightened out nice. Then the mill took off and made a profit again. I didn't need to fire him. He could see the handwriting on the wall, so he quit. He didn't have a mean streak and I didn't treat him mean either.

> **We built that mill because we wanted to provide employment for more of the family. Our sisters had husbands and our wives had brothers.**

At that time, we didn't have a dryer. When you're cutting wood, it can pile up pretty fast. We tried to dry it ourselves by hand, using hot plates, where you'd put it on the wood and take it off and put it on again. Otherwise, the veneer would break up. Finally, Metzelburg said, "You ought to get yourselves some kind of a dryer. Haven't I paid you enough money?"

Ernst went out looking for a dryer. That's when another fella took over. I'll call him Chester.

I was at a Lutheran Hour meeting in Chicago. Their founder, Dr. Meier, had died. I had to come from California for the funeral. I was in California only about a month that winter when Ernst went to look for the dryer. I had to come right up to Petoskey that night after the funeral because Chester was taking over. I wasn't at enmity with him and Ernst wasn't. But we were both gone, and he saw his chance.

He tried to get the union in there from Detroit to jack up the wages. He stirred up all the employees to go on strike. You see, the mill was very young when Chester did this. It had only been running maybe four years. And he was bound to destroy it. He had a great hate, for nothing! What did he want to do it for? You can't make hay by destroying all the machinery! I guess he wanted more money. The love of money is the root of all evil, you know. A lot of wars start over money and power! We've been watching it from a distance and now our boys were in the thick of things over in Europe.

> **The love of money is the root of all evil, you know. A lot of wars start over money!**

June 6, 1944

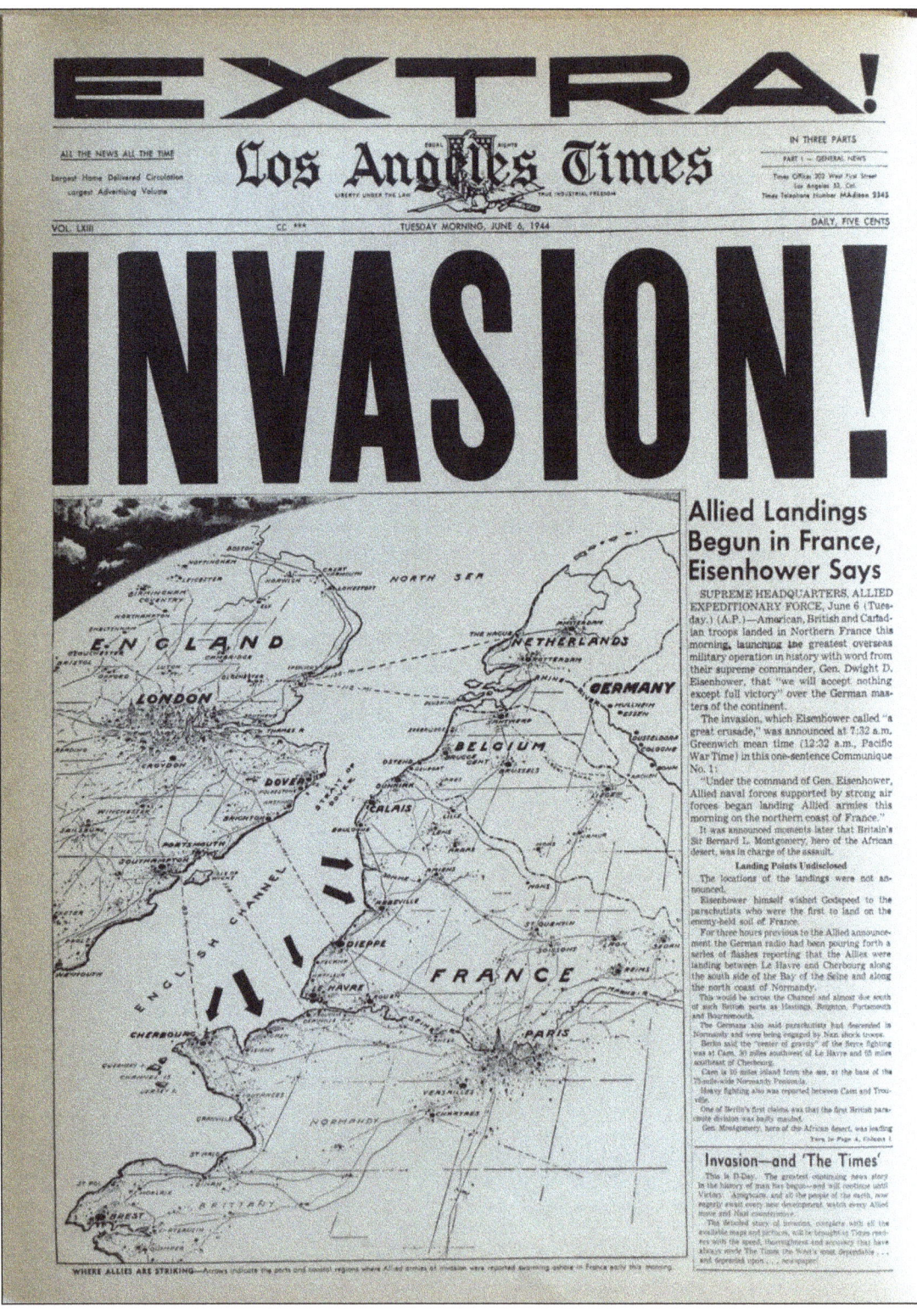

October 26, 1944

We're praying that brother Bob is safe and sound in the Pacific.

May 7, 1945

This is great news for brother Herman
in the European Theater.

August 15, 1945

Finally, the news we'd all been waiting for! The war was over!
The Behling brothers were coming home alive!
Unfortunately, not all families could say the same.

Ted: 1947 A New Venture—Property Acquisitions

Ted

Our lot in Lynwood, California, was right along the boulevard where 800 automobiles went by every hour. We had two little children, David and John, who were still toddlers, and twice I caught them out in the middle of that boulevard. Man, I thought, if I could only get 'em to shore (safely across two lanes to their own yard). It was hard to do when they were out on the grass with cars going by on each side. I said to Mary, "We gotta move out'a here."

Before that, John needed a tricycle, but they cost $30, and we couldn't afford to pay that much. So we didn't buy one new. We waited until we saw an advertisement; "Tricycle for Sale - $4." This guy would go to the dump and pick out the wheels and frames and put 'em together and sell 'em cheap for four bucks. One night we went down to see this guy and I asked him if he knew where there was any land for sale. That's how you'd greet the other guy them days. Land was really selling good.

The guy said, "Yah, I know a place down in Huntington Beach." He bragged it up real good.

So I said, "Why don't you buy it?"

He said, "I would like to buy that place, but my wife won't go down there." She was too high and uppity to go to a dumpy place like that. But he wanted us to buy those twenty acres.

John was trying out the tricycle and we seen that the wheel on the front of the tricycle was too small. He said "I'll find another wheel pretty soon and bring the tricycle up to you if you'll take it for four bucks."

Sure enough, in about two weeks he came up and had a nice wheel that fit that tricycle just right. And the first thing he said was, "Did you go down and look at that place?"

"Nope, didn't get a chance to go down there yet."

"Well," he said, "you gotta go down and see it." That's all he talked about the whole time he was there.

I kept saying, "Yeah, yeah yeah."

Finally, he went home, and I stayed there and I forgot all about what he said.

One day, just before we were coming back to Michigan, we were walking down the street to the bank in Compton, and I met this same guy on the street. The way he greeted me was to say, "Did you go down and look at that place?"

I felt a little bit ashamed. "No, I didn't go down yet."

So, he said, "You go down and look at that place! If you don't, you're going to be sorry."

I said to Mary, "This sounds awful funny. For this complete stranger to keep talking to me like that, it must be from the Lord. " So that's when we went down and looked at those twenty acres. We finally bought that place for $10,000.

We liked real estate, Mary and I. We had something in common there. We both liked real estate and the Lord had in mind that inheritance of mine. I didn't know what it was, but that real estate was always enticing to me. Everybody in Huntington Beach thought we were crazy to buy that place for $10,000. But I liked that place.

There was one house on our property when we bought it. That's the one we lived in. The second house behind it was used for a stable and a granary. We made a nice place out of it and called it "The Pink House." By golly, that was a nice place to live. Then we built those cottages. We didn't have much money in it, and we rented them out for about thirty years. We made a lot of money on that.

We ran a little sawmill there and a cement plant. There was also a gravel pit on it. When John and David were in high school, I got 'em an old truck and found an old loader. They trucked gravel over to the next lot.

Eventually, we got $5000 a month from a company that made floats for the ocean. I made a lot of money on that place, whether I used it or sold it. It always made me a lot of money.

I think we made close to $2 million off of it. Ain't that somethin'? The inheritance, see? And that's not all it did. It paid the down payment on that land up north that we sold for $5.5 million. (We had close to a million in it, but we cleared 4.5 million!) Those twenty acres in Huntington Beach gave me enough cash so I could tackle that mountaintop. Our boys have still got a chunk left up there (2.5 acres) and they're asking $1 million for that yet.

> **That guy was right. If we hadn't gone and looked at that place and bought it, we would have been sorry. See how the Lord leads? That's "dressing the earth"!**

So that guy was right. If we hadn't gone and looked at that place and bought it, we would have been sorry. See how the Lord leads? We did real good on that place. That's dressing the earth. Without dressing the earth, you starve to death.

Ernie: 1947 My Life with Margaret

Ernie

After finally finding a woman I could really love, only four years and nine months later, the Lord took her home. You'd wonder why the Lord first gave her to me and then took her home. Those things are in the hands of the Lord and we don't question His knowledge because it's way past our finding out. I know that she's better off in heaven than she would have been with me.

The last time I was with her, I remember coming home in the car and thinking, "My, it's like riding with an angel."

We enjoyed working, playing, and raising our children together!

Herb   Paul

Judy

I had a funny feeling that she might go home, even before she got sick. Not long after that, she died. She'd had no sign of being sick. Another thing, she was pregnant, maybe two months or so. The Lord took them both home at the same time.

When I first asked Margaret to marry me, we knelt down, and prayed the Lord's Prayer together. And that's the last thing we prayed together before she left this earth.

She died of viral encephalitis, which attacks the spinal column, and she became paralyzed. We were only married four years and nine months.

I don't know why the Lord took Margaret home. But I'm pleased and very happy for this one thing: I know that she died a real Christian mother who believed in her Savior. That is something to rejoice over.

> **When I first asked Margaret to marry me, we knelt down and prayed the Lord's Prayer together. And that's the last thing we prayed together before she left this earth.**

Cousin Irv's pastor in Traverse City sent me a real nice letter of comfort.

Memories of Margaret

Margaret and Ernie Manth.

Married January 31, 1943 at Immanuel Lutheran Church in Grand Rapids

Margaret died on November 27 1947

Herbert Born January 21, 1944

Paul born on January 19, 1945

Margaret & Paul Herb & Ernie

Herb, Judy, Paul

Judy was born on February 26, 1947

Ernie: Comfort From the Lord

I had a dream three weeks after Margaret died. I said, "This is it! I'm going to have to dig her up!" So, I got a shovel. This dream is just as plain as I sit here and see this room and it happened thirty-five years ago. I took the ruler out of my pocket (I always had one for log-buying) and measured down three feet. It was heavy clay, but the ground was fresh where I was digging because she hadn't been there for long. I dug down three feet and measured. Then a hand came up out of that dirt and pointed and there lay *her* Bible!

I knew immediately what it meant. There was no need for digging. My comfort was not in that shovel, but in the Word of the Lord. I jumped out of bed and took her Bible, and she had lovely markings in it, so I read her Bible. I knew immediately that my comfort and joy was in the Word, not in digging.

I've told people about that dream, but it's not something to be written in the Bible. It was for *my* benefit. The Lord still talks to us individually and gives us comfort and strength if we trust in Him. That was my comfort. I also sang hymns while I was driving in the car or truck. One was my confirmation hymn.

"In the hour of trial, Jesus plead for me
Lest by base denial, I depart from thee.
When Thou seest me waver, with a look recall,
Nor for fear or favor suffer me to fall.

Should Thy mercy send me sorrow, toil, or woe
Or should pain attend me on my path below,
Bring to my remembrance sad Gethsemane
Or in darker semblance, cross-crowned Calvary.

Another hymn I loved to sing was "My Jesus, As Thou Wilt."

My Jesus, as Thou wilt, oh, may Thy will be mine.
Into Thy hands of love, I would my all resign.
Through sorrows or through joys, conduct me as Thine own.
And, if all strength should fail, my Lord, Thy will be done.

> **I knew immediately what the dream meant.**
> **My comfort was in the Word of the Lord.**
> **The Lord still talks to us individually and gives us comfort and strength if we trust in Him.**

Those old Lutheran hymns are so wonderful. They preach a sermon all by themselves! They comforted and helped me in my time of grief.

When I lost Margaret, I thought, *Now how am I going to raise these three children?* Mother was here and she helped take care of them. Judy was still in diapers. (Now there's an outstanding fine girl too. Judy does an exceptional good job.) The Lord gave me these children and I had to raise them with the help of my mother.

Margaret had asked me to visit her friend in Grand Rapids and thought maybe something would work out because the children would need a mother. I went and visited her and we talked awhile, but it was not the Lord's will. We were friendly. She thanked me for visiting her as Margaret's husband. She said Margaret was a very good friend of hers. I think her father sold pianos. They were a good Christian family. They had a music store and played for the church. But the arrangement was not to be. Man thinks and the Lord leads. I only saw her that once. The reason probably was because Ted said, "Why don't you and Mother come to California? Spend a couple months and get away from everything. Come out and visit us." So I did.

Ernie

Ernie: 1948 California Here We Come

When Ted encouraged me to come out to California and rest a while, I took Mother and the children and pulled a trailer to California that winter of '48. We had already bought the trailer because Margaret and I were planning to go for a trip and take Mother to California. Then Margaret died, so just Mother and I and the children went. We camped right next to Ted's place that winter.

Ernie and Mother 1948
"Traveling West"

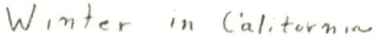
Winter in California

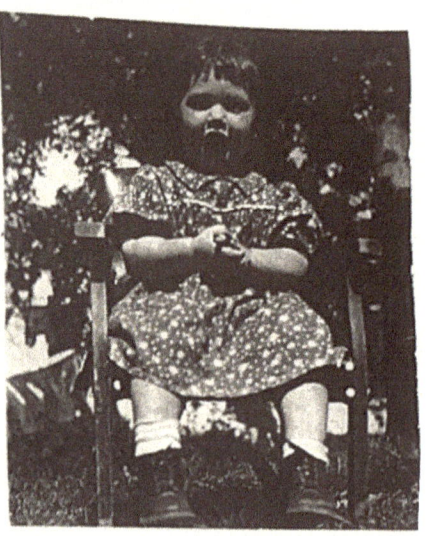
One-year-old Judy

That's how I got acquainted with Cora. I thought the last thing I would ever do would be to marry one of Mary's sisters. Mary was somewhat of a general, and I resented taking advice from another woman, because Ted and I were always partners and Mary was a third party. I didn't feel that she should have a voice in our decisions because she had nothing to do with establishing the business. I resented that and the last thing I wanted to do was to marry one of her sisters.

So, there I was in California and Judy got awful sick. Mother also got quite sick and couldn't help me with Judy. Mother said, "You've got to take her to a doctor right away. There's something wrong with that little girl."

I said, "Well, what will I do? I've got to drive and can't take care of her at the same time."

Mother said, "Go and ask Cora." She was living with Ted and Mary at the time, helping with the children. "Maybe she'll go with you."

I asked her and Cora said, "Sure, I'll help."

Cora took little Judy, put her on her lap and we went to the doctor. Cora is very motherly and sympathetic, having come from a big family. The doctor gave Judy a shot and, boy, she started snapping right out of it. She was dehydrated, but after the shot, it wasn't long until she started perking right up.

Then the doctor said, "My, you two have a lovely little daughter here." I didn't say nothin,' and Cora smiled a little but didn't say anything either.

When I got home, I told Mother what the doctor had said. Mother thought that was very nice. I said, "What do you think of Cora? She seems to be a very nice girl."

Mother said, "If Cora ever loved a man, she would be very faithful. A good Christian wife."

I dropped it for a while after that. Then one day I said, "Mother, what would you think if I asked Cora for a date?" I had a lot of respect for my mother's wisdom. "Well," she said, "why don't you try? I don't know if she would go with you. But if Cora ever loved a man, she would be very faithful and true. She's a fine girl." Mother knew that, see?

> I had a lot of respect for my mother's wisdom. She said, "If Cora ever loved a man, she would be very faithful and true. She's a fine girl."

I had asked Cora for a date before I married Margaret, but she was too young. She was only eighteen years old and wouldn't go with me. She was nearly twenty-five when I asked her that second time, and she was still single. Look how the Lord works. He preserved her for me!

I asked her for a date, and she went out with me. I took her down to Laguna Beach, one of those beautiful places overlooking the ocean. We visited together and I could see that Cora was a very fine girl. Then I asked her for another date, and we went out a few more times. I found out that she was a very lovely girl, just like Mother had thought.

Then I asked Mother, "What would you think if I would marry Cora?"

Mother said, "Cora is a good woman, and she will be a very faithful and fine wife." That's all she said.

I kept dating Cora while I was still there in California, and it wasn't long before I realized that she was the girl that I wanted to marry. I knew that I could love her. She was such a wonderful woman. I asked her to marry me! Cora was nice to court. She was a sweet girl, very appreciative of things. She was even nice to kiss! She was also very attractive. She's still very attractive for her age. When she'd go with me, I'd be kind of proud of her.

> **I never prayed for the Lord to give me another wife. I liked Margaret! But man thinks and the Lord leads. Cora was nice to court. When she'd go with me, I'd be kind of proud of her.**

Cora took Margaret's place about as well as is possible. Man thinks and the Lord leads. I never prayed for the Lord to give me another wife. I liked Margaret! But the Lord took her home. So, then we have to say like Job said, "The Lord hath given and the Lord hath taken. Praise be unto the Lord! In all things, give thanks unto the Lord."

Ted: Black Gold for the Gospel

Ted

I met a fellow in Huntington Beach by the name of Jimmy Thirst. He was thirsty for money. He bilked (cheated) us out of quite a bit of dough. I guess he was a pretty good guy, but he was an expensive man. We bought our equipment from different outfits because there were quite a lot of companies around Huntington Beach that were flourishing. The first well they dug came in at 10,000 barrels of oil a day. That's a big well. We picked up our machinery from companies that were servicing the oil fields. We'd buy their old equipment when they improved a well and upgraded. We picked up derricks and all the tools you have to have to go down and make a hole. These oil guys down here in California had connections up there in Canada. They came to visit me right there in Huntington Beach, and they had leases to sell. It's very easy to get sucked into something like that.

Ernie: Ted Convinces Me to Go to Canada

Ernie

In 1948, after Margaret died and while I was getting to know Cora, we drilled an oil well in Canada. It was my brother's idea to give this project momentum. He was a great promoter and optimist. Everything looked on the bright side to him. So, he put this whole oil plan together. He got all those things lined up to keep me real busy.

First, he bought the oil pipe and equipment. Then he called me one day at the veneer mill and said he thought we should go up to Canada and drill an oil well.

I said, "I don't know why we would want to drill an oil well! I've got my hands full with the mill and trying to raise these three children alone. If you think we should drill an oil well, *you* go drill it! I don't think I'm too interested.

"Oh," he said, "you should be in on it!"

Well, I wasn't too convinced that I wanted to be in on it, but a few days later, he called to tell me that he had bought this equipment on the veneer mill money, and we better get going on it!

I said, "What in all the world are we getting into the oil business for?"

"Well," he says, "we're going to drill an oil well so that the results go to the spreading of the Gospel! The Lord could bless that and make it very good!"

So that's how we got going on an oil venture. Ted got all those things lined up for me to keep me real busy.

> **We're going to drill an oil well so that the results go to the spreading of the Gospel!**

We hired an attorney by the name of Abrams. He had a big office, a whole flat in one of those big buildings in Los Angeles. He set up our whole operation and we paid him a good sum of money for that. He also made arrangements with an attorney in Calgary. We called it "Interior Petroleum" in the United States and "Exterior Petroleum" in Canada, which I thought was a good name. We got all the legal arrangements made to proceed into Canada. A man by the name of Mr. Pillings was supposed to handle our Canadian venture. Mr. Abrams handled our United States venture.

I took Mother and the kids back to Michigan in the trailer that spring. I was very leery about making a venture like that, especially if it was to serve the Lord's cause, so I stopped in Missouri on the way back to Michigan to see Dr. Walter Meier, who was the speaker on the Lutheran Hour radio broadcast at the time. I thought I'd bring this matter up to him and ask him to pray about it, as long as it was going to be serving the Lord's cause. I didn't know anything about drilling an oil well, so I made an appointment with Dr. Meier and told him what we intended to do.

He said, "Is this your earnest intention?"

I answered, "Yes, it sure is. We intend to spread the Gospel with the money that the oil well would produce, above the cost." We were not going to use it for ourselves.

He said, "If that is your earnest intention, then we'll kneel down by this chair and pray about it." So, we both knelt down, and he made a very good prayer. Then he put his hand on my head—I remember that as plain as day—and he said, "The Lord be with you. Go in peace." That's what I remember of that prayer the best. "The Lord be with you. Go in peace."

Then I came back to California and went to Canada in June to set up the oil well. I started thinking that maybe Cora and I could get married and work this thing out together. I think that's when we became engaged.

Here's the way I think real love goes. I wouldn't do anything to hurt my relationship with Cora. I was very careful about what I did. You put your best foot forward all the time and polish that shoe too! Once I knew I could love her, then I was very cautious not to do anything that would hurt her feelings nor our relationship. I wouldn't even let out a pooh (passed gas)! I got to thinking an awful lot of Cora. I wonder now if I'm not as warm to her as I ought to be. The children think a lot of Cora, too, and that makes me happy.

We didn't date very long. Then I said, "Boy, why should we wait? I'm getting older. Maybe we should just get married." I told her, "I really love you. I can see that."

She said, "I love you, too."

Cora was a Christian and I was a Christian too. I'd tell her a lot of things about the Bible. She said she had always prayed for a devout Christian husband. The Lord must have put that in her heart.

I asked Cora to marry me just before I left for Canada to set up the oil well.

Goodbye letter as Ernie is heading to Canada...

*Sure am glad that you love me, Darling. Sure is a wonderful thing when one is lonesome for the family and a sweet wife.
Hope that nothing on my part will ever be done knowingly to injure this beautiful thing which the Lord has given!*

*   Goodbye Sweetheart,
    Ernie*

Ernie: A Tricky Border Crossing

Ernie

We loaded our equipment on an old Mack chain-drive truck. We put several tons on it and that outfit traveled *very slow*— probably 20-25 miles per hour at best. Most of the time, it was doing more like 15-18 miles per hour! It was a slow operation.

It took us most of two weeks to get from Los Angeles to Sweetgrass, Montana. Some of the big trucks could make that trip in 2-3 days, but it took us two weeks!

That was when I was held up on the border. On the other side of Sweetgrass, MT was Coutts, Alberta. The sign said "International Goodwill," but it sure didn't feel like that to us! We sat at that border for seven days! One day, two days, three days... and every day we'd contact Pilling, our attorney, who said he was definitely working hard every day to get us in... Fourth day, fifth day, sixth day, and still we were sitting there on the border with no place to go. I had my crew, trucks, and machinery sitting there, just waiting to get into Canada.

Finally, at 4:00 in the evening, Mr. Pillings calls me up and says, "Manthei, I have exploited all of my possibilities for getting you into Canada, and I have to report that I *cannot* get you into Canada!"

What a revolting situation! Here we sat, with all that machinery and two carloads of machinery already on site at Kitscoty, Alberta, waiting to be unloaded from the track, and I'm sitting here at the border and can't do anything…with expenses mounting!

I was very unhappy and disappointed and asked him, "What can I do?"

He replied, "You'll have to call Honorable "Monkman" (MacKinnon) and explain the situation yourself."

I asked, "What good will that do when you've already explained it all to him and exploited all your possibilities as an attorney? What good could I do?"

He says, "Well, Manthei, you can talk pretty well. You have nothing to lose and everything to gain, so I suggest you do that.

"But it's 4:00 on Saturday afternoon! He isn't even in his office."

"Oh yes, he is!" says Pilling. "I just got done talking with him."

I said, "Okay." I felt about two inches high, because here the big moguls couldn't do nothing, and I'm supposed to call this big shot in the government. He was the Minister of Mines and Resources. He was a big gun in the government, and I was just a small potato, and by this time, he probably didn't like me much either. I didn't know the man from Adam, so I said a prayer and then I called.

He asked, "Who is this?"

I said, "This is Ernie Manthei from the Exterior Petroleum Company."

He said, "I have been bothered hearing your name all week. I am full up to the neck and I don't want to hear any more. Furthermore, tomorrow is Sunday. I suggest you go to church!"

Look how man thinks and the Lord leads. Dr. Meier had prayed that the Lord bless me on this trip, and here was the key word: Church!

Immediately, I grew up to be a full-sized man and said, "Don't you tell *me* to go to church! I go to church without you telling me! Furthermore, we intend to come into Canada and drill an oil well where the proceeds will go to the spreading of the Gospel, but you won't even let me in!!"

> I said, "Don't you tell *me* to go to church! I go to church without you telling me! Furthermore, we intend to come into Canada and drill an oil well where the results go to the spreading of the Gospel, and you won't even let me in!!"

He says, "Repeat that please!" I repeated it, and he says, "Monday morning at 6:00, I'll have a Mountie there with a permit for you to proceed. I want you to come to my office. I'd like to shake hands with you and talk with you a little."

Well, I felt pretty good and realized right away that here was the hand of the Lord answering our prayers. It was not our engineering or "smarts" in putting together a company—it was God that made the difference. The attorney and all the money we put out was worthless, but because we prayed, God put it in that man's heart to say the right thing to get me talking and telling him my side. That part he had never heard from Attorney Pilling.

Monday morning at 6:00 am, here was the Mountie with that permit. He said, "I can't understand this! I had strict orders to keep you from even walking into Canada, and here I have a permit telling you to proceed. I can't understand this!"

He didn't have to understand, but I understood. I don't remember if I explained it to him or not. But the conversation I remember word for word because it was so impressive to me.

When we got to Edmonton, I stopped into the office and discovered that the Premier of Alberta, Honorable Ernest Manning, was a very God-fearing man, and a minister! He used to preach over the radio every Sunday. He preached very good Gospel sermons. He was a very fine man, and he had surrounded himself with Christian officials. So Honorable Monkman was one of his Christian officials in charge of mining. This was an outstanding thing. I saw how prayers work and how man thinks and the Lord leads.

Now, as I look back, I see that through all my life. Man thinks and the Lord leads, and the Lord blesses. The Lord wants us to take all these things to Him in prayer and communicate with Him, to stay in touch with our Creator, that His name be glorified. Strictly in this whole thing, I have to give glory to God. I cannot take any glory for myself because there wasn't any. All our efforts were for naught, but the Lord had His hand in this. That was while I was single, before I remarried, but Cora and I were engaged before I took the equipment up to Canada in June of '48 to set up the oil well.

> **The Lord wants us to take all these things to Him in prayer and communicate with Him, to stay in touch with our Creator, that His name be glorified.**

Excerpt of a letter from Ernie to Cora, June 28

"I bet you wonder why I am over 600 mi from Kitscoty again. Well, they won't give us no extra money for our American Dollar in Canada and then take 12% off. So, I came back to Great Falls to change dollars into their money here. Then I'll go back with it to pay our freight and expenses and have more money to work with, because $7000 with 10% increase is $700, which all helps.

I drove my car 330 miles to Calgary, then left it in a garage for a checkup from hitting bad holes in the road. Rode the train 130 miles, then hitchhiked over 200 miles back here to Great Falls, all in one day. So, you see I got quite a little life in me yet, but I am very very tired now."

Letter from Cora to Ernie

Wednesday – July 7th

My Darling,

I looked for a letter from you today, but it didn't come so maybe it will tomorrow. Honey, I sure wish I could be with you on your birthday Saturday and every other day too. I didn't buy you a present yet but will spend the money on that phone bill and when you come home, Darling, I'll make you a nice cake and try to make the rest up in love. Will that be alright?

This morning we drove to Santa Ana and bought apricots for canning, so I have some work ahead of me yet. Dornfelds aren't back from San Diego yet, but I suppose they will come today. Ed has a job coming up in the peat pit on Saturday.

Sweetheart, I love you more than ever and pray that you will come back to me soon. October seems a pretty long way off and I would go with you in a minute now if you still wanted me. I realize now my place is with you and the children. The Lord Bless and Keep You, my Darling,

Your loving Cora

Letter from Ernie to Cora

My Very Sweetest Darling,   *July 7, 48 Kitscoty*

My, you sure write me sweet letters, and I love you a lot Darling. The Lord sure blessed me richly with Love like yours because of its sincerity and pureness. I pray that the Lord bless me with faith and strength to walk humbly before Him and always thank Him for this great blessing that He has given me.

Kitscoty is a small wooden-structure town about like the ghost town at Knotts Berry Farm.

Herman told me last night that the girls in this town are pretty fast, so he is going to be careful I guess, but he has not met any Lutheran girls yet that I know of. So there still might be hope.

Darling, the way the money goes in this business makes me very nervous. It certainly takes a lot of money. Last Sunday I talked before the Lloydminster Lutheran Church and told them all about this new venture which is to be to the Glory of God. First, I brought them the greetings of Dr. Meier and Dr. Bertermann. They were all very happy over that and nearly everyone invited me to dinner at their house.

You know, Darling, I need a fine Christian wife to be with me and pray with me that we might be stronger together in doing the Lord's work. And I guess with the Lord knowing all things like He does, knew that I had need of this thing. Having mercy on me, blessed me soon with this richest of all blessings.

Darling, we need casing equipment badly, and it looks like I will have to chase some down, maybe your way, but I will try along the way because the Lord's angel might lead me to some before I get there and then the freight would not cost us so much. Ted and Herbie are sending $15,000 more out here, which they borrowed from the bank. Stock is not moving back there. The location we have looks very good and should bring in a good well because it is surrounded by about sixteen producing wells. Slim thought it best to take this new location and let all of Allen's property go back at present because leases are easy to get up here, he says. Everything is unloaded now. Was a big job to do. We hired only one man steady.

Darling, don't you think I better stop now? You will have to stop me sometimes when I talk too much because that is easy for a Manthei to do. The Lord Bless and Keep you in His Hands of Love.

Your Love, Ernie

Excerpt from Ernie's letter to Cora, July 11

"The roads up here are terrible hard on a car. All my shock absorbers are shot to pieces and a stone flew up on the gravel road and broke my windshield so we really gotta work hard to earn this all back. Mr. Theriot has no money either. But I do know that the Lord will bless the efforts of our hands if we serve Him all the time. Darling, with lots of love and sweet thoughts of you.

I am your Promised Husband in Christ,
  Ernie"

In mid-July, I had to come back down to pick up some drill pipe in Los Angeles for the oil well project.

While I was down in California, I married Cora on July 21st.

We got married in St. John's Lutheran Church in Orange. We had no big wedding. Our folks weren't there. Ted and Mary were back in Michigan. Cora's brother, Ed, and Mrs. Gesch (the pastor's wife) were our attendants.

Our honeymoon was spent traveling back to Canada with the rest of the oil equipment. I think Ted and Mary brought up the trailer later. Grandma and the children stayed on the farm.

Wedding Day: July 21, 1948

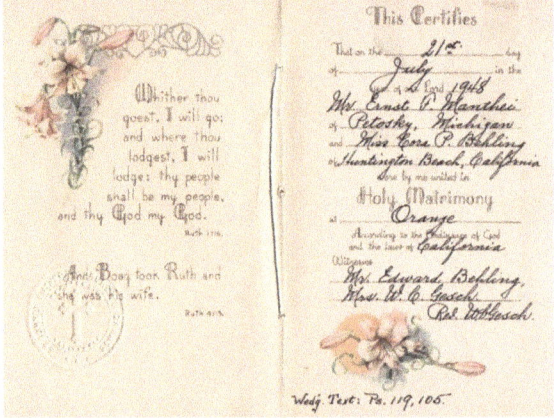

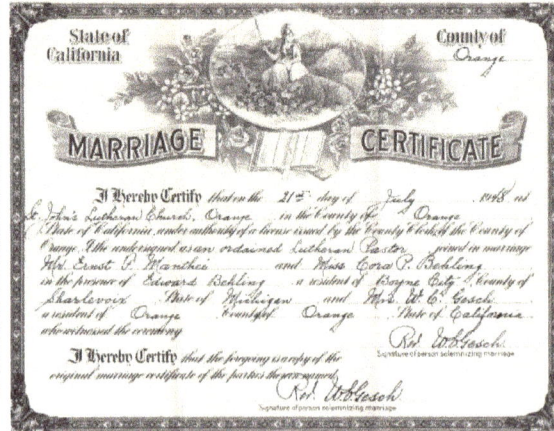

Ernie: Yes, We Got Oil!

Everyone wants to know if we got oil. Yes, we got oil!

We drilled an oil well. Now that is an interesting thing. The man who we got to drill the well was supposed to be a real sharp man, but he did a lot of foolish things. He never did bring the oil in and, eventually, he ran away, leaving me with the oil well. I didn't know anything about an oil well! His name was Slim Terrio. I came home that fall and we still didn't have a well. But we didn't give up. The next spring, we went back with the children and rented a house in Lloydminster, Alberta.

Traveling back to Canada

1950 - Our house

Lloydminster, Alberta

I had a New Yorker Chrysler, a pretty nice-looking car, and I drove up to the supply company. We still owed them in the neighborhood of three-thousand dollars. The man watched me drive up and said, "You have a nice automobile there and you still owe us some money."

I said, "Do you like that car?"

He said, "My, yes!" Cars were still pretty scarce, right after the war. Nice cars were not available. He said, "Yes, I think that's a beautiful car."

I said, "Would you take that car for what I owe you?"

He answered, "You'd let us have that car for the amount of money you owe us?" I said I would because I'm an honest man. He said, "Hold on. I'll call the president of the company." That was Mr. Reed, from the Commonwealth Oil and Drilling Company. Mr. Reed called to Ottawa and they said, "You take the car for the money. We'll arrange for customs."

The deal was made, just like that! So now I was on foot. I said, "Now I have to get home, out in the country where my wife and children are."

They said, "Okay, we'll let you use our company pickup for ten days until you find some other transportation."

I used their pickup until I found a little old V-8 Ford pickup with a small engine called a Ford 60. It was only a one-seater, so I would pile the three children up on the ledge by the window. They crawled up there tight and, that's how we'd go to church and town and wherever we wanted to go. One could sit on the seat between us and the others sat on the ledge in back.

Well, I was kind of a joke there in church because, when we first came to church, we had a nice big car and now we came with this old Ford. They wondered what happened. So, I'd tell them, "My good car went down the hole and this is all that's left."

I paid $600 for that old Ford. We owned a coring line on a wench, which was used for coring oil wells. Another company needed that wench and gave me $600, so I could pay cash for that pickup. I had no money because our money was tied up in the well.

Somehow Mr. Reed heard about this whole thing and said, "I want to meet Mr. Manthei." We met and he said, "I was so impressed with what you did that we had a meeting and decided to service your well. We know you've got oil. We'll put the necessary equipment there, the oil tanks, jacks and everything, get it pumping, and give you half of the production until the well pays back the money we have in it. Then we'll turn it over to you: lock, stock, and barrel!"

That's exactly what they did!! They installed their equipment, took half of the production until their supplies were paid for, and then turned the well over to us. The money we made went for buying Bibles for Japan.

At that time, World War II had just ended and General MacArthur had made a plea for Bibles for the Japanese people, who were desirous to hear the Word of the Lord. He asked for ten thousand Bibles and said, "I'll see that they are distributed, even if I have to do it myself!" The American people were still mad at Japan for what they had done at Pearl Harbor. Nobody wanted to do anything good for the Japanese. My brother and I figured that if the Japanese wanted to learn the Word of the Lord, that's what they needed more than anything else. So, from the proceeds of that oil well, we made the money available to distribute Bibles through the Lutheran Hour in response to General MacArthur.

> **He was so impressed with what I did to pay my debts that he decided to service the well and provide all the necessary equipment we needed in a way we could afford.**

We never made big money from that oil well, because it was tar-sand oil; heavy gravity oil, which they used for greases, transmission oil, and 7% diesel fuel. There was no gasoline because tar-sand oil is too heavy for that. Today, that oil would be very valuable, but then we got only $1.50 per barrel. Today, that same material would be worth $25-$28 per barrel.

Figuring all our expenses and machinery costs, it was not good management. We could have dug that well for much less money if we had farmed it out. But we were used to doing things ourselves. If we had continued drilling oil wells, we probably would have done okay because we had all the machinery. Then we dug only one well! But the money we made *was* used for spreading the Gospel to Japan and we did hold to our agreement with the Lord. We sold the oil well the next year.

THEODORE W. MANTHEI, PRESIDENT

ERNST MANTHEI, VICE PRESIDENT

INTERIOR PETROLEUM COMPANY
INCORPORATED UNDER THE LAWS OF THE STATE OF NEVADA

7391 EAST TALBERT AVENUE

HUNTINGTON BEACH, CALIF.

OFFICE AT
PETOSKEY, MICHIGAN

Ted: Tithing is important!

Ted

The Lord ordained in His all-knowing knowledge that the earth must produce to His glory. That's how we came up with "Dressing the earth to the glory of God." There's no other dressing than dressing the earth to the glory of God. All these guys, like Henry Ford and others, *are* producing things to the glory of God but they're not getting the credit for it with God because they're doing it for their own materialistic rewards. But God is honored by it because the Christians are making use of their products to His glory.

> **Tithing is important! The Lord ordained in His all-knowing knowledge that the earth must produce to His glory.**

That's how it worked with the oil venture. We used that equipment to help send Bibles into Japan for God's glory.

Our well in Canada was an experimental well. That's why it cost us so much money. For one-fourth that money, we could have had a good production up there that would have paid out. But it was an experimental well, what they call a "pre-packed gravel-packed liner." We had to drill an extra-big hole, which took so much more work, and then slip that liner down the hole. Well, it plugged up overnight. Then they had to pull the whole thing back out and produce oil like the rest were doing. That whole experiment was a waste. An oil well like that can take your motel and farm and a whole lot of other stuff down the hole with it in a hurry.

Old Chimmy Curtis the banker said, "Boys, you're gonna have to quit this." We had to borrow money from our banker to dig that old hole, you know. We lost money but the mill was running good, and she could pay off the debt.

It wasn't all bad. We did our best for the glory of God. None of this stuff was easy but it gave us a lot of knowledge and we gained wisdom from it. You can learn a lot from your mistakes, you know.

> **The money we made *was* used for spreading the Gospel to Japan and we did hold to our agreement with the Lord.**

Once Ernst agreed to the tithing, we always gave 20% of our net income from our mills for Gospel work. That's the pattern we followed. Nobody could believe it. That banker couldn't believe it. My mother couldn't believe it. But we did it! We didn't ask anybody for permission. We just took the cash out of our safe. We had no interest to pay, and we were doing most of the work with our own hands. We all got paid well and none of us suffered.

That's the way we got the Gospel into Japan.

Ted: Another Vision (1949)

Ted

It was about the time Chester was making so much trouble in the mill that I had this vision from the Lord.

I was standing on top of a valley that ran down and I seen something coming, and it was a great wonder. It was a boxcar. Just like a full-size box car on a train. Fifty feet long. And it was coming at me at a pretty good clip. I would say 35 mph. I wondered how something could move that fast when I couldn't see an engine or mode of power. There was no vehicle hood, no tractor, and no engine.

When it got close enough, then I began to see the mode of power. A tiny white beast was pulling that huge load. This was something that was impossible. He had to have help from somewhere. This little beast looked like an oversized goat, and he had two horns and a good heart. His heart's purpose was to get this thing through the valley, and he had to work hard to do it. He was pulling this terrible load, you know. He didn't want to fight but if he had to, he would, and those two horns were his tools to do it.

He went down the hill on an impoverished road which was narrower at the bottom. Just narrow enough for one unit to go through to a time. The sides dropped off into a ditch. And right in the worst spot where he was the most vulnerable, there lay another beast. He looked just like the first beast and he was laying there just hoping this good beast would take for the ditch. But he wasn't about to take for the ditch! He gave way to the side all that he could, but he wasn't going to tip the load over. He was determined to go on through and do his work the way it was supposed to be, so the other beast had to back up. He had horns too. He backed up enough so the first beast could get by. He hadn't shown his cards yet, his temper. Since he couldn't tip it over into the ditch by laying in the road, he tried to push it over by bucking at it with his horns when the load passed by him. And that broke his horns off, you see. When he bucked against that, it ruined him.

The good little beast knew that this was his enemy who would go to no ends to destroy his work. While he was pulling that first unit along, a second unit attached itself to the first.

Now the little beast had two units to pull uphill! Not downhill. But he didn't slow down a bit. That was another wonder! He went up that hill just as good as he went down the hill, at a good clip, you know.

When he got into the level area, there was a little cabin. He detached himself from those two units and went to stand in the doorway of the little cabin, half in and half out. He was preparing for battle. Then I was transferred into the scene, and I wanted to get into that building quick for protection. I pushed that little beast so I could get inside, and he moved a little for me, but he didn't leave the door. He stood firm.

The one-room cabin had a partition and I walked around behind it and crouched down to hide because I was awful fearful of the battle that was going to take place. The little beast just stayed out there in front by the door, even when he heard the hoofbeats. Loud hoofbeats! The fella down in the valley got all his cronies together and they were coming to fight. I wondered if that building would stand up under that terrible battle. But the little beast wasn't afraid. He stood in the door and every time he heard the noise get a little louder, he'd put his head a little lower so he could hook a little harder. Good golly! He was courageous. Finally, the hoofbeats died down and it got real quiet. The little beast finally left the door. He knew there wasn't going to be a war after all.

As I crouched behind this partition, I glimpsed a man walking by. He was Asian and a wife followed him with a little child. They came in the cabin and drew something on the wall. I couldn't see because the partition was between me and the wall. It took him quite a while. When he finished, he came around the partition and he picked me up by my left arm and he helped raise me up from my fear, you see. And we walked around the partition to where he had drawn something, and he had a covering over it. He pulled the covering off and there was the emblem of the Japanese flag. Just as plain as day. He said "Behold the glory of OUR God!" And I just squeezed and hugged him. Our God. He was my friend.

Then I woke up. This dream happened while I was in Michigan.

God reassured me through that dream. Enemy at the door. Hoofbeats and footsteps. Tremendous battle. But then it died away and didn't affect us at all. I can still see in my vision when he rammed against that unit going by and it knocked the horns right off his head. He was bucking against something too strong for him. He was in bad shape when he got done with that thing!

> **God reassured me through that dream. There would be a battle, but it was all for the glory of our God.**

I didn't treat Chester mean. But we had to get him out of there when he made trouble bringing in the union. Chester wanted to get back in the mill and he went to court over the thing. He filed for reinstatement with back pay. The insurance company was really riled up about that. He had a life disability deal in there and everything. He got three union lawyers from Detroit to come up here. We had to fight that case.

Just to show you how he would do it... Chester had been down in Florida and came back broke with no money. Ernst wanted to help because he could hardly feed his family. That's how he got into the mill. Ernst helped him with land and a house. When he didn't need his trailer anymore, we told him there was a fellow down at the mill that needed a home. Our boiler-man. We said, "Maybe you could sell the trailer to him, and he can park it on the mill grounds so you can keep an eye on it till he gets it paid for. That way you're safe and you'll get your money." Chester turned that whole case around and made that guy be a witness against us and for himself. The guy had arthritis and we paid him 24-hours-a-day as a watchman and a boiler-man. Easy work. But they took advantage of us. Some of those guys were wicked. And Chester put them up to it.

Chester was telling him that the trailer was using too much juice (electricity!) He wanted the Manthei Brothers to compensate him for all the juice the trailer was using. To Chester, it was not a mill. It was a trailer. He could twist it out of shape in any way to get anywhere.

But our lawyer had that under control, I tell you.

The referee said to Chester, "I understand there's a mill hooked onto that line!"

Then Chester turned around and fought for our side, making himself look like he was concerned that everything went well for us. That shows how corrupt he was. Then the referee wanted to know who the manager was down there.

Chester said, "I'm the manager."

Then they asked me "Who is the manager down there."

I said, "Herb Trier is the manager down there."

They said, "How long has he been working for you?"

"Oh, about 5-6 years."

He asked how long Chester was there. I said, "Oh, a few months."

The referee could see right away. Chester was out there really deep. They got him out of here.

Chester finally said to our lawyer, "The Lord will judge you."

Our lawyer laughed and said, "He's already judged you!"

That union lawyer never should have come up here. He was in the wrong department and there was nothing for him to stand on.

That was something in our lifetime that should never have happened at all. Chester could have been well off. He could have been an honorable citizen and had an established family. He had a little trouble with faith. That guy could have done real well, like the Behling brothers did. Al and Bob and Jim—all the boys that worked with us did well. They all came out independently wealthy.

That Petoskey plant was the main mill that made things go. Our other endeavors were just offshoots from it. Those are the repercussions that came out of it eventually.

Chapter 7
1950s: Growing Families and Enterprises

1950	Apr 6	Mark is born to Ernie and Cora
1951		Ted and Ernie begin to build the Soo Veneer Mill
	Nov 17	Jim is born to Ernie and Cora
1952	Jan 15	Constance dies
		First broadcast to Japan
	Oct 28	Stillborn baby Peter is born to Cora and Ernie
		Purchase White Swan freighter to haul logs
1953	Feb 18	Phil born to Ted and Mary
	Aug 2	Dedicate Soo Veneer Mill
		Ted builds Krueger & Peters Ready Mix
1954		Ernie sponsors Dunkel family from Canada to work at the mill
		Ted finds investors to buy 40-acre tract of land in Huntington Beach
1955	Feb 25	Ben is born to Ernie and Cora
		Ted finds MI investors to buy more CA land
		Chet Cone graduates as Reverend
		Babe has a stroke
1956	Nov 28	White Swan sinks
	Dec 25	Ruth is born to Ernie and Cora
1957		Ernie sponsors Wally Dunkel from Canada
		Ernie buys and converts the Mackinac Islander; hires Dick Lyons

Grandma's Last Christmas (1951)

Paul, Mark, Herbie and Judy

Paul
Mark
Herb
Judy

Christmas 1951

Grandma's last Christmas on Earth

↑ In Kingstree, So Carolina where Father was taking down a dryer for the Soo Veneer Mill

← Jim joined our family on November 17, 1951.

Jim's 1st Birthday
November 17, 1952

Ernie: Grandma Constance (January 1952)

Our mother died of colon cancer, after a surgery from which she never woke up. Thankfully she got to see baby Jimmy and to celebrate Christmas together with us before she was gone. She wrote a lovely letter to the family in her journal the night before her surgery.

Ernie

A LETTER FROM GRANDMA CONSTANCE

(This letter was written on Monday, January 7, 1952 at Lockwood Hospital in Petoskey, when Grandma Constance was facing surgery, from which she never awoke!)

I am not afraid, the Lord will take care of me.
His angel will be around me.
I have mutch to thank for in my life.
I was led up and down, but always protected by the Lord.

I pray for my Family, for <u>peace</u>
and never to loose there Fayth in God, their Maker.

If it is the Lord's Will that I go Home,
<u>There</u> I want to see you all again.
Not one should be missing.

I love you all,

    Mother

Note of interest:
While Father was growing up, Grandma told him that she did **not** expect to see Jesus return in her lifetime, that Ernie **might** see Him, his children **probably** would, but she felt quite certain that his grandchildren **would** see Jesus return in their lifetime!

*Constance Manthei
25ᵗ Dez. 1940.
born 21 of May 1884.
in Oblatzkowo Pro. Posen
Germany
Maiden Name. Menzel.*

The Soo Veneer Mill

Ted

Ted: It All Started with Logs (1953)

We didn't need those fancy logs like they're using now. We could use a low-grade tree of the kind of cuts we were making at that time.

Here's the story. Poplar in our country isn't much good for veneer. They have too many limbs on them. These limbs die and leave a hole. Then the tree grows around it and when you cut it, that hole just pops through all the way to the center. In Canada the season is short, so those limbs stay small and are broken off by the heavy snow. Canada has a shorter growing season with longer winters. Poplar is a dense wood. It isn't good face material, but it's strong, so it's good cross-band material. They don't use it now because they're just cutting high-quality face veneer.

We thought maybe we'd try some of that poplar from Canada. I and a pastor from Flint went up for a small vacation and to do a survey of some trees they had up there. We stayed in a fancy hotel, and I did a little reconnoitering to find out about those trees. Ernie didn't go. I was the guy who pioneered that. I was the first one to order a carload to come down with about 34,000-40,000 pieces. We trucked it down from Soo Canada to our Petoskey plant and processed it, just to see what kind of stuff it was, you see? It turned out very good—80% nice cuts. It was high yield.

Then we thought maybe we could save on trucking if we just built a mill in Canada. That's why we flew in that plane to Ottawa—to see what the setup would have to be. But there were too many complications and restrictions for an American to set up a mill in Canada, so we backed off and built our plant on the American side. We came across the border to the Soo (Sault Saint Marie) in Michigan, and the logs came across the border too. That's how that was done.

Ernst went up and bought the machinery wherever there were machines for sale. Escanaba had some clippers for sale. They were minor and not too hard to get. It's a small machine. Our long-term customer Metzelburg found us a brand-new lathe in Lockport, New York. There was a big dryer for sale in southern Michigan that we bought, and it was still in good shape. It did a lot of good work. And so on, don't you see?

We bought an old dance hall, converted it into the Soo Veneer Mill, and dedicated it to the Lord. Dressing the Earth to the Glory of God!

Dressing the Earth to the Glory of God!

I stayed in Michigan 'til the mill started running that winter.

Ernie: The Soo Veneer Mill (1953)

Ernie

After the veneer mill was running well for quite a while, we decided to start a second mill in Sault Saint Marie, Michigan. It was just this side of Canada, and we figured we could find unlimited resources of logs in Canada. So, we went up to the Soo to start a second plant.

Ted always said that we needed to dress the earth to the glory of God. He said God created the earth for our benefit and we were given the job to take care of the ground, to nurture it and cultivate it. We were to grow things and build things and be good stewards over the earth. That's what we did, both in farming and in logging trees to produce veneer.

We bought up an old dance hall there in the Soo and converted it into a veneer mill. When we dedicated it to the Lord, we hung up a big banner in front that said, "Dressing the Earth to the Glory of the Lord." Think of that! The same building that was once used for the devil's work was now being used to further the Lord's kingdom, the proceeds of which would go to spreading the Gospel!

Then we sent Herb Trier and Cora's brother, Bob, up there to run the plant. It took some work to get it running, but once it got on its feet, those two boys did real well to manage the plant and keep it going.

> **God created the earth for our benefit, and we were given the job to take care of the ground, to nurture it and cultivate it, to grow things and build things and be good stewards over the earth.**

> **Soo Veneer sounds a lot like "Souvenir." When Ruth first told Yosh about the Soo Veneer Mill, he asked: "What kind of 'souvenirs' did your family make?"**

OUR MOTTO

"Dressing the Earth to the Glory of the Lord"

Dedication Program

for the

SOO VENEER MILL

SAULT STE. MARIE, MICHIGAN

Sunday, August 2, 1953 - 3:00 p. m.

"Bring ye all the tithes into the storehouse that there may be meat in mine house, and prove me now herewith, saith the Lord of Hosts, if I will not open unto you the windows of Heaven and pour you out a blessing that there shall not be room enough to receive it."

—Malachi 3:10

Words of Information and Appreciation

The plans to establish a veneer mill at Sault Ste Marie were formulated in 1951. It was due to the wonderful interest and cooperation of Mr. Clifford Everett, President of the Industrial Commission of Sault Ste. Marie, that we decided to locate in this city. We want to take this opportunity to thank Mr. Clifford Everett, other members of the Industrial Commission, Mayor Freeman, and all city departments for the helpful assistance which they have given us.

The building in which the veneer mill is housed was formerly the old Gould's Pavillion. Most of the work of rebuilding was done by us, together with three other workers. Production started in March of 1952. The manager of the mill is Mr. Herbert Trier, who is also a partner in our business.

At the present time we are employing about 25 men at the mill. For our veneering purposes we are using a species of Canadian poplar. The veneer is sold in Michigan, Indiana and Wisconsin and is used as center stock for plywood and die panels in the auto and television industries. Very shortly we shall be in a position to flitch Canadaian birch.

We want to take this opportunity also to thank our employees for the cooperation which they have given us in our undertaking. In addition we want to thank all others who have assisted us in one way or another in getting this mill into production.

"Whatsoever ye do, do it heartily, as to the Lord, and not unto men; knowing that of the Lord ye shall receive the reward of the inheritance; for ye serve the Lord Christ."
—Colossians 3:23-24

A lot of birch veneer has rolled from the Soo Veneer plant at Sault Ste. Marie, Mich., in eleven years. And a story lies behind the biblical message which, as shown here, greets all visitors upon entering the plant.

Soo Veneer Co. — a Dedicated Michigan Birch Veneer Plant

In-plant photos by PLYWOOD Magazine

Back in 1953, after operating successfully for more than a decade at Petoskey, Mich., Theodore and Ernst Manthei of that city decided to branch out and establish a second mill at Sault Ste. Marie, Mich.

The Petoskey plant had been specializing in select white hard maple, and in the move to the birch country of Sault Ste. Marie it was only natural that the new mill there would specialize in select white birch.

The James La Grand Lumber Co. of Grand Rapids has been exclusive sales agent for the maple veneers out of Petoskey, and the firm was given similar status with respect to the new Soo mill. The Manthei brothers also invited James La Grand, president of that firm, into partnership with them in the Soo venture.

Herbert Trier and Bob Behling, manager and assistant manager of the Soo plant, also became partners. Other partners are Al Behling and a sister of the Mantheis', Mrs. Robert Notestine.

There's one unusual and very worthy aspect of this operation—enough, certainly, to cause all men in the veneer and plywood industry to take a second look. The Manthei brothers had been devoting a good share of the profits of the Petoskey plant for philanthropic purposes and for the spreading of the gospel. A unique part of their management-partnership agreement at the Soo lies in the fact that the full amount of the profits allowed by the U.S. Government is devoted to philanthropic purposes.

Theodore Manthei advises that this includes several mental sanatoriums, Christian Education Grants, and especially missionary work, not necessarily along denominational lines, but strictly to causes stressing the Orthodox and Evangelical position with regard to the spreading of the gospel. He mentions especially the Wycliffe translators, who aim to publish the Bible in every known language, the Lutheran Hour, the Back to God Hour, the Billy Graham crusades, etc.

Visitors to the mill are very much surprised to note, as they enter the plant, the large dedication announcement prominently displayed in the center of the mill. It carries the message "Our Motto—Dressing the Earth to the Glory of the Lord—Dedicated August 2, 1953."

The Soo mill operates a freighter capable of carrying from five to eight carloads of logs. It is the "Mackinac Islander," which operates between the
(Continued)

Bob Behling is assistant manager at Soo, and a member of the Soo partnership.

The Mackinac Islander, above, is chief provider of log supplies for both the Soo and Petoskey mills. Below, the Soo mill utilizes a very sizable reeling system.

The careful effort to achieve this damage-free packaging of veneer crates at Soo depends upon special veneer stalls (shown in photo at right) and the steel strapping equipment.

Herb Trier, Soo manager and a partner, displays stalls used for building up crateloads of veneer. Veneer sheets drop into stalls with perfect vertical alignment of edges.

177

PETER H. ELDERSVELD
MINISTER - DIRECTOR

RALPH ROZEMA
PRODUCTION MANAGER

C. J. DEN DULK
BUSINESS MANAGER

THE *Back to God* HOUR

10858 SOUTH MICHIGAN AVENUE
CHICAGO 28, ILLINOIS
PHONE COMMODORE 4-8773

April 16, 1956

Mr. & Mrs. Ernest Manthei
Route # 1
Petoskey, Michigan

Dear Mr. & Mrs. Manthei:

We have received from Mr. James La Grand a check in the amount of $1,252.96, and he has told us that this represents one of your monthly tithe checks.

As we wrote to Mr. La Grand, we are sincerely grateful not only for the gift of money, welcome as it is for use in the work of the Back to God Hour, but especially because of the information which he gave us relative to the fact that as Christian partners you have committed yourself to the principle of tithing. To find individual Christians who are consistent tithers is beginning to be a difficult matter, but to find a company which is committed to this principle is certainly a rarity. Therefore, we certainly commend you, and praise our God for you. May you find much joy and happiness because of your action, and we know that God will richly bless you for it.

We know that you are all aware of the work of the Back to God Hour, and we would urge you to continue to pray for us. We are humbly grateful to God that He has given us such a large ministry, and that there are those like yourselves who are willing to help in this work of bringing the Gospel to so many thousands.

Once again we thank you most heartily for your kindness and generosity, and we wish for you God's choicest blessings.

Most cordially yours in Christ,

THE BACK TO GOD HOUR

By C. J. den Dulk
Business Manager

CJD:js

THE LUTHERAN HOUR
SPONSORED BY THE LUTHERAN LAYMEN'S LEAGUE

3558 SOUTH JEFFERSON AVENUE
SAINT LOUIS 18, MISSOURI
PHONE: PRospect 2-4000

Bringing Christ to the Nations

Mr. and Mrs. Ernst Manthei
Petoskey, Michigan

March 5, 1956

Dear Cora and Ernie:

I can't begin to tell you how tremendously thrilled I was over your very lovely communication of February 29 and over its marvelous contents.

I certainly am tremendously grateful for your magnificent check to The Lutheran Hour in the amount of $8,000. It was marvelously kind of you to remember the radio mission in this way, and we thank you for it with all our hearts.

I note, of course, that you have designated this for the purchase of Japanese station time and we will be very happy to see to it that this is used exclusively for this purpose.

I believe this is the largest single such communication, and I join you in thanking God, too, for the remarkable blessing which it represents. I know that this blessing comes because you dedicated yourselves and God's gifts to you for the upbuilding of His kingdom.

I am leaving tonight for the commissioning in Chicago of Missionary and Mrs. Del Schneider to go to Japan. It happens that Mrs. Del Schneider, is as you know, the daughter of Pastor and Mrs. W. C. Gesch from Orange, California, now from East Pomona, California. We certainly will be thinking of you up there. The significance of Missionary Schneider's going to Japan is that he will become The Lutheran Hour branch office manager when Missionary Del Glock returns to the States on furlough.

On coming Sunday, March 11 I am scheduled to speak in Los Angeles in connection with the Kick-off meeting for the Hollywood Bowl Lutheran Hour Rally. I am looking forward to the pleasure of meeting Mary and Ted at that time, and of having an opportunity to sit down and talk things over.

May God bless you mightily for all you are doing in this way for the preaching of the saving Gospel throughout Japan! Many immortally precious, blood bought souls will praise God in heaven for the preaching of the Gospel which your generous gift has made possible.

With heartfelt personal greetings and a prayer for God's overflowing benediction, I am

Yours in the Savior's service,

Eugene R. Bertermann

ERB:ds
cc: Mr. and Mrs. T. Manthei

89-F

strawberries
The Story of the Manthei Brothers

Ted and Mary and Family

THE DATE WAS AUGUST 2, 1953. The scene a large industrial plant — a veneer cutting mill — at Sault Sainte Marie, Mich. On this summer Sunday afternoon a rather unique service was taking place in these unexpected surroundings. Hymns were sung, prayers spoken, sermons delivered, addresses given by civic, industrial, and religious leaders. And dominating the entire scene was a large banner proclaiming: "Dressing the Earth to the Glory of the Lord"!

This motto, prominently emblazoned near the northern boundary of the United States, is the guiding principle which has governed the lives of two remarkable Christian couples: Mr. and Mrs. Theodore Manthei of Huntington Beach, Calif., and Mr. and Mrs. Ernest Manthei of Petoskey, Mich.

The story of how the Manthei brothers rose from poor farm boys to liberal supporters of the church's work in the United States and foreign countries is a fascinating one.

As farm lads they cut, split, and piled firewood on their farm in Petoskey at sixty-five cents a cord. However, at four cords a day, their earning powers were severely limited. So in 1924 they hit upon the idea of raising certified navy beans and seed oats and received the highest honors in the certified-seed world.

Their career began in earnest over twenty years ago, when they decided to go into the strawberry business. They became interested in the Fairfax and Dorset varieties, strains which had been developed in England. Although their fruit was large, delicious, and beautiful in appearance, nevertheless the United States Department of Agriculture listed them as commercially unfit for production because of their low yield.

Theodore and Ernest determined to experiment with four-acre fields of strawberries. In spite of careful cultivation, they were severely disappointed the first year by a crop which was low in yield and poor in quality. During harvest time they discovered that one place in the center of the field grew large and beautiful berries. Soil tests were taken, and it soon became apparent that the conditioning of the soil with commercial fertilizer played an important part. Careful pruning, too, was a significant factor. Each plant was permitted to grow only two baby plants a year. The production of strawberries was furthermore benefited by a system of irrigation and a unique water cannon capable of irrigating two and one-half acres at one setting.

In the third year the plants paid off with a remarkable yield. Soon, with heavy straw mulching, these plants were made to produce up to 14,000 quarts an acre. The largest picking for one day was 529 crates of sixteen quarts each. These fancy berries were a unique feature at the convention of the governors of the United States held at Mackinac Island in 1945. The late Henry Ford, too, was among their ardent admirers.

FROM THE BEGINNING, the two feminine partners in the Manthei enterprises, Mary and Cora Manthei, have played their important part. These two sisters, daughters of Mr. and Mrs. Henry Behling, stem from a fine large Christian family of Boyne City, Mich., of which two brothers have entered the ministry, one sister has married a minister, and another sister took up mission work in Hong Kong.

Strawberries led Ted and Ernie Manthei directly into another far-reaching undertaking, the veneer business. In 1939 and 1940, the start of World War II made it increasingly difficult to secure berry boxes and crates, of which the growing business required 80,000 a year. The most practical solution appeared to be the erection of a small plant on their own land to produce their own crates. Although they had no previous knowledge of this business, it was a great success.

The Petoskey veneer mill, which originally employed five or six men, soon required twenty-five, not including those engaged in logging operations. It cuts into veneer about one and a quarter million log feet of basswood and maple logs annually. The veneer is sold in Michigan, Indiana, and Wisconsin and is used as center stock for plywood and die panels in the auto and television industries.

As they look back on their past years in Petoskey and recall how they were led from one business into another, they are always ready to acknowledge the Lord's leading. They recognize it also in their further enterprises. When for reasons of health, Mary and Ted

From Strawberries

and stewardship
by Eugene R. Bertermann

moved to California, they founded a ready-mix concrete business which proved to be such a success that the bulk of the profits were devoted to Christian work.

ANOTHER VENTURE WHICH the Manthei brothers ascribe entirely to the blessing of God is an oil-well undertaking at Lloydminster, Alberta, Can. After careful surveys and prayerful consideration, the Manthei brothers embarked upon this undertaking in 1947. The entire project was under the spiritual guidance of Dr. Walter A. Maier, Lutheran Hour speaker, and the Reverend William C. Gesch, pastor of Saint John's Lutheran Church in Orange, Calif.; and from the very outset they agreed that the oil well, if successful, must serve the glory of God.

The story of the drilling of the oil well is a heroic and interesting chapter. They purchased a 1934 Mack truck with trailer for $2,000. Equipped with drive chains, it had thirteen speeds forward. They brought into the oil fields of Canada two carloads of heavy drilling machinery. After many discouraging experiences, they started drilling in July 1948. Again and again it seemed as though the project would fail, but finally in June of 1949 the well came in. The proceeds have been used in great part for the spreading of the Gospel in Asia and for the support of other religious, charitable, and educational causes.

In 1951, again under circumstances in which they see the hand of God, the Manthei families began to make plans for a second veneer mill, to be erected in the Upper Peninsula of Michigan. They purchased an abandoned dance hall, called Gould's Pavilion, at Sault Sainte Marie, and adapted it for use as a veneer mill.

It was dedicated to the glory of God and the upbuilding of the Savior's kingdom on August 2, 1953. And to demonstrate graphically to the entire community the fact that their time, talents, and treasures were devoted to the Savior's kingdom, Cora and Ernie, Mary and Ted Manthei prominently displayed their guiding motto: "Dressing the Earth to the Glory of the Lord."

The Mantheis not only personally guide their own lives in accordance with the principles of Christian stewardship but zealously encourage others to tithe and give generously for the cause of Christ's Gospel. They see in their experience a clear demonstration of the promise: "Prove me now herewith, saith the Lord of Hosts, if I will not open you the windows of heaven and pour you out a blessing that there shall not be room enough to receive it."

Their lives fully demonstrating that Christian consecration leads into constantly greater opportunities of service, the Mantheis are convinced that every individual Christian can do great things for Christ if he will take God at His word and wholeheartedly dedicate himself to Christian service.

IN COMMENTING ON THE blessing of God upon those who practice the Bible's principles of Christian stewardship, Mr. Manthei stated: "America, the richest nation on earth, has the Savior's great commission to 'preach the Gospel to every creature.' Far too often, however, we have been lulled into a selfish, 'do-nothing' state of mind, in which we misuse our New Testament liberties as an excuse to do little or nothing for Christ. How often our giving runs less *(Continued on page* 41*)*

Ernie and Cora and Family

to Concrete

to Oil

to Plywood

Ted: Saving the Soo Veneer Mill

Ted

The following year, that mill was running in the hole like nobody's business! The Soo mill was losing so much money that the broker, Jim LaGrand, and the partners all felt like we had to junk it. By that time, the Soo mill already owed the Petoskey plant $80,000 for logs alone! And they owed us about $50,000 for labor. We were trying to make the payroll down here in Petoskey, so we started losing money on the little mill in Petoskey too. And it really looked bad. Oh, it looked bad!

One day, Lou Fochtman said, "Why don't we have a little lunch together?" Lou ran the Fochtman Part Store in town and his father was one of the main operators in town. They ran the dry goods store and they were uppity-up. Lou was about our age, so we met him for lunch.

He said, "I hear you're having a little trouble up there at the Soo. "

"Yeah, we're having trouble."

He said, "Old Weck from Boyne City had a sawmill. He went up there and went broke. We went up and lost out too. Seems the Soo is kind of a bad place to do business. Then the Mantheis went up and if they lose out, nobody's going to go up there anymore."

Well, we had dedicated that mill to spreading the Gospel, so that just cut me like a knife. I didn't know what to say.

We went home and had a meeting. Ernst and LaGrand and all the small partners came, and I gave some suggestions of what we could do up there.

They said, "If you think you're so smart, why don't you go up there and try to run it?" That included Ernst. He said, "Go up and see what you can do."

Boy, I just did not want to go. I felt awful bad. But then I had a dream.

In the dream, I was sent to the Soo and it was a big worry on my mind. I got up there early in the morning when people were going to work in our mill, and it was running in darkness. All the lights were turned off! I said, "Why don't you turn the lights on?" When we built this mill, it was all lit up like a Christmas tree. Now, there were no lights! I could hear the machinery running and oh, that was impressive to me, that darkness. Our manager was in his office in the loft, and it was darker there than the darkness in the plant. That showed me where the trouble was. Not that he was a bad egg. He was a good guy! But something had overwhelmed him. He proved himself later to be a fantastic operator up there. But anyhow, I just felt so bad about that darkness, and I finally woke up.

I didn't go up to the Soo yet. I stayed home. But I thought about that dream. Our manager had managed our mill on the Petoskey side working with Ernie. Now he was up there by himself. He was not a dumb guy. He was a good guy! Maybe he was overcome by that prestigious job. All those people bowed down to him and I think his wife just loved that idea. I think it had an effect on him. As the situation went along, I felt awful bad about it.

Then I had another vision. I dreamed that I was in a compound and it was told me that there was a lioness down there in the compound. It wasn't too bad, but it wasn't good either. Here were all these great big tools. In the veneer industry everything is big, you know. I was supposed to view them, take inventory. You get the point? I was supposed to go up and look at these tools! At what's happening up there. And it was a mess. These tools were all leaning against the rack. The crowbar was a fantastic huge thing! And the wrecking bar was about five feet long and thick. I wondered, by golly, how would you pick that thing up? And as I was walking, I had turned my back on the lioness. In other words, I wasn't facing the problem. I had turned my back. You get that? And she came up out of a hole and snuck up behind and bit me in the back end and took off a piece of cloth. When I turned around, she went halfway back to the hole, which was about 75 feet away. She sat on her back end and watched me. I had to give her a good tongue-lashing. Boy, I gave her the works in every way I knew how! And she just sat there with her ears back and looked at me.

Then I turned my back again, which wasn't the right way to go, you know, and as I was looking at the tools, she came and bit me again and took a piece of my skin! This time she only went back about 20 feet. She sat down on her back end and looked at me. This time I knew I was in trouble. I had to do something. I had to get mad. But I didn't know what to do because I was helpless standing by the rack with her sittin' over there. I was between the devil and the deep blue sea, and I didn't know what to do! I thought if I gave her another good tongue-lashing, I might be able to hold her off long enough to get my eye on the rack and figure what kind of tool I could pick up to defend myself. Right next to me was the wrecking bar. She came up while I was turning to get the wrecking bar and she severely wounded me. Boy, was I mad!! I was enraged and I did get my hands on that old wrecking bar and this time she wouldn't back up. She was right up against me and I couldn't quite get a good swing at her—because she was too close, you see. I couldn't give her a good wallop with that old wrecking bar. If I could have gotten a good swing at her I could have given her the works. I hit her in the head just close enough so I could feel her fur on my hand and knock a little skin off her head. She backed up a step and I backed up a step, and I hauled off and came down on that head with that wrecking bar. Oh my, the blood squirted up against the stand and it was a bloody mess if you ever seen one! I blinded her and she had to sniff her way back to her hole. And then I reviewed the rest of that stand by walking backward and keeping an eye on that hole.

> **(In my dream) I had turned my back on the lioness. In other words, I wasn't facing the problem. Now, I had to go up there and run that mill. I had to do it! Nobody else.**

You get the point? I had to go up there and run that mill. I had to do it! Nobody else.

I said to Mary, "I've got to go to the Soo." I didn't eat breakfast. I jumped in my car and drove up there.

When I took over, the manager's wife said, "What are the people going to say?"

And I said, "What are they going to say if we go broke?"

I stayed in that trailer they left on the lot that they had used when they were building the mill. Mary didn't go at first. I don't know what I ate. I could've ate nails, I was so sore all over from the evil that was going on in that mill. It was really terrible. Here's what I found...

Our manager, who had all this knowledge about veneer, was sending our customer carts of inferior panels, eight feet long and four feet wide. They had all kinds of defects in the wood and some of the pieces were two inches short. Three inches short. Four inches short. And they shipped out four huge trailer loads of this stuff to Wisconsin. Of course, the customer shipped the stuff back! I had to re-process those four big loads of veneer. The wood was good but we had to clip out the defects and splice it again into panels. I did that at night when the mill was down. I worked til 2-3 o'clock in the morning. Pretty soon, Bob Behling came and helped me. After a while, our manager and his wife helped me, and my family came up and helped too. Everybody worked nights till 2 o'clock in the morning to re-process that stuff.

The second time we shipped it out, it went through the works just the way it was supposed to. When the truck came back the second time, they kept the good veneer and out of four truckloads, they only sent back a little bit of rejects on one pallet that they had graded out. Once we processed it properly, it was good wood.

Then I discovered that the loggers were bringing in bad materials to run that mill. That was one of the aspects running it into the dump. We would pay big money for them as veneer logs, when actually they were sawmill logs that we were buying. There wasn't a veneer log among them, to speak of.

Then I went to the boiler area at night. The boiler man, who's supposed to feed scrap chips into the boiler, was feeding the left-over cores into the boiler. They burned longer and that way he could lay down and sleep. Those are expensive cores that we sold for firewood.

We were splicing up there too. There were about six people, probably good people, but they had no idea how to splice that stuff. They were breaking and wrecking so much of it.

Then I went over to the clipping department. We were cutting poplar and the operator was putting forty logs a day through the lathe. That's nothing! That's about standing still! It didn't take me long and we put 200 logs a day through that lathe! I trained Bob. He was very willing and cooperative. He's a good man!

Then I had to go to the clipper and here's a guy clipping out the defects one piece at a time. Normally they always hit about 10-15 sheets at a crack. That veneer comes off the lathe pretty fast and you can't let the sheets pile up and have the lathe man waiting until you get that corruption out of the way. You need to stack it up in sequences and let the knife hit it. That clipper man had a major in forestry, but I had to fire him! He didn't want to make a mistake. I said, "Make a mistake! There's nothing wrong with that. They can always come back and be re-clipped if you make a mistake. But you've got to hit more than one at a time to make this thing pay out. Those are by-products and you only get $20/1000 so it pays to save them only if you do it fast." I couldn't make him see it.

There was nothing running right in that mill. I went up to the dryer and here comes old Wysocki, one of our buyers from Wisconsin, with a bunch of bad veneer under his arm. I asked, "That didn't come out of this mill, did it?" He said, "Oh yes it did!" They bought a lot of stuff from us at that time so we couldn't afford to lose their business.

I went over to the dryer man. I had worked with him a whole week showing him exactly what I wanted him to do when he was feeding the machine. It went real good for about two weeks. But he wouldn't mind me, that guy. So here comes Wysocki with more bad veneer under his arm.

I went over to the dryer man and told him, "Go down to the office and get your check and don't come back." He said, "Who's gonna run the dryer?" I said, "We don't want to run the dryer under this basis." Believe me, that boy about pulled the hair out of his head. Then I hired some ladies to feed that machine and they did a nice job. Really wonderful! And we also used girls on the matching take-off end.

They did a marvelous job! They worked for us 'til the mill was sold. That first guy came back after a while and became the best dryer man they ever had. He learned his lesson. They hired him back after I left.

While I was there, we got a new order coming into the Soo mill through Metzelburg. He was in business with us and bought that big lathe. It was a lucrative order—the first white birch order that came into our mill.

This was a touchy order. The company buying it was reluctant because they knew that color was hard to keep in the wood. You had to process it awful fast in order to save it. We had sent out a sample and they had accepted it.

I said to the boiler-man, "Set the temperature at 112 degrees. Not boiling. Just a little heat and no more."

I got up at 2 o'clock in the morning when I didn't hear any noise and here he was, snoring away and the boiler was at 212 degrees! We cut the order out and the color was ruined. We shipped it out anyway. In the meantime, this same company sent us another order. Like $2000... a small order... just a sample to see how it would turn out. When the first order got to their shop, the telephone rang and I went to answer it.

They said, "We can't use that veneer. The color is way off."

That guy had boiled it and the color turned yellow. I said I had another order in hand and he said, "Don't send it down if it's anything like this one."

I said, "Can't you use it for cross-banding or something?"

He said, "Nope, it's boiler fuel."

A lot of this was experimental, you see. You've got to have good judgment when you run a mill like that. You can't run it any old way, helter-skelter. You've got to run it right. We were already losing money and then to lose that order on top of it was bad. That really hurt.

I fired the boiler man and got another guy on the boiler who would mind me. I told him 112 degrees and he kept it there just right! And sure enough, 112 degrees would cut that birch just perfect!! It preserved the color! Finally, after all that grief, we landed the order that made us millions of dollars. Then we got an order from the west coast for yellow birch. Metzelburg brought in the order, and I said, "I don't want to cut this order. I'm afraid they will reject it."

"No," he said. "They won't reject it. You go ahead and cut it."

And I said, "OK, but I'll just cut a small carload. Not the full order. Because I'm afraid they'll reject it."

The telephone rang about a week later and they said, "The veneer is wonderful. We want a big car." I had $7000 in the bank after three months and paid all those debts back. You can make a lot of money with a thing like that when it rolls over right, you know. And you can lose a heck of a lot if you're not doing it right.

So, it was just like the dream showed me. Everything was running in darkness there. Our manager was a very nice guy, and I don't think he corrected those guys. It seemed like he didn't have the gumption to straighten things out.

That happened down in the Petoskey mill too, under that other relative. I had to go down and take care of that problem too. What a poor manager! My oh my oh my. He was losing $30,000 a month instead of making $30,000 a month. He could run that mill backwards just as good as forwards.

> **That's the kind of a guy that I am. When I take a hold of something, I'll make a go of it even if it kills me.**

When I came back to Petoskey, Ernst wouldn't honor me for what I'd accomplished. Nobody honored it. They didn't thank me or give me credit for that. But I had that mill running smoothly and a year later she cleared a quarter of a million dollars that we couldn't explain to the Internal Revenue. Ain't that somethin'? The same manager was running it but he got down to brass tacks! We straightened it out and we made a lot of money in the Soo after that.

That's the kind of a guy I am. When I take a hold of something, I'll make a go of it even if it kills me. I was up there 3-4 months. Plenty long for me. It did about kill me. I got very sick after that. I was on my feet just about 24 hours a day. It took the sap right out of me. I came out to California after that and went to the hospital and almost died of pneumonia. I was throwing up quarts of pus every day. I was wore out. I was so weak I had no strength left. I couldn't get over it for a whole year.

But don't you see how that goes? This is the kind of a guy you have to be to salvage a thing like that. I had trouble with the Union and, boy, that was Union up there! But I wouldn't back down to the Union. I tell you, I had those guys to where they would crawl in a hole when they seen me coming.

But the Lord was with me. He gave me the strength to go through with it and we made a fabulous mill out of it. He gave me the vision and I understood the vision. That old lioness never bothered me again, outside or inside. She did mortally wound me because that experience almost killed me. But in the end, I clobbered her over the head, and she didn't bother us after that.

That conversation with Fochtman was remarkable. He said everybody who went up to the Soo lost his eye teeth. If the Mantheis, who are impregnable and can really run a thing were to lose out, then the rest of them had come by it honest. We showed them, I tell you! He ate those words after a while. That was a slam in the face.

> **But the Lord was with me. He gave me the strength to go through with it. He gave me the vision and I understood the vision.**

We had dedicated our plant to the spreading of the Gospel. She was the one who was supposed to take the Gospel into Japan through that broadcast. But it didn't come easy. I had to fight for that. The Lord wanted *me* to go up there. Nobody else but me.

So, you see how that other vision also turned out? First, we had to face down that Chester beast and his union cronies. Then the second boxcar joined the first one and that was the Soo Veneer Mill. Then I was transferred into the dream, and I pushed the little beast aside for fear of the battle. It turned out I did push people out of the way, from our own manager to the guys I had to fire. It took a terrible toll on my emotions. I was crouching in the corner afraid of losing my life, which nearly happened from the battle to save that mill. That pneumonia nearly knocked me out. But it was worth it in order to bring the Gospel to those Japanese, who were our enemies in the war but became our friends through Christ.

Saving the mill was a brief victory in this life. But the salvation of their souls is a victory that will last forever!

> **Saving the mill was a brief victory in this life. But the battle was worth it in order to bring the Gospel to those Japanese, who were our enemies in the war but became our friends through Christ. The salvation of the souls of their souls is the victory that will last forever!**

Ted: The Japanese Man

Ted

We came back to California and there was going to be a talk in the Long Beach auditorium by the Japanese ringleader who flew those planes that bombed Pearl Harbor. Mary and I wanted to hear what he had to say.

Just as we barely got into the auditorium, a Japanese man walked across the stage and I said, "That's the guy I saw in my vision!" He gave his talk and everybody booed him because they hated the Japanese for the attacks on Pearl Harbor. He was a courageous man, you know. He said he didn't blame them, but he said he was converted. He found the Lord and wrote, "From Pearl Harbor to Calvary." It's fascinating! At first, he didn't know what to do after the Japanese got smitten down. He didn't know whether to commit suicide or what. But he found the Lord and came to be a Christian. I don't know what happened to him after that. But I had a chance to talk to him in that auditorium. He was a brilliant man. He picked up the English language in three months so he could give his talk in English. Imagine how the Lord is able to help people do the impossible.

That was the guy in my dream! We were meant to go into the Far East with our Gospel program. And that's exactly what we did. But first we had to go through some hard things. God led us step by step… through a battle in court and building a second mill and drilling an oil well. It was a wonder! Like Bowman running that radio tower into the Far East. Now who'd of thought it would turn into something like that? Fellow can't believe it! It was something so big! Fabulous thing!

That dream gave us a clear-cut picture of what to do. Before that, The Lutheran Hour couldn't get those stations into Japan. There were no transmitters that could be used for Gospel broadcasting. But when the war ended and Japan opened up and the terms of the armistice were signed, we were able to open a big station in Gregoria. Ernst and I had our finger on it even before it was ready. Rudy Berteman was the negotiator. He did all that work and dealt with the governments. He was a wonderful guy. He came up and said, "Which way do you want to go? There's this thing opening up in Europe and there's this transmitter opening up in Japan." And we said we'd take Japan. Ernst knew the dream. Europe had heard the Gospel already. But Japan had not. I won't forget that.

It was given me to know that this little beast was our little veneer operation, no doubt. Ernst and I were the two horns and we had a good heart to serve the Lord. We didn't have the ability ourselves. We needed help from God to pull that business to where it needed to go. When the Lord gives you something to do, it may be something pretty big! Sometimes bad things happen. The Lord says that "Even the enemies of God praise Him." He works it out so that it makes sense, and He is glorified. The enemy gets hurt by tackling the Lord. We saw that the second beast would go to no ends to destroy the business, but he lost his horns and the hoofbeats died away to nothing, so we knew the Lord would win.

> **The Lord says that "Even the enemies of God praise Him." He works it out so that it makes sense, and He is glorified.
> The Japanese enemy became my friend.**

The second boxcar was another mill, you see. Old Chester tried to get in the way at our first plant and there was a severe battle in the court. Terrible! He brought up three union lawyers from Detroit.

I was afraid because there was going to be a fight, you see. But there was a purpose to the battle. To beam the Gospel into Japan. When the Japanese man said "Behold the glory of OUR God," he revealed that my God was his God now, you see. This was after WWII when we fought the Japanese in the Pacific. Our bitter enemy became my friend.

Ted: Land Acquisitions in Huntington Beach (1954)

Ted

There was a guy in Long Beach who had been picking up lots when they went up for sale. He had a big section just down the road from our place. This was an oil subdivision, a swindle they used to pull in those days in the oil business. They sold 25 x 50-foot lots for $300. *(The people basically bought the oil rights, so they'd make a percentage if they struck oil.)* There was no access to their lots. Just little pieces of land with no streets on them and the original swindler kept the rights of entry. He could get onto the land, but the other owners couldn't. Of course, there was no reason to get onto it cuz who's gonna want a chunk of land in God-only-knows-where and what good would it do you? So it was an oil swindle, you know. That Long Beach fellow had bought up 800 of those 12x50 lots in a tax sale.

This piece of ground was not attractive to anyone because it was under the Torrens Act. *(Instead of owning a deed, they just signed their name in a county registry to show ownership.)* You didn't need any attorneys. All you had to do was sign. So, the people who bought the land had no title. The Torrens Act did not clear even the tax titles of that land. And none of the owners had signed off. We were about to buy the whole kit and caboodle, but Bing Crosby Enterprises bought it away from under me, in the court in Long Beach.

Just before it was time to go back to Michigan for the summer, the telephone rang, and Bing's boys were ready to sell it to me. They had looked at that title which couldn't be cleared and changed their minds. I bought those forty acres for $8000. What they sold me were the squatter's rights. No title at all. Just squatter's rights! I had merely squatted on it. Get that?

In order to clear that title, it took an act of legislature. Sure enough, 6-8 years went by, and they outlawed the Torrens Act! That would sling it back into the conventional mode of doing business. But that meant we had to go to every lot owner all over the world and clear that title. Most of them were here in CA. We had to have everyone sign off. A lot of them were dead and gone, or there was a filling station or skyscraper at their address instead of a house. So, you could see what we were up against. It took 25 years to clear that title! That was a pretty colorful thing.

Then Frank Bucella, an investor from Huntington Beach, came along and there were 18 lots that we hadn't cleared yet. We were kind of mad at those owners. These people wanted $5,000-6,000 per lot. Bucella knew the value of it, and he paid them whatever they wanted for those 25x50' lots. He finally cleared it up.

That was a valuable piece of ground. We should have hung onto some of it. It's worth about $250,000/acre now (1986). When we sold it, we averaged about $40,000/acre. That's not too shabby considering we paid $8000 for the whole forty acres!

We agreed that Ernst could come in on this thing if he wanted to. He could have the benefit of what we would do here and have part of the money if there was money to be made. That was a 5.5 million dollar deal there! Ernst and the Browns went in on that deal. It was a fabulous proposition. They just went in on it to keep us company. And it cost a little money to clear that title, you know.

The Lord sent us a lawyer who worked for nothing—Ray Overacker, the City Attorney for Huntington Beach. It was a very sophisticated piece of legal work he had to do there to make that lawsuit. There were so many papers. That title suit weighed a quarter of a ton! Those papers had to be delivered to people all over the country. Another title lawyer, Baker, did that for free. I gave her some of that land and she came out smelling like a rose. Ray Overacker never got a penny out of it. He did quite a bit of work on it too, but he died before we sold it.

I went to court three times to get the right of entry to the property. Some lots were holdouts that we had to buy. It was especially hard to clear because the original swindler had the right of entry on those lots. But those that went to the state had a clear entry and most of them were from the state. On the others, we had to have an act by the county to outlaw the swindler's deal and give me the right of entry.

Then the darn banks wouldn't honor it. For five or six years, we fought around with those banks trying to get them to honor it. You can't sell a piece of ground unless you have the right of entry. Couldn't get on it! But we finally got that. They saw there was enough legal work to clear it, so it was safe to sell, and the banks finally did come around and honor it. It took a long time. Just recently it got resolved. It was a long hard battle and we fought that through, Mary and I. Now it's all sold. I got $85,000 for selling it.

> **So, you see how that worked? We did our part by dressing the earth and we received an inheritance.**

So, you see how that worked? We did our part by dressing the earth and we received an inheritance.

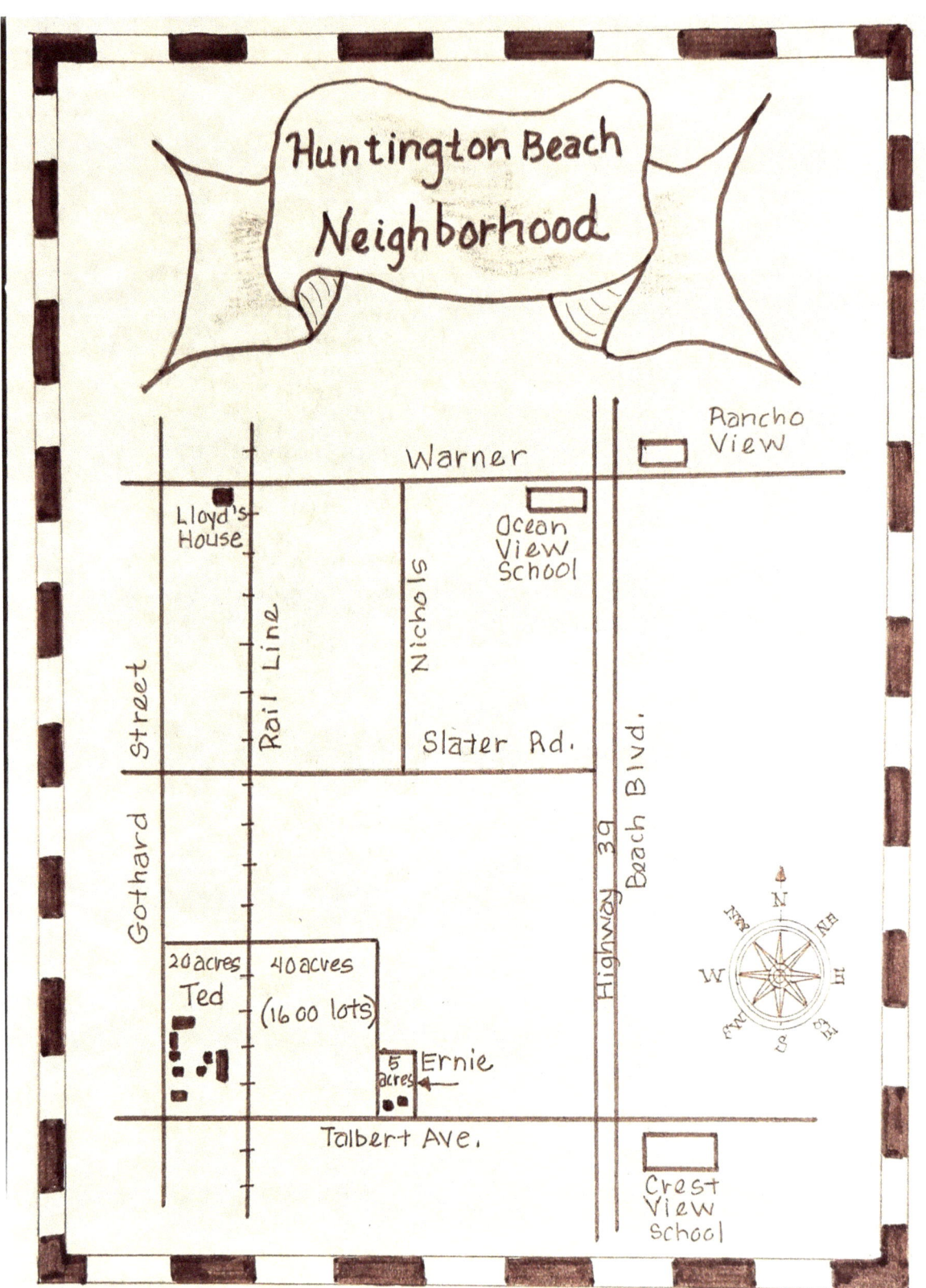

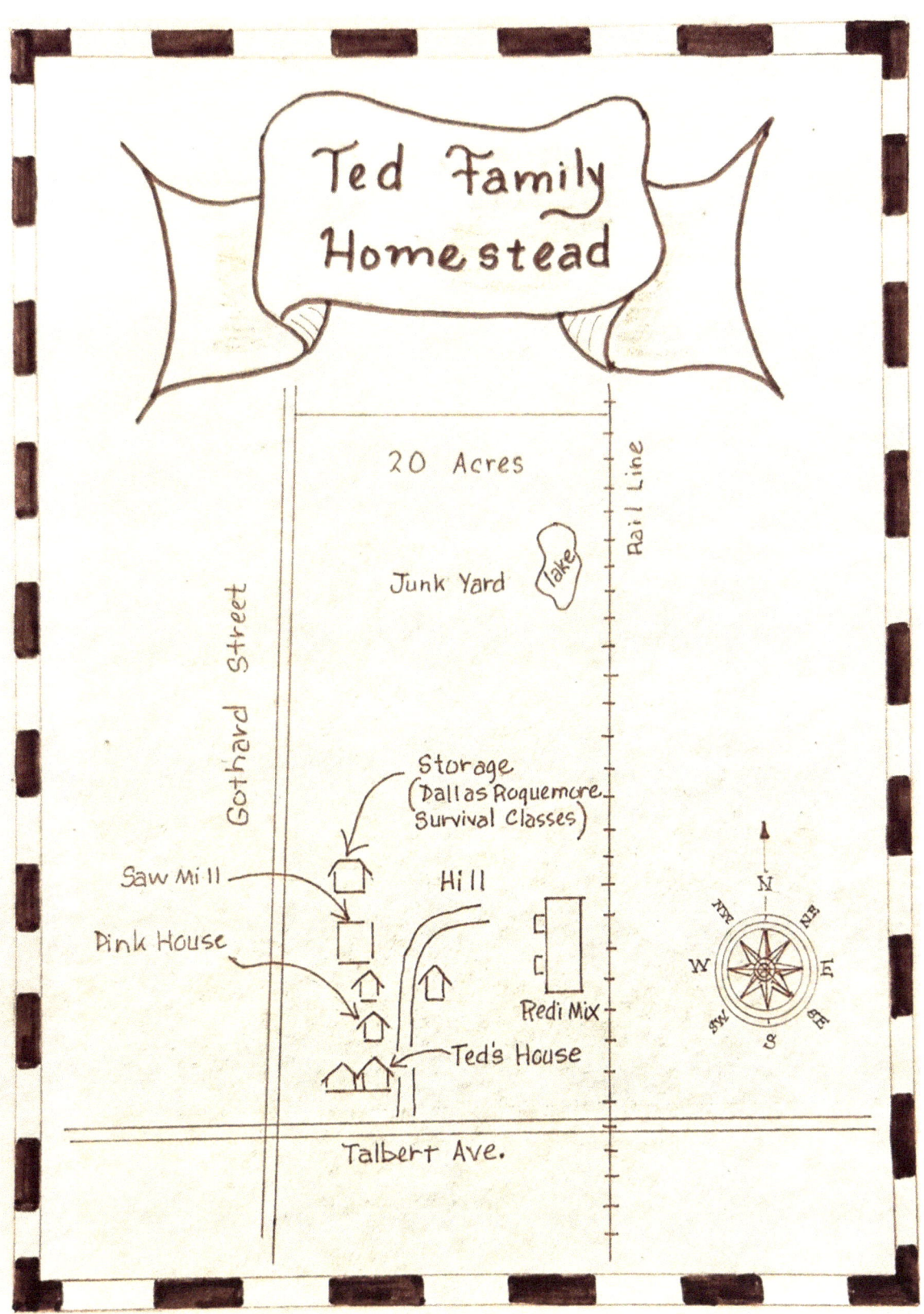

Ted

Ted: Redi-Mix and Sawmill

I needed to do something productive on my land and keep my boys busy. Over the next few years, we started a redi-mix plant and set up a sawmill.

Teaching my boys to work at an early age.

Little Phil helping me cut logs at the end of a cross-cut saw.

Ernie

Ernie: Our Families

While we were busy building our businesses and enterprises, we were also raising our families in the nurture and admonition of the Lord. The Bible says that children are a gift from the Lord and blessed is the man whose quiver is full of them. Both Ted and I were abundantly blessed.

Ted & Mary's Family
Back: John, Dave, Dan
Front: Tim, Phil, Tom

Ernie & Cora's Family
Back: Herb, Paul, Judy, and Mark
Front: Jim, Ben, Ruth

Logging the Islands

Original Manthei Bros. Veneer Mill

First Semi-Truck used to deliver veneer to customers. Bob Notestine was driver.

The White Swan

Ernie: Sponsoring the Dunkel Family (1954)

Ernie

Around 1954, I met Don Dunkel in Canada while I was scouting around for logs. He seemed to know a lot about buying logs and trucking them around. I asked if he might be interested in coming to work for me and, sure enough, he said yes. I sponsored him and his family to immigrate to America.

At first, I moved the granary to the front of our homestead and converted it into a little house for them to live in. As their family grew, they moved into the Edgerton house. Later they bought their own land and built a nice house of their own. They still live in the neighborhood to this day.

Don was such a good worker that the boys ended up taking him into business with them after the mill burned down and was rebuilt as Manthei Inc.

NEW CITIZENS. Eight persons passed their final examinations Tuesday in Emmet circuit court and were presented their citizenship papers. The group included six Canadians, one British and one German subject. In the group are, front row: George E. Fick, Detroit, examiner; Dorothy Louise Ballou, Harbor Springs; Menno Burkhart, Brutus; Anna Maria Rose, Pellston; Catherine Gunderson, Cheboygan and Circuit Judge Edward H. Fenlon, who presided at the special session. In the back are Donald Gordon McClellan and Doreen McClellan, Petoskey and Lucille Dunkel and Donald Ernest Dunkel, Petoskey. (News-Review photo by Fred Lovelace)

Ernie

Ernie: The White Swan (1956)

We started having difficulty getting enough logs to keep two good mills running. We bought our first freighter, the White Swan, from Dick Lyons. He was one of the best captains on the Great Lakes, but he decided he was *done* with sailing and sold his boat to us. Then, he took up bartending for a relative in Detroit.

I didn't know anything about running a ship, but I didn't think it could be all that complicated. Well, I found out real quick that it was quite different from running a speedboat. You couldn't just throw her into reverse. You had to get a message down to the fellow in the engine room and he would pull the lever to put the engine go into forward or reverse. Then, it took time for the boat to respond and change its speed and direction.

Our first trip was to Beaver Island. We were going along real nice and, as we got close to the island, I saw people waving on the beach. I thought, *My, the folks here are friendly!* Then, I found out they knew something that I didn't. I was approaching the shore too fast. By the time I figured out the problem and got the message down to the engine room, it was too late. By golly, I ran that ship right up on the beach!

Well, I gave up my career as captain right there and set out to find a real ship's captain.

Ernie

Ernie: A Real Ship's Captain

We hired a man by the name of Gus Linell, a young Swedish fellow. On his last trip of the season, in late November, he was bringing the boat down from the Soo to over-winter in Charlevoix. I'm not sure if the buoy shifted or if he just decided to take a short cut, but he ran the ship aground on Skilligalee Reef (aka. Ile Aux Gilet). That was bad enough, but what he did afterward was really *dumb*! If he had been smart, he would have thrown off all the logs and lightened the load so the boat could work free. But instead, he threw in the anchor!

That reminds me of a joke I heard recently. A man in Sweden got in some kind of accident and had to go to the hospital. While they were operating, they removed half his brain. The doctors got called out of the operating room and, when they came back, the man was gone. It took them a while to locate him and, when they did find him, do you know where he was? That man was teaching seamanship at the University of Stockholm!

Man on left is Gus Linnell, Skipper of White Swan

From the way our Swedish captain handled the situation with the White Swan, I could almost believe that joke was true! Then, lo and behold, if my son, Jimmy, didn't grow up and marry a Swedish school teacher! But Marlys is a lovely person and an excellent musician. When she plays that cello, the notes are so clear and her timing perfect. She sounds just like that woman on Lawrence Welk!

Anyway, that was the last voyage of the White Swan! There she stood, stuck tight on that reef. There was no way to move her. We got the crew off and saved some of the equipment. If it had happened earlier in the year, it wouldn't have been so bad. We maybe could have saved her. But this happened in November, when the seas are stormy and rough. (To understand November weather on the Great Lakes, listen to *The Edmond Fitzgerald* on YouTube.)

Cora didn't want me out there on the water trying to salvage stuff off the boat, with six children at home and her being eight months pregnant. But we had just installed a nice new Cummins engine and, fortunately, we were able to salvage that off before it was ruined. It didn't take long before the White Swan broke up and went down in pieces. We sent down divers to bring up a few things that weren't too heavy.

In the spring, someone found a cabinet lying on the shore by Sturgeon Bay. It was off the White Swan and was fully encased in ice. When they opened it up, inside they found the ship's Bible, just as perfect as could be. Isn't that marvelous? It goes to show how the Lord preserves His Word.

> **"All things shall pass away, but My Word shall not pass away." We saw the truth of that when the ship's Bible was found on shore in perfect condition.**

Cora and I have a plaque hanging over our bed that says, *"All things shall pass away, but My Word shall not pass away"* (Matthew 24:35) We saw the truth of that when the ship's Bible was found on shore in perfect condition. Jimmy refinished the cabinet, and we have it hanging right here in our kitchen so I can show it to people and tell them that story.

FEAR WHITE SWAN DOOMED

Swan Skipper Says Shifting Buoy Caused Grounding

An attempt to save the 81 foot White Swan, aground off the Skillagalee light house has been about given up, according to its skipper Gustave Linell of Petoskey.

Linell said however, that an attempt is still being made to salvage the logs and a mobile crane, aboard and this will be done as soon as arrangements can be made for a barge from St. Ignace.

In relating the accident to The News-Review, Linell said that he was supposedly on course when he neared the buoy marking the reef west of the lighthouse. However, he learned later that the buoy had broken loose from its moorings and had floated some 1300 feet over the reef into 'dangerous water' and he said this had not been reported by the Coast Guard.

The buoy, according to Linell, shifted during a heavy storm the day before Thanksgiving. The White Swan went aground November 28 when it was enroute to Charlevoix from Lime Island.

PETOSKEY, MICHIGAN, SATURDAY, DECEMBER 1, 1956

Tug Races To White Swan To Remove Crane

A salvage tug out of Cheboygan was called this morning to aid the White Swan, aground on a reef off Skillagalee near Cross Village.

Coast Guardsmen today advised the owners, Sault Veneer Mill and Manthei Brothers Veneer Mill of Petoskey, to have the log-lifting crane removed. They felt it might be possible to salvage the 81-foot, 99 ton vessel and its load of logs if the heavy crane was removed.

The vessel was listing badly today and taking water, apparently in several places. The Sundew was pumping water from the stricken vessel.

* * *

The Swan went aground about 5:30 p.m. Thursday enroute to Charlevoix from Lime Island in the St. Mary's River. Skipper Gustave A. Linell, about 32, Petoskey, and his two-man crew were removed.

A HAWSER BROKE aboard the Sundew early this morning when it was attempting to free the Swan. Yesterday a line got tangled in the prop of a 40 foot Coast Guard vessel from Charlevoix and it was towed back by the 65 footer.

White Swan Goes To Bottom In Wind Last Night

The stricken 81 foot White swan, aground off Skillagalee light house off Cross Village on Nov. 28, completely disappeared from sight last night during the height of the severe wind storm.

Group Commander Joseph Etienne of the Charlevoix Coast Guard said today that its disappearance was reported to him this morning by men of the lighthouse who had been watching the ship since it ran onto the reef.

The Swan had broken loose from the reef last Monday but stayed in sight, moored to an anchor, although shipping water.

According to Commander Etienne, only small effects were salvaged from the ship. The crane and lumber was not removed as planned by its owners, Manthei Brothers of Petoskey.

Ernie: The Mackinac Islander (1957)

Ernie

After we lost the White Swan, we still needed to buy logs for our two veneer mills and we knew it was a good idea to get them off the islands, since they were much cheaper that way. The islands had good virgin forests, if only we could transport the logs to shore. So, I got busy that winter, trying to locate a ship and a captain.

I heard Dick Lyons had got knifed in Detroit and had moved back to Charlevoix, so I tracked him down in a bar where he was working and asked him if he would consider coming to work for us. He said he wasn't the least bit interested! He had just retired and wanted nothing to do any more with the life of a sailor.

Captain Dick Lyons

Well, I had to think pretty hard, but I gave him an offer he couldn't refuse. He thought it over good and finally agreed to give it a try. We'd hit it off pretty good when I bought the White Swan from him, and I think that helped. I think he liked me and I learned to respect Dick very highly. In fact, all our kids liked Dick. He became the family hero! Even though he smoked and drank and used colorful language, he was very good at what he did, and we all thought a lot of Dick.

Well, Dick set out and he found us the Mackinac Islander. She was a steamer hauling passengers between Mackinac Island and Saint Ignace. About that time, the Arnold line went to more modern boats with diesel power. The Mackinac Islander used boiler power, which was very labor intensive. She was slow, dirty, and obsolete, no longer useful as a ferry. They didn't want her anymore, so we bought her.

We put her in dry dock and got busy converting her into a freighter. We had to make a lot of changes. Mostly reductions. We cut out the middle section to build cargo holds for the logs and took out the boiler. We also moved the pilothouse to the back of the ship.

The thing that made the Islander such an ideal ship for our purposes was that she had a *sponson* (air tank for stability) around the sides, which provided extra buoyancy and made her much more stable on treacherous seas. Because of Dick's experience, he recognized the benefits of that!

You can see the changes in the pictures. Then we put in a new diesel engine and installed a crane for moving the logs from the shore onto the boat, and back to shore.

From Ferry ...

...To Freighter

Renovated Islander Becomes Heroic Sailer

THESE TWO VIEWS of the Mackinac Islander show a "before and after." The top photo was taken when it was owned by the Arnold Line and ran to Mackinac Island, the lower photo taken yesterday by Carl Rosenow at Charlevoix showing the 96-foot, 97-ton vessel in Charlevoix harbor after it was converted for Manthei Brothers Veneer Mill here and the Soo Veneer Mill of Sault Ste. Marie. It shows how the stack was removed for a diesel exhaust, the pilot house and cabin are cut away and moved back, the center deck cabins and part of the forward section cut off and the aft section enclosed in steel. A new crane was added amidship.

The Mackinac Islander, converted from a passenger vessel to a lumber carrier, has tied up in Charlevoix for the winter after proving itself a hero to the new owners the last week in November.

The Islander was proceeding past St. Joseph and Sulphur Islands with a load of lumber when its ship-to-shore phone rang with an urgent plea from the Canadian buoy tender Heillier which had fouled its propeller in a buoy chain and had drifted aground, threatened with being dashed on shore.

Answers S.O.S.

Ernest Manthei, who was engineer for the converting since its sale this past fall, said the Heillier was a 200-footer and a bad storm was threatening to wreck the vessel. He said the Islander was pulled in as close as possible, but had to spend several hours vainly trying to get a line to the stricken Heillier.

The Heillier finally rocketed a line to the Islander and it was secured and the vessel (buoy and all) was hauled free with the new $21,000 V-12 Cummings 600 hp Islander engine, straining with the dead pull.

Rescue Well Done

The Heillier worked the chain out of its prop while being towed and then signalled to be free. Manthei said he was pleased with the way the Islander handled during the towing and gave special praise to Capt. Richard Lyons of Charlevoix who is skipper. Lyons is the former owner of the White Swan which was sold to Manthei Brothers and was lost when it went aground off Cross Village a year ago when Skipper Gus Linell and his crew of two were saved.

Convert the Islander

The Islander was secured through efforts of James and Prentiss M. Brown, jr., of St. Ignace. Coast Guard Commander Cronin of St. Ignace drew a design for the changes the company had in mind and Ernest Manthei did the engineering work with technical and seafarer advice. Theodore Manthei, a brother, and the sons of the two men also assisted in the ship converting.

Logs will be hauled to Charlevoix from Beaver Island, Canadian Island, Batchawana Island, Manitoulin Island, Cockburn Island and other ports, Manthei said. Investigation will also be made on the possibilities of using Petoskey harbor and dock. Logs or lumber brought to Charlevoix are hauled to the plant on R-1 Petoskey near Walloon Lake.

New Rigging

Equipment installed on the vessel includes a Little Giant crane, a $21,000 engine with full pilot house control, radar, a fathometer, ship-to-shore phone and other equipment necessary for moving logs or lumber. It is completely modern.

Part of the salvaged equipment of the White Swan is at the Manthei Mill here and will be sold

PETOSKEY, MICHIGAN, WEDNESDAY, DECEMBER 4, 1957

Renovation in process

The crew hard at work

Unloading logs in Charlevoix

Chapter 8

1960s: Land, Logging, and Loss

1960   Soo Veneer Mill partners buy 80 acres in Sky Valley

1961   Ted gets group of MI and CA people to invest in 50 acres in Sky Valley
                 Ernie buys and renovates the Galster Building in Petoskey
                 Mackinac Islander collision with a Greek ship

1962   Communist scare and Dallas Roquemore
                 Ted buys 2000 acres in Cohasset, CA after three other partners back out

1966   Ernie starts logging on Hog Island
                 Ted buys out Soo Veneer Mill partners in Sky Valley 80 acres

1967   Veneer mill burns in September
                 Manthei Brothers partnership is dissolved

1968   Ted and Ernie help sons rebuild the veneer mill as Manthei Inc.
                 Mackinac Islander is sold to King Crab Corporation

1969   Soo Veneer Mill is sold

Ernie: Winter 1961

We couldn't do logging in the winter, but I like to keep busy.

When the Galster Building on Howard Street in downtown Petoskey suddenly went up for sale, I jumped quick on the opportunity and bought that building. I figured that, considering the 13-year age difference between Cora and me, I would probably die first, and Cora would need a steady income for many years after I was gone.

> **I invested money in a rental property because I figured I would probably die first, and Cora would need a steady income for many years.**

One side of the building was the Brock Eckel Drug Store. The other side housed the defunked Palace Theater. That first summer, I kept our teenage kids busy gutting the theater for renovation. Many artifacts and wooden theater seats were carried out. When the project was done, Kilwin's Candy Kitchen and Russell's Shoe Store moved into the downstairs units. The upstairs was converted into apartments.

Galster Building

A Pup for Payment

One month, the dentist upstairs in the Galster Building couldn't pay his rent and convinced me to take one of his German Shepherd puppies instead. That's how Bruno came into our lives!

Tim spent a winter with us. He and Bruno became good friends.

October 23, 1962

The Cuban Missile Crisis:
The Little Story that Rocked our World!

Ernie: The Communist Scare

Ernie

As youngsters, our mother told us horror stories from the news as the Bolsheviks overthrew the Czar in 1917 and massacred the royal families. We learned that millions of Christians were imprisoned and martyred under the brutal Marxist regime that was attempting to build their own version of a utopian society apart from God.

In 1949, the Soviet communists aided the Chinese in the Chinese Communist Revolution. Our sister-in-law, Lorraine Behling, was a missionary in western China and was rescued and flown out just as the soldiers were entering her city. She served refugees fleeing to Hong Kong to escape the brutality of the new communist government. We watched as the continent of Asia was engulfed in atheistic communism.

In the early '60s we learned firsthand the brutality of these regimes when we hosted John Nobel, who wrote, *I Found God in Soviet Russia.* He was touring America after spending years in the Gulag.

Now, in 1963, the Communists was coming close to home! They had conquered the island of Cuba and set their eyes (and missiles) upon the United States of America! We were living in California that winter and met Dallas Roquemore, who wrote a survival guide called, *Get Ye Up Into The High Mountains,* in case our own nation was attacked and overrun by the communists. He taught us many things and added a very colorful chapter to our family history.

We all breathed a sigh of relief when Khruschev announced that they would not conquer America with guns and wars. However, they laid out a plan for the communists to take over America slowly and quietly from the inside through the education system, news media, arts, and entertainment. They would spread their atheistic humanism through the troubadours and influencers. Having been warned, we hoped that the American people would be too smart to let that happen.

Ernie: Back to Work

We ended up getting most of our logs off Hog Island. The reason it got that name was that it was full of snakes. The rattlesnakes were the worst. They were poisonous! Someone figured that, if they put a lot of hogs out there on that island, they would kill the snakes. Well, I didn't see any hogs out there, but I sure did see a lot of snakes!

Ernie

The logging operation was very interesting. We took loggers out to live there for the summer and cut down the trees. They brought along their horses to pull the trees to the shore. Watching them load and unload the horses was quite a feat. Those horses had big harnesses around their bellies so the crane could hook onto them and hoist them up into the hold of the ship, and back out again. When we got to the island, they'd swim to the shore.

We were told that these particular logs will run "15-16 per thousand," which means it will require 15-16 logs to equal one thousand board feet of lumber. Weight-wise, the double-axled truck is usually loaded to legal capacity, which is 1600 pounds per axle.

One night, we were loading logs from the barge onto the Islander at Hog Island. I was on the barge, hooking the logs so Dick could lift them up with the crane. I somehow stepped too far backwards and fell off into the water, right between the boat and the barge. I remember going down, down, down in those heavy boots. I had to swim really hard to get to the top and came up right between the boat and the barge. It was a big sea and, at any minute, the waves could have pushed that barge against the boat and I would have been crushed. I kept trying to climb out, but I was too cold and had on all those heavy clothes! The other fellows couldn't pull me out either. Dick saw what was happening and, lickety-split, he was out of that crane and jumped down onto the barge. He reached down and, next thing I knew, I was lying on the barge. I don't know yet how he pulled me out so quick. That man must have had incredible strength! It was a real tribute to Dick that he was able to run that crane and still see what was happening. He saved my life!

Another time, a fellow named Kenny Mousseau worked for us, and he was on his fanny more than he was on his feet that summer. One time, he got his feet tangled in a cable as it went over into the water, and it pulled him right under. Dick just happened to see him going into the water and he quick-jumped over and pulled Kenny loose from the cable. If Dick hadn't seen him, he certainly would have drowned.

Dick fell off the boat once himself when we were docked in Charlevoix. He liked to tip the bottle when we were in port, and he was pretty well inebriated. Willard had painted the rub rail, and it was still slippery that night. When Dick staggered up onto it, he slipped and went right down between the boat and the dock. He hit his head going down, but the cold water brought him to and he came up against a piling, so he knew just what that felt like. He was hurt pretty bad. Hit his head and broke some ribs.

> **Many times, we were in a dangerous situation and the Lord always watched over us and blessed the efforts of our hands. As I look back, I wonder if our protection had anything to do with the fact that we took the Lord into partnership with us. We tithed faithfully and did our best to use our profits to further His kingdom. It could also be that He just loved us as His own.**

Chuck Kiebel was hurt once, too. He was in the habit of jumping from the dock onto the railing and then onto the cargo deck. One night, he forgot that the hatch was left open from loading some scrap iron and he jumped straight down into the hold. It was a long way down and he landed on top of that iron! He could have been severely injured, but he only broke his wrist. He must have fallen fourteen feet!

The Lord watched over us and the fact that no one was ever killed is an absolute miracle. I think of that often.

As I look back, I wonder if our protection had anything to do with the fact that we took the Lord into partnership with us. We tithed faithfully and did our best to use our profits to further His kingdom. It could also be that He just loved us as His own. Many times, we were in a dangerous situation and the Lord always watched over us and blessed the efforts of our hands.

We had many close calls. Like the time the diabetic went into a coma during a storm made it into the paper. Bob Clock liked to write about the Mackinac Islander, and he did an excellent job of reporting this grease gun story. He made it very entertaining!

We also had a problem when that Greek ship ran into us in the fog. That was in the paper, too. Again, there were no serious injuries. It could have been a lot worse, but the Lord always preserved our lives.

Manthei Brothers Claim Zermatt Disregarded Calls

Theodore Manthei, co-owner of the ill-fated Mackinac Islander which was rammed in a heavy fog Wednesday off Gull Island, told the News-Review today that the Greek freighter Zermatt disregarded the Islander's warning signals several minutes prior to the collision.

He said the ship's captain, Richard Lyons, told him and his brother Ernie Manthei that he (Lyons) had the Zermatt on the Islander's radar screen for six miles before the collision and he was sounding repeated warning signals for the Zermatt to give the right of way.

He also said the Zermatt disregarded the signals, struck the Islander and continued on, stopping at the Mackinac Bridge an hour and 27 minutes later when they picked up the calls of the Islander and the Coast Guard on their radio. The Zermatt did not return to the scene, Manthei said.

Manthei said Lyons had the Islander in full reverse when the collision occurred off Gull Island.

Manthei said his brother reported from Manistique last night that the Islander suffered damage to its bow and rudder controls in the accident. Ernie is due to arrive in Petoskey today.

The Zermatt was involved in another accident earlier this year near Holland, Michigan. It is a converted Liberty ship from World War II days and flies a Greek flag.

Damage done to the bow of the Mackinaw Islander

The Great Divide:
The End of the Manthei Brothers Partnerships

FIRE DESTROYED the Manthei Veneer Mill on Walloon Lake today. This photo was taken about noon. (NEWS photo by Kirk Schaller.)

Fire Destroys Manthei Mill

BULLETIN

Fire late this morning destroyed the Manthei Veneer Mill in Resort township on Walloon Lake.

The mill was burned to the ground and fire spread into adjoining fields.

Firemen from Resort-Bear Creek were joined by Petoskey firemen and conservation fire fighters and fire fighting equipment in bringing the spreading fire under control.

The mill was a mass of flames before firemen arrived.

Cause was not immediately known.

The mill was operated by Theodore and Ernest Manthei of Petoskey. According to News-Review files, they employed some 25 men and at one time were cutting a million and a quarter log feet of basswood and maple a year which were converted into veneer and marketed in several states.

In 1953 the brothers dedicated a similar plant they operated at Sault Ste. Marie "to the Lord" with God as a partner in the profits and the proceeds were used for church and mission work. The brothers tithed profits of the plant here as well as other operations which included a cement mixing plant in California, an oil well and farm operations.

They also operate a ship, the "Mackinac Islander" to haul logs from logging operations to their plants.

Ernie: The Mill Burns (1967)

Ernie

Eventually, the mill here on Walloon Lake burned down! Ted and I were getting older and had enough of wrangling with all the problems that went into running a business, so we decided it was time to retire and let our boys build up the new mill under their own name and corporation: Manthei Inc.

Not long after that, we got an offer on the Soo Mill and we decided to sell that plant. It wasn't too profitable anymore, and that way the boys could concentrate on building up the mill at home.

The mill burned in September 1967

At that time, the environmental movement was starting up and they were complaining about harvesting timber on state land. They wanted to see the islands being used for wildlife preservation, so the state started refusing timber sales. That environmental group was a pimple on the arsh of progress! We could see the handwriting on the wall. If we couldn't buy timber off the islands there was no reason to keep the boat, so we had to sell it.

The sad and dismal remains

Ernie: The End of a Legend (1968)

Ernie

Dick Lyons and the Mackinac Islander captured the imagination of a local journalist in Charlevoix, who enjoyed featuring Dick in his stories. This article was his final tribute to the true character of Dick Lyons. I got my biggest laughs when I would read this to my audiences!

Clock Wise
By Bob Clock

For one reason or another, sea-faring men have always been numbered among the world's best story tellers.

Herman Melville drew upon his experiences on the South Seas to write "Moby Dick." And Richard H. Dana put plenty of autobiographical material into his "Two Years Before the Mast." Even England's Robert Louis Stevenson crossed both the Atlantic and Pacific to gather material for his "Treasure Island."

This penchant for story-telling is still commonplace today among the men who sail America's inland seas. A case in point is Dick Lyons, former skipper of the Mackinac Islander -- a tramp freighter which has carried logs from Hog Island to Manthei mills at Walloon Lake and Sault Ste. Marie for the past several years.

The Mackinac Islander is tied up in Charlevoix this spring and reliable sources report the mill owners would like to sell her -- ending the era of the tramp freighter on northern Lake Michigan.

But regardless of what happens to her, Dick Lyons'' adventures aboard the spunky little logger will continue to live so long as sailors bend elbows and swap yarns at the Topside and the Town House in downtown Charlevoix.

My favorite Lyons story is about a diabetic seaman named Hubert who sailed with him for a season on Lake Superior. Even today diabetes is a serious illness, but it can be controlled and the victim may lead a fairly normal life so long as he maintains a proper balance of sugar and insulin in his system. Too much of one or the other can send him into a serious shock requiring prompt medical attention.

On the lakes, Hubert had no trouble adjusting his insulin intake to his sugar consumption. He ate well and he took his insulin shot every morning and he was fit and hearty.

It was lay-overs in port that nudged Hubert off the narrow dietary gangplank he was forced to walk the rest of his days. Like most sailors, he enjoyed a beer, or two or a dozen and sometimes he drank so much he forgot to take his insulin or he'd take it too often.

When this happened, poor Hubert went into shock and it was up to his buddies to ply him with orange juice until he regained consciousness.

However, one blustery November night when the Mackinac Islander was bound for the Soo from Duluth, Hubert went into a deep coma which gave Lyons some of the most anxious hours he had ever known on water.

The crew had spent a long weekend in port and Hubert as usual was the life of the party. He drank lustily, sang boisterously and swashbuckled up and down the steep streets of Duluth. And he took insulin whenever the spirit moved him.

Needless to say, it was a pretty sorry Hubert who helped pull in the mooring lines the next morning. After the ship was underway, he went immediately to the crew's quarters and didn't appear in the galley for lunch.

"He's a sick man," Willard Pischner, cook, first mate and jack-of-all-trades, told Lyons at the dinner table. "He looks sort of green and this heavy weather isn't helping any. He's not just hung over; he's seasick."

That evening Willard again checked on his condition and reported back to Lyons.

"He says he doesn't want any dinner and wants to know if there is something we can do to stop the ship from pitching so."

After the meal was over, Lyons himself looked in on poor Hubert, but it was too late. He already has slipped into a heavy coma. Lyons had Pischner prepare a pitcher of orange juice and together they propped Hubert up in bed and held a glass of the juice to his lips. Hubert wouldn't take any. And when they finally forced some down, up it came. Hubert was indeed seasick -- on top of his insulin shock.

Lyons repaired to the bridge and managed to get in touch with Hubert's family doctor at the Soo on the radio-telephone. The doctor said to keep trying with the orange juice and confirmed that the patient might die unless he got something sweet into his digestive tract.

Again and again Lyons and Willard tried the orange juice treatment without success.

In the meantime, the storm was picking up alarmingly, the ship's clutch was beginning to overheat and all manner of blips began appearing on the radar screen, any one of which could have meant imminent danger.

As the evening wore on, Hubert's pulse grew weaker as repeated attempts to give him orange juice failed.

Finally, in desperation, Lyons began fiddling with the radio and picked up a public health doctor in Rogers City. He explained the situation and asked for advice.

"If he can't keep anything down, your only hope is to give him an enema of sugar water," the doctor said.

"An enema!" Lyons roared. "Do you realize I'm in the middle of Lake Superior in the worst storm of the season -- with a bad clutch to boot -- and you want me to give this man an enema? I'm not even equipped to give enemas!"

The doctor quietly explained it was Hubert's only hope.

Lyons snapped off the radio and sat alone a few minutes in the bridge. Finally he called down to Willard.

"Find a grease gun -- the cleanest one you can find -- and boil it in water," he ordered. "Then mix up a sugar solution as thick as you can make it and let me know when you're ready."

"We've got the grease gun," Willard said, "but we're out of sugar. The only sugar we have is mixed with cinnamon -- the stuff we use on cinnamon toast."

"Use that then," Lyons said wearily. "It can't do him any more harm than the grease gun."

So that night, in the crew's quarters of the Mackinac Islander, poor Hubert was the recipient of what is probably the most unusual enema in medical history.

But it worked.

When an Ontario Provincial Police motor launch met the Mackinac Islander in Batchawana Bay the next day, Hubert was well enough to climb over the rail -- unaided -- and wave a fond farewell to his shipmates.

When we sold the Mackinac Islander to King Crab Corporation, Captain Thompson sent Captain Lange down from Alaska to pick her up. He piloted her down the Mississippi River and through the Panama Canal, then up the West Coast to Alaska.

Willard Pischner, our cook, went along on that trip. He told me they had to stop in Chicago and cut off the pilot house, then put it on hinges and re-mount it so they could flip it back to go under some of the low bridges on the Mississippi River. That must have been an exceptionally interesting trip!

That boat is now being used in Alaska as a fishing vessel for King Crab Corporation. Cora and I went up to Alaska to see if we could find it and, sure enough, she's still running. Now she's called the Bellaire.

Willard Pischner

Capt. Thomsen, who purchased the Islander, sailed it to Seattle for rebuilding into a crab fishing boat.

CAPTAIN THOMSEN

U. S. Coast Guard
1940-1952

Alaskan Businessman – 1952-1964
– Founder and President –
Aleutian Marine Transport Co., Inc.
Aleutian King Crab, Inc.

After rebuilding, the boat was renamed "Belair", and joined the crab fishing fleet on Kodiak Island, Alaska.

Ernie standing on top of pilot house.

Ernie

Ernie: Transition to Retirement (1967-1969)

After Ted and I dissolved our partnership, we sold the Soo Veneer Mill and the Mackinac Islander. Then I helped the boys rebuild the veneer mill as a corporation and they named it Manthei Inc.

Logs brought into mill by semi truck ①

Gilbert Morford operating lathe

1st Retirement Project: Helping sons rebuild the mill

Wet logs enroute from vat to lathe

Ready to deliver veneer to customers

Ernie

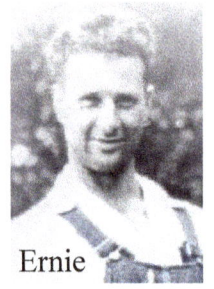

Ernie: A Walk on the Moon (July 21, 1969)

I lived in the best of all times! I went from carrying water and traveling with horse and buggy to traveling the world in cars and planes and watching men land on the moon on a television! The Bible says that in the last days, there will much running to and fro, and knowledge will be increased on the earth (Daniel 12:4). Isn't it a marvel? I watched it all happen in my lifetime.

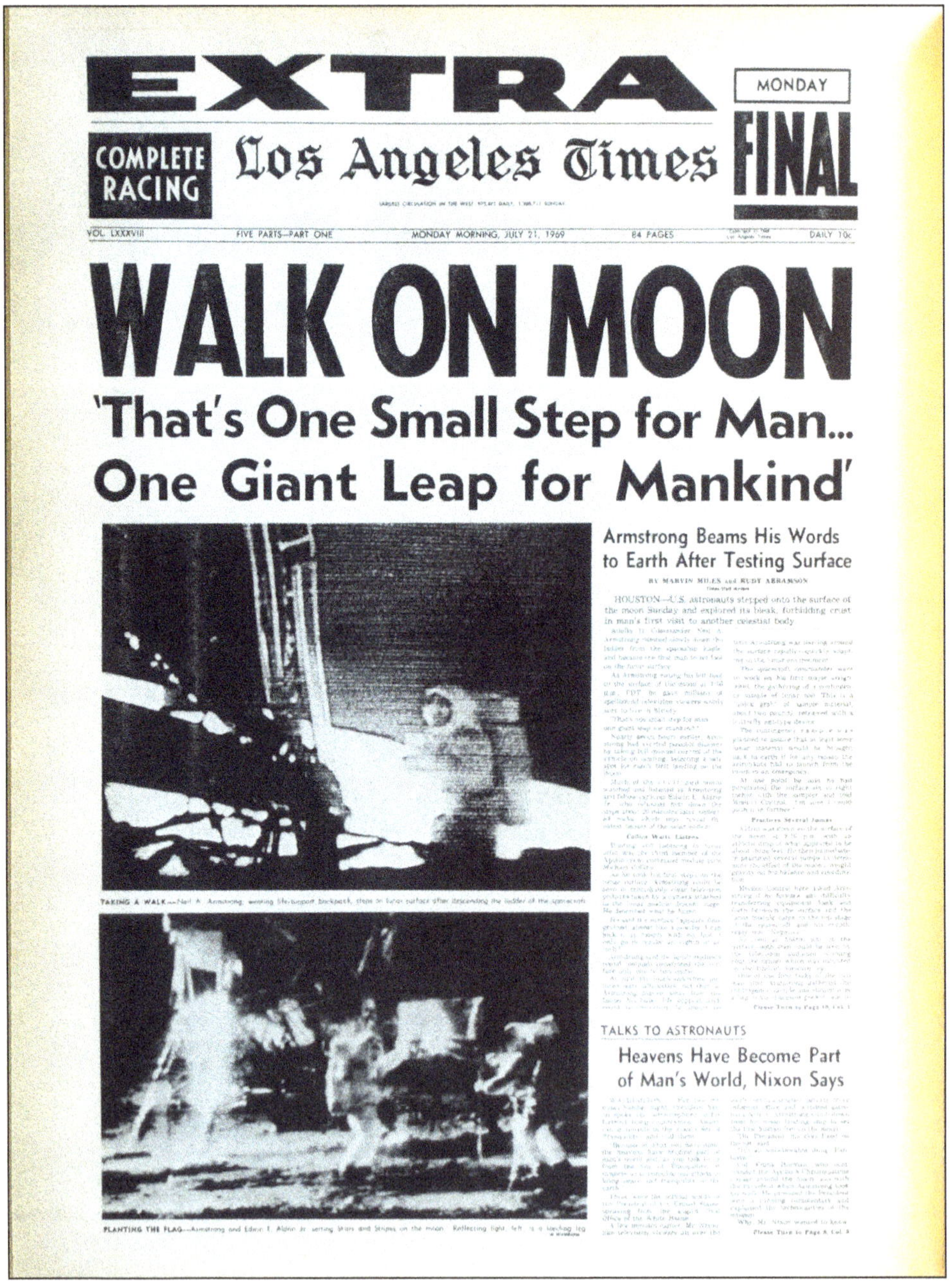

EXTRA

MONDAY

COMPLETE RACING

Los Angeles Times

FINAL

VOL. LXXXVIII | FIVE PARTS—PART ONE | MONDAY MORNING, JULY 21, 1969 | 84 PAGES | DAILY 10c

WALK ON MOON

'That's One Small Step for Man... One Giant Leap for Mankind'

Armstrong Beams His Words to Earth After Testing Surface

BY MARVIN MILES and RUDY ABRAMSON

HOUSTON—U.S. astronauts stepped onto the surface of the moon Sunday and explored its bleak, forbidding crust in man's first visit to another celestial body.

TALKS TO ASTRONAUTS

Heavens Have Become Part of Man's World, Nixon Says

Chapter 9

1970s: Retirement Projects

1970   Ernie and Cora acquire foster children, Jack and Mary Sue
             Ted's son, Tim, begins developing Ted's land in Sky Valley, CA
             Ernie helps sons launch Manthei Development Corporation

1971   Ernie and sons build Pine Bluff Condominiums

1973   Ernie and sons crush stone and gravel on Charlevoix property
             Ted starts selling CA properties

1974   Ted and Mary start wintering in Sky Valley, joint family Christmas in Sky Valley

1976   Ernie and Cora start wintering in Sky Valley

1977   Ernie and Cora visit Ruth in Peru, family conflicts with the Lutheran church

1979   Ernie helps John Shep launch radio ministry into Ukraine

Sky Valley (1970)

How the heck did we end up in the desert?

It all started with arthritis! In the early '60s, Ted and Mary invited Papa and Mama Behling to escape the cold winter in Michigan and come to California. Papa was suffering terribly with arthritis, so Mary found a mobile home park near Desert Hot Springs with hot mineral pools called Healing Waters. Later, when Ernie's family came to California and visited Mama and Papa, Ernie stopped into a real estate office and discovered a piece of property for sale in Sky Valley with a little five-room motel. Ted put together a group of investors and they purchased the land.

In the years that followed, Mary kept asking one son after another to do something with the land. No one was interested until Tim, son #4, graduated from Chico State and said, "Sure, I'll give it a go!" Since Mary had experienced RV life traveling across country and Mama and Papa had enjoyed living at Healing Waters, she thought an RV park would be a good idea. Tim's high school buddy from Huntington Beach, Lloyd Pedersen, came on board, and Sky Valley Resort was born! Mary incorporated her gift of hospitality into Grandma's Kitchen and the chapel ministry.

Ernie

Ernie: Retirement Projects (1970s)

When the mill burned down, I was only 58 years old. I still had a lot of gumption. I wasn't ready to sit around and do nothin.' So, I found many ways to stay busy and productive and serve the Lord.

1. Helped sons launch MDC: Manthei Development Corporation (1970-1980)
    a. Building driveways with Ben
    b. Buying crusher and crane to start sand and gravel operation
    c. Purchasing equipment and running errands

2. Building Pine Bluff Condominiums (1971)

3. Hospitality
    a. Home Church and VBS (1965-1970)
    b. Foster Children (1970)
    c. Welcoming spouses and loving the grandchildren (1966-1985)

4. Travel
    a. Wintering in Sky Valley (1976-1984)
    b. Searching Alaska for the Mackinac Islander (1981)
    c. Celebrating 35th Anniversary in Germany (1983)

5. Helping start new Mission Programs
    a. Peru: Faith Mission Society (1977)
    b. Ukraine: Thoughts of Faith radio program (1979)

6. Entertaining through Slide Shows (1980)

7. Preparing for Eternity (1985)

Retirement Project 1:
Helping Sons Launch MDC:
Manthei Development Corporation (1970-1980)

Associated Underground Contractors, Inc.

Serving the Public and Industry

SpreadSheet
Fall 1993

2nd Retirement Project - Helping sons start M.D.C.

From gravel to underground construction, Manthei Development Corporation has grown

When Ernest Manthei went into semi-retirement, little did he know that out of a few pieces of land would grow a northern Michigan contracting company, but that's how it happened for Manthei Development Corporation in Charlevoix.

Manthei began his work life as a farmer, first growing beans, then switching to strawberries. A wrong piece of equipment purchased with the intention of making the thick veneer used for berry crates led him and his brother into a more profitable venture — hardwood veneer.

"By the time my father retired in the late '60s, they had veneer plants in Petoskey and in Sault Ste. Marie," says Mark Manthei, Ernest's son and president of Manthei Development. "They sold the Sault Ste. Marie plant, and the Petoskey plant burned down in 1968. My brothers and I had worked in the Petoskey plant, and my father offered to help us rebuild it. The fire was sort of a blessing in disguise because we were able to build a much more efficient plant. We, along with some of our cousins, still own that veneer plant in Petoskey."

Around the same time he was going into retirement, Ernest Manthei decided he wanted to develop several pieces of land he owned in Charlevoix and Petoskey. One piece of land he wanted to turn into a subdivision, but that never came about. He built 12 condominiums on another piece of land, but they sold slowly.

"I worked with my dad during the summer while I was in college, and when I graduated in '72 I went to work with the company full-time," says Manthei, who now runs the compa-

(l. to r.) Mark, Ben and Jim Manthei are proud of the way Manthei Development Corporation has grown since their father Ernest founded it in the late '60s.

Retirement Project 2:
Building Pine Bluff Condominiums (1971)

Demolition of Old Folks Home

Old Folks Home on Bluff Property

Pine Bluff Condos

1st Phase

(Early 70's)

3rd Retirement Project - Developing Pine Bluff Condominiums

Ernie, Mark and Mary Sue on steps down to Lake Michigan

THE MANTHEI Development Corp.'s Pine Bluff Townhouses on US-131 are completed and ready for residency, but only one is still for sale. The five, two-level, one-family residences are split one, two and two, with the two pairs sharing only a lawn and stone pathway. The townhouses sit high above the Lake Michigan waters, with a steep incline for a backyard, but a pair of stairways totaling 127 steps lead to the beach. (NEWS photo by Jeff Blake)

PETOSKEY NEWS-REVIEW Monday, July 2, 1979-18

ERNIE MANTHEI, head of the Manthei Development Corporation, takes a walk down the 99-step stairway leading from his new Pine Bluff Townhouses on US-31 to the Lake Michigan shore. Actually, the 99 steps only lead to level ground above the shore, but connect with another 27-step stairway to reach the beach. The five one-family dwellings, 135 feet above the water, are ready for residency, with four of the five already sold. (NEWS photo by Jeff Blake)

Retirement Project 3a:
Hospitality:
Home Church and VBS (1965-1970)

From 1965-1979 we belonged to the Evangelical Lutheran Synod. Our new congregation, Faith Lutheran Church was served by Rev. Robert Moldstad from Suttons Bay. For several years worship services were held in our living room on Sunday afternoons. Vacation Bible School was held in a big tent in our backyard.

Two farmers from Pakistan were our guests for a few days. They were invited to visit our area by the local Farm Bureau.

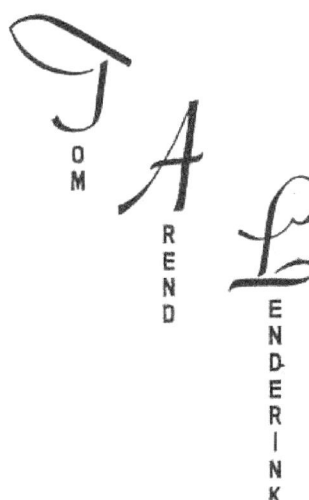

October 28, 1975

Mr. and Mrs. Ernst Manthei
Route #1, Townsend Road
Petoskey, Michigan 49770

Dear Mr. and Mrs. Manthei:

Thank you both so much for the kind hospitality you showed me. Your Christian home is very warm and enlightening.

The breakfast was supurb, but most important were the discussions about your beliefs. Your life style and the general feeling in your home caused me to do a great deal of soul searching. The special feelings I left your house with had a lot to do with my decision to begin tithing and to truly accept Christ as my savior.

Thank you so much. God Bless you both.

Sincerely,

Tom A. Lenderink

Jack & Mary Sue at their snow house in the back yard.

Mary Sue and Jack Keeder came to live with us as foster children in 1970, when they were 8 and 10 years old, at the request of Pastor Moldstad. They had been removed from their home in West Virgin and placed in foster care a few months earlier. Jack lived with us for 2 years, Mary for 10.

Mary Sue was little and sweet. She was eight years old and wore size 6x

Mary lived with us until she got married at 18 years old.

Retirement Project 4:
Searching Alaska for the Mackinac Islander,
Now Called the "BelAir"

Retirement Project 5a:
Helping Start a Mission Program in Peru:
Faith Mission Society (1977)

15 de Enero 549, San Antonio, Lima 18, Peru

October 13, 1977

Mr. and Mrs. Ernst Manthei
Route #1 Townsend Road
Petoskey, Michigan 49770

Dear Ernie and Cora, and Boys,

Ruth has been here now a month by the time you get this letter. She is doing fine, and we are happy that she is here. She mentioned that you, Ernie and Cora, are planning on coming down for a visit in November. I don't know whether to believe it or not, after all these years. But I'd like to belive it, so I will.

She also has told me about the problems in the family over the fellowhip question. This is sad news. I hadn't heard about it. I had heard that there were some disputes over something. But I thought these were more like the knock-down, drag-out sessions that we had together, which one time half-scared Grandpa to death and almost ruined one corner of the kitchen table.

How many days and hours did I spend at your house over the years? I'd be broke if you added up my account, and all the good food that I didn't pass up!

But most of all, I enjoyed the fellowship that we had, and the opportunity to study together in depth such things that many other families wouldn't have been interested in.

Now it happens that this fellowship question is one of the six doctrinal subjects that we have listed here in Peru as a distinctive Lutheran doctrinal possition.

Do not fuss over the point that the boys want to be zealous about getting the Word of God out to people. This is wonderful! Just so it is done without any compromising of the Word whatsoever. That is what the doctrine is all about. The doctrine should be a motivation to us to get the <u>pure</u> Word out to the people. It should not be an excuse for not doing anything in evangelism.

I am looking forward to this study and your visit. Even heresy serves a good purpose as it seperates those who really want to follow God's Word perfectly (1 Cor. 11,19). Let me hear from you on this soon because November is very close.

Because Rev. Fred Schmugge is your pastor, and because he has been working on this with your family, I will send him a copy of this letter. This is also to assure him that I am not intending to do anything behind his back.

Greeting to all of you from all our family. Ruth, during the month of October, is involved mostly in language study. We are all fine and in good health. Ruth is adjusting nicely.

Greetings to all, love,

Retirement Project 5b:
Helping Start a Mission Program in Ukraine:
Thoughts of Faith Radio Program (1979)

behind the
IRON CURTAIN

September 1982

FIRST ANNIVERSARY ISSUE

Cora and Ernie Manthei of Petoskey, Michigan were two people God used as tools to chisel out John Shep's dream of Thoughts of Faith. See Page 3.

Retirement Project 6:
Giving God the Glory through Slide Shows
Sky Valley and Petosky (1980)

Friday, February 22, 1980
DESERT MOBILE HOME NEWS

Sky Valley News Quips

By JEANNE ROBERTS and FRANCES KASUBKE

How's the world treating you? Say by the way, today is the day for sweethearts — young or old. So. "Happy Valentine's Day" to you all.

Once a week the folks here in Sky Valley Park get to enjoy films from all over the world. However we just weren't prepared for the entertainment we would get as Ernie Manthei showed his slides of his 17 year logging operation on the Great Lakes. Most of his slides were made from old newspaper clippings. At several points in the showing, the dialogue became so funny that the laughter drowned out the narrating. Ernie, we think you should be writing lines for Bob Hope! Needless to say there will be a repeat performance.

Ernie Manthei Knows Where Credit Belongs

Looking 'Em Over by Jim Doherty

Ernie Manthei, who has enjoyed considerable success in a variety of family ventures in his 71 years, says he knows where the credit belongs.

Their program to serve the Lord with 10 percent of their earnings plus other offerings, he said, have contributed greatly to their success in blessings and direction.

He also knows all about rolling up his sleeves and going to work.

And Ernie said, in a humorous slide talk to Petoskey Kiwanians Tuesday, that he knows what causes gray hair. When he and his wife were married many years ago he was aware that she had more schooling than he and was better at figures so he asked her to take charge of paying all the bills. She did, he said, and after all these years she has the gray hair despite being 13 years his junior. One would have to look close to find a gray hair in his head.

The speaker has been in many business activities since he and a brother, four years his senior, started as partners on a farm. It has ranged from building berry crates, running a veneer mill, logging, developing business blocks, condominiums, remaking and operating their own ship and much more. And he related some of the stories about how these things came about.

When he and his brother built up their berry business, they found they needed 500 to 600 crates a day. They decided to get the machinery and make the crates. For $50 they bought an old barn, tore it down and built a building. Then they bought a lot of used equipment, but they didn't know how to utilize it.

A couple years later they contacted an expert on such equipment and learned what they had purchased was excellent for veneer making, but not exactly what they needed for berry crate making. Once they were trained, they had a sawmill running. And then they decided they needed a boat to haul logs from the U.P. and from islands such as Hog in the Beaver chain.

Manthei threw in considerable humor telling of his first—and last—adventure as captain of the White Swan log carrier. He landed high and dry on the shore of Beaver Island because he forgot how long it takes to signal the engine room and for them to carry out an order to stop or reverse engines when approaching a landing.

The 110 foot White Swan went to the bottom some time later when a former Swedish fisherman he hired as captain ran it aground on Isle Au Galet Reef with a load of logs. Their veneer mill burned to the ground with $35,000 worth of veneer ready to ship and they, he said, had no insurance.

Manthei said this was a humbling experience for them, but a good blessing in disguise. They have rebuilt since the fire and the sons are running the mill, which he described as one of the most modern available. It has 24,000 square feet of space at its site at the end of the West Arm of Walloon Lake. They also bought the former Arnold Line Mackinac Islander, once a steamship used by the Coast Guard to break ice. They converted it to diesel so it could haul logs with a crew of three men. They did the converting themselves at Cheboygan without going to a shipyard.

He showed photos of their lumbering and ship loading at Hog Island where they built 15 miles of road to get at the birch they were cutting under a contract with the federal government. They worked with small crews using cranes, barges and trucks.

He included some News-Review photos and excerpts from a hilarious story by Bob Clock based on an interview with Captain Dick Lyons a dozen years ago. It told how Lyons had to administer a fruit juice enema to a crewman in a diabetic coma, using the only means he had available for such a task: a grease gun. He had been told by a doctor via ship's radio that without getting fruit juice into the man's digestive tract he would not survive until the vessel reached shore.

Manthei said "we give glory to God, he leads us."

Robert Doctor was program chairman.

PETOSKEY NEWS-REVIEW Wednesday, July 30, 1980-5

Chapter 10
1980s: The Last Days

1980		Ted sells all CA properties except Sky Valley
	Oct 8	Babe dies
1981		Ernie and Cora visit Alaska to track down the Mackinac Islander
1983		Ernie begins slideshow presentations at Sky Valley and Rotary Clubs
		Ernie and Cora celebrate 35th anniversary with a trip to Germany
1985	Oct 11	Ernie dies

Worldwide Challenge

July/August 1984 $2

A Bimonthly Magazine of Campus Crusade for Christ

ERNST MANTHEI
Petoskey, Mich.

"OUR CHURCH never taught tithing and I think they made a big mistake. We started tithing when we started our own business, my brother and I. We figured that the Bible said in Malachi to 'bring your tithes and offerings into the storehouse of God and prove me herewith if I will not open the windows of heaven and pour out a blessing that there shall not be room enough to receive it.' Now we believed that, Ted and I. We figured if the Lord makes that promise, He must really mean it.

Everything comes and goes. You're born, you get old. You buy a new car, it gets old. You build a new house, it gets old. But we look forward to eternal life. Jesus says He's going to build mansions for us where we will dwell with Him forever. *That's* what a Christian looks forward to. With that hope, he can enjoy this life, regardless if he has money or not! Because through faith in Christ our Savior, we have eternal life.

The Lord has ways to show His love for us by—we call them hardships—but they actually come from a loving attitude of our Heavenly Father—because He wants us to come close to Him and follow His precepts, or recipes. I like to call it a recipe. The closer you follow the Lord's recipe, the closer you are to His promises.... How can the Lord bless you if you're not following what He's telling you to do? It gets clearer and clearer to you as you get older."

TED MANTHEI
Petoskey, Mich.

"I THINK young people should follow the biblical principles. I didn't go by what my church taught me, I went by what the Bible taught.

I never inherited a nickle, but the Lord blessed the work of my hands. I met a man who had 2,100 acres for sale up in the mountains, timber land. Timber wasn't evaluated much then, $10 on the stump. I bought it, and after I had it 12 to 15 years, it had risen to $200 on the stump. Two years ago that piece of ground sold for a bonanza! The children took this money and they lopped off 30 percent for gospel work. Part of it went to build a Far East broadcasting tower in Saipan in the Pacific, to broadcast the gospel into China, Russia and India.

I told the Lord I wouldn't change my pants any different because of His blessings. I tried to live the same and treat my friends the same as before. I drive a 10-year old car. I try to skimp so we can do the things that need to be done out there in the Far East and around the world to spread the gospel so that many might find their way to heaven through faith in Christ Jesus as their Savior. I want to be a good steward over what the Lord's entrusted me with."

Worldwide Challenge, July/August 1984

Tithing has been the byword for every business ever operated by the Manthei brothers. Ernst, 75, and Ted, 79, practiced it back when they were trying to cultivate the perfect strawberry . . . and then again when they started their wood veneer business. They've both been surprised at their successes. With delight, they've channeled large portions of profits into gospel work.

Worldwide Challenge, July/August 1984

Ernie: Looking Back from the End (1985)

Two Wives

My first wife, Margaret, died in November on Thanksgiving Day of 1947, and I married Cora the 21st of July in 1948. It wasn't that I was a fast mover. As much as I thought of Cora, I could not forget Margaret. Whenever I saw a woman that reminded me of Margaret, I'd have to go and talk to her. It always seemed that maybe she was still around somewhere. As much as I thought of Cora, I never figured I could love another woman. I loved Margaret. She was the mother of my three children, and I thought a lot of her.

Cora won me over when she said, "I hope that I can fill the shoes of Margaret. She was a fine person." That won my heart over. Cora was a smart woman. She let me talk as much as I wanted to about Margaret.

For a young woman to take over a family like that was not easy, but she was always willing to carry responsibility. She has a very loving and kind spirit. I don't think the kids could have had a nicer mother. Cora was also a very Christian girl. She took the place of Margaret just perfectly.

It was hard on the older children having to change mothers. Cora always tried to be kind and just to the children. She loved babies, though, and mothered her little babies and took good care of them. Maybe the older children felt that she loved them more than the older ones. But she was a good mother. That was a special blessing, when the Lord sent her to me to make my home complete.

I loved Margaret, then married Cora and loved her too. Then I dreamt one night that Margaret came back, and I thought, "My, what am I going to do now? I love them both. When I try to choose between the two, I love them both! I don't know what to do." Finally, I thought, "I know what I'm going to do. I'll keep them both!" Then I woke up thinking how terrible it must be to get a divorce if a man loved his wife at first. It must bother him all his life to have it end up that way.

When the Lord took Margaret home, he replaced her with a woman who had the same Christian qualities but with the other things added. Cora was pretty, very cooperative, and always a nice person to be with. She helped me overcome my grief for Margaret.

I loved Cora a lot and thought a lot of her. I still do! I'd like to help her more yet, but I guess I can't no more. I'm about to leave this earth. Our lives are in the hands of the Lord. *"The Lord hath given, the Lord hath taken. Praise be unto the Lord."*

After I'm gone, you can give Walter my slippers. Tell him, "Nail them up on your garage there and write above them *Running Bear loved little White Dove*." (Great song… You can listen on YouTube.)

Child-Rearing

Ernie

I'm really concerned about my children and grandchildren that I'm leaving behind. They haven't had to endure the kind of hardships that we did growing up. I pray that they keep the faith and remain steadfast through whatever trial they may face in the future, and that they will raise their children in the nurture and admonition of the Lord.

This story happened in our home when my sons were young. One day, the boys came downstairs and said, "Father, there's a bad book in our house!"

I asked, "How did that bad book get into our house?"

We were keeping a young lady here while her mother was in the hospital, and she was connected with a "Book of the Month" outfit. That's how this dirty book came into our house.

I said, "Boys, bring that book down." They brought it down.

It was morning, so I said, "Today we'll have devotions out of this book." I started reading out of it, and then read a portion out of the Bible. Then I said, "We're all around the table here, and we're going to decide which one of these books we're going to keep."

My family all decided to keep the Bible.

I said, "All right, what about this young lady?" Well, she wanted to keep her book.

> **I'm really concerned about my children and grandchildren that I'm leaving behind. They haven't had to endure the kind of hardships that we did growing up. I pray that they keep the faith and remain steadfast through whatever trial they may face in the future, and that they will raise their children in the nurture and admonition of the Lord.**

I told her, "You don't want this book and I'll tell you why. The Bible serves the Lord, but that book you've got serves the devil. There's only one place for that and, since we've all agreed that there isn't room for both books in one house, that book has got to go into the fire."

I had a good fire going in the kitchen stove so that's where it went. There was not room in this house for two kinds of books, so the book of the Lord had to stay, and that other book had to go.

That's what the Lord is eventually going to do with all the devil's works, including the devil himself. He's going to burn them up in a lake of fire.

Ernie: Silly Stories

The boys had a snowmobile once, and I wanted to test how much compression that engine had, so I gave it a little pull on the rip cord. I was straddling it. When I gave the cord a little pull, that thing took off like a ruptured duck! Shot right out between my legs. It was a cold winter evening. The throttle was frozen, wide open! That snowmobile shot across the road and hit a big snowbank, and there it stood and scratched. Then it fell on its tracks and headed down the road. Really fast!! With my dog behind it!

When Paul heard the thing take off, he started chasing it. Paul just had his socks on, and it was winter! That snowmobile shot down the road and through a fence with Bruno tight behind, heading straight for my neighbor's chicken coop. Holszchu had a lot of chickens! Oh, I could just picture all those feathers starting to fly! Just as it reached the chicken coop, it quick veered off to the right and went out into his field. Then all of a sudden, it stopped. The throttle thawed out and it stood there idling, just as peaceful as could be.

In the meantime, Bruno stopped off at the neighbor's chicken coop and got into a fight with their dog. By the time I arrived, Holszchu was swinging his boot, trying to hit my dog over the head. He had only one sock on too!! It was a revolting situation.

I was trying to explain to him what all the rumpus was about. Paul was there too. We each had a different story to tell and nobody paid any attention to the other guy's story.

I'll never forget that. What a mess a guy can get into by making one little pull!

****

Our Kopenkosky neighbors ate a lot of cabbage. They were Polish and ate lots of sauerkraut and cabbage. Oodles of cabbage! Old Man Kopenkosky had eight or nine children, every one still living except one who died. They're all getting up there in years now. Johnny used to be my brother's partner, and now he's eighty-three. George is about seventy-eight. Louie, Tom, and girls—that whole family is still living, except one. They ate a lot of cabbage!

I always told the kids that the stork brought them right past Georgie Kopenkosky's house and up the hill to our house.

Ernie: The School of Hard Knocks

I remember, as a little feller, sleeping upstairs with Father and the covers coming off. Us boys had to tough it out! But it was good, because we grew up to be healthy and tough, like the Eskimos. Their babies are warm even when bathing undressed in those ice igloos! They adjust to the conditions and survive. I learned to survive too.

We went through a lot of hardships on the farm. For example, we had no running water. We had an outside toilet. We went to the barn to do our job instead of sitting in the house where we eat. It actually is a dirty thing to eat in the same place where you go to the bathroom. We had to go to the barn or outside. Same thing with water. We'd take a bath maybe once a week. We had to carry the water about ¼ mile from the lowest part of the farm. Father dug a well down there and we had to carry the water up; first with a yoke over the shoulders, then later with a barrel and a horse.

We had to be very conservative on water when we bathed. Mother would warm water on the stove, then put it in a big washtub where she did laundry. She'd put that in the middle of the floor. Father would take the first bath. He was usually the dirtiest of them all! Mother would take the next bath, then Herbie, then Ted, and by the time it got to me, the water was very dirty!
I always said I was washed in a swill pail and that's why I grew the best! I got more vitamins that way and I grew the tallest. Those things are all in the head. I washed and got clean. It didn't bother me to be the last in the tub. I was thankful to have water to wash up! It was pretty thick and muddy by the time it got to me, but it was still wet, you see. I have no regrets whatsoever. I didn't know any different.

Mother bathed the girls on a different basis. I think she used clean water for the girls. I don't remember them ever getting into that washtub at all. The rest of us were conservative with water.

To this day, I can't see wasting water. I still let Mama (Cora) wash first. I figure she's the cleanest because she doesn't work out in the fields and get sweaty like I do. Then I wash in her water. Look at all the water I've saved over the years! I'm happy and thankful to wash in her water. It's nice and warm and all set to go. No water wasted. I've done that all my life. Ted does the same thing. Why? Because we had that kind of training.

This wasting of water is bad! Let me tell you something about that. Out in California, they're very wasteful with water. People shower long and water their lawns. I heard recently that the salt water is breaking into the fresh water supply and they're getting into trouble in many places close to the ocean. They're now learning to value and be conservative with water.

Water is an exceptional blessing from the Lord. We don't appreciate and realize how valuable clean water is. Without fresh water, you couldn't live no time on this earth. You'd die! It's very valuable. I drank enough dirty water in my life that I know how precious clean water is.

I feel sorry for you children! You were not brought up under hardships and you actually missed some university training there. It's the finest training you can get. You get closest to the Lord when you get into tight straits. That's when you get down on your knees and say, "Lord, have mercy on me, a sinner. Lord, help me. I'm in trouble—bad trouble!" You do your best praying when you're really in trouble. That's when you walk closest to the Lord.

Therefore, don't ever complain and say, "Why did the Lord send this trial to me?" No! The Bible says, "In all things, give thanks unto the Lord." Why does it say that? Because "whom the Lord loves He chastens." When the Lord is willing to take you into the woodshed and give you a spanking once in a while, He *loves* you! You should thank the Lord that He still loves you enough to take that much interest in you.

I would never trade anything for growing up under hardships. Everything after that was easier, regardless of how hard it was. I could never have gotten that kind of training in a college or university. It was the Lord's way of teaching my brother and I patience and endurance. Not to be afraid of hardships, but to have courage. With that kind of a rearing and by the grace of God, Ted and I were able to accomplish things in this life that, without that training, we probably never would have been able to do. Everything we did after that seemed to come easier and easier.

I would say that one of the biggest secrets of running a business is knowing "the law of economy." You have to be efficient. You can't be wasteful. That's one problem in the United States. We've been trained to throw away cans and bottles. You use things once and throw them away. It's a throw-away system. If you want to be successful, you have to learn to be efficient and economical. That's one thing. But how do you arrive at that?

Well, before the Lord can use people, He always takes them through a hard school. I believe that those hardships we had on the farm forced us to learn to help ourselves. We were raised up so poor. We had to figure things out for ourselves. I believe that was a special blessing from the Lord. When you read the Bible, you see that, before the Lord could use a man, he always took him through a hard school.

Look at Shadrach, Meshach, and Abednego. They had to go into prison, and then were thrown into a fiery furnace. And look what marvelous things came out of that! When the king saw all of that, he said, "From henceforth I make a new decree. Everybody in my realm shall pray to the God of Shadrach, Meshach, and Abednego" (Daniel 3:28). Look at Joseph. He had a nice home. He was loved by his father and had exceptional godly parents. He was a good boy! The Lord loved Joseph and He wanted to raise him up to do a great thing, so he took him through a hard school. The Lord arranged it so that he was sold into Egypt as a slave to Potipher and cast into prison unjustly. In order for the Lord to really prepare him and train him for the very high position that He had in mind for Joseph to do, Joseph had to sit in that prison for 3½ years! Then look at how high he rose. He became second-in-command to the king and had tremendous power. But he was humbled and trained so that he could do his work very well and efficiently.

So, you can see why the Bible says, "In all things, give thanks unto the Lord" (1 Thess. 5:18), regardless of how things go and how we may think it's not right. God knows all things and makes all things work for the best to those who trust in the Lord. Those hardships were only a training school.

Many times, we get into predicaments by being rebellious and not obeying God as we should. We make it harder for ourselves than it needs to be. Before the Lord can use us advantageously, he has to wear us down and prepare us for the work he has for us to do. Often, that's through hardships.

For instance, take Jonah. The Lord had a job for Jonah. He was given a hard assignment. It was not easy to go to Nineveh and tell those people that they would be destroyed in forty days. There was no gospel in that story. Now that was a difficult mission. Those were ungodly people. God says that their great wickedness came up before His throne.

So, God said, "Jonah, you go tell them what I'll have to do to them to straighten them up." There again was a hard school.

Now, Jonah could have had a nice boat ride to Nineveh if he had only obeyed. We know he had money because he bought a ticket going the wrong way! So, the Lord had to put Jonah on His *own* boat!! He could not use Jonah until he put him through a rough school. That old whale was a tough boat. No toilet, no windows, no air conditioning. But that was his ride because he did not obey God. He had to go through that smelly whale's belly before he finally said, "Lord, if you get me out of this terrible mess that I'm in here, I will serve You and do what You want me to do.

Then, the old fish took him over there and spewed him out on the beach by Nineveh and it must have taken him 3-4 days, maybe even a week, just to get cleaned up. He must have been a mess! But he cleaned himself up and then he did the Lord's work.

So that's how it goes with us. Many times, we go through a lot of hardships because we don't listen and mind the Lord as we should. Sometimes, we wouldn't do it at all if the Lord didn't put us in hard predicaments where we couldn't help ourselves.

> **Many times, we go through hardships because we don't listen and mind the Lord as we should. Sometimes, we wouldn't do it at all if the Lord didn't put us in hard predicaments where we couldn't help ourselves.**

So also is it with God's children. They wanted to stay at home and be comfortable. They weren't going out to spread the Gospel around the world as they were supposed to do, so the Lord spread them out. Through persecution, He gathered them up and spilled them out of the basket to witness around the world. That's how we heard about Christ dying on the cross for our sins. The only way to spread the news was by word of mouth, by witnessing. There was no TV in those day, no radio, and no modern transportation.

All through the Old Testament, you'll find that the Lord had to take people through a special training period before he could really use them to carry out His work. That's why we, too, should pray continuously and ask the Lord's blessing on our work and efforts.

As we went into the machinery age, we were so excited. There were no cars when we were born. We would jump up from the table to watch a car go by. The entire machinery age came about in our lifetime! Airplanes, autos, trucks, rockets, radio, TV, modern ships, submarines. Before that, they brought lumber into Petoskey in big sailboats. Think of the tremendously interesting era we lived in.

Daniel 12:4 says, *"At the time of the end, there shall be much running to and fro, and knowledge shall be increased."* I see knowledge being increased tremendously in this era. Before, they were able to help themselves and accomplish outstanding marvels, but it wasn't the same kind of knowledge we have today. To be able to go to the moon, send rockets and control them from the earth—all this came in my lifetime!

We always prayed and called on the Lord's holy name. We had devotions at the table and read the Bible. We survived the hardships and then went on to do the greater things in life He had prepared us for.

We did what we thought were some dumb things in life, but the Lord turned it all for our good. He blessed the efforts of our hands. Like when we built the veneer mill. We went to an auction and bought machinery. We wanted to make crates. Never made a berry crate! But the Lord showed us the machinery to buy and later we became one of the more successful veneer mills in the industry. Look how man thinks and the Lord leads. To Him be the glory. Amen.

It seems whatever we took into our hearts to do, the Lord would bless. He gave us "fields, house, cattle, and all that we need to support this body and life" (Luther's catechism). We were able to give generously for the Lord's work. I thank the Lord for giving me the opportunity to do that.

. . . But we also glory in tribulations, knowing that tribulation produces perseverance;

and perserverance, character; and character, hope.

Now hope does not disappoint, because the love of God has been poured out in our hearts

by the Holy Spirit who was given to us.

Romans 5:3-5

Ernie: Preparing for Eternity (1985)

Ernie

I once read an evangelism tract called *The Greatest Fool*. In it, the king sent his court jester out into the kingdom to find a man more foolish than the jester himself. He searched in vain for a full year. When he finally returned, the king was on his deathbed and the jester asked him, "Have you prepared yourself for eternity?"

Surprised, the king said, "No. I haven't even thought about it."

The jester smiled and said, "I've finally succeeded in finding the greatest fool in the kingdom!"

That story really impressed me. I wanted to make sure I never found myself in that position. I've been thinking about that for many years. We never know when it will be our time. I prayed that God would spare me from a fast and violent death, and now God is giving me this time to prepare for eternity.

My devotion book has a quote that says, "The choicest delicacies in the pantry of heaven are reserved for those suffering." This is my special time of visitation from the Lord.

****

While I was in the hospital, a young lady was in the hospital handing out Christian literature. I started talking with her and it turned out that her grandfather was a schoolmate of mine by the name of Stuart Swenor. All at once, the whole story came back to me. We were playing war at school and my brother, Herbie, and Stuart were the captains. It was winter at Maplewood School and time for snowball wars.

I said to her, "Do you happen to be related to Stuart Swenor?"

> **My devotion book has a quote that says, "The choicest delicacies in the pantry of heaven are reserved for those who are suffering." This is my special time of visitation from the Lord.**

She said, "That's my grandpa."

I said, "If that isn't something! I was in school with him, and you know, he made a terrible mistake."

She said, "What was that?"

I told her, "When he chose soldiers to fight, Stuart made the mistake of choosing me for his side. When the fight started, I snowballed Stuart something ferocious. Stuart's team took a bad lickin'. I couldn't fight against my brother! That wouldn't work."

She laughed and said, "That's probably the first big mistake he made in his life!"

****

This sickness that I have is not a good sickness. I've never seen myself go down that fast! They all say you really go down. I would be a real miracle if I am healed. Only the Lord could do that!

The doctors say there's nothing they can do. There's one chance in three that radiation can prolong my life, at the longest, maybe two years but probably more like three to six months. What is that?

If a man was a worldling and wanted to stay here as long as he can to live it up, maybe he would like to do that. But a Christian doesn't do it that way. A Christian looks forward to heaven. "For me to live is Christ, and to die is great gain."

> **If a man was a worldling and wanted to stay here as long as he can to live it up, maybe he would do that. But a Christian looks forward to heaven. "For me to live is Christ, and to die is great gain."**

****

Since I've been sick, I had a terrible dream that was very impressive to me.

I was walking down the street of a city, looking for a certain man. I noticed the street was very unkempt. The sidewalks were broken, with big weeds growing up through the cracks. There was litter all around. There were people leaning over the balconies, talking and laughing and they didn't seem to care at all about the terrible condition of their street. There were broken things lying around and all they could do was talk and laugh.

I couldn't find the address of the person I was looking for and I kept trying to ask people if they knew where he lived, but no one would listen to me. Finally, I succeeded in getting someone's attention and they said, "Oh, you won't find him around here!" He was a Christian man, and these people were foolish and didn't care.

I got to the end of the street and there was a cart loaded with garbage. When I reached the wagon, I fell down in the dirt next to the garbage and couldn't get back up again. Then Cora came running so fast that her skirts flew behind her in the air.

She tried to carry me, but she couldn't. She looked up at those people to help her, but nobody paid any attention, so Cora took hold of my hand. She wanted to push the cart at the same time to get it out of the way. She pushed it and held me by the hand, dragging me and pushing the cart. Her hand would slip out of my hand. She grabbed my hand again and pushed the cart to get it out of the way. She tried to hold my hand and pull me. She wanted to help me so bad but she couldn't! I was too sick to help.

That was the end of that part.

Then Cora and I were together, coming back down the other side of the street and I said, "Cora, look! There's a platform up there on the left side." There were no balconies or people on that side.

I said, "There's a platform and there's an old woman sitting up there. That's odd. Let's go and look at that."

We had to sort of climb up a hill. It was an old, dilapidated deal. Here was a platform. This woman looked like a gypsy. She was unkempt and looked like she fit into that situation.

In the middle of the platform was a little dog, trying its best to climb into a boot and hide himself. He was scared.

Down on the right side of the platform was a canvas lean-to, real sloppy looking. In there was a vicious-looking animal, like a beast, sickly green! He had a narrow snout and big teeth sticking up.

I knew then why that little dog was so scared, but I said to the lady, "Is that animal tame?" She was sitting there, not too worried.

She said, "Oh, NO! He's very wild!"

So, I said, "Cora, let's get out of here fast!"

Then it came to me that the beast was the devil. He was on that side, and he snarled at me and showed his teeth terrible. Then I knew that he had those people under his spell. He didn't want me around there. That's why he snarled at me.

I said, "We've got to get out of here fast!"

The more I think of it, I read John where the Lord Jesus says, *"I tell you the truth. I came in the flesh to save you from eternal damnation, that you might be saved through faith in me. But ye will not harken."*

They just wouldn't listen. They were just enjoying life, living it up and letting their children grow up in weeds. Here was Satan and all this danger, but they just lived it up.

That's what's happening to this world. That's why the Lord had to destroy the world at the time of the flood. He had to destroy Sodom and Gomorrah. There were no Christians left!

That's why we should warn the people that the end is not too far away. With the homosexuals and all this pornography and TV, all the things going on is leading many people to hell. That's all there is to it.

When the devil gets them about so far into the morass, then he says, "This is the end. You might as well finish it up and kill yourself. "

That dream was so sad. That's the picture the Lord showed me of what Satan really is doing in this world. Satan is a very vicious enemy. Very wrathful, as the Bible says, *"knowing that he hath but a short time."* I can see why the Lord is going to make a lake of fire and burn him. He deserves it. He came down here into God's kingdom of love and led us astray.

Then Jesus came down, personally, and suffered this terrible agony that you and I should have suffered, to redeem us. What a great love! He came down from the Kingdom and died on the cross for our sins. He bought us away from the clutches of Satan.

Satan is very angry now. All those who believe on the Lord Jesus do not have to spend eternity in hell. We've got a beautiful promise in heaven. Co-heirs with Christ. That doesn't mean just a small inheritance. We are co-heirs with Him in heaven. I'd be happy if the Lord will just let me get in there. But He says, we will be co-heirs with Him in eternity.

What a beautiful thing that will be! To see Elijah, who went to heaven in the fiery chariot, and Daniel, and Shadrach, Meshach, and Abednego. All the patriarchs and our loved ones. And then to see the Lord Jesus in all His glory. What a beautiful sight!

Why should I pay and fight to stay three to six months and take radiation? Why, it's foolish! I can be with you all during this blessed time we have right now.

Now to an atheist, I can see why he would fight for each precious moment. But to a Christian, that is not so important at all. This is a time of grace, during which we prepare for life hereafter. That's why I pray, *"Lord, preserve me from a fast and evil death."* You don't have time to take account and pray to the Lord. I'm using this time to thank people in my life, to ask forgiveness where it's needed, and have important conversations with my children. This is a beautiful time to encourage one another in the Lord! What a more beautiful time could you have on this earth? We can enjoy it together. I'm not expecting any big crowns when I get to heaven. If I can just make it through the door, I'll be very grateful.

> **Now to an atheist, I can see why he would fight for each precious moment. But to a Christian, that is not so important at all. This is a time of grace, during which we prepare for life hereafter. That's why I pray, *"Lord, preserve me from a fast and evil death."***

****

I had another dream where two angels came and brought me a silver package. They said, "This will help you over your sickness and you'll feel better."

Then, in the dream, Dr. Ledingham came out and said, "Let me smell of that." He smelled it and then he said, "My, that has a lot of onion in it. That's good."

The angels left it for me and said, "Now when you get feeling worse tomorrow, you eat some of that."

That was really something! Shortly after that dream, the doctor prescribed Brompton's Mixture for the pain. I didn't want to take it at first because I was afraid of addiction, but Ruthie reminded me of the silver package in the dream that made me feel better. The first night I took it, Ruthie misread the dosage and gave me a tablespoon instead of a teaspoon. I barely slept that night, but I felt young and light like I was in my twenties again!

****

You know, it must be confusing to the Lord. The people at Jimmy's church are all praying that the Lord will heal me, and the Lord loves them and hears their prayers. But I am praying that the Lord will shorten my days. I believe I'm being called home. Death is not a decision. It's a calling.

I think I'm going back to my Creator. But sometimes, I don't know. Maybe the Lord has got some work He wants me to do yet. You can't tell. I might fool the doctors by the grace of God and maybe live another two to five years, who knows? That has happened a number of times. Walter and I were planning to start a junking business next year after he retires; scavenging, fixing, and re-selling junk. But I don't know if it's God's will for me to stay that long.

****

One thing Dr. Ledingham told me tonight. He said, "Your case is an exceptional case. We're not familiar with this."

I told this woman in the hospital that they ran this tube right through the liver, down the bile duct and into my intestines.

"No," she said, "they just put it into the liver to bleed out the bile."

She couldn't believe the tube was able to go all the way into my intestines. Normally they would drain it into a sack attached to your body, but I didn't need that. So, I asked Dr. Ledingham again in front of her and he said, "Yes. That is what surprised us all. It is an exceptional thing. That's done very, very seldom."

He had told us that cancer is like cement. He didn't think the chances were good of running that small tube down through it if it were like cement. But then it went so easy. He couldn't get over it, the whole procedure went so easy.

Then, they wondered why I went into such terrible chills. They figured there was bacteria loosened up in the liver which caused the severe fever and chills. The liver didn't want to accept this. They marveled over my case, that they could run that tube right through the obstruction. They thought it would take hours.

The doctors had a meeting to discuss my case and Dr. Ledingham's associate, Dr. Carpenter, said they got pretty wild about it. They discussed it for hours and really hassled around about surgery. Dr. Ledingham figured that, if he'd operate, it would do more harm than good. Ledingham is a fine, Christian man.

It would mean another month in the hospital, very sick. I don't see any sense in it.

Here's an odd thing. The Lord may have something else in mind. I don't know why this is, and it's not what they expected. It might be something special.

Cora told Dr. Ledingham, "When you gave us all the options before Ernie had this test, that one you didn't even mention!"

He said, "I know. It's so rare that I didn't even think of it." He said the man who performed the procedure couldn't get over it. It's the easiest one he ever did.

A lot of people were praying that the Lord would guide his hands. When they told us the verdict, they felt it was terrible that the tumor was so high they couldn't operate. But we were relieved because we didn't know if I'd make it through the surgery.

Ed Warner prayed that I be healed, but he committed me into the Lord's hands. "Thy will be done." But if it were possible to heal me, that the Lord would do that. He prayed strong and earnestly.

This case was new to that lady and to the doctors. That's the reason they argued so over it. But Dr. Ledingham didn't want to do surgery, even though it meant less money for him. He called me "my Christian brother." Isn't that nice?

****

When I think that the Lord will send His angels to come and take me out of this world, then I realize what a beautiful thing the Lord Jesus really did for us. I think that's what Bill Bright means when he says to "Lay all your life before Christ." Put on Christ.

I know I used to like to watch TV, but when I got in the hospital, facing these problems, I read the Bible. I didn't even want to watch TV! It distracted me from these wonderful thoughts from the Lord. I can see what the devil is doing. He's using that TV to distract people from reading the Bible, getting on their knees and praying to the Lord. It's getting worse and worse and worse.

The Bible says, in Daniel, that people are going to get weaker. Physically weaker, but wiser. That's exactly what's happening today. People have sore backs because they don't work hard physically and get that exercise like we used to before all the machines. If a guy complained of a backache, he was just a pantywaist. Rarely did anyone go into the hospital with a bad back. He would be thought of as a lazy guy.

To pull thirty acres of beans by hand, stooping over and pulling and pulling all day long, ten to twelve hours, stacking them up! Ted and I did that year, after year, after year, for about ten years until we hit it! Then, we made good money and paid off all our debts.

That's the way the Lord works it.

He says, "You be patient. *In the sweat of thy brow shalt thou eat thy bread all the days of thy life and I, the Lord thy God, shall bless the efforts of thy hands.*"

That's what the Lord did. Then He blessed us, and we had, not half a load, but one full boxcar load of beans from two years. Then we got eleven dollars per hundred. Think of it! All your life, you're always in debt. Then, all at once, you're paid up!

Look how the Lord blessed the efforts of our hands. We were the poorest people in the neighborhood. Nobody was poorer than we were. Today, we might be the richest people in our community, with children, home, and spiritual blessings. And the thing that pleases me is that I don't hang my heart on anything here.

I can see the blessings of the Lord and praise His holy name. He was so good to me. I enjoyed my work, even pulling the beans! The Lord gave that joy to both my brother and me. We enjoyed our work. That was our reward. The blessings came on top of that, like icing on the cake.

In those days, we had no TV, telephone, no terrible pornographic literature. No drugs or all this scary stuff.

You'll have to do a lot of praying and teaching your children so that we all meet in heaven. That nobody be missing. That's going to be a great reunion!

****

I'm so thankful that I have children who want to continue to serve the Lord and use these blessings to further His kingdom, as long as they have power over them. It might not be long before they are stripped of all their power.

I think this country is fast going into atheistic communism. It's going to be a terrible existence. For how long does the Lord say this "abomination which maketh desolate" is going to last? It sounds like three

> **I'm so thankful that I have children who want to continue to serve the Lord and use these blessings to further His Kingdom, as long as they have the power to do so.**

years and six months. Then the Lord is going to cleanse it. Now, just how long our time is compared to God's time, I don't know. But look what's going on in Russia. Many of those poor people are suffering. It's going to really be something. It hasn't gotten here yet, but our time is coming when we're going to suffer too.

I believe that we are living in the time of fulfillment, just before the great catastrophe prophesied. I believe we're going to have a one-world ruler, one-world government, a critical, severe time of tribulation for Christians.

Then, the Lord says, "Immediately after these days shall the sun be darkened and the moon shall not shine by night and the stars shall fall from heaven. Then shall you see the Son of Man coming in all his glory with all his angels, to gather the elect from the four corners of the earth. So shall they ever be with him in the air" (Matthew 24:29-30).

He will then raise all the dead and the Christians who fell asleep in Jesus shall be raised from the dead. Those who did not accept the Lord Jesus will go to their sad reward. I hope and pray that people will not have to go there, because it's not necessary. They just need to hear and listen to the Word of the Lord and enter into eternal life by grace through faith in Christ our Savior.

I'm afraid you children may go through a lot of suffering. That's why you should always pray hard that the Lord gives you strength! Scripture says, *"Fear not, my little flock. For lo, I am with thee, even unto the end"* (Matthew 28:20).

That's what you want to tell people when they're suffering. This life has an end. But eternity has no end. So, when we believe in Christ as our Savior, we will be in everlasting life, where there will never ever be any more sorrow, pain, or grief. But eternity in hell, just think of that. Think of the terribleness of that! People should know that. There's not enough preached about it. To spend eternity in hell would be a terrible thing!

****

Nancy came by today and told us about a dream that she had last night. She saw me in heaven at a big table like The Last Supper. I was sitting with a lot of Bible characters and eating bean soup!

I asked the man on my right, "Who are you?"

He said, "I'm Abraham."

Then I asked the man on my left, "And who are you?"

He said, "I'm Jacob."

I shook their hands and said, "Oh my, I've got grandchildren on earth by those names!"

Isn't that something? She dreamt all that!

Then she asked me to look up her father and brother when I get to heaven and give them her greetings. I told her I would be very happy to do that.

****

The other day, Ruth was talking with Mary Sue's girls, Amy and Joy, about heaven and hell and asked them if they wanted to go to heaven to be with Jesus. They both said, "Yes!" Then Joy asked about her mother. Ruth said, "If she trusts Jesus as her Savior, she'll go to heaven, too." So, Amy asked, "What about Daddy?" Joy quick said, "Oh, he's going to Texas!" I don't think she quite understood.

I'm surprised at little Jamie. He'd like to go to heaven with Grandpa, too. Isn't that odd for a little child to say that?

Mother also wanted to go to heaven with her sister. She lay outside her sister's bedroom door, covering the crack so when the angels came, they'd see her and take her along, too. That was a very stirring story Mother wrote.

My mother is in heaven. I have wonderful thoughts of her. She was a very Christian woman. Mother instilled in us wonderful things about the faith. She was a devout, God-fearing woman, a Christian mother. She read Christian stories and read the Bible to us. We always prayed at the table and thanked the Lord for our food. It was probably the most delicious food I ever ate. To this day, I can still taste her delicious vegetable soup and bean soup. Now my appetite is gone. I'm not well. I'd love just one more time to have a healthy appetite and eat her bean soup. I think I'll have to wait and eat it with her in heaven. I remember her that way and look forward to seeing her in heaven. I'm sure my mother is in heaven, and my brother, because he saw the angels. I'm sure Father is in heaven, too, because he died a Christian. I'm very much looking forward to seeing my loved ones in heaven, along with the angels and my Lord Jesus Christ.

My father was ½ Jew, ¼ Polish, and ¼ German. His deaf-mute mother was not capable of raising him, so his grandmother raised him. His grandmother spent much of her time in the beer gardens.

Father was a stern character, very hard on my older brothers. I think that's why Herbie died young. When he was sick, Father made him go out and cut wood. Herbie said he had pain in his lungs, but Father made him cut wood and carry it in when he should have been in bed.

Father was brought up under hardships and it was hard for him to get away from those. After Herbie died, Father sometimes took out his anger on Ted. I was down the line aways and escaped some of that. Ted got the brunt of it because he was four years older.

> **I'm sure my mother is in heaven, and my brother, because he saw the angels. I'm sure Father is in heaven, too, because he died a Christian. I'm very much looking forward to seeing my loved ones in heaven, along with the angels and my Lord Jesus Christ.**

Sometimes, we still get into problems innocently, like Joseph. The Lord has his ways to train us. The Bible says, "In all things, give thanks unto the Lord."

That's the way we were brought up. It was probably hard for Father to conduct himself in a Christian way sometimes. Yet, he did see that we went to church, were baptized and confirmed, and had family devotions and prayers. So, we have to excuse and forgive the other-mistakes that he made.

Father was sick at the end for 2½ years. He got water dropsy (congestive heart failure with edema) and gangrene set in. The flesh rotted on his own body and the stench was terrible. It was a very trying time for Mother, but she cared for him faithfully.

I know that 2-3 weeks before he died, he became a humble Christian. Ted kept talking to him all along. Ted read the Bible a lot and told him about his sin, that he must repent and accept the Lord Jesus Christ as his Savior and Redeemer, and truly believe that Jesus died on the cross for *his* sins.

At the end, Father did say, "I know now that my Redeemer lives. That my Lord Jesus will forgive my sins and that I am saved by grace through faith in Christ." So, I know that he died a humble Christian and that he's in heaven.

Father died in this old farmhouse. Herbie died here too, and maybe the Lord will allow me the same privilege. I'm looking forward to seeing my father, as well as my mother and brother and all my loved ones. Above all, to see the glory of the Lord Jesus when we get to heaven. That's going to be a beautiful time.

****

The Lord made this earth out of nothing. He didn't tell us just *how* He did it. We don't need to know. He just said He created it and the glory be to Him!

A Christian believes that. If you doubt it, you get no joy or blessing out of it. But the Christian gets a blessing out of it. He knows that the Word of God is truth. If the Lord says He did a certain thing, he did just that!

One of the things we definitely know, for sure, is that the Lord said, "*The day thou eatest thereof, thou shalt surely die.*" That has never changed. They ate from that tree and death has been going on ever since.

Death will be the last enemy to overcome, the Bible says. It will be done away as the last enemy when Jesus takes the world over. The Christians won't need to die any more. We'll be with Christ in heaven forever and ever.

We need to die here and get down into the ground so the Lord can raise us. We are buried in corruption and raised in incorruption. That's what He means. We will be raised in glory, not in dishonor. Just like a potato. It is planted in dishonor but raised in honor. For those that believe in Jesus, what a beautiful future!

The thought of death used to bother me more, but it's so nice now when I think of where I'm headed. Probably, Lord willing, I'll soon be there.

Mama Margaret used to tell me, "You're going to be very happy that we had a girl. (Ted had all boys and I thought, "Boy, I should have had a third son, too. But here the Lord sent me a girl!) She said, "Someday, you'll be very thankful that the Lord sent you a girl because girls are also very nice. They are also a blessing in their own way." Judy has been a blessing in many ways. I see that more and more. She loves Cora, comes up and visits, does her best and raised a large family, all Christian.

> **The thought of death used to bother me more, but it's so nice now when I think of where I'm headed. Probably, Lord willing, I'll soon be there.**

Mama Margaret had a lot of wisdom, but she didn't have anything on Cora. They have different gifts. Margaret was a nurse. Cora is an exceptional housekeeper and cook. Comes from a big family and learned to work. They had different gifts. Both were good women. Twice the Lord gave me fine, exceptional Christian mates. But why the Lord took Margaret home, I cannot answer. It was not my idea. It's not my idea to leave now. Death is not a decision, it's a calling! Man thinks and the Lord leads. That's the way it goes.

It was odd because Margaret was a young mother taken away from her children. The last thing I asked the Lord to do was to take her. She knew her duty was to raise her family. Margaret's life was in the hands of the Lord. But the Lord took her and so fast. She was only sick three days.

I said, "Margaret, you can't go. We have children to raise."

She'd say, "I'll try." About ten minutes later, she'd say, "It's no use. I've got to go!"

I'd say, "Try again."

So, she'd try and then say, "It's no use."

The first thing we did together when we were married was to pray the Lord's Prayer, and that's the last thing we did before she died. Death is not a choice. It's a calling.

A Telephone Conversation with Dave Fero

Ernie: My bile duct just plugged up about a month ago and then I turned yellow as a pumpkin. Otherwise, I was doing pretty good. All of a sudden, people noticed me getting yellow. The liver doesn't have many nerves, so I didn't have any pain.

Now I'm nauseated and can't eat anything. I must have lost seventy-five pounds. You wouldn't want to see me like this. But if you wanted to come, Dave, I'd love to see you. I've always considered you a close friend.

I'm not too desirable a character now. I have to take medication, so I'm not in much pain most of the time. But I'll tell you one thing. I could never play any more shenanigans with you!

I marvel yet, how did you learn to hook up that radio so we could broadcast that German program? That was an accomplishment!

Dave: You know, Ernie, all these years in the service and then in the trucking industry and even after I've retired, the Lord must be with me because some of the things that come to my mind... Don't ask me where they come from because you know, Ernie, *I* don't even know! It must have been born in me. I come up with some of the darndest things that it even surprises myself!

Ernie: It's good to hear your voice, Dave. To tell you the truth, when Ted let you go, I felt very bad for six months to a year afterward. I missed you. I sure thought a lot of you. We got along real good. You had so much on the ball. You fished good. Ted is a great fisherman today, and if he only knew what a good fisherman you were, I think he would have changed his mind. We were younger then and Ted was older. He thought differently than we did. He didn't have the patience with me.

Dave: He didn't have patience with either one of us!

Ernie: Dave, it was always fun! You made life so interesting for me and I have such wonderful thoughts of it that it makes me feel good just to hear your voice!

Ernie to Ruth: Dave had a lot of personality and qualities that the average young man doesn't have. He's something like Dick Lyons. Even in his voice. When Ted fired him, it hurt me a lot. I felt bad for six months to a year afterward. Mother liked Dave, too.

Ernie: Final Reflections

Ernie

Now, looking back over my life, I would trade nothing for that training that the Lord took me through. It's also easy for me to leave all these things. I think of the joy that awaits us in heaven and the beauties of heaven. It's easy to leave all these things. This little time we spend on this earth is peanuts compared to eternity, which is forever and ever and ever with no end!! We can spend that in heaven with our Lord and Savior! Of the beauties of heaven, the Bible says, "No eye has ever seen and nobody has understood the wonders of heaven" (1 Corinthians 2:9). It must be a beautiful place.

Think of it. God is so wonderful and so great that He can take these millions of tons of weight and hang it on nothing in the air. This earth is also turning at 1000 miles per hour. Actually, we should be flying off this earth! But we don't, because God has put a magnetic field here so we can walk around like an ant or fly on a ceiling. He hung that moon up there and it functions beautifully. He put the sun there, many, many, many times bigger than the earth. So big is the sun that it warms the earth, and it functions perfectly so that the seasons work within a minute. Now that is a great God! He holds it all in His hand. What a big hand that must be!! How great God really must be! We need to value that.

> **I only hope that all my children remain faithful, and their wives and children also will remain faithful unto death and receive the crown of life—that none be missing in heaven, no not one. That we all spend eternity in heaven with our Lord forever.**

My children are all faithful children and Christians, so they will take care of things as long as the Lord gives them the strength, ability, and power to do it. I'm very thankful for that.

I always kept the place looking pretty decent. Now I can't do it any longer, but I enjoyed doing it while I could. I doubt that I'll ever be able to trim the hedge again, unless maybe there are hedges to trim in heaven!

When I went into the hospital, I thought I'd just slip in without anyone knowing. But I had more visitors and phone calls and letters. I couldn't get over it! There was no chance even to rest.

This morning, Rev. Peterson called from Wisconsin and quoted some nice, comforting Scriptures. He said, "The Lord has gone to prepare mansions above."

I told him, "I'd be glad if the Lord just lets me be a doorkeeper."
I'll be thankful to get into heaven through faith in Christ. We've really been enjoying Pastor Force's tapes from the Sky Valley Chapel.

This is not a good sickness. It's probably one of the worst you can get, but it's a shortcut to heaven! My father was sick many years and suffered. That is hard. Cora's father got to be ninety-three years old. He always said, "It isn't easy getting old." He couldn't walk or get around by himself. Had to be carted around. I'm glad that I can help myself a bit yet and not cause too much trouble for the family. That's a blessing.

I don't in any way feel bad that I'm going home soon. I just thank the Lord for the many blessings he has showered on our family. I only hope that all my children remain faithful, and their children also will remain faithful unto death and receive the crown of life—that none be missing in heaven, no not one. That we all spend eternity in heaven with our Lord forever. Praise be unto the Lord. Amen.

Ernie's tombstone says: "Be thou faithful unto death, and I will give thee a crown of life."

CORA'S JOURNAL OF ERNIE'S LAST DAYS

This is the history of Ernie's illness and last months here on earth before he departed for his heavenly Home on October 11, 1985.

The Certificate of Death states the cause of his death to be liver failure due to cholangia carcinoma—interval between onset and death: six months.

Diagnosis of the cancer took place exactly four weeks before death, but looking back now, we can more plainly see the signs as they developed over several months.

It seems as if Ernie's real symptoms began in July. He was more tired than usual and decided he should be taking Geritol to give him some extra energy. He also had a severe backache, which I believe came from moving the washing machine out for repair and another machine back in. Finally, on July 20th, he went for chiropractic treatments, which helped both his neck and back tremendously. He picked most of the strawberries, really enjoying the fruits of his labors. He was so proud of the delicious Fairfax berries.

Judy and her children came on July 5th for ten days, and they were busy days indeed. Ruth came home on the 7th, having finished her project at the Seminary in Fort Wayne, and on the 8th, we had a luncheon party on the Star of Charlevoix dinner boat. Ernie had excitedly planned the party and made all the arrangements, and we had a happy time. During much of this time he wore his back brace, which he had had since back surgery thirty years before.

After the strawberries were finished, the raspberries started to ripen, and we picked every day. Ernie and I would get up early every morning and pour out each pint container picked the previous day, removing any bad or moldy berries, and then he would deliver them to his customers.

When Judy went back to Illinois, her daughter, Valerie, stayed behind. She and Ruth helped us pick raspberries and we had a busy but happy month, visiting away the many hours in the garden as we filled our pails and stomachs with lovely berries.

Several times that month, Ernie told me he was concerned that he was losing weight for no good reason, but I always told him that it was because I was going to Weight Watchers and not cooking as much, and besides, men lose weight twice as fast as women. He was also having some stomachache, which he thought began when he started eating so many strawberries.

He told us a number of times that he felt his days on earth were not going to be many more. He often sat with us on the patio in the evening, looking up at the sky and telling us of glories that awaited us in heaven, as promised in the Bible. He told us how much he looked forward to being there with loved ones gone before. Once, he said, "You know, I've traveled a lot over the years, and I've seen some beautiful places. I have no hankering to see anything more on this earth." Then he'd get a twinkle in his eye and point toward heaven. "That's the next big trip I'm looking forward to!"

Much of the time, Ernie didn't feel like eating. He would tell us he had eaten his way through carloads of food in his lifetime and maybe it was time to slow down now and leave some for the rest of us!

In August, another concern of Ernie's was the fact that his urine had turned "as dark as German beer." The end of August, we drove to Stoughton, Wisconsin, for the annual Thoughts of Faith board meeting.

Ernie was tired and definitely not feeling well, and he asked me to drive more than usual. When we arrived back home on Saturday night, Ruth greeted us with the news that Dr. Wakulat called about his test results. He made it very clear that Ernie needed to call in immediately when he got home. He told Ruth that "This is not something he's going to cure with carrot juice!"

The first week of September is when the medical tests began in earnest. By that time, Ernie was becoming severely jaundiced.

A few hours before he was admitted to the hospital for testing, Ernie came home from a quick trip to town and found me up on a ladder in the orchard, picking pears. He was afraid I would fall, and he made me get down so he could pick the pears himself before he went to the hospital. The next thing we knew, we heard a THUD and Ernie was lying on the ground at our feet! Thankfully, he landed on soft sawdust and wasn't hurt. When we got to the hospital, he got a real kick out of telling that story.

Dr. Wakulat asked Dr. David Ledingham, a general surgeon, to examine Ernie and when he came in, it was quickly established that the Lord had sent us a sincere Christian doctor to minister to Ernie. A bond of fellowship was immediately formed.

On Wednesday, they decided that a special test should be done on Friday morning by Dr. Gietzen, the liver specialist, with surgery following immediately if indicated. A tube with a light would be threaded down his throat, through his stomach, and into the duodenum, where they expected to find a malignant tumor. Dr. Ledingham would be standing by to remove the tumor.

Ruth and I spent most of our time in the hospital and the boys came every evening after work. Thursday was a quiet day. Dr. Ledingham drew a picture that evening, showing us what they expected to find during testing the next morning. He also prayed and asked the Lord to guide the doctor's hands. Judy and her daughter, Kathi, arrived at the hospital just before visiting hours were over.

On Friday morning, Ruth, Judy, Kathi, and I arrived at the hospital at 7:00 a.m. Ben and Mark joined us for prayer, and we all followed the gurney carrying our family patriarch down to the room where the testing was to be done. Paul joined us in the waiting room where we kept vigil until Dr. Ledingham came out to report that they found the location of the blockage at the common bile duct and would need to perform another test an hour later. They returned Father to his room and, when he woke up in good spirits, he told us that he dreamed he was picking mushrooms and had a wonderful time.

The next procedure was much more traumatic. We met Dr. Ouimette who was doing the test, which involved shooting dye through a long needle into the liver and through the blockage in the bile duct. The doctor then threaded a perforated plastic tube over the needle, which would drain the bile out through his side into a bag.

When the procedure was done, Dr. Ledingham showed us the X-rays and informed us that Ernie had a malignant tumor in the bile duct that was spreading upwards into the right liver lobe, and he probably had 4-6 months to live.

We had all expected news of forthcoming surgery, but I was not prepared for this death sentence. I learned later that both Father and Ruthie had felt bad intuitions that Father would not have survived the surgery, and they were both relieved that we were given the gift of extra time before the Lord took Father home.

Finally, the gurney rolled out of X-ray with Ernie aboard and we followed him back upstairs to his room. He was in good spirits but felt cold and asked for blankets. Then he started to shiver. He had been through so much this long morning!

Dr. Wakulat stopped by to see how things had gone. As he and Ernie joked about how the attorneys should be shot, Ernie suddenly started to shake so violently with chills that it was impossible to hold him still. Dr. Wakulat started barking out orders to the nurse, who couldn't find his chart since it had been left in X-ray. Dr. Ledingham came and they called for a respiratory therapist to administer oxygen. Dr. Wakulat ordered a blood test, but Ernie was shaking so hard that the nurse couldn't get the needle into a vein. Dr. Ledingham drew the blood himself from Ernie's leg.

I tried hard to comfort Ernie the best I could. He was having a hard time breathing, along with the awful chills. Judy, Ruth, and Kathi sat along the window ledge and cried while Mark and Ben paced the floor. Paul had already gone home, and Jim had to work that day. It was such a tense time!!

Finally, with the oxygen, his breathing improved, and the shaking became less intense. Then Dr. Wakulat issued the order for an immediate move to intensive care. The doctors theorized that, when the needle was pushed through the liver, a big slug of bacteria had been riled up, causing the violent reaction. In intensive care, they started an IV with powerful antibiotics.

We all felt better that he was receiving such good care, but now we were only allowed to stay in his room a few minutes at a time. The nurses had to ask us to leave several times, as groups formed outside his door. We learned to wait outside, but still visited him more than the "rules" allowed. The waiting room was filled with his visitors the rest of that day, keeping vigil while the condition of our patriarch stabilized. What a blessing and comfort we had in our large caring family!

By evening, all of us were exhausted. Gwen cooked a big family dinner and Jim and Marlys informed us they had just received news that their adoption had gone through and they were getting a baby from Korea. The same day we learned that we would be losing a beloved family member, we also learned that we were gaining one. When they showed Ernie their picture of Bethany, he said: "Oh my! The Lord gives, and the Lord takes away. Blessed be the name of the Lord!" (In the year following Ernie's death, the Lord added three new members to our family: Bethany, Lindsey, and Christina!)

> **The same day we learned that we would be losing a beloved family member, we also learned that we were gaining one. When Jim showed Ernie the picture of little Bethany who they were adopting, he said: "Oh my! The Lord gives, and the Lord takes away. Blessed be the name of the Lord!"**

When the cancer/radiation doctors explained the options for radiation therapy, Ernie told them he was prepared to meet his Savior in heaven and saw no reason to postpone his going any longer than necessary. In fact, he was eager to go! Dr. Hilal was from Syria and probably Muslim. Dr. Dulal was from India and probably Hindu. When Ernie started talking about heaven, they had nothing more to say and left. However, in the tumor board meeting, they fought for surgery so they could have slides in their files. Both Dr. Ledingham and Dr. Wakulat told them they had no intention of putting this ill patient through prolonged surgery for no real benefit. We respected them for their stand!

Ernie stayed in the hospital for a week until the IV antibiotic therapy was finished. During that time, get-well cards, telephone calls, plants and flowers kept arriving. Visitors remarked that when they came in, they felt sad and didn't know what to say. But when they left, they were smiling and uplifted because Father had such a positive joyful attitude toward going Home to be with the Lord. Ernie referred to his illness as his "shortcut to heaven" and felt like he was putting one over on the IRS because he "wouldn't have to pay any more taxes!"

These were hard days for me at the hospital. I and the children would stay until all the visitors had left at night. Then we had devotions with Ernie and prayed together. After I did everything I could to make him comfortable and finally left for home, I felt so alone. I was used to *always* being with Ernie. The idea of soon having to face life without him beside me was, at times, overwhelming. For nearly ten years, we had been together daily doing everything as a team; traveling, shopping, gardening, visiting. The few times I did go somewhere without him, the first thing I did upon returning home was to look for him and find out how his day had gone, and we just enjoyed being together again. Now, I did not want to face the fact that life for me was going to change drastically.

> **Ernie referred to his illness as his "shortcut to heaven" and felt like he was putting one over on the IRS because he "wouldn't have to pay any more taxes!"**

On Monday, September 23rd, after giving me a lesson on how to care for his drainage bag, Dr. Ledingham released Ernie and I brought him home. When Ernie commented to the doctor that we had always slept together and maybe things would have to change because of the "bag," the doctor said that would make absolutely no difference and he would be very disappointed if we changed our life pattern. It was so good to have him home again!

Ernie wanted to come to the table for meals, but he ate very little and before the meal was over, he would feel sick and have to lie down in his chair again. Eventually, we set up a card table in the living room and ate dinner there, so he could just lie back when the nausea hit him.

On Friday night, Ernie called Dr. Ledingham and invited his family for Sunday dinner "while he was still able to enjoy the company."

On Saturday, he drove the car for the last time, taking me grocery shopping. Mark's and Ben's families came out that day and the boys clipped out the raspberries and stayed for lunch. Ernie walked down to the garden several times and showed Ben how to turn off the water underground, getting down on his knees to position the wrench correctly while Ben pulled.

The Ledinghams came for dinner on Sunday and their children played their violins for him. About 4:00, Judy and Dave drove in. It was a complete surprise! Some friends had arranged to fly them up by private plane to visit for a few hours. Ernie was so pleased, and we had a great family time together. By the time everyone left, he was completely exhausted, and I put him right to bed, keeping him there all the next day, as he was getting much weaker. Dave later told us he knew that coming two weeks later, as they had planned, would be too late.

The next week, Ernie called old friends to let them know how much he appreciated them and to ask forgiveness for any offenses. Dr. Bunkowske called from the Lutheran seminary to encourage Ernie. He reminded Ruth to read the Bible to him, especially about heaven, because that was the road map to his new reality.

Tuesday, October 1st, was my birthday and all the children came in the evening, bearing cards and gifts. Louise brought a birthday cake. Ernie spent the evening in his chair, visiting but lying down much of the time. The next morning, as soon as he woke up, he told me he had a dream and all he could remember was that he heard the Lord say, "TEN DAYS." He didn't know if it meant that in ten days he would be healed, but he thought it was ten days until he would be Home with the Lord. He had been praying daily since his diagnosis that the Lord would shorten his days, and this seemed to be an answer to his prayers.

On Wednesday, Mark came with papers from the attorney for Ernie to sign, but he was too weak to sign his name. We propped him up and held his hand while he made an X. Gwen, Nancy, and Mark then witnessed his "signature."

During his last ten days, when the intense pain episodes came and Ernie would double over in agony, Ruthie would lay her hands on Father's stomach and pray for the Lord to take the pain away. Then he would lay back, sigh, and ask, "Where did you learn to do that?" When she told him someone had prayed over her hands for the gift of healing, he said, "Maybe the Lord was guiding you after all when you left the Lutheran church." Often, during the day, she would bring her guitar and sit quietly on the floor beside his bed and sing his favorite hymns in her sweet voice. She sang scripture choruses too, which he loved, and again remarked that the Lord knew what He was doing when he let her go to those other churches. It was a time of real healing in their relationship, restoring the breach that had developed when Ruth left the Lutheran church.

A bad spell before sleep one night was followed by a dream in which two angels brought him a silver package and told him, "Take this. It will make you feel better." Because his pain was becoming frequent and intense, I called Dr. Wakulat and he suggested we call Hospice for home health care. He also phoned the pharmacy for a prescription of Brompton's mixture for pain. Father was not anxious to take such strong drugs, including Morphine, but Ruth reminded him of his dream of the silver package making him feel better, and the doctor told him he didn't need to worry about addiction. That night, Ruth accidentally misread the dosage and gave him two tablespoons of medicine instead of two teaspoons. He said he hadn't felt so good in years. He lay awake much of the night, feeling young and strong. He thought about working hard in the fields and had the most wonderful night!

One morning about 5 a.m., while Ruth was sitting up with him, Father woke up and groaned. When she asked what was wrong, he said he had been hoping he would wake up in heaven. She told him it hadn't been ten days yet and he asked, "Well, how many days has it been?" She calculated the dates and told him it was only Day #6. "Okay," he sighed, "I guess I can make it another four days."

Wednesday, October 9th, Dr. Ledingham stopped by to visit on his day off. He sat on the corner of the bed by Ernie's head and told him he came as a friend just to sit with him. Ernie was so pleased and happy to see him. He was hardly able to talk any more, but he tried so hard. Dr. Ledingham read scripture and prayed with him. He fed him water from a spoon and told Ernie he loved him. Ernie immediately fell asleep. He woke up about twenty minutes later, smiled at Dr. Ledingham, and said, "I love you too." Those were the last words he was able to speak on earth.

Thursday, October 10th, was the ninth day after Ernie's dream. Pastor Bernthal came to give Father communion and Ed Warner also stopped in to visit. Such beautiful prayers were offered up to the Lord, asking the Lord to take Father out of his suffering. That evening, when the boys were with us, we all laid hands on Father and released him from us, asking the Lord to take him to heaven.

Then we read to Ernie the verse he always quoted as his confirmation verse, Revelation 2:10. *"Be thou faithful unto death and I will give thee a crown of life."* What none of us had realized until that night was that the part he always quoted was the second part of the verse. The first half says: *"Do not fear what you are about to suffer. Behold, the devil is about to cast some of you into prison, that you may be tested, and you will have tribulation **ten days**."* There it was again, *ten days*, just as Father had heard on the night of October 1st. During those ten days, Father's body became his prison and he truly suffered tribulation. He seemed to age five years for every day. At the time we read it to him, we were only two hours away from October 11th, which was ten days from when Father had heard those words.

He was not able to talk anymore and didn't even open his eyes, but when we asked him if he could hear us, he nodded his head, "Yes."

That night, he had so much mucus in his throat, and he was too weak to cough it out. The tension was so great that I had to leave the room several times to work it off. I went to the kitchen to wash dishes and Mark split wood and fired the stove. Around 1 a.m. Friday morning, Ben took me to the sofa and insisted I lie down for a while, promising he would call me if necessary. Ruth took the phone upstairs and called Ruth's best friend, Vicki—her way of relieving the tension. Jim rested for a while, and Mark, Paul and Ben stayed with Father.

Around 3:15, they called us to "come quick!" Father opened his eyes, and his lips were moving. I asked him if he was trying to tell us something and he nodded, "Yes." Then his last breaths sputtered out.

For days, he had eagerly looked forward to seeing the angels come to take him Home, and we would say, "Father, when you see them come, tell us so we can know, too." I am so certain now that he was trying to tell us the angels had arrived, but in the last seconds of his life here on earth, grief overtook us, and we forgot to ask if he was seeing the angels. But I know they came for him!

It was exactly ten days from the time the Lord had spoken to him. Father always loved to study Daniel and Revelation, and often talked about the 3½ years of tribulation in the last days. We found it interesting that the Lord took him home just 3½ hours into the tenth day!

It was exactly four weeks after his diagnosis, when the doctors told us he had 4-6 months left to live. Surely the Lord was gracious and honored his prayers to "shorten his days" and deliver him from his pain and suffering. His faith in Christ was so strong, and he longed to leave his sick body and go to be with the Lord. My dream in August and Nancy's and Vicki's dreams confirm to us the fact that Ernie is in heaven.

After Ruth called Vicki during those last hours of Father's life, Vicki was not able to sleep. Finally, about six o'clock, she fell asleep and dreamed she saw Father in heaven, sitting in a gilded chair. All those around him were clothed in white robes, but he had just arrived and was still wearing his earthly clothes. He was beaming with joy. <u>Home at last</u>!!

It was about 5 a.m. when Paul called Georgia to tell her that Father had gone Home. She told us later that she looked up at the sky over our house and saw the brightest star she'd ever seen. She said it stayed there even as the sky started to get light. We were reminded of a verse Father often liked to quote: *"Those who lead many to righteousness shall shine like the stars forever"* (Daniel 12:3). Father certainly loved to talk to people about God in an attempt to lead them to righteousness, and we believe the Lord brightened that star to acknowledge his welcome Home!

In August, I had a dream in which Ernie and I were supposed to walk to a lake, and to get there we had to climb over a hill. We started out and when we got to the hill, it turned out to be a solid concrete wall reaching up into the sky. Ernie climbed right up, but I couldn't even get a finger or toehold into the concrete. I began crying to Ernie: "Come down, come down! You're sick! You'll never make it!" He kept right on climbing, faster and faster, as I fell to the ground, exhausted and still crying out to him to come back. All at once, his voice was beside me asking: "Well, did you have a good trip?"

I puzzled over this strange dream as I recounted it to him. Then I forgot all about it in the busyness of berry picking. Once, during the week before Ernie went to heaven, I told it again briefly, but it still didn't make much sense.

On the morning of October 12th, after his Homegoing, the Lord revealed to both Ruthie and me the meaning of the dream. Ernie was much more ill than we realized at the time, and he was going <u>up, up</u> to heaven and I could not follow. How clear it became! The Lord had been trying to forewarn me, but I was not able to understand or accept it at the time. When Ernie's voice in the dream asked if I'd had a good trip, it indicated that, in heaven, there is no time and when I arrive, he will greet me as though I followed him quickly.

What a comfort to me now to know that we will surely see each other again in heaven, where we will spend eternity around the throne praising God!

Ernie went home to heaven on October 11, 1985, and his lifeless body was laid to rest on October 14. It was a beautiful day with the trees at their peak of red and gold. Years earlier, his sister, Christel, had dreamed that Ernie had died, and the golden leaves were falling on his grave. That's exactly what happened. It was the season of the year he loved the most. He had lived a long, busy, colorful, and happy life in his love for the Lord and for his family. His greatest legacy to us is the golden promise of God by which he lived and by which he wants us to live.

"Be thou faithful unto death, and I will give thee a crown of life" (Revelation 2:10). Father is now wearing his crown in his heavenly Home!

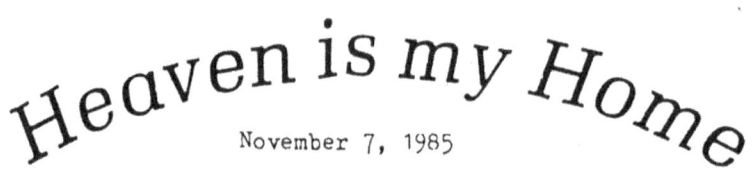
Heaven is my Home
November 7, 1985

GREETINGS in the name of Jesus, in whom we share the blessed hope of eternal life in heaven.

With mixed sorrow and joy, I'd like to tell you about the HOMEGOING of my father, Ernie Manthei. He left this world of sin October 11, and now lives with his Lord Jesus in heaven forever! (Oh, that we were there!) Those of you who met him know that he was a man whose presence in a room was always felt, and so now is sorely missed. Yet I praise God for the many blessings and insights our family has gained through this "special visitation of the Lord", as Father called it.

"I will talk to my brothers about GOD my Father,
Together we'll sing His praises."

Let me start by saying that God called my father to faith in Jesus his Savior at a very tender age, thus setting the tone not only for his life and work but also for his attitude toward death. Father has been looking forward to being Home with the Lord for years, so he greeted the news of terminal cancer almost with enthusiasm, calling it his "shortcut to heaven". Upon hearing the prognosis of 4-6 months, he began praying immediately that God would "shorten his days". "After all" he figured, "if I'm too sick to live a full life here any more and am headed for heaven, why linger?" With a twinkle in his eye he would recall his many travels and remark that "This will be the greatest trip ever." Or he'd chuckle and say "I won't have to pay any more taxes!"

Many friends prayed fervently for his healing (Thanks!), but Father would recall the words a wise man once told us while dying of cancer: "Healing is a blessing, but it is an even greater blessing to walk through this valley victoriously." Father received that blessing and set a tremendous example for our family. He died as he lived, by faith, praising God for so great a salvation through Jesus Christ our Savior. He not only taught us how to live, but how to leave ... with that golden key to heaven gripped tightly in his hand. I must say, the crux of Christianity snapped into focus during this "time of visitation". He grieved over his past sins, yet ever remembered that "By grace ye have been saved through faith, and that not of yourselves, it is the gift of God and not of works, lest any man should boast."

As you can see, God provided comfort and cheer through Father himself. And beside that, friends sent cards of encouragement and called to pray with us. (Another thanks!) Hymns and Scripture sprang to life like never before. One verse that especially comforted me was: "Precious in the sight of the Lord are the death of His saints." Indeed, it was a precious time.

Even our dreams seemed heaven-sent! I will relate only the most significant one here. As I mentioned, Father was asking God to shorten his days and would awaken mornings a bit disappointed to find himself still on earth in a sick body. After being home from the hospital one week, he awoke October 2nd to relate a dream in which the Lord told him "TEN DAYS". For him it was a call to patience. For us, acceptance. During those ten difficult days we watched him decline incredibly fast. The evening of the ninth day, we gathered around him in prayer and read him his confirmation verse, noticing for the first time the context of that verse: "Fear none of those things which thou shalt suffer: behold, the devil shall cast some of you into prison that ye may be tried; and ye shall have tribulation TEN DAYS: Be thou faithful unto death and I will give thee a crown of life." (Rev 2:10) Father's body became a prison indeed for those ten days.

And that dream, confirmed by Scripture, became reality at 3:25 AM on the tenth day! Great is God's faithfulness. As for shortening his days, the 4-6 month prognosis was reduced to exactly 4 weeks from date of diagnosis! I hope that this story encourages you in the faith as it has me.
...Together we'll sing His praises!

I cannot say that my father "died", for JESUS says "He who lives and believes in Me shall never die. Though he die, yet shall he live!" Death has been swallowed up in victory. Father often told us that we are "born with the seed of death", that some day we will "lay down this old coat" because "flesh and blood cannot inherit the kingdom of heaven." He is more alive now than all of us, he just lives at a new address!

Rejoicing in hope —
Ruth

The Family Ernie Left Behind

1987

Paul, Jim, Mark, Herb, Ben
Ruth, Cora, Judy

Ted

Ted: Looking Back from the End (1986)

Broadcasting the Gospel

We got connected with The Lutheran Hour radio program through Rudy Berteman and Dr. Meier. That's how the Gospel went into Japan. We were the first ones to beam the Gospel into Japan.

Then I got to meet that Japanese pilot in California. He'd been converted to Jesus Christ. He had changed from being an enemy of the Gospel to being a child of God! He thought he was doing right, you know, when he bombed Pearl Harbor. Like St. Paul killing the Christians. Paul thought he was doing right too. But when he was stopped by the blinding light and met Jesus, he became a Christian and served the Lord.

I've had some terrific visions. I had one that showed how the Word of God was not to go into Muslim lands where it was so hard oppressed, like Iran and Iraq. At that time, they were not ready to receive it.

In that dream I was standing alone in a review stand (stadium) with loudspeakers around it and there was a pond of water before me, nice and quiet. There were six or seven little vessels (boats) on the pond. They were not very big—just small vessels. There was a great reef running between the pond and the sea. A big voice boomed out through the loudspeaker.

"None of these vessels will be able to ram through the reef and get to the sea."

This was a confined pool that represents the Muslim faith. They were cut off from the sea by this awful reef running around it. I was standing there watching. The vessels had no engines in them. There is a spiritual aspect to this. They were powerless to come against that reef. One by one, these small vessels rammed against that reef and boy, did they suffer shipwreck! They experienced great violence, like hitting a hammer mill that crushes rocks with repeated blows of hammers. It just ground those vessels into pieces. I walked around the edge of the pool where the boats had rammed the reef, and I couldn't find any pieces bigger than my finger. Those ships were ground up so bad that they were just destroyed. The impact was ferocious!

Then I went back to my reviewing stand and a mist formed over the water. This is the interesting part. And from out of the mist there was launched a vessel from up above. It was a small vessel like a canoe—not nearly as big as the other vessels. When that vessel hit that reef, the reef buckled! I was immediately transferred into this vessel as it was going through the reef. It cut a clean channel right through that reef! When it got out to sea, I was transferred onto the water and I asked myself, "What must the bottom of that ship look like after cutting through that reef? How did it grind through all that rock to cut a channel?" The thought was brought to me to run my hand over the bottom of that vessel, and it was shiny smooth, not a mar on it. Perfect! This was the physical aspect of the dream. Then I woke up.

A couple minutes later I fell asleep and was back in the dream again and now comes the spiritual aspect. I was in the land of the Mohammedans. There are a lot of them running around the world, you know!

They held a council, and their chief was a nice-looking man. He wore a turban, and they were haggling about something with different groups of people from the west, like the United States and Great Britain. It was very important that they got together to find a peaceful arrangement! But they couldn't agree. It was a tremendous conflict. Finally, this great big Mohammedan guy stood up and before him unfolded the Scripture, wide open.

He pointed at it and said, "How is it written in there?"

I jumped to his side and said, "It is written that the Gospel shall be preached to all the whole world and to every creature."

He said, "Then that's what we'll have!" He was greatly relieved to find a solution.

Now both of these dreams are alike. The small vessels were trying to do something worthwhile, to break through that barrier, but they just couldn't agree on anything and became broken themselves. They directed their efforts at this impossible reef, which was this false faith of Mohammed. Not a saving faith. It had them locked into this small stagnant pool of water where they couldn't get out to the life-giving sea and have free sailing. The vessel from above was the Word of God which was launched and when I was transferred into it, I was riding on the Word of the mighty Living God! In the second vision, I explained that life-giving message of the Scripture to that big Mohammedan and that vessel didn't suffer shipwreck. He accepted it gracefully from me.

Then I woke up.

The vision showed us the sequence of what countries to support with our tithes. That's when we chose to first beam the Gospel into Japan and then later into the Muslim countries.

You see, after WWII President Eisenhower was concerned that Japan was so destitute, they might fall prey to communism. So, he asked Americans to buy Japanese products and to send them Bibles. We figured the best way to help rebuild the people was to give them the Gospel, the good news that their sins could be forgiven, and they could have eternal life with God. In Japan, 20% of all the believers got converted through the Lutheran Hour and 90% knew of the program.

Later, we got acquainted with Far East Broadcasting and started going into Asia. By then, they were more open to receive it. That tower was over 600 feet high. Fabulous thing, you know. It took a lot of power to run that and it was the power of God unto salvation for everyone that believes. He is a powerful, wonderful God.

Mary and I supported 3-4 stations ourselves. We always bought stations in the Bible-less areas. They were strong in India too. Eventually those broadcasts went all over the earth. And marvelous things happened.

Ted

Ted: Perspectives on Historical Events

Our family never felt anything from the Temperance Movement. Uncle Walter made moonshine, but when he heard that the Feds were coming, he dumped it in the pig trough. The pigs were pretty drunk when the Feds arrived, but they had no evidence to prove anything. We ourselves never had any problem with liquor.

We didn't feel the Depression much when it hit. We never had nothin' anyway, so we just had a little less of nothing. Couldn't tell the difference. We had a few chickens and a little slop to raise a pig. You have no idea how we lived. We lived on nothin.'

We had our own fuel from the forest, and meat and milk, cheese, butter, eggs, hens in the old chicken coop. We'd raise a little grain and corn and potatoes. We didn't need anything else. All we had to do was make a few payments. Our folks owed $600 on this farm and all they had to do was pay a little interest. But it was very hard to make that 6% interest.

> **The Great Depression? We never had nothin' anyway, so we just had a little less of nothing.**

We never went to a show.

I was 14 years old during World War I and was too young to go into it. Everybody in the neighborhood that was old enough went. My father was already too old.

When World War II hit, I was too old. They would have drafted Ernst, but they needed veneer to make certain packages. Ernst cut some of that stuff at the mill. And he was a farmer. We got into pigs for the war effort. We were going to supply pigs for the army. That was really something. We raised two-legged pigs out there. We should have gone into the Ringling Brothers Circus with that stuff! We probably had 6-8 sows. There was an inbreeding problem and they had only two legs, just in the front. We only did that for a year or two.

As for politics, did you know that only 6% of people in the press are Christians? That means 94% of the journalists are not Christians. They will never print anything that would go against their majority. So, you have to be careful what you believe about what they say. They dig up anything they can find to go against a good regime. The communists are doing that. In Russia, the communists are never in the majority. The communist minority has to work hard to get the majority to follow their corrupt ways. Now (1986) they are infiltrating us through our press and schools, just like they said they would. They are brainwashing us with their corrupt thinking.

Ted: Life Lessons

Ted

I've had a very colorful life. We lived off the land mostly. Trapping, farming, milling trees, selling real estate. It all was tied to the land, you see? And now that I'm old, I like to go fishing off the end of the dock and work in the garden. I still love the ground. I am a dresser of the earth!

The people who won't dress it, like in Africa where they don't drill wells, they starve to death. Ninety percent of the sweet water on the earth is underground. Did you know that? The Great Lakes and all those sweet rivers are only 10% of the sweet water in the world. The rest is underground. Just like in the desert. There's tons of water under there. Without it you'd die. But you've got to dress it. Dig a hole and get that water out so you can use it.

Some people don't want to dress the earth. They might get welfare or a disability check for the rest of their lives. They might live off money that somebody else works hard for, fighting it out day after day, while they won't work at all. It might seem like they came out the best, but spiritually, I think it might be the worst. It's not dressing the earth, and I don't know whether the Lord is for that or not. If we dress the earth, there's a reward. But I believe if you don't plant, dig the copper, or use the ripe trees for veneer and don't dress the earth, you shouldn't get paid. The Bible says, *"He who doesn't work, neither should he eat"* (2 Thess. 3:10).

I always loved the Scripture, and when we found that section in Malachi about tithing, we just had to do it! There's a blessing that comes with doing what the Bible says, you see. And then I had those visions which gave me courage to do some hard things, even things that nearly cost me my life. And the Lord rewarded me with that inheritance.

So, you see how that dream came out for our inheritance? I never dreamed I'd get to be a millionaire overnight like that. A multi-millionaire. I didn't need all that money myself. I divided it up into portions for my children so they can dress the earth with it. They built mobile home parks with it and invited Ernst's boys to join them. They like those boys. They're nice kids.

I'm so tickled about those children of mine. They work together well. They are really something, all those boys. God's word says, "Behold how good and how pleasant it is when the brethren dwell together in unity" (Psalm 133:1). It's wonderful how they work together. Just out of this world!

> **I'm so tickled about those children of mine. They work together well. They are really something, all those boys. God's word says, "Behold how good and how pleasant it is when the brethren dwell together in unity." It's wonderful how they work together. Just out of this world!**

I had to laugh at Danny. He told me one of the boys had an idea to build something that could save thousands of dollars if they could make it work. Then Danny went ahead and figured out how to build that machine!

You see how the brain works differently on each one? One guy has the idea, and the other guy figures out how to build it. Ain't that fantastic?? But that's the way it is. Then they all benefit from it. That machine saved them thousands of dollars in building the parks.

And Tom, his job is to keep everyone together. When anyone gets in a fight out in the parks, they always send Tom out there. He'll win the battle. It doesn't matter how sore it looks on the outside. He'll come back the next day with praise in his pocket. That's Tom. He's the oddest guy you ever seen. They say he's terrific in public relations, even in his own crew. He could talk things over with a crook who was running away with his money.

Our children can work together because they aren't stubborn. They listen to each other. Ernst and I had our controversies, but we couldn't get away from each other. We just had to hang in there come hell or high water. Ernst said that if a person were to stick with Ted and listen to him, you could really go places in life. So that's what he did! There were times when he realized that he needed me so bad, and naturally, we would get along real good then. Then there were times when we wouldn't. But I knew his heart. Everybody's got his own opinion and one thing you have to give him credit for is that he did a pretty good job with that mill after it got going. We did alright. And one thing about Ernst that I like real well was that he wasn't crooked. His spirit was honest. He was a real honest guy. Stubborn but honest.

Yah, there was a lot of color in there. But if you look for the good, there were a lot of good parts that came out of it. It was not good for us both to be there in Michigan all the time. You can't have two ambitious stubborn bucks working together in the same place. It just don't work!

I needed to get out to California to pick up my inheritance and fulfill God's purposes out there for our family, you see? Sometimes you've got to go through some hard times before the blessings come. It's like crossing a river by jumping on stones this way and that. Sometimes you might even fall in the water. But those stones get you to the other side.

We did a lot of Gospel work with the money we made on all that land in California. I had to leave Michigan, or the family never would have landed in Sky Valley and those parks would never have come into being! Many people have been blessed by those parks.

So, in a way it was good that we had our controversies. Man thinks and the Lord leads. Blessed be the name of the Lord.

> **Sometimes you've got to go through some hard times before the blessings come. It's like crossing a river by jumping on stones this way and that. Sometimes you might even fall in the water. But those stones get you to the other side.**

Ted's Family

1987

Back: John, Tom, Dave, Phil
Front: Tim, Mary, Ted, Dan

THE 50TH YEAR UNION OF TED AND MARY MANTHEI

Thanks for helping us celebrate the 50th wedding anniversary of our dear parents. Their marriage is truly a unique blending of two very different people.

Father, the spirited, creative visionary, and mother, the calm shrewd plodder, together tackled large projects, seeing them through to completion. These strong believers in the work ethic started their romance appropriately working together in a strawberry patch in northern Michigan. After marriage, work continued in the well-manicured 16 acre berry patch. The berries led to the start of a veneer mill operation (strawberry boxes were made from veneer). Father's health forced them to winter in California where he invested in twenty acres of Huntington Beach real estate, forming the base of a great inheritance. This led to a ready-mix plant, a sand-and-gravel operation, a sawmill, and a junkyard. Father, the entrepreneur, used this twenty acre investment to purchase other properties launching them into the real estate investment field.

Mother was Dad's constant helper. Excelling in homemaking skills, business management and—her finest achievement—bearing and rearing six sons. Mother comes closer to the Proverbs 31 woman than anyone else we know.

Father and Mother have indeed been blessed by God and they in turn were faithful to be a blessing to the world God placed them in. They have given generously to various Christian endeavors. Together their blended lives have made a positive impact on their generation. The six sons and their wives plus twenty-five grandchildren and two great grandchildren rise up and call them blessed. We thank them for their hard work. We appreciate their sacrifices and the truth for which they stand.

Thanks, dear Dad and Mom, for a godly heritage. We honor you today on your fiftieth wedding anniversary.

Chapter 11
1990s: Ted's Journey Home to Heaven

1991   Ted and Mary celebrate their 50th anniversary in Sky Valley

1993   April   Ted talks to an angel
        May 25   Ted dies

Ted's Final Dream (1993)

As told by John, Son #2

Ted

I went down from northern California to see Dad and Mom for Easter one year. When I drove into Sky Valley, Dad said, "John, come on in here. I want to tell you something." This experience was fresh in his mind; it had just happened. He was sitting in his chair. Dad had been in a lot of pain the last couple of years. He had some operations, and he was getting tired. He was around 88 years old.

Dad had been praying and telling the Lord, "It's time for me to go. It's time for me to leave. Life isn't fun anymore. It's time for me to go to Heaven."

He believed in the Lord that way. He believed in the substitutionary atonement of Christ. He understood that. And so he was in bed in his mobile home and he fell asleep and he had a dream. There was a brilliant white angel standing at the foot of his bed.

Dad started talking to the angel and he said, "Did you come to take me home?"

The angel said, "No. No, Ted. I can't take you to Heaven in the condition you're in. You have too much hard feeling toward Ernie, and I can't take you to Heaven like that."

So, there he was. He was in a dilemma: he wanted to go to Heaven and the angel was telling him I can't take you like this. So, he was having a discussion or an argument with an angel.

He said, "What do I have to do?"

The angel said, "You have to forgive Ernie. You have to forgive him."

Dad said, "Oh, I don't think I could ever forgive him."

"Well," the angel said, "The Lord can help you forgive him."

So, he stewed on this for a couple weeks, I think.

His argument with Ernie was that Dad didn't like machines and Ernie liked them. So, Ernie was down there trying to run the mill with his old worn-out machinery. He couldn't hold tolerance on the veneer. So, Ernie went down and bought a new lathe, so they could cut straight veneer.

He called Dad and said, "I bought a new lathe for $18,000 bucks."

Dad didn't like that. He wanted his dividend of half the $18,000. Forget about buying a new lathe.

So, Ernie kept reinvesting in equipment this way over the period of the twenty-five years that the mill ran and they were partners. Dad resented it. Or course Ernie was right. You can't cut straight veneer with worn out stuff. Ernie didn't want to crawl under a truck in the snow and try to fix it on the side of the road. Instead, he'd go and buy a new truck and call dad and tell him what he'd done.

Dad thought that he was being mistreated. He didn't like that approach. So, he had a grudge against Ernie. He had a New Testament just like the rest of us and he should have known that you can't have bitterness in your heart and be at peace with the Lord. You just can't do that. Finally at the end of his life he was in this dilemma. He was 87 years old. He wanted to go to Heaven pretty bad.

> **You can't have bitterness in your heart and be at peace with the Lord. When Dad said the words, "I will forgive Ernie," he told me, "It was just like a ton of weight rolled off my back. I should have done it fifty years ago!"**

But he had to forgive. He didn't want to do that. So finally, he said, "OK, Lord. I'll try. I'll try."

Dad told me that when he said the words "I will forgive Ernie," he said, "John, it was just like a ton of weight rolled off my back. I should have done it fifty years ago!"

Who can find a virtuous woman? For her price is far above rubies.

The heart of her husband doth safely trust in her.

She will do him good and not evil all the days of her life.

Proverbs 31: 10-12

PART THREE

Legacy of the Ladies

When the Manthei brothers married the Behling sisters,
they discovered treasures indeed!
As Ted married Mary and Ernie married Cora,
not only did the Lord bless them with life partners,
but also with extended-family partnerships.
The Behling brothers worked closely with the Manthei Brothers
managing their veneer mills, driving trucks,
and co-laboring with the Lord in Lutheran ministries.
Papa and Louise lived in Ernie and Cora's guest house.
The two families are knit together forever!

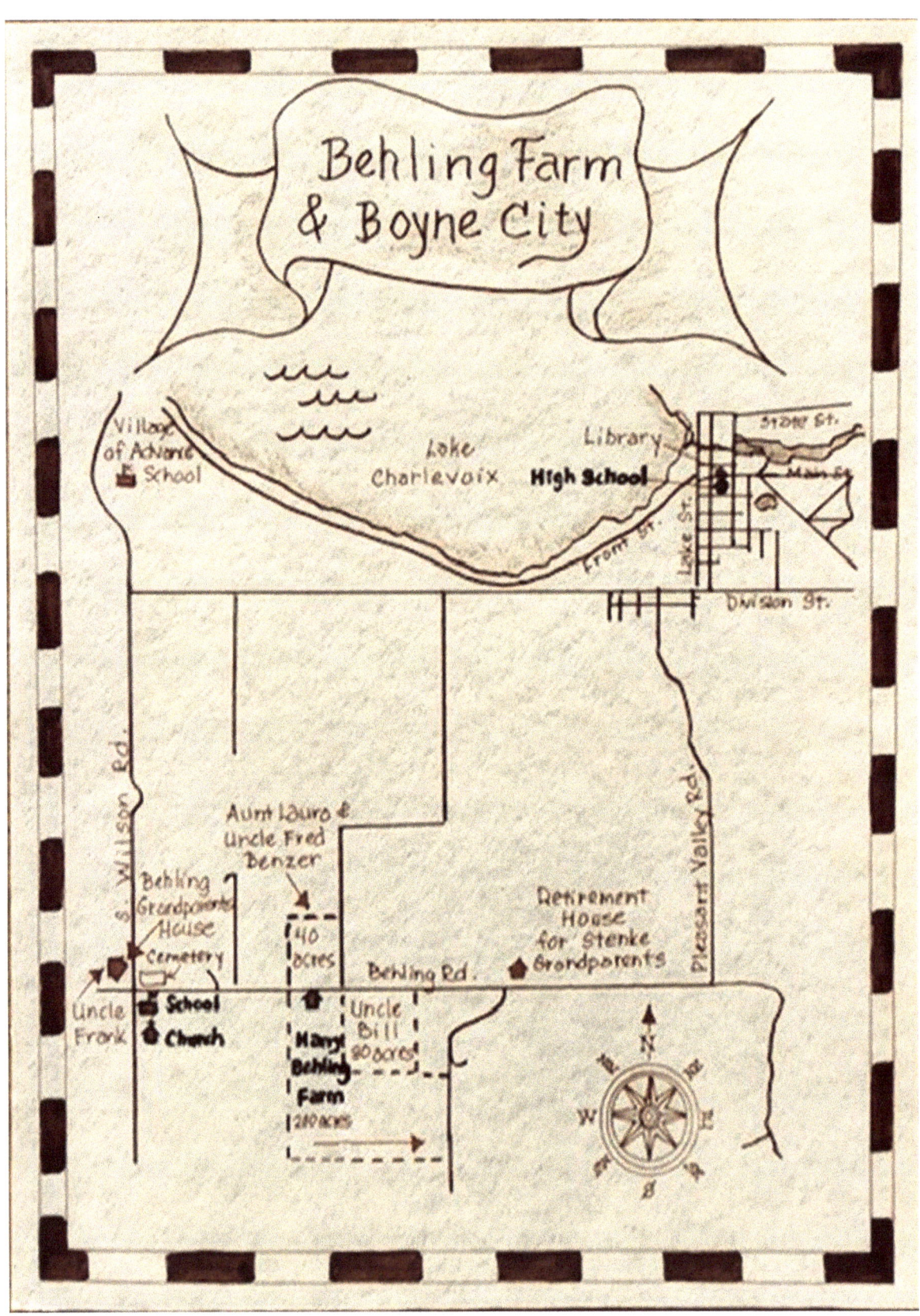

The Behling Family

Harry Behling
Son of
Frank Behling &
Augusta Schultz
Immigrants from
Koerlin, Prussia
German Empire

Gertrude Stenke
Daughter of
Fred Stenke &
Marie Shirvon
Immigrants from
Koenigsburg, Prussia
German Empire

Married April 15, 1911

Back: Herman, Bess, Bob, Cora, Lorraine, Ed, Helen, Al
Front: Jim, Louise, Mama, Papa, Mary, Henry

Mary Augusta Behling Manthei

I thank God every day that He placed me in a Christian family that loved the Lord.

I was born on April 12, 1912, at home on our family farm. We lived in a rural community on Behling Road in Wilson Township near Boyne City, Michigan. My parents were Harry and Gertrude Behling, both new immigrants from Germany. I was named after my grandmothers, Marie Stenke and Augusta Behling. My name is Mary Augusta Behling Manthei.

My father and mother had built a house on a farm they homesteaded in Wilson Township. It was covered with timber, so Dad cleared the land and sold the logs in Boyne City to the sawmill. He cleared most of the stumps by hand but sometimes needed horses and dynamite. They had no tractors.

The house had a kitchen, dining room and parlor downstairs. We had three bedrooms upstairs and a basement or cellar under the house. A furnace was in the cellar, but we couldn't use it much as the cellar was full of potatoes that needed to stay cold, so Dad put a heating stove in the dining room. We had no heat in the parlor. Parlors weren't used much in those days. They were saved for Ladies Aid meetings, funerals, and special occasions.

> **I thank God every day that He placed me in a Christian family that loved the Lord.**

The house had no insulation. It was built using boards with lath and plaster made of bone, sand and horsehair. It was cold. Snow and wind blew in around the windows and water froze solid upstairs all winter.

As the family grew, we always slept two and three in a bed. Our mattresses were made of straw ticks. By the time summer came, the straw was worn flat, and the mattresses were hard and dusty until we threshed and got fresh straw.

We had no electricity, so we used kerosene lamps and lanterns. When I was about ten, we got a carbide plant and had bright lights. We had no bathroom, only a toilet in the backyard. Dad put a pump in the kitchen to bring up the rainwater we collected in a cistern in the basement. We used that for washing dishes and for baths. We had a well in the back yard for drinking water and for the cattle. Later Dad put in a windmill and cistern for running water in the barn and the kitchen. We heated water in a boiler on the stove. We put a washtub on the kitchen floor for baths and for washing clothes. We scrubbed them by hand on a washboard and hung them out to dry. Drying clothes in the winter was hard. They always froze. I had very few clothes—just two dresses a year. I had a work dress for every day and a nice dress for Sunday.

When I was a teenager, Dad built an addition on the house with a bedroom, bathroom, and a woodshed.

The bathroom had no water. We still heated it on the stove and carried it into the tub, but it had a drain. We also got a chemical toilet that needed carrying out every day. Everyone washed by the little pump in the kitchen during the week. Baths were for Saturday night and the whole family used the same water. When I was about fifteen, Dad put a water heater by the stove. Then we had hot water in the bathroom and kitchen sink whenever we had a fire in the kitchen stove. That was a luxury! Eventually we got a telephone. About six families were on a line and everyone had their own ring. Some people always listened to everyone!

We went to a one-room country school one mile from home for eight grades. We walked unless it was too stormy. Then dad took us in the sleigh with horses or we stayed at Grandma's overnight as she lived right near the school. Later I went to Boyne City High School and graduated in 1930.

I worked as a domestic for a year before studying for one year at Charlevoix Country Normal School where I trained to be a teacher. After that, I taught one year at a little one-room country school in Advance, Michigan. I found out I liked teaching, but I wanted to teach in a Christian school, so I enrolled at Concordia Teachers College in Seward, Nebraska, and studied there for a year. I was then given a "call" to teach at a Lutheran school in Annandale, Minnesota. After a year in that cold country, I accepted another "call" to teach in a Lutheran school in Mount Clemens, Michigan, where it was much warmer and closer to home.

When I was twenty-nine, during summer vacation I came home and worked in the strawberry harvest on the Manthei farm near Petoskey. I had known the Manthei brothers for many years through the Walther League church group and activities, but we became better acquainted in the strawberry fields and a romance developed. I liked Ted because he was an enterprising person.

We got engaged in August. I went back to Mount Clemens that fall to teach for one more semester. Ted started building the house in October. We were married on January 25, 1941. For our honeymoon, he took me to the warm climates of Texas, Mexico, and California.

After we were married, Ted and I raised strawberries during the summer and helped develop a little mill to make berry boxes that fall. We came up with the idea of the mill so we could employ more of the family. This grew into the Manthei Brothers Veneer Mill and then we added the Soo Veneer Mill. Our businesses were dedicated to the Lord, and we were blessed!

Ted and I didn't enjoy the cold winters in Michigan so we decided to go to California and see what we could develop there. We started out in Lynwood, then bought a farm in Huntington Beach. We ran a sawmill there for many years.

I was a busy mother, raising six sons and helping Ted with land investments and developments. Eventually we sold our land in Huntington Beach and helped our boys develop Sky Valley Mobile Home Park in the desert. As it grew, I spent many hours in "Grandma's Kitchen" making soup, bread, and pies, and also making wonderful friends!

Now I would like to talk to my children and grandchildren about the faith. I believe God instituted two sacraments: Holy Baptism and Holy Communion. Sacraments use God's Word together with an outward physical element. Water is the physical element used in Baptism. Bread and wine are the physical elements in the Lord's Supper. Both sacraments were instituted by God to forgive sins.

In Holy Communion, all the Gospels say, "This is my body and blood" when Christ gave the bread and wine. To human logic, we can't understand how it can happen, so the Reformed churches say the bread and wine "represent" the body and blood of Christ. God made the heavens and the earth. We believe He can also put His body and blood into the bread and wine just as He says.

In Holy Baptism, God grants forgiveness of sins. The Bible says we are born in sin. In sin did my mother conceive me. To be saved, this sin must be forgiven no matter what age. Nothing is required of the recipient. It's a gift of God in baptism. As a child, he receives faith like any other gift.

Over the years we have tried to improve on God's Word and invented baby dedication to replace infant baptism. In dedication, no sacrament is used. It doesn't forgive sins, which is necessary for eternal

salvation. It takes some of God's work and places it on the child. The child has to be old enough to be accountable for his sins and confess them and ask forgiveness. This is **not** what God's Word says. God is able to do what He says and needs no help. He is able to do it right Himself if we follow His Word. We can never improve on God's way. The Lutheran church uses Confirmation when the child is older to accept his place in the kingdom.

Mary's Q&A Book

How would you describe yourself?

My eyes are brown. I have freckles. As a child I had dark brown hair but now it's white. It turned gray early. My adult weight is 130 pounds, and my height is 5'2" at age 86. I'm right-handed. A distinguishing physical trait that runs in our family is wide thumbs.

As a child, I would describe myself as homely, shy, bashful. I had very few clothes which weren't very good. We had to wear long underwear and handknit stockings which were not comfortable or pretty. I would watch my Grandma Behling sit by the hour and spin yard to knit stockings and mittens for all of us. There were no snow suits or warm clothes like now.

What was your childhood like?

I spent most of my time helping Dad with the chores and farm work and helped my mother with the housework. We were always washing with a washboard and tub. We had to heat all the water on the stove and got a bath every Saturday in a round washtub. Dad built a windmill when I was about ten and piped cold water into the house. If the wind didn't blow, we had to pump the water. We didn't have many friends until I went to high school. There was a family of four girls one mile away and two boys and a girl another half-mile away. Sometimes we played with them on Sunday afternoon.

Back Row:
Louise, Al, Herman
Bess, Mary, Helen

Front Row:
Cora
Cousin William

What do you know about your family history?

My grandparents were all immigrants from Germany who chose to settle in northern Michigan and make it their home, together with friends and relatives.

Dad's parents, Frank Behling and Augusta Schulz, met on the ship enroute to the United States in 1873 and married in Chicago in 1881. Dad was born in Chicago July 22, 1883. They moved to Wilson Township, Michigan and settled with squatter's rights on a 40-acre homestead at the northwest corner of Wilson Road and Behling Road. Augusta was a hardy woman who would don her husband's overalls and help clear the forest to create farmland. They had seven children. Augusta died February 21, 1941, and Frank died of a broken heart six months later. They both lie buried in the Wilson Township Cemetery across the road from their farm.

Mother's parents, Fred (Fritz) Stenke and Marie Shirvon, immigrated from Koenigsberg, Prussia, when our mother was eight months old. They arrived at New York Harbor aboard the Amalfi on April 3, 1891. They came to Mancelona with two children, Helena and my mother Gertrude, before they settled in East Jordan and farmed. I don't know if my grandparents went to school.

Dad made it through 7th grade and Mom only through 3rd.

Life was hard. These pioneers encountered difficulties and endured many hardships, which we of a later generation can hardly imagine. They came here with little or no funds. There was an abundance of fish and game. The giant maples furnished sugar. Yet often there was no bread for weeks and supplies were very meager.

Where we glide around in comfortable automobiles, our grandfathers trudged along narrow, winding trails or drove a horse and buggy over sandy roads. Yet these pioneers bore their hardships with Christian courage. Thus we, the younger generation, have entered an inheritance which our fathers and grandfathers obtained through fierce outward and inner conflicts. We praise the mercies of God who so clearly manifested His faithfulness in His dealing with them.

I had one great-grandmother who came to Michigan. Her name was Louise Behling. She was buried in the Wilson Cemetery before I was born.

I knew all my grandparents. Frank and Augusta Behling lived one mile from us. We went there often. My Uncle Frank always got a big pan of apples from the basement when we visited Sunday afternoons. They were so good. Apples were our only fresh fruit in the winter.

Fritz and Marie Stenke, my mother's parents, lived ten miles away. We didn't see them often until we got cars. None of them talked about their relatives in Germany. Grandma had an Aunt and Uncle Sherbrat who had a tailor shop in the flatiron block in downtown Petoskey. They lived above it. They came to see us once in a while. They died when I was small.

Northern Michigan didn't have churches yet in 1880, but a missionary-at-large held services in schools and homes around the country. He was a Missouri Synod Lutheran man. In 1886 Pastor Truelzech was ordained in Petoskey and installed to serve Boyne Falls, Advance, Ayr, Mancelona, and Bear Creek (which later was renamed Petoskey.) In 1891, due to ill health, he left for warmer climates and Pastor Schauer, resident pastor in Mancelona, served these communities with the aid of a student assistant. In 1896, Pastor Schweppe took over his duties as a regular pastor. In March 1903 a meeting was held to organize a congregation. This first meeting was held in Wilson Township, and it was decided the new church would be built there. Plans for the new church went ahead rapidly. While the church was being built, services were held in the schoolhouse in Wilson Township. Every member helped and cooperated and by May 3, 1903 completion was done and plans to dedicate the new church were made for June 28, 1903. Both German and English services were held. The same year, five cents a month was asked from each member to establish a library. In 1904, the first confirmation class was confirmed in August. My grandparents and parents were involved with it all.

What was your elementary school like?

I went to Knop School on the corner of Behling and Wilson Roads. It was a one-room school with grades K-8. The toilets were in the back yard. We had a pump for water. School was one mile from home and we walked. When it was too stormy, we stayed at Grandma Behling's overnight, right near the school. We had one teacher and about thirty students.

I don't remember discipline problems. At recess we played baseball a lot. We played Move Up. Winters we went out and played Annie-Eye-Over, throwing a ball over the school's roof. Mostly we swept the floor, washed the blackboards, and cleaned up during recess or carried in wood and kept the fire. Our classes were 10 minutes long. With eight grades, there were a lot of classes.

I couldn't talk English when I started school, but I don't remember any problems. I made Kindergarten and First Grade the first year. Two more girls were in my class all the way through grade school—Dorothy Behling and Violet Staplry. Then Violet moved to Montana.

What was the grocery store like when you were little?

We went to town with a horse & buggy on Saturdays. There was a water trough and a place to tie the horses in front of the store, which was about 15x30 feet. We took eggs, dressed chickens, butter or whatever we had to sell and traded them for groceries. The first thing I remember in the store were about three barrels of soap. You put what you wanted in a sack and the clerk weighed it. There were boxes of cookies which you also put in a sack. We gave the clerk a list and they brought the items and put them in sacks and weighed them. No one walked around the store.

Meat was in a butcher shop. A clerk cut and weighed it. Hamburger was about .25 per pound. Stores didn't carry bread or milk. Farmers had cows and a few people around town had a cow and sold milk to their neighbors. People made their own bread and only cookies were sold in stores.

Later an ice cream parlor opened. Ice cream was 5 cents a cone. We always bought a watermelon on July 4th and sometimes two quarts of ice cream. They always had oranges and bananas at Christmas, so we each got one. There was a dry goods store too.

What did you most enjoy doing with your family as you were growing up?

We lived on a farm and spent lots of days in the fields hoeing, putting up hay, cultivating, husking corn, shocking grain, or digging up potatoes. Our parents, especially Dad, worked with us. Mom always sent a good lunch at mid-morning and afternoon. Fresh bread sandwiches and coffee cake and coffee with half milk. We never took vacations. We often went to Grandma and Grandpa's on Sunday afternoon, but we had to be home for chores by 5 pm. The chickens and pigs needed feeding, eggs gathered, cows brought from the pasture and milked.

We either spent holidays at our Grandparents' or they came to our house. In the evenings, we just talked or played games after chores or did homework. Mom played the organ, and we sang a lot. We usually baked a pan of apples or squash to have at bedtime.

We didn't have a telephone, radio, TV, or electricity when I was little. We got a Model T Ford Touring Car when I was five. All the roads were dirt and we usually had to push the car up the hills.

What was the Christmas season like when you were a child?

At Christmas time, we always had a program at school and church. We all memorized poems, had little plays and songs. Dad hitched the horses to a big sleigh and put straw and horse blankets in. Mama heated soapstones in the oven, and we put our feet on them to keep warm. Everyone got a sack of candy and nuts at school and a gift of three pencils from the teacher. We also got a sack of candy at church. The church had a big tree with real candles. The elder, Mr. Schultz, had a long hollow stick and always stood near the tree to watch the candles so the tree wouldn't catch fire.

At home, we went in the woods and cut a tree and made paper chains to decorate it. We also strung popcorn and cookies. Mama usually got us each a present if she had any money. Usually, she spent a dime for each present. We also got an orange and banana. That was the only time we got an orange or banana. One year, Grandma Stenke knit a pretty pink purse for me and one year, Grandma Behling gave me a doll. I treasured those for years.

What were the main problems you remember having?

My real concerns when I was young was… how to know I was going to heaven? It bothered me for years until I understood. Just believing God's promises of faith and showing my faith by doing God's will. Go ye.

The other concern was… how does a person earn enough to build a house? We were so poor. It was hard to get any clothes or shoes or a car. There was no way to get ahead it seemed. Everybody was poor.

What was your church life like when growing up?

I was baptized May 5, 1912, by Pastor O.H. Trinklein. My sponsors were George Stenke, Marie Stenke, Augusta Behling, and Laura Benser. I was confirmed: May 13, 1928, by Rev. Helmuth Schultz.

We had a church one mile from home. It was a white country church. We had church every other Sunday when I was small. One time German and the next time English. The minister came by train to Boyne Falls on Saturday and Dad picked him up. We kept him overnight. We went to bed early so he could study. He needed the lamp and quiet. About thirty people came to church.

Confirmation instruction was very meaningful to me. Learning about God was such a serious thing. Dad had a big German Bible with lots of pictures. We gathered around his chair while he read to us a lot.

Rev. Succup and Rev Ofsty were outstanding to me. By the time I was 15, we went to English services and the minister got a car. More people got cars and we visited other people on Sunday afternoons. We had a mission festival every summer with a big dinner outside where we drank pop and ate ice cream cones. They were real treats. We started a youth group, which was lots of fun, when I was about 18.

What have been your most enjoyable travel/vacation experiences?

In 1933, I went to Chicago alone to spend a week with my relatives, the Leib family. They took me to the Field Museum and the stockyards. The smell at the stockyards was so bad I could hardly breathe. We saw them bring in the animals and butcher them and prepare meat for sale, make sausage, render the lard, and process all the products. We rode the street cars and elevated trains, and we visited some parks.

We didn't go on vacations, as there was too much to do just to make a living. The train ride was interesting as I had never been on one. I remember most the street venders with the carts. They were constantly calling out their wares for sale and some were buying rags. It was never quiet from these peddlers in Chicago.

What was your father like?

Papa was a man to be feared in love. I respected him and never thought of doing anything to hurt his feelings. He was respected by the whole community. He was school treasurer for many years and Justice of the Peace for years. He went through the 7th grade in school. He read the Bible a lot and took the whole family to church every Sunday when we had church. Many of the men drank and always liked to fight at the church meetings. My father got so upset and always tried to keep order. He was good to all of us kids, but we all knew we better do what he said. Acts of love were never shown, but our home was always peaceful.

What was your mother like?

Mama was a hard-working lady, a good cook and helped Papa in the fields and always had a big garden. She canned a lot and provided good meals with what she had. She usually invited a new family at church for Sunday dinner and always baked a cake on Saturday. She got into the 3rd grade in school and then had to help at home.

My mother was good-looking and kept a nice home. She had migraine headaches and was often sick. She had 12 children and no washing machine until the youngest boy was born. Papa took care of the money and paid the bills. I don't remember much about her conversations. Mama was always busy taking care of a little one and we kind of just lived and learned things by ourselves.

My siblings:

Louise Harriet (Krenz)	8-20-1913
Helen Martha (Ott)	3-17-1915
Bessie Ann (Schwyn)	11-11-1916
Herman Walter	8-22-1918
Albert Frank	1-10-1920
Cora Pauline (Manthei)	10-1-1922
Lorraine May (Sonnenberg)	5-10-1924
Robert Lewis	4-9-1927
Edward Fritzrick	11-25-1928
Henry William	2-28-1932
James Clare	11-10-1935

We were four girls and two boys, then two girls and four boys. Papa said it took twelve to even out the boys and girls.

What was your typical date like?

I never dated much. I went to Normal School in Charlevoix and studied for one year after high school and then taught for one year before going to Concordia College to become a Christian Day School teacher. There was no one around that I wanted to date until I found Ted. We went to some movies and some Walther League meetings in his new Dodge car. After a month, I left for my teaching job in Mount Clemens. He came down once and then brought me home for Christmas.

On our first date, we hauled a load of strawberries to Detroit. We left at 7 p.m. and got there at 2 a.m. We unloaded and started home. After a couple of hours, we stopped and rested a while and got home at 2 p.m. We learned a lot about each other on that trip. I had seen Ted a few times at Walther League meetings before, but not enough to want to date him.

What were the circumstances under which you met your spouse?

I met Ted occasionally at youth meetings but, during the summer of 1939, his mother asked me to work in the strawberry patch, checking pickers and packing berries for a month. I did this and we got acquainted as Ted helped load the truck each evening.

Ted asked me to go with him to Detroit on the last load. We did a lot of talking. After the season was over, we dated a couple times a week and went to a movie or just talked. We only had a month until I went back to teaching.

Before I left for teaching, we had decided to get married at Christmastime. I couldn't get off until January 25, as they couldn't get a replacement teacher. Ted came to Mount Clemens once for help in building a house and again to get me for Christmas.

I felt Ted was a good prospect for a husband. He was a Christian and very industrious, which are both needed for a happy home.

I would advise all my grandchildren to look for a Christian mate first. Check the quality of their temperament and actions. Do they serve God? Are they conservative in spending? Wasteful? Do they spend time with God every day? Are they hospitable? Are they interested in developing a Christian home? Comfortable in raising a family?

> **I would advise all my grandchildren to look for a Christian mate first. Check the quality of their temperament and actions. Do they serve God? Are they conservative in spending? Wasteful? Do they spend time with God every day? Are they hospitable? Are they interested in developing a Christian home? Comfortable in raising a family?**

What was your wedding day like?

January 25, 1941, was a cold, stormy day. It was a little scary to wake up thinking my life would be so different. Ted was very loving and kind. I had a white satin dress. He had a dark blue suit. I had three bridesmaids. I had a small wedding in the church where I had attended all my life. Then we had dinner for just the family at my parent's home. We couldn't afford to have much. We drove to Petoskey and had pictures taken after dinner. Then we left for our honeymoon.

Where did you go on your honeymoon?

We went to Texas, Mexico, and California. We borrowed $200 for the trip of two months and had a little money left when we got home.

As we were driving north to the US from Mexico City, there were very few places to eat along the dusty gravel roads. We would stop at small bakeries along the way to get sliced bread for picnic lunches. At one of these stops, several young men surrounded us and asked for money. Ted was thinking about fighting them off, but I saw that the young men were hungry… so I threw one of them a slice of bread. He grabbed it out of the air and started devouring it. I threw the next slice a little farther away. The banditos scrambled after it. I kept throwing bread slices farther and farther from the car and told Ted to get in and start the engine. Finally, I threw the last slice as far as I could, jumped in and off we sped. We learned to be careful about where we stopped for lunch after that.

It was amazing and a blessing from God that, in all our trips between Michigan and California every year, we never had a serious accident or incident. We did have a close call once. We were nearing the Rockies and I wanted to stop and cross the mountains in the morning. Ted wanted to keep going and make good time. We stopped for gas just before heading up the mountain and, lo and behold, the car wouldn't start. Ted looked for a mechanic only to learn that it was too late to get the car fixed. I was relieved and we enjoyed a relaxing supper. The next morning, the car started up immediately without any problem! I turned on the radio just in time to hear the news that a car had been held up on that very road the night before. The thieves stole their money and killed the people. That could have been us! We thought maybe our guardian angels made the car stop running because God had more work for us to do here on the earth.

> **Ted often told me his long life was due to the good care I gave him, the good food I prepared, and how happy he was with our marriage.**

What was your spouse really like?

Ted was a very interesting man. He read a lot and could talk on any subject. He loved farming. He loved to study the Bible and never neglected going to church. He always wanted devotions with the family at suppertime. Sometimes he had a temper and got upset over things and was not diplomatic, but he had a kind heart and was always ready to help people.

He always wanted me with him whatever we did, and we did lots of things together, like gardening, fishing, clearing titles on property and traveling to locate people in real estate work. We traveled to every state but Maine. We went to Mexico and Canada. He often told me his long life was due to the good care I gave him, the good food I prepared, and how happy he was with our marriage.

I don't remember any special times as we had many really good times together.

John Manthei tells us about his mother, Mary Manthei

I think mom had a pretty good handle on who God was and what He expected. Of course, everything she did was from a Lutheran perspective, having gone to Lutheran university.

She made sure we learned and memorized the Ten Commandments. We had to memorize the Lord's Prayer and the Apostles' Creed. I remember Mom reading the Gospel of John out loud when I was little. I can't remember what age I would have been then, but I remember her reading it.

I think her mission was to serve the Lord, and she did that through serving her family. She was very devoted to Dad. She took a lot of guff from him. She didn't have to, but she did.

> **I think her mission was to serve the Lord and she did that through serving her family.**

Mom had that steady Behling-approach to life. She didn't have high and low emotions. At least she didn't display them very much. But Dad sure did. It was good that she was there, I can tell you that. Good that she was there! I remember two examples of how Mom brought balance and protection into our family.

My first such memory was as a nine-year-old boy. You need to understand something about Dad. He was single-minded. He could only think of one thing at a time and when it came time to discipline a child, he was very serious about that. I think he was not as drastic as his own father, but he still had too much of it, whatever it was! I observed him spanking one of the younger guys and I literally thought, "He's not going to survive!" Just then, Mom showed up and said, "Ted, that's enough." When Mom said that, he would always stop.

Another time, I was the one in danger. We were crossing the Rocky Mountains. Dad wanted to get to Pueblo, Colorado to stay overnight with someone we knew. When we started up Wolf Creek Pass, there was a sign beside the road that said, "Chains Required." Well, Dad didn't have chains and he didn't want to turn around to get some, so he just kept going. It was snowing hard as we got near the summit, which is 11,000 feet high.

We were driving a '51 Hudson. The windshield wipers ran off the engine and when the engine was pulling hard, there wasn't enough vacuum to make the wipers work. The summit was steep and pretty soon the snow was building up on the windshield so Dad couldn't see. He'd let off on the gas so the wipers would work. Then he'd push on the gas and they'd stop. It was a miserable situation! Suddenly Dad had a brainstorm.

"Mary, you gotta diaper?"

"Yeah."

"Give it to John. He's going to get out on the hood and wipe the snow off the windshield."

If you know anything about the '51 Hudson, it was a very aerodynamic car. There was nothing to hang onto out there. No hood ornament, nothing! Dad was going to put me on the hood to be the windshield wiper! Mom said, "No, Ted, no. John's not getting on the hood!"

Just then, the car did a 360-loop in the road. I was sitting by the window in the backseat and looked down over the edge into the canyon. It was probably four thousand feet down to the river at the bottom. And Dad wanted me out there on the hood! Thankfully I was still in the car when we stopped on the upside of the mountain. Six big guys came along in the next car and lifted us out of the ditch. Dad finally said, "OK, we'll go down and get a set of chains." By the grace of God, we made it safely over the summit to Pueblo, Colorado.

Mom didn't withstand Dad face-to-face very often. But when she did, he always listened. She was as determined and passionate as Dad, but she didn't show it very often. She had enough common sense to know when something was dangerous.

It was very important to Mom that we were honest and that we worked. Mainly that we worked hard.

The good thing Mom did was that she always had good food for us. We came home from school and there was hot homemade bread with strawberry jam and honey. Of course, she always made good meals. Great dinners! She took very good care of us that way. We always had plenty of food to eat with good vegetables from the garden. Mom took very good care of us that way.

I would like my grandchildren and great grandchildren to know that Mom was a very conscientious person. She knew how to work. She knew how to organize things. Mom took care of all the money. Dad never knew what he had unless he'd ask mom. She took care of all the banking and paid the bills. She did a lot of the business. I can't help but think that Mom had some Jewish ancestry. She sure was good at all that stuff. I understand that Grandpa Harry Behling was good at the farming business too. He knew how to make money and modernize and was always able to loan money to the neighbors when they needed help. He held offices in the local government. Mom was the eldest child so, in effect, she helped Grandma raise eleven children before she had children of her own.

Mom had education. She had the equivalent to a bachelor's degree except for the last semester. Dad talked her into quitting school and marrying him. She was teaching already, but somehow, she didn't finish the last year. That was before I came along, but it's what I picked up over the years.

Hospitality was very much a part of our home. We always had someone over for dinner. Mom would set a nice table with good food, plenty of it, tasty, good recipes, and a lot of variety. I was always a good eater, so I appreciated that very much growing up.

As for pitfalls to avoid, the folks always talked about not getting married very soon. We were supposed to wait until we were thirty-five. Dad set that example, so we were all supposed to wait until we were thirty-five.

Another pitfall was a great flaw in the way we were raised. There was never an emphasis on being kind or loving to your brother. There was a lot of ridicule, cutting someone down emotionally and verbally. That should have been addressed, but it never was. Of course, Mom didn't do that to us. Dad was the ringleader in sarcasm and harsh words and criticism.

I think Mom would want to be remembered as a conscientious person. She would want to be remembered as a good mother. She would want to be remembered as good at business. She did all that and, of course, took care of the house and food preparation. Dad always washed the dishes.

From the time I was about five or six until the time I left home when I was twenty, Mom was helping Dad clear the title for forty acres of land next door where somebody had perpetrated a fraud back in the '20s. This guy had bought forty acres and figured out how to swindle some money. He divided it into

25x50-foot lots. 1600 of them! No roads. No access to their lot unless you owned one of the few along the public road. He sold the lots as oil land since there was an oil boom going on at that time in Huntington Beach. He hired a bus to come from every major city in the Los Angeles basin, as well as Pasadena, Long Beach, Los Angeles, Santa Ana, Anaheim. The guy put a full-page ad in the newspaper stating that if you'd get on the bus, you could ride down to Huntington Beach for free, have lunch at his expense, buy an oil lot and go home. He spent twenty years in jail for doing that.

Dad came along and decided he was going to buy the land and get this mess cleaned up. Ray Overacker, the city attorney for Huntington Beach, was my wife's grandfather. Ray had redeemed the land by paying the taxes on 1500 of those lots. Most of these people had quit paying taxes. Ray picked up on the tax thing and when he was ready to retire, he sold those 1500 lots to my dad. He really didn't have anything to sell because he had no patent deed on any of it. Then Dad went to the ones that had not let them go for taxes and by then, the original owners had died, and their children were scattered all over the United States. Dad found them and offered their money back. Some haggled with him. He ended up buying all the lots. Ray Overacker and a local judge helped with the paperwork until they finally got a patent deed to that forty acres. Then they found another twenty acres next to it and they did the same thing. Then they bought another eighteen acres up the road. They cleared the titles on all three pieces of land so they could sell the property.

Mom kept track of everything. She suffered through all of that! It's mind-boggling, but they finally got the patent deeds. By then the land had gone up in value from $500 an acre when he bought his first twenty-acre farm to $135,000 an acre. It took them about twenty years, and Mom was the one who did all of the bookkeeping. She knew who everyone was! It was dad's idea, but Mom implemented it. She took it on with Dad, and they worked at it for many years. When it was all done, they had a substantial piece of money. It was worth doing!

They were a rare combination, Mom and Dad. I think Mom was one of the most faithful people I've ever known. She was faithful to Dad, and she was faithful to what she believed. She was faithful to her family.

Mom instigated much of what you see at Sky Valley and Caliente Springs. She got Tim and Tom going on the resorts. She encouraged each of us boys to do something with that land until finally Tim said, "OK, I'll do it." Dad was against it at first, so Mom loaned Tim the money to build the first section. She shepherded Tim through building the different phases of the park.

Mom had a vision of how to treat people to make them want to come back. She liked people and had the gift of hospitality. She cultivated relationships. She sat on the front porch and greeted people as they went by. She knew everyone by name. She started the restaurant. She was the one involved in getting the chapel program going at the Park. She instilled the Christian emphasis there, with the chaplain and the chapel program. She was very much at the root of all that. Mom helped keep the vision going to fruition. That place would still be a little patch of desert if it weren't for Mom. It's because of Mom that the parks have touched so many people's lives!

Cora Pauline Behling Manthei

Senior Picture

Enjoying brother Bob

Our Grandparents

Grandpa Frank Behling was born in October 1853, son of Martin and Henrietta Braatz, in Moerling, Prussia, Germany. In 1873 he immigrated to the United States with his widowed mother, four brothers and three sisters. They settled in Chicago, IL.

Grandma Augusta Schulz was born in Germany in 1861 and came to this country in 1875, on the same boat as Grandpa, when she was 12 years old. She probably came with others of her family and also settled in the Chicago area. She and Grandpa were married in Chicago in 1881 and their first two children, Laura and Harry, were born there.

Shortly after that Frank, along with his little family, his mother and brothers, Fred and August, moved up to Charlevoix County in Michigan. They settled with squatters' rights on a 40-acre homestead on the north west corner of what is now Behling and Wilson Roads. Fred and August settled on nearby homesteads. Other children, Emma, Harriett, William, Frank and Louis were born to Frank and Augusta.

Grandma Augusta died in February 1941 of pancreatic cancer, and Frank died six months later from a broken heart. They both lie buried in the WilsonTownship
Cemetery across the road from their home.

My sisters and I all remember our grandmother spinning wool yarn on this spinning wheel, and knitting socks and mittens for the family.

By Cora Behling Manthei

Cora: Daily Life in The Olden Days

We were very poor on the farm. My dad raised potatoes to sell. In fact, one year he was elected as the Potato King at the fair. We grew grain for 10-12 cows and sold cream to the creamery. Every morning and night they would milk the cows and run the milk through the cream separator. That separator was an amazing thing! At that time, we didn't have electricity, so we had to turn the crank round and round. The cream came out one nozzle and skim milk came out the other. We put the cream into a cream can in the basement and once a week the creamery truck came by and picked it up. The skim milk was fed to the calves. Our family drank whole milk that was set aside before it went through the separator.

Those were the days before refrigerators and freezers. Since there was no electricity, we had a big old wooden ice box. The ice went into the top and bottom of the chest. There were a few shelves where we could keep things cold in the summertime, like milk and butter. In the winter our dad would go down to Boyne City and cut big chunks of ice out of Lake Charlevoix. He'd load the wagon and bring them home. We had an icehouse full of sawdust next to the shed, and we could keep ice all summer long for the ice box. We kept the ice box out on the closed-in porch, which was screened in the summertime and had windows in the winter. We didn't need the ice box in the winter because the porch was cold, and we kept the food out there. Life was very different back then.

We were fortunate to have a windmill, so we didn't have to carry water in buckets like Ernie did. Our windmill pumped the water up to a cistern on the hill, and then the water would run back down into the barn and the house. We had one cold water faucet in the kitchen sink. We had a bathtub in the bathroom but no running water, so we would heat the water in a big wash boiler on the wood stove, then carry it into the bathroom and dump it into the tub. We only took a bath once a week. Two or three of us would use the same bath water. We didn't have a septic tank. Our bathtub drained through a pipe in the wall to the outside lawn. The kitchen sink drained the same way. In the winter we used a chemical toilet in the bathroom, but in the summer we all used the outhouse. Before electricity we had carbide lights. Carbide is a chemical like salt. We had a tank in the backyard. My dad would pour the carbide in the tank and then add water. When they mixed it, it would make gas. He ran a gas line into the house, and we had one gas light in each room hanging from the ceiling. A carbide light was a lot brighter than a kerosene lamp. When the electric company promised to deliver power to our farm, my dad disassembled the carbide system. Then something happened and the electricity was delayed, so we had to go back to kerosene lamps for a year or two. That was terrible.

We also had a little two-burner stove in the house that my mother used once in a while in the summertime, when it was too hot. The rest of the year the big wood stove heated our food and water and kept the house warm. We had a furnace in the basement, but as long as I can remember, we never used the furnace because my dad stored his potatoes and other food in the basement, and he wanted to keep it cool down there. We had a big wood heater in the dining room. It kept the downstairs warm and the heat went up through the register to the upstairs rooms. The parlor door was kept closed unless we had company, and then it was heated with its own stove. When Uncle Louie came down from the Soo, he and Papa would sit in the parlor and smoke cigars. We had a Reed organ in the parlor that you pumped with both feet. Both Mama and Helen played the organ. Helen took lessons with Mrs. White in Boyne City.

We always had chores. With so many kids in our family, we had lots of chores! Although we didn't all live in the house at the same time. Louise was already married, and Mary was away teaching, and when they came home one weekend for a visit, to everyone's surprise, Jimmy was born! Nobody knew Mama was pregnant! Lorraine and I were the girls who helped Mama raise the youngest four boys: Bob, Ed, Henry and Jim.

Our chores were doing dishes and helping our mother in the kitchen. We cleaned the house and hung up the wash. We didn't have dryers yet. When I was growing up, during those early years, we had a wash tub and scrubbed the heavy clothes on old wash boards. Detergents hadn't been invented. We used bar soap for laundry and for dishes. The dirty dishwater went into a swill pail to feed the pigs, along with table scraps and peelings. After we girls did the dishes, the boys would carry the swill pail to the pigs. It wasn't easy. It was a hard life.

We hardly ever had new clothes. I was number seven in the family and wore the same clothes my four older sisters had outgrown. We younger ones grew into their hand-me-downs.

We didn't have many toys at all. When I was seven or eight, our mother bought one doll for Lorraine and me. Lorraine was my best friend because she was just twenty months younger. We had cousins up the road and would go to their houses to play with them in the summertime, or they would come to our house. We played outside. We played tag and we played Annie-Eye-Over, throwing balls over the two-story roof of the house to someone on the other side. It was good exercise. The boys played horseshoes. We didn't have bikes or tricycles or anything like that.

We girls worked mostly in the house. The older boys, Herman and Al, did the field work—setting up hay and milking the cows. In the summer, my dad raised a lot of potatoes and corn. The cultivators were pulled between the rows by horses. The cultivators had big tines on the bottom, going into the ground, and my dad and brothers would hold onto the handles while the horses pulled the cultivators.

Lorraine and I had to ride the horses and, when we got to the end of the rows, our job was to pull the reins and turn the horses around to go up the next row. We spent a lot of hours doing that when the corn was fairly short. We didn't have saddles, just horse blankets to sit on.

When you work on a farm, accidents can happen! One summer we were back in the "middle-forty" field with woods all around it. When we were done cultivating, they put the cultivators on the wagon and hitched up the horses to pull the wagon home through the woods, on a choppy, rough road. Lorraine and I were sitting on the back of the wagon and Papa said, "Now watch those cultivators so they don't fall off." We went through a big hole, and I turned to make sure the cultivator stayed on and my foot got caught in the wagon wheel. They were big old wheels with wooden spokes. I hollered and my dad stopped the wagon and got my foot out. It was turned totally sideways. Papa turned my foot back and took me home. They tried taking me to the doctor several times, but he was never in his office. Every day I would soak my foot in warm water with Epsom Salts. I didn't have crutches so I hopped around on one foot that summer for about six weeks before I could walk again. Rough time!

Another time I put a pitchfork through my foot. We had been thrashing wheat and the neighbor left his pitchfork behind when he went home. My dad said, "Take this out and put it in the ground by the mailbox so he can pick it up when he passes by." I was barefoot and, when I stabbed it into the ground, I stabbed it the wrong way and one of the pitchfork tines went into my foot between my toes. It didn't break any bones, but that foot took a while to heal up!

There was a pickle factory in East Jordan and my dad had contracted with them to grow cucumbers one summer. When the cucumbers were mature, the whole family went out and picked them. One day Aunt Myrtle and Uncle Bill next door had company, a bunch of young people from Chicago. One of the boys had brought his 22 gun and was shooting at birds. He missed and shot Louise instead. She was bending over picking cucumbers and the bullet hit her in the back of her leg. I don't remember if my dad took her to the hospital in Petoskey or to the doctor in Boyne City, and I don't know if they ever got the bullet out, but she always talked about "getting shot in the pickle patch!"

Christ Lutheran Church
Wilson Township

When baby brother Jim was about five years old, my dad had a pick-up truck sitting in the yard. Jim was climbing around into the back of the truck, and he fell and splintered his elbow. My dad took him to the hospital in Charlevoix and somehow, they got his arm put back together, but he's had a crooked arm ever since. He's eighty-two years old now and his arm is still crooked! But he's been able to farm and drive his truck, and he's in good health in spite of it all.

The boys slept upstairs above the kitchen and Papa would call up the stairs in the morning for the boys to get up. If he didn't hear any noise of them moving around up there, he would pound the broomstick on the ceiling. That's why Aunt Lorraine wrote that verse in the family song for the reunion: *I hear the broomstick on the ceiling. "Boys get up!"* It was a totally different life in those days.

Mama and Papa were both Commanders-in-Chief. Mama was very active in church. Sometimes she played the organ. She was active in the Ladies Aid. Our minister lived in Petoskey, and we went to the little country church in Wilson Township, so he would often stay overnight with us after the late service. My parents practiced a lot of hospitality. I think we learned it from them.

Papa was well-respected in the community and quite progressive in his farming. He would loan money to neighbors in need. He held local township offices. He was church treasurer and president of the church council for a while. He was very active in our country church and school.

The Behling Farm after Haying

School Days

Our school started at 8 o'clock. Our country school was a mile away over a couple of big hills, and we had to walk. When it was raining our dad, or Uncle Bill from next door, would take us in our old Model T Ford. In the winter when the snow was too deep to walk, they would take us with the horse and sleigh. We sat on hay bales and covered up with horse blankets. We didn't have school buses or warm down-filled clothes like they do today. The girls didn't wear slacks. We had long underwear and long stockings. One time it was 40 degrees below zero and my dad hitched up the horses and loaded us kids in the sleigh, covered us with horse blankets and drove us to school. We were the only family there! The teacher sent us home and we got a day off.

In the spring when the roads were thawing out, there was a very bad stretch through a marsh just a little way from our house. The marsh would flood, and we'd have to walk around it through the field on the muddy ground. That wasn't any fun! I went to that school from Chart Class (Kindergarten) through eighth grade.

I was quiet and shy, especially in high school. There were a lot of strange kids in Boyne City that I didn't know. When my four older sisters were in high school, they drove the horse and buggy those five miles into town and left it at Aunt Laura's, a few blocks from the high school. But when I was in ninth and tenth grades, I was pretty much on my own since the older ones were grown and Lorraine was still in grade school. There were no buses running yet and I had to find my own way into Boyne City. Some of that time my brother Herman worked at a business in town, and I would ride with him in the morning. Other times I would either walk that five miles home after school or stay until he got off work at six o'clock. In my junior year they closed the country schools and consolidated, so all the country kids went into Boyne City, and then Lorraine and I rode the school bus back and forth.

I graduated in 1940 and worked a few years in the NYA (National Youth Association). It was a government agency under Franklin Roosevelt during WWII. Early in the war, Herman joined the army and went to Africa and then to Europe. Bob was in the navy somewhere in the Pacific toward the end of the war.

My Family

My parents worked hard to raise us as Christians. Even though our parents talked mostly about work, they always took us to church. They taught us that church was very important!

Later Helen married a pastor. Ed and Henry also became pastors. Lorraine became a Christian Day School teacher for a few years before she went to seminary in Springfield to prepare to be a missionary. Then she went to China. When she came home on furlough one year, she stopped off in California to visit Ted and Mary and speak in the Lutheran churches there. While teaching Sunday School she met little Bruce, who had just lost his mother, and Bruce introduced Lorraine to his dad, Al Sonnenberg. Just like me, she had three children when she got married! She and Al ran a Christian retreat center, and in her later years she was a prayer warrior.

Mary went to Normal School in Charlevoix and studied for one year after high school so she could teach in the country school. She taught for one year in the little one-horse town of Advance, on Lake Charlevoix halfway between Boyne City and Charlevoix. Then she went to Concordia College and became a Christian Day School teacher and taught in Mt. Clemens down by Detroit for a year or so.

That's when Ernie and Ted had the strawberry fields and were looking for pickers during the summer. Mary came up to pick strawberries, got acquainted with Ted, and they were married the next January.

The Manthei and Behling families became very close. Two of us married Mantheis, and four of my brothers (Herman, Al, Bob, Jim) worked with them in the veneer mills. So, the six of us who were not in full-time ministry were connected to Ted and Ernie, who gave generously from their businesses to promote the Gospel of our Lord Jesus Christ.

Louise went to work for Aunt Harriet, who was married to Mr. Stone. He was a millionaire in Grand Rapids, and they introduced her to Clare. He was quite a bit older than Louise and they never had children. Bess married Ray who was an engineer with General Motors.

Before I was married, Mary and Ted were in Huntington Beach and wanted Mama and Papa to come out for the winter, because Papa was getting arthritis. They took little Jimmy to California with them, but Bob, Henry and Ed were still in school and kept the farm going. Mama and Papa asked me to come home and take care of the boys that winter. Henry said that was his happiest winter on the farm! They didn't have any big authorities to boss them around, and I liked to keep things peaceful and pleasant.

When Papa's arthritis got so bad, Ted took them out to Healing Waters RV Park in the desert. That's when we learned about the property for sale in Sky Valley. Later Mary had the vision for Sky Valley Resort and convinced Tim to build the park. The park's chapel program and restaurant for hospitality were also Mary's vision.

> **In the dream she went to heaven and saw family and friends gathered on a grassy knoll around two empty thrones. The crowd parted and here came Mama and Papa to sit on the thrones. The Lord was honoring them before her eyes.**
>
> **Ruth said, "Lord, what's this about? They were simple potato farmers." Jesus answered, "Yes, but they were faithful, and look at the family they raised!"**

My daughter Ruth had a dream one night that she went to heaven and saw family and friends gathered on a grassy knoll around two empty thrones. The crowd parted and here came Mama and Papa to sit on the thrones. The Lord was honoring them before her eyes.

Ruth said, "Lord, what's this about? They were simple potato farmers."

Jesus answered, "Yes, but they were faithful, and look at the family they raised!"

Ruth's dream was a beautiful sign that God was pleased with Mama and Papa Behling for raising our family to love the Lord and serve Him with all our hearts.

Courtship and Marriage

I knew Ernie from Walther League. There was a Junior League for young teens and a Senior League from age sixteen to singles in their forties. The churches in Petoskey, Boyne City and Wilson Township shared the same pastor. The Mantheis attended the Petoskey church, and we went to the little church in Wilson Township, south of Boyne City. Sometimes the Walther League would meet in Petoskey, but most often at the church in Boyne City because that was more centrally located. The Junior and Senior Walther League met at the same time. Ernie was thirteen years older than me, so he was in the Senior Walther League with my older sisters. Our families knew each other for years and years. Sometimes our pastor would have a combined service where we all worshiped together.

Eventually Ted and Mary got married and the Manthei/Behling families were joined through marriage. The year I turned twenty, Ted and Mary started going to California. They already had Dave and John and Danny was on the way. They asked me if I'd like to go to California with them to help with the kids. I was free, working here and there, so I agreed to go. They had bought 40 acres on Talbert Avenue and put a few houses on it. I stayed in the big house with them, and Mama and Papa stayed in one of the little houses. I continued to go with them to California for the next few years.

By that time Ernie had met Margaret at a Walther League camp and they were married with three children: Herb, Paul, and Judy. I was in California when Margaret died suddenly on Thanksgiving Day, 1947. Little Judy was just nine months old! Margaret had gotten the flu and it turned into Guillain-Barre Syndrome, which paralyzed her, starting from the feet and going up her body until she could no longer breathe. That was a shocking tragedy for the whole family!

Ernie and Margaret had already bought a travel trailer and had planned to spend that winter in California with Mary and Ted. After Christmas, Ernie brought his mother and the three kids to California.

They celebrated Judy's first birthday in California, at the end of February. Shortly after that, Judy got very sick, and Grandma Constance was also ill. I was helping Ted and Mary with the kids, so Gran told Ernie, "You take Judy to the doctor and maybe Cora will go with you to hold her in the car." So, I went along and the doctor said, "My, you two have a lovely baby!" A short time later Ernie asked me to go out with him. I think Grandma told Ernie, "Cora is a very nice girl. You should talk with her."

Ernie took Grandma and the kids back to Petoskey in the spring. My brother Ed and I had stayed in California that summer to look after Ted and Mary's place.

Meanwhile Ernie and Ted got very interested in the oil drilling in Canada. They had met someone in Huntington Beach where there was a lot of oil drilling going on, and that guy talked them into going to Canada to drill a well. So, Ernie and Herman came back from Michigan to California, bought a big old oil truck and drove it up to Canada with a big load of pipe. Herman stayed in Canada to set up the oil well and met his wife, Pat, in her parent's boarding house.

Ernie drove the truck back to Huntington Beach and, on the way, he stopped in Utah and bought an engagement ring for me. When he got back to Huntington Beach, he asked me to marry him.

We didn't have a long courtship and some of it was long-distance while he was traveling, but I could see that Ernie had many fine qualities. He had a strong faith in the Lord, he read the Bible a lot, and he was good to his mother and his kids. He was a Christian. I respected him and really liked him for that. I was 24 years old and felt I was ready to get married and have a family. It seemed like the right thing to do, and I loved and respected him. It didn't bother me that he had children because I was used to kids. I had helped Mama raise my four little brothers at home and was helping take care of Ted and Mary's kids. I liked kids! I was foot-loose and fancy-free, and I wanted to settle down. So, I said yes!

> **I could see that Ernie had many fine qualities. He had a strong faith in the Lord, he read the Bible a lot, and he was good to his mother and his kids. He was a Christian. I respected him and really liked him for that.**

We were married in July of 1948 at St. John's Lutheran Church in Orange, California, and spent our honeymoon driving from Huntington Beach back to the oil field in Lloydminster, Canada. We pulled the little travel trailer Ernie had brought to California and lived in it from July to November.

Grandma Constance

Ernie and I returned to the family in Petoskey in November of 1948. That's when I took over the care of Herb, Paul and Judy and became a mother. Grandma had been taking care of them after Margaret died.

Grandma and I got along good. We had no problems. That first winter she went with Dr. Chevy to Florida. Dr. Chevy was the personal physician for Mrs. Lobe, who owned what is now Castle Farms. They probably met when Dr. Chevy bought strawberries from the Mantheis. Dr. Chevy was also from Germany and those two got along famously. They loved and appreciated each other.

Grandma lived four years after we were married, and she helped a lot in the kitchen. She was a good cook. But she wasn't well. She was a big, heavy woman and had an ulcer on her leg that bothered her. She died of colon cancer in January 1952, when Jim was a baby. She went into the hospital for surgery and never came out of it.

Life in the Manthei Home

Our daily routine was getting up around 6:30–7:00 in the morning. Ernie would build the fire in the wood stove while I made breakfast and lunches for all the children. We always said Luther's Morning Prayer after breakfast. Once the kids were off to school, the kitchen floor had to be swept and the beds made. There was always a lot of housework to do with laundry and cooking and raising a family.

We ate dinner together as a family and always had devotions afterward. When the kids were little, we used *Little Visits with God* and *At Jesus Feet*. We prayed *Luther's Evening Prayer* and sang *Holy, Holy, Holy* or *The Lord's My Shepherd*. No one could leave the table until devotions were done. Some of them would get very antsy. Herb especially wanted to get up and go, but he had to stay until devotions were done.

Most of those years we had a big Home Comfort stove in the kitchen that was half wood-burning and half gas. We had a wood box to the left of the stove. The bathroom was on the other side of the wall behind the kitchen stove, and the hot water heater for the bathtub was connected to the wood stove. After the natural gas was put in, we got a gas water heater.

We didn't have downstairs bedrooms when we got married, except for Grandma's bedroom off the kitchen, which later became the den. The north side of the house was just a porch. Ernie and I slept upstairs in the north room to the right of the stairs, which was later Herb's and Paul's room. It wasn't nice like it is now. We did a lot of work in that house. When Ben was a baby, we built the two downstairs rooms on the north side of the house, which became our bedroom and the nursery. The nursery had a crib and the junior bed. The utility room was just a little step-down pantry with shelves on the wall when we got married. Mark was very bashful, and I remember that when people came to visit just after we got our first television, he went and hid in the utility room. So, that means it was already built by the time he was 3-4 years old. The big living room and bathroom in the front of the house were built just before Judy got married in 1966.

Ernie traveled quite a bit for business, but when he was around, I never knew how many people he'd bring home for lunch. If Jim LaGrande, our veneer broker, was up from Grand Rapids, Ernie would always bring him home for dinner. If there were businessmen visiting the mill, Ernie would bring them home. He would say, "Add a little water to the soup." We always had enough food in the house. I ground our own wheat for fresh homemade bread. I made a lot of chocolate chip oatmeal cookies, and we ate a lot of soup.

Ernie was the head honcho of the veneer mill. Ted was his partner but spent most of the year in California. He came back summers but wasn't active in the mill. They couldn't agree or get along. Ted criticized Ernie for everything he did, so it was good that Ted had his own business in California. Ernie met Herb Trier in church when he moved to Petoskey from Fort Wayne due to allergies, and Ernie hired him to manage the mill. They became very good friends. They got along well, took each other's advice, and were very close.

They were getting a lot of logs from Canada and for some reason they wanted to expand the logging operation, so they bought the White Swan to harvest logs from the islands. It sank off Skilligalee Reef in November 1956, just before Ruth was born. That was a very stressful time. I was in my ninth month of pregnancy, with six kids at home, and Ernie was risking his life to salvage everything he could off the White Swan. He was stuck out on that reef in the Great Lakes with rough December storms. Later they replaced the sunken White Swan with the Mackinac Islander, which they converted from a ferry boat to a freighter, after the Mackinaw Bridge was built.

When they built the mill in the Soo, Herb Trier and my brother Bob moved to the Soo, and my brother Al took over managing the mill here in Petoskey. They hired my little brother, Jim, to deliver the veneer. He drove for quite a few years until he had a serious accident and jack-knifed the truck. It happened on Judy's graduation day in June of 1965, and Ernie had to miss her graduation to go help Jim.

Who is God to me?

God the Father is the Creator of the earth. He created everything out of nothing. It's almost unbelievable when you think about how the human body was made, how he created all the creatures and they're still the same after thousands of years, and how the earth was made and everything in it, and how everything works together like clockwork. Then He sent Jesus, His only Son, to be our Savior and our Redeemer. He came as a human being and experienced the same kinds of hurts and joys that we do, but yet He died on the cross for us so that in believing in Him as our Savior, we will go to heaven after we leave this earth. He also sent His Holy Spirit to strengthen our hearts and live in us and help us to believe in Him. I expect to die believing all these things about our Lord and Savior and Master and King! Amen.

Experiences along the way that helped me know God is real and I can trust Him!

The Lord has led my life from childhood on! I was baptized in the name of the Father and Son and Holy Ghost. I was confirmed when I was thirteen. I've always believed and trusted in Him. I prayed for many years that He would send the right mate, and He sent Ernie into my life. That was an answer to prayer, because I was single and floating along and had never met anybody I was interested in. It helped my spiritual journey when the Lord answered my prayer and sent me the right mate for life. Ernie was very much a spiritual leader and inspiration. I had not dated anyone in high school. I had gone to California and met a couple of brothers in the Walther League. Ruth Goebel and I went to a few places with those guys but there was never anything serious at all. Then when Ernie came out that year with his mother and three little ones after Margaret had died, that was it. The Lord was leading and that's why I wasn't married yet.

We went to church every week. We both belonged to the Missouri Synod all our lives. But when there was that upheaval in the seminaries and they were beginning to teach wrong doctrines in St. Louis with Seminex, we left the Missouri synod and joined the Norwegian Synod. They were sticking very close to what the Bible taught. Pastor Bob Moldstad was our pastor, and he was very interested in mission work. He wanted to go to Peru in the worst way, so we really supported him. At that point the church had no mission in Lima Peru, so Ernie and I were very instrumental with the Lord to help him start a mission in Peru. A few years later, Ruth went down to help Pastor Moldstad, so we visited and saw how the Lord was working in the barrios and the mountains. Later, after we met John Shep, we were very interested in his radio work in Ukraine and helped him start the ELS magazine and radio program, *Thoughts of Faith*. After WWII, we also helped Dr. Walther Meier start The Lutheran Hour radio ministry into Japan. We were big supporters of Far East Broadcasting. We met Dr. Bowman through Mary and Ted. He was the main speaker for the organization and Far East Broadcasting now ministers into many parts of the world. I still support them and the Lutheran Hour. Ted was great about tithing, so we've tithed for many years.

Hospitality

Ernie liked to share the Lord with everybody who came his way. He talked about God with anyone he brought home. Jim LaGrande was a very strong Christian and, whenever he came to Petoskey, they talked and talked about the Lord and the work they were doing. Ernie would bring hitchhikers and bums home for dinner, and sometimes they would spend the night. He was very good about sharing the Lord with them. Maybe we will meet some of them again when we get to heaven.

One time he picked up Stanley the bum. Stanley wore a business suit and top hat and that was his profession, traveling around and being a full-time bum. He would come downstairs in the morning, and if he didn't like what we were having for breakfast, he'd ask for something else. He overstayed his welcome and finally I said, "Ernie, either he goes or I go."

One of the first black people we got to know was right in our own kitchen. Ernie picked him up as a hitchhiker and brought him home for the night. We had that little 2x4 bedroom upstairs on the front of the house and that's where the bums slept. That's where Pastor Moldstad always slept too, when we belonged to the ELS and had afternoon services in our living room. He stayed overnight and visited shut-ins on Mondays. That room housed a lot of people over the years. You kids would bring friends home from college. And then there was that guy from Traverse City, Jim Thompson. Pastor Moldstad brought him to us. He was married and had 5-6 kids and got kicked out of the house for having an affair with another guy. He stayed with us for a year or so. I was always afraid to have him around Ben.

We were not prejudiced against people. It didn't matter if they were black or gay or bums or missionaries or family or friends or hillbillies from West Virginia. We just wanted to help out whoever needed the help.

One summer Mary Thompson stayed with us. She was the pianist from Bethany whose father was a professor. Pam's sister, Leah Kooyers, whose father was a missionary in New Guinea, spent a summer with us. Ruth's college friends, Karen Geisendorfer and Alice Lam and Karina Atrops lived with us different summers. Bert and Faye stayed with us when Aunt Babe had her stroke. Dan, Tom, and Tim stayed with us during different winters when their folks were in California and the lodge was closed up. We often had house guests.

We took in foster kids, Mary and Jack, who were 8 and 10 when they arrived. Their brother David went to church in Traverse City and told Pastor Moldstad that they had to leave their home in West Virginia because their mother was disabled and their father was molesting them. We asked to have Jack removed from our home because all he could think about was sex and would crawl in bed with Mary Sue at night. We needed to protect you girls.

How did it come about that the family had such an open heart of hospitality and we would open up our home to whomever?

I think the Lord must have put that in my heart. We always had people in our home growing up. We had a big family and another mouth to feed was no big deal. We never had a resident pastor down in the country when I was growing up. Our parish shared a pastor with Boyne City and Petoskey so, when he would come to Wilson Township for an evening service, we would always keep him in our home for the night.

My spiritual journey was a day-by-day living out the Gospel by offering hospitality and nurturing our family. Even now, after Father has been gone and I'm getting older, we've hosted many dinners and housed many people in ministry. Hank Paulson, with Eastern European Bible Missions, was way too tall for the bed so I put the twin bed crossways at the end of the queen bed to make room for his feet. He said I was the first person who had ever thought to do that for him.

> **My spiritual journey was a day-by-day living out the Gospel by offering hospitality and nurturing our family.**

We've hosted Ken Ham from Answers in Genesis, General Able with Campus Crusade Military Ministry, Kent Hunter the Church Doctor, Ed and Candy Holtz with Campus Crusade in Europe, Chaplain Cooper and Chaplain East of Sky Valley Ministries, and many friends and family. We've supported Ruth and her friends with Campus Crusade for Christ, along with William Lim from Singapore. He traveled with Mark, Jim, Ben, and Tom in China. I met William with Ben on our trip to Hong Kong, and he brought his family to visit and stay with us. William is my Chinese son and Alice Lam is my Chinese daughter. I'm "Mama Ruth" to her friends Vic and Lorna, who would visit when they all lived in California, and I still treasure them as friends. They came to my 95th birthday party for our Octoberfest at the barn.

I especially love having my children and their children stop in. Many grandkids visited me in California while going to college, like Josh and Jake and Jeremy when they were at Arizona State University and Emily and Katie going to college in Orange County. Elizabeth would often come out for spring break. Ruth would bring her friends while she worked with Campus Crusade in San Bernardino and also while going to college in Irvine. I've met many wonderful people through my children!

How did I choose my career?

My main career was marrying Ernie, raising a family, and offering hospitality. Before that, I had taken shorthand and typing and worked in several offices in Boyne City. I worked in the Federal Land Office and the NYA (National Youth Association.) Then I went to Grand Rapids and worked in the Michigan Trust Company with my sister Bessie. Mary and Ted went to California and asked me to go along to help with the kids. John remembers that as a very special time in his life, according to his book. The Lord used my time in California to bring Ernie and I together. Building a family with him was my career.

What would I like my grandkids to know about their Grandpa Ernie?

Your grandpa read the Bible every day. He was very interested in everything it had to say. He especially liked Ezekiel, Daniel, and Revelation. He loved the prophecies. I learned a lot about the Bible through 35 years of being married to him. He liked to visit the grandkids and loved to tell them what he was learning in the Bible. He was always interested in what his boys were doing in their business and taught them a lot too.

What can the grandkids learn from their Grandpa Ernie?

To always have devotions with their families. One thing I wish we would have done is to pray with the kids before they left for school in the morning. I would like to encourage my grandkids to do that with their children. I know the men are rushed to leave for work but having devotions every day with your children is very important.

Other important principles we employed in raising our kids?

Teaching them to work! Family chores—around the house and in the yard and garden. They had to learn how to work from the time they are little and while they are growing up. Our kids had to split and carry wood. Ben had a cow and he had to get up early every day and milk that cow before he went to school. He didn't want to smell like a cow barn, so he had to get up real early, milk the cow, shower and put on clean clothes before he went to school. The girls did dishes and helped cook and clean the house. We didn't have a dishwasher and we had a big family, so we had to wash lots of dishes. Father found work for the other boys at the mill. They all had chores to do. Everybody had to learn how to work. We did a lot of gardening and canning and washing windows. Father trained the boys, and I trained the girls. With my 95-year-old brain there are a lot of details I don't remember because there are too many things stored up there.

How does my home reflect who I am?

Many people who have come into my home say how peaceful it is. It may not have been that way when we were raising kids, but now in my old age it is peaceful. It looks comfortable and inviting. I like to keep it clean with dishes done after every meal. People can stop by any time and it's ready for company. When the kids were young, it wasn't picked up all the time, but on Saturdays all the toys had to be picked up and floors mopped and carpets vacuumed. I had to have a clean home. That was important to me. Clean clothes. Clean bedding. I like cleanliness. I always have and probably always will as long as I live. I like a lot of pictures of family around me, and also religious pictures. That's very important to me too. I like soft comfortable chairs. You don't see rocking chairs in many homes anymore, but I like rocking chairs and recliners. I like soft colors, blues and mauve and pink. Not dark brown or maroon.

What do I enjoy about my grandchildren?

I'm very proud of my grandkids. They do good work in their jobs, and I'm very proud of them. They are wonderful Christian people. I'm proud of the way my children and their spouses are bringing up their own children as Christians and their grandkids. I'm very proud of all of them. Many of the kids hold responsible jobs and are very conscientious. They do a wonderful job.

Other words of advice?

Make sure they follow the way the Lord tells us to live. There are many important things to learn in Proverbs. Follow the Ten Commandments, which show us how to live our lives.

What would I change if I had it to do over again?

I can't think of a thing. After 95 years of living, that's pretty great!!

Counsel for the wee ones?

Don't fight. Try to keep peace in the home. When you do something wrong, ask forgiveness. Forgive those who hurt or offend you.

How would I like to be remembered?

As a warm loving mother and grandmother!

> *What would I change if I had it to do over again?*
> *I can't think of a thing.*
> *After 95 years of living,*
> *that's pretty great!!*

Ernie & Cora Manthei
Tune: A Bicycle Built for Two
Written circa 1977

Mama, Mama, give me your answer do
My three babies need you and I do too
I promise you lots of children
While I farm and mill run
We'll drill for oil. We'll work and toil.
Come grow old with me. I love you.

Ernie, Ernie, you were so young and bold
You thought big and everything turned to gold
You brought me to your homestead
To cook and clean and make beds
Our kids are grown. But they've come home.
And with grandchildren swell our fold.

Herbie, Herbie, you were the black sheep one
Chasing girls and trading cars just for fun
When you said, "I'll quit school."
Your dad said, "What a fool!
Come back and float upon the boat.
Don't be a poyatz, son!"

Paul, Paul, asked Dad how he hatched.
Dad said, "Right past Georgie's tomato patch."
The navy ordered "Cast off!"
The black gang polished you off
Now since you reached your Georgia Peach
You've found your perfect match!

Judy, Judy, girl with the ready smile
Had a wedding we won't forget in a while
When Dave and Father scuffled
Your feathers sure were ruffled
But now you're grown. The coop have flown.
And we all admire your style.

Mark, Mark, the brummer in the crowd
Just so quiet, hardly talked out loud
You graduated then
Began to study Gwen
He's not so shy. He's quite a guy.
The construction world is wowed.

Jimmy, Jimmy, pretending he drove a tank
Steered a buggy over the condo bank
He rode it like a trooper
Without a single blooper
Till with a lurch he hit a birch
We won't live down that prank!

Benny, Benny, psychiatry was your thing
But that gravel now makes your shovel ring
A strawberry was a prize
That lit up Father's eyes
Then your fancy turned to Nancy
Now you sing lullabies.

Ruthie, Ruthie, long hair and long-legged
Heard the cry when those in darkness begged
Peru's her destination
She says "It's no vacation."
But P.T.L! All will be well
She's got her goals pegged.

Now dear Father, here is a gift from you
All those words with meanings so strange and true
Your grandchildren all now yammer
We hardly stand the clamor
They're crubbling now. That kotching—Wow!
And they endlessly peeper too.

Mama, Mama, how can we ever you pay
For your hairs that we all turned so gray?
You raised us all with such love
May God smile on you from above
His blessings give long as you live
For this we all daily pray

Thirty-Five Years

(Anniversary Poem written circa 1983
by Judy Manthei Schillinger)

Thirty-five years, where did they go?
I, for one, would sure like to know.

Father married Mom, that was the start
Three kids and Grandma, they were all part.

"Consider them a bonus," our dear Father said,
"and as for this house, I'll always be head."

For the following eight years
Our Mom gets all the cheers.

For added to Herb, Paul, and Judy
Were Mark, Jim, Ben and Ruthie.

As Father worked the mill and the boat
Mom kept kids and house afloat.

Last, but not least, one child still came.
She grew up in this house, Mary by name.

The years passed swiftly, as they will.
The children were growing, the house to fill.

Weddings took place, apron strings tore.
In-laws were added, more and more.

Those unions were blessed as years went by
Sixteen new births like stars in the sky.

The folks are retired now all these years
Busy as ever, holding no fear.

Through joys and trials this family still stands
Because we possess the Manthei bands.

Those thirty-five years, where did they go?
They were spent raising Christians, as surely you know!

PART FOUR

Our Families Remember . . .

Ted Manthei Family

David Theodore 1942-2013

John Mark 1943-2020

Daniel Robert 1945

Timothy Alvin 1947

Thomas Edward 1949-2020

Philip Harry 1953

Theodore Walter Edmund Manthei 1905-1993

Mary Augusta Behling 1912-2006

1941

Ted's Family Remembers

John: (Son #2)

Dad was a very passionate man. He felt very deeply. However, the resentment that he felt toward Ernie was not an accurate representation of what Ernie was doing. At the same time, the Lord was gracious enough to shepherd him through this. If you're going to write a book about him, make sure you put that in there. The Lord was kind enough to come to him and give him the manifestation that he needed in order to forgive, in order to come out at the right place. A few weeks later he died.

> **Dad was a very passionate man. However, the resentment that he felt toward Ernie was not an accurate representation of what Ernie was doing. The Lord was gracious enough to shepherd him through this and give him the manifestation that he needed in order to forgive Ernie before he died.**

Our emotions are very real and we feel them very deeply. But emotions are not always accurate. Emotions are very real to us at the time, but it may not be an accurate feeling. I think that was the case with Dad. Nobody's all bad or all good. He did have a relationship with the Lord.

Dad was always kind of a salvage guy. He liked to salvage something that was in trouble or messed up. But as far as running a conventional business with employees and encouraging and keeping them happy, he couldn't do that. He didn't mind stepping on somebody's face if he felt the need. Mom rolled with the punches. Mom saw the potential in dad, but she was the one that implemented his ideas. She brought them to fruition. Every visionary needs somebody who can make it happen. Ernie could implement his ideas too. If it hadn't been for him, the veneer mill never would have run, in my opinion.

Dad felt very strongly that he should be involved in missions. He took the money he made on his real estate venture there in Huntington Beach, and he didn't spend that money on himself. He gave it away. Most of it went to foreign missions. I don't know how much, but it was in the millions. He made a vow to God that if he made money, he wasn't going to change his pants any, meaning he wasn't going to strut around and be fine. He was still going to buy used shoes and stuff from Goodwill. He stuck with that. Bowman, the director of Far East Broadcasting, said that the Mantheis were the single biggest donor to Far East Broadcasting in their entire history. He also donated to Wycliffe Bible Translators.

Mom instigated much of what you see at Sky Valley and Caliente Springs. Dad was against building an RV park because there were too many people involved. He was good at finding a piece of real estate that was going to be valuable in the future. He could find it, buy it, hold onto it for a while, and then sell it to someone who was going to use it. But as far as being involved with people, he just couldn't do that. He never got along very good at church, but he felt very deeply that he should be involved in foreign missions because those people were on the other side of the world. They were far enough away to not be trouble. When you get personally involved, then it gets tricky. I'm not saying that was right or wrong. I'm saying that's the way it was. Dad talked to everyone, but he never listened. Mom cultivated relationships with people. She was the glue that held people together. She hosted the Behling family reunions and made sure we stayed connected to the relatives by visiting them and hosting their visits. She was the one involved in getting the Chapel program going at the Park, which became the hub of community-building activities. She started Grandma's Kitchen. She was the one that shepherded Tim through building the different phases of the Park and bailed him out when he got in trouble with people. She liked people and had the gift of hospitality.

Dan Manthei: (Son #3)

Father and his Beans

Father and Mother both came from low-income families and that affected their thinking the rest of their lives. Every bit of anything had value and was not to be overlooked. This worldview controlled their lives.

When Father was just starting in farming, he spent lots of time reading the Bible. One day, he tripped across Malachi 3 that refers to "robbing God of his rightful portion" when you withhold the tithe. He took that literally and thought it applied to him personally. He talked it over with his brother, Ernie, and he agreed. The two of them talked it over with the banker, the lawyer and their pastor. Those three all disagreed with Father and Ernie. I have learned that, where Father and Ernie agree, it doesn't hurt to pay attention. God had to be involved in the mix in order for them to agree. The folks chose to track with the Bible instead of their human counselors and take the Bible literally. Father would say they were just smart enough to know what the Bible said and not smart enough to know it couldn't be done. They made a vow to be faithful to give back to God his portion and went about their business of farming.

Father formed a partnership with Ernie and started working with Michigan State University professors, who taught them a lot about crop rotation, fertilizer, and pesticides.

Then came the crunch. One year, the crop rotation said to plant beans. The State of Michigan had a 13-million-bag surplus from the previous year and beans were selling for just $.95. That was below cost! After some not-so-civil discussions, just guessing about the tone, Father won, and they planted beans. They had a good crop, but it was a wet fall. All the beans had to be pulled by hand and tied on a pole so they wouldn't rot in the field. Have you ever tried to pull 10 acres of beans by hand? I would guess most of you reading this don't have any idea about the work involved in pulling beans, but take my word for it, it's back-breaking work. When you come across "personality disorders" in our parents, try to remember where they came from and give them a little grace. Father was a survivor and would do whatever it took to save his crop. There was no welfare or crop insurance. Survival was up to them.

The next spring, the 13-million-bag surplus disappeared. The wet fall prevented the big bean farmers from using their heavy machines to harvest their beans in the muddy fields, so their beans rotted. Can you imagine a crop failure over the entire state? I don't think it ever happened before or after that year. Because Father insisted on pulling the beans by hand, Father was one of only three farmers in the state with Certified Seed Beans. He sold his crop for $13-a-bag instead of $.95-a-bag. Did God have something to do with that or was Father just smarter than the rest?

Who was Father?

When I hear stories about Father, they range from A to Z. I'm sure the stories are true from the perspective of the storyteller, but to get a picture of who Father was and why he acted the way he did, I think it's important to try to understand Father's mindset, his world view.

To set the stage, let me tell a little story. This is totally from my perspective and others may have a different perspective, and that's OK. Let them tell their story.

Every year we traveled from California to Michigan by car. We had a Hudson Hornet. It's about the size of a Chevy Malibu. We would pack eight people and all the luggage for six months into that little car with a small trailer behind. After I became a parent with three kids and a wife, I discovered that a 32-foot motorhome with a TV, kitchen, and bathroom was on the small side. Well, all eight of us piled into the car and, for seven days, that was home. Mom brought our food along and she would make sandwiches as we were driving and pass them out to each of us, one at a time. Sometimes we got cottage cheese sandwiches. Two slices of bread with cottage cheese in the middle. Appetite is the best seasoning. Very filling. I never remember eating at a restaurant.

Phil was a 1-year-old and Pampers were not invented yet. There was a new invention—paper diapers. That added a little extra color to the atmosphere in an already tight situation. About four days out, things are getting a little edgy in the back seat. Everyone has their own personal space staked out as much as you can in a little car. "Don't touch me. You crossed my line…" and the war is engaged. It doesn't take long to spread and soon the back seat is in turmoil and about this time it spreads to the front seat. At first, it's verbal commands. "You kids better settle down or…" Then the long arm of the law shows up. This is a small car and Father can reach the whole back seat and, at this point, justice is blind because he is looking forward and he doesn't care who touched who first! He just wants peace and quiet. From the kids' perspective, we're all innocent, sensitive little boys just doing our best to be good. It's the other guy that started it, so why am I getting punished? These little dustups happened from time to time. Every few miles. Later in life, I was with Mom one day, watching a family with several little kids acting up like little kids do, and the parents were doing their best to bring a certain amount of order to the situation. I asked Mom, "Did we ever act like that when we were little?" Mom never answered.

One winter, Father bought a 1947 Cadillac limousine. A real upgrade. It was long and jet black and had two jump seats in the middle. We were traveling west, coming into Albuquerque NM and, as we came down that long canyon into town, the traffic got real slow, and there were more and more people on the sidewalk and Mom finally figured out that we were following a parade and we were the last float in the parade! Here we were with Father in the driver's seat of his limousine with his straw hat on—he always cut holes in his hat with a pair of scissors for better ventilation—with six kids in the back and towing a trailer. I think that's where the idea for the Beverly Hillbillies came from!

Father was a flawed human being like the rest of us, and his mission was to provide for his family. Feelings weren't always on the top of his list of considerations. At this point in his life, our feelings might not have even been anywhere on his radar. But we never went hungry or frozen. We had a warm clean dry place to sleep and clothes to wear. There were times we got cold, but that was our fault. Father was a good provider. All of us reached our full-weight potential.

Father was driven. He didn't have time to babysit us. He was mission-focused. Get up and get going. Carry your weight or be considered lazy. This was his personality. This was his experience growing up. I'm not defending him. I'm trying to explain how I understood him. Every personality has its strong points and its weak points. Father was not an exception to that.

Father had a strong personality—a definite Alpha male with a mission. Father's strong point was that he was ambitious and got things done. Father started the farming. Started the strawberries. Built two veneer mills, plus a third in Marquette that was sold immediately. Promoted an oil-well venture in Canada. Built a concrete plant in California. Bought and sold a number of properties for a fair profit. And raised six boys. As a family, we traveled to about 40 of the lower 48 states and supported lots of charity work.

He had a passion to spread the Gospel to the unsaved and he supported organizations like Far East Broadcasting and Wycliffe Bible Translators. Those organizations worked with people-groups that didn't have access to the written Word of God. He had a special passion for those people. He wanted everyone to hear about Jesus.

Father was very generous to charity and to his family. He worked with us through the 70s on estate-planning and successfully transferred his estate to his six kids so we paid no estate taxes when the folks died. According to estate-planners, it seldom happens that estates are passed without taxes. He gave us very little money, but he gave us lots of potential. He passed on a good name and a good work ethic. He had several pieces of property that he sold to us so he could provide an income for himself and Mom until they both passed. Father did all this about 15 years before he passed. We then developed the properties to launch ourselves into the businesses we have today. He got a lot of pleasure out of watching us build things and develop projects. I would hear him brag about all of us to visitors when they stopped in. I think Father finished well.

Father felt very responsible. As a kid, he got up at 4 a.m. to run a trap line so he could help his folks buy shoes for the family. He was quite ambitious and, I would say—driven—along with several other quirks that showed up along the way. When one starts putting all these personality traits under one roof, it's hard to know what direction the next move is going to be. One thing that's predictable: there will be lots of energy dedicated to the project and people's feelings will not be on the top of the list of considerations.

> **Father gave us very little money, but he gave us lots of potential. He passed on a good name and a good work ethic. I think Father finished well.**

One of Father's weak points was that he was mission-focused and people were down the ladder, if they were on the ladder at all. It's not that Father didn't care about people. It's just that feelings were not a priority. The mission was the priority and people were somewhere down the priority list. There's nothing wrong with being mission-focused but, to be most effective, it should be balanced with understanding people.

Father was not an easy person to work for or with. He was a very ambitious person. His mind never stopped for long. There was always some potential out there that needed to be taken advantage of and, if he didn't do it, someone else would. In business terms, he was pure Catalyst—A visionary. That worked great if he could talk someone into following-up and doing the day-to-day work to bring his vision to fruition. Father didn't always have the skill set to follow through and make his ideas successful. It took other people to run the business. This is all well and good, but one of the skills he was missing was the skill he needed most. That was how to find good people to put wheels on his ideas.

That's where Ernie came in. Ernie was much more mechanical than Father and he had a personality that worked well with people. That's something Father didn't seem to understand or appreciate. As a result, it caused a lot of trouble. I don't think Father and Ernie understood each other. They didn't have the books on "personality types" that we have today and, as a result, they interpreted everything the other person did through their own filter. Total disaster. Today we have all the books and counselors and still seem to have trouble getting along.

When Father started farming, that was a lot of hard work, and he was OK with that because he was a hard worker. But as he started getting older, the work kept getting harder and harder and the bed kept feeling better and better. I'm drawing on my own experience here. The older I get, the earlier that sun comes up every morning, so I can identify with Father. About 6 a.m. I would hear, "Danny, get the fire going!" We didn't have a furnace. Well, there was a furnace. But as long as I would cut the wood and build the fire, well, you get the idea. As Father aged, he mellowed a lot.

Who was Mom?

Mom was quite an ambitious lady. All her brothers called her the Iron Lady. She was very intelligent and a very fitting partner for Father. Mom was always very encouraging and supportive of us kids. At least that's the way I felt. Mom had faith in us.

Mom is the one that pushed us to build the little log cabin next to the lodge. At that time, I didn't know much about building. One day, a truck showed up at our place with a load of wood. It was a a pre-cut cabin kit. All the lumber was cut-to-length and like a jigsaw puzzle, you just had to find where each piece fit. I was in high school. Mom had a lot of confidence in us, but she also had a backup plan. She hired Earl because he had put these together before and had a good idea of how it worked. We unloaded the truck and spread the lumber out all over the yard. Now what? We had to lay out the foundation and it was all pre-cut, so it had to be right and it had to be square. It was 80 degrees and humid and the foundation needed to be 42" deep, hand-dug with a pick and shovel in hard clay. Most of you reading this won't know what a pick is. It's not something you use to clean your teeth. A pick is a tool that you swing like a sledgehammer, only it has two long sharp projections on it, and it's used to loosen dirt so it can be shoveled. The trench needed to be 42" deep to get below the frost line. This was before they invented backhoes. At least we had never used one and the thought never crossed our minds. We had a pick and shovel and some strong young boys that needed something to do to keep them out of trouble. Without Mom, it never would have happened. I'm not sure if she wanted a guest house or a job to keep her boys busy. We had a lot of energy and if left unguided, who knows what direction it would go. Either way, we learned a lot about building and it turned out to be a good move. A lot of things need to happen before a cabin can be built. It looks so easy, but someone needs to cut the trees and bring them to the mill. An architect creates a plan so the mill knows what to cut. A salesman makes arrangements with the buyer. There's a big back-story before the load of lumber magically shows up and, poof, there's a cabin.

Mom is the one that encouraged Tim to start Sky Valley Park. Without Mom, there probably would be no park. She gave Tim the seed money to get started.

Mom ran Grandma's Kitchen for a number of years. Mom and Aunt Louise would bake fifty apple pies and they would be sold by noon. Her cinnamon rolls were the best I ever had. They knew how to make things taste good and their food was always in demand. There were twelve kids in Mom's family, and they learned how to cook. Father insisted on running the cash register; only we didn't have a cash register. We only had a change drawer. It was funny watching Father trying to make change for a hamburger. He could make a million-dollar deal on a piece of property but had a difficult time making change for a hamburger. Mom kept all the books. She kept the banking straight.

One day, Mom gave Father $100 cash and sent him down to the local orange grove to buy some citrus. He spent the whole $100. Father had a big Imperial car and filled that whole car full of grapefruit; the back seat was level full up to the windows and the trunk would barely close. When he got home, Mom looked at his haul and said, "TED, WHAT DID YOU DO!?! I can't even trust you with $100!" Father knew he was in trouble and all he could say was. "That Mexican got me again!"

Mom started the chapel service in the park. She would invite a speaker from one of the mission organizations that she supported and found a song leader in the park, and we had a chapel service. The service outgrew the existing space, so we built Force Hall. Force hall is named after Rev. Force. He was an outstanding teacher and at one point we had up to 1000 people attending service on a Sunday.

> **One day, Mom gave Father $100 cash and sent him down to the local orange grove to buy some citrus. He spent the whole $100. Father had a big Imperial car and filled that whole car full of grapefruit; the back seat was level full up to the windows and the trunk would barely close. When he got home, Mom looked at his haul and said, "TED, WHAT DID YOU DO!?!**

Mother and Father left an impressive legacy. They raised six Alpha boys in one household. As I look back, knowing what I know now, that is no small accomplishment. I think Mom was thankful she had six boys and not six girls.

What is Hospitality?

I remember one night in Huntington Beach when all us kids were home, and the folks were out visiting. About 9 pm, the front door opened, and the folks came in with a very sick man. He was out of his mind. He was so sick he didn't know who he was or where he was, and he sure didn't care about either. The folks brought him in and put him in the spare bedroom. We learned that, while they were out, they had stopped by to see Mr. Thomas. He was an acquaintance of the folks and they thought they should see how he was doing. They found him passed out and very sick. He was a known drinker, and they didn't want to leave him by himself and didn't know what was wrong, so they brought him home and took care of him until they could get him to a doctor.

It was a different time and a different culture. You took care of your neighbor. You looked out for each other. We would be driving down the road and Father would say, "This is where so-and-so lives. Should we stop and see them?" Often times we did and often times people would stop in at our house. We thought it an honor to have someone stop by and visit and Mom would always have something to serve to make them feel welcome. If it was dinner time, they were invited to stay and share what we had.

I remember one time some missionaries stopped by about 9 pm. Mom fixed them a nice little dinner and offered them a bed, but they had to keep moving. Many times, Father would bring someone home from work and Mom would just set another place and share what we had. I remember just about everyone showing appreciation for the hospitality and for something to eat. I never heard a word about the floor not being swept. The only exception was when Ernie brought a bum home. Ernie liked his potatoes hard, and the bum was making a big show of how hard it was to mash his potatoes. Ernie didn't take well to the bum criticizing Cora's cooking, especially when she was following his instructions. The bum didn't have to be a genius to get the message that this is the way Ernie liked his potatoes and he was not interested in a cooking class by a bum. The bum proceeded to cut his potato with a knife.

I was talking to one of my nieces about this and she said she has a friend that, when they go there for dinner, before dinner is over, she has the vacuum out and is cleaning things up. My niece feels more comfortable at a different friend's house where not everything is perfect. The place looks lived in. When you fill someone's need, they normally overlook everything else.

We live now in a different culture. I'm very careful who I stop by and visit unannounced, unless I know the person well.

Hospitality is a great way for the host to focus on others instead of themselves. To give instead of receive. It can be a great help to bring a person out of depression, for the host even more than for the person being hosted. There is a satisfaction one feels when he gives.

Property Acquisitions

I'm going to tell this story from my memory, the way I experienced it from my point of view. Others will look at it differently, and that's OK. Let them tell their story. I'm starting in the early 50s and that's about 60 years ago and things can get a little fuzzy and even come up missing some details altogether.

Father loved property and, wherever he went, he saw the potential for what he could do with any given piece. This is where Mom comes in. She had to write the check. I don't think Father ever wrote a check and I don't think Mom was about to teach him, for good reason. Anyway, Father found a nice 20-acre piece in Huntington Beach, and we moved there to live on the property. Right next door was a 40-acre tract. This was during an oil boom in Southern California, kind of like the Gold Rush. California was the Wild West. There were all kinds of scams and swindles going on and the 40 acres next to Father's was one of them. It was put up for auction and Father bought it. It had lots of title problems, so it couldn't be used until the title was cleared. Father found a title lawyer, Ray Overacker, and a judge, Baker, who started working on the title.

It turns out that the lawyer had a granddaughter named Cheryl. They lived in Corona, about 20 miles from us, and we had a great time target-practicing and shooting rabbits at their place. There was one girl and a bunch of us guys. Everyone wanted to take a look, but it didn't take long to realize John was the Alpha dog in this hunt and the rest of us scattered before any serious collateral damage occurred. Cheryl was conservative Baptist, and we were conservative Lutherans and, when those two types meet, there is usually fresh blood spilled on the ground somewhere, and this was no exception. Cheryl and Father didn't hit it off, especially after Cheryl let it be known Lutherans didn't fit the qualification requirements for heaven; we might want to upgrade to Baptist to have a better chance at a more comfortable life in eternity and she would be happy to show us the way. Father and Mother had a problem with that. I'm sure Mom and Dad did a lot of soul-searching at this point to determine how to deal with this one. Remember, they had lots of boys and this was a new experience. I think they did the right thing. They didn't try to change John and Cheryl. They chose to accept them and pray. They didn't like it, but they thought it would save broken relationships and allow time for things to cool down. Then they would go and visit the grandchildren.

John and Cheryl got married and moved to Chico, California. The process had to be expedited. Nine months after marriage, Steve was born right on time and the folks went to visit. Steve was their first grandchild, and he came out of the chute full of personality.

On that trip, John introduced Father to Crenshaw, who introduced Father to Mr. Rose, who had three-and-a-half square miles of timber property for sale. Father loved both property and timber and when you put those two together, it's a marriage made in heaven. It was totally irresistible, and he bought it on the spot. He had convinced three other partners to invest with him, so he put money down. When it came time to close the deal, all three backed out and Father was left standing at the altar in his underwear by himself. Looking back, that was the best thing that could ever happen. I chalk that up to God's protection.

To buy that much property by himself was really stretching him, but he didn't want to lose his earnest money, so he talked it over with us and we all agreed to go ahead. There were times when we couldn't make the payment even though we all pitched in with what we had in our little piggy banks. Mr. Rose was a great guy and several times he let us put off making a payment.

Tim and I were in college during this time and, every fall, we would cut Christmas trees to help pay our tuition. We had a 1947 International pickup truck with a 4-speed stick shift on the floor. We drove all over the mountain picking up Christmas trees and bringing them in. We used a big truck and trailer to haul them to town and even down to Huntington Beach. That was a great time. We loved spending time in the woods doing something productive to accomplish a positive outcome.

That's when we met a guy we called Bigfoot. He got so used to us running around in his territory that, one day, he introduced himself. He wanted to know what we were doing with all his trees. He was curious because usually people cut the whole tree and don't just take the top.

We bought the property for $125 per acre and, twelve years later, it was still worth $125 per acre. By now we were becoming aware of taxes and estate planning. We talked it over with the whole family and decided it was a good time to divide the property between us six kids. Each of us got a half-section. After talking to an accountant, we all decided to donate 30% of our property to the Manthei Charitable Trust.

About this time, it became public information that Japan was buying huge amounts of timber from the west coast, causing a timber shortage and a huge spike in lumber prices. John and I visited several big lumber mills and decided it was time to sell the property. We discussed it with Tim and Frank and decided to ask a real estate lawyer, Marsha, if she could help us or recommend someone that could. Marsha was fantastic. She said she would love to do it and had the time to help. Marsha and I started putting an auction together. So much paperwork… so much detail—surveys, appraisal, timber cruise, advertising. In a couple months, we went to Chico and held an auction. Two of the biggest lumber companies in the US were bidding at our auction. The property sold for $2200 per acre. It went from $120 per acre to $2200 per acre in one year. That's an increase of 18 times, after twelve years of no increase. Was that our superior intelligence or did God have something to do with it?

The special circumstance was that Japan was buying up all the timber in the northwest which caused a timber shortage. This was in the Carter years with an interest-rate of 18 percent. Due to these economic things, the prices went wild. That was the only year it ever happened.

I met Tom Wolfert, the forester, about ten years later who said that was the top sale in Northern California of all time. A few years later, I ran across the buyers for Louisiana Pacific who were bidding on the property. They told me how much they appraised the property for, and their number was very close to mine which was $1000/acre. LP put the highest price they could on the property. It sold for twice either of our appraisals. This was a huge increase!

Is that just a coincidence? Or did God have something to do with that? The 30% that we donated to the Trust all went to charity.

God says in Proverbs that the heart of the king is in the hand of the Lord. He can turn hearts to benefit those who love and serve Him. God's hand was on our family, and He blessed the work of our hands and turned even bad things into good, because He trusted us to pass the blessing along to others. He did this with the beans, the berries, the veneer mill, the resorts, and all of our companies. We hope and pray that the next generations will continue to follow the examples of Ted and Ernie, giving God His portion to bless others… that His mercies may endure forever throughout all generations.

> **We hope and pray that the next generations will continue to follow the examples of Ted and Ernie, giving God His portion to bless others… that His mercies may endure forever throughout all generations.**

Wolf Creek Pass

This is a story I lived, along with my five brothers. I have heard it told numerous times by various people. Sometimes I recognize the story and sometimes I don't. I thought I would tell it from my perspective.

Our family traveled across country from MI to CA every year. This year we were in a 1951 Hudson Hornet. It was the stock car King of the Year, and we had a small trailer in tow. I would estimate it weighed about 1200 pounds. There were six of us boys and Mother and Father in the car. It was getting late in the season and that's why we were going south. I remember Mom reading the map and saying we would have to cross two mountain passes on the route. We were on one that was about 10,000 feet. When we left Pueblo, CO, the weather was nice so Father decided to try it. Something you should know about my dad. He was adventurous. Always looking for a new road to travel, and we had never been across this road before to my knowledge. We had a good car, and everything was going well so… "Let's give it a try!" Father also liked to make good time, as he would put it. I remember driving across Nevada one time, and I was sleeping in the back seat. I could feel the car slowing down and thought maybe something was wrong, so I ask what the problem was. He said, "No problem. I just had to slow down to pass a car." When we got to the mountain, the weather started looking a little dark but… "So what? We'll give it a try!" Father was not one to be intimidated by a little bad weather, so up the mountain we went.

Now this was pre-interstate. We were on a little two-lane road headed over the mountain. Everything was fine until it started to snow. This was the first snowstorm of the season, but we kept going until we could go no further. We dropped the trailer and headed back down the mountain. It took some time, but we finally found a tire store that had a set of chains. The chains were the wrong size but a little creative work and some haywire and we were on our way back up the mountain. Now we had lots of power and great traction in the snow and Father liked to move right along so we would get over the mountain before dark. Father was driving. Mom was on the right side with Philip on her lap and I was sitting in the middle. It was snowing and the wipers were having a hard time keeping the windshield clear. Father was always thinking about how to solve a problem and suggested that one of the kids should sit on the hood and keep the windshield clean. It didn't take Mom long to squelch that idea and Father knew better than to push it any further.

It was just about then that he lost control of the car. It was headed for the edge and over the cliff. As we got to the edge of the road, we hit something that redirected the car to the other side of the road and into a ditch. It was a miracle we didn't go over the cliff. Now we were stuck up on the mountain in a snowstorm. Father sent me down the road to wave down traffic so we wouldn't get hit. Remember, this is the early 1950's on a mountain in Western Colorado in a snowstorm, and it's getting late in the day. In a few minutes, a car comes by! Six big guys get out, see our problem, surround the car, pick it up and set it back on the road. The whole family was happy to be on the road again. They all piled into the car and took off as I was standing down the road in the snow watching them leave. One of the men saw me and managed to wave Father down so I could catch-up. I guess he didn't want to care for an orphan. We then retrieved our trailer and continued over the mountain without further incident.

Father and his Cow

Father grew up as a farmer. He never did well with animals except for cows, cats, and a stray dog once in a while.

Grandpa Behling gave Father a cow—a big Holstein cow.

After we moved into the lodge, Father had to have a cow. We had stopped to visit Dr Albright who told Father to eat raw butter for his ailment.

Now, we didn't have a place to keep a cow, so we got a good solid stake and a chain and staked her out in the field. Twice a day, someone would have to take her down to the lake so she could drink. That was usually my job and, two times a day, she had to be milked. That was Father's job, I thought. When Father determined that I was big enough to milk the cow, I became a convenient substitute. This was before we had a barn.

To milk the cow, we would take her some grain and tie the cow to a post and milk it. That kind-of worked most of the time unless it was raining. Then the water would drip down off the cow into the milk pail. But who cares? We had a good strainer at home.

Pretty soon, Father decided we needed a barn. That was great. It took care of the water dripping in the pail off the cow's back. That was a big improvement but, as usual, when you solve one issue you create two more. We had a nice dry place to milk the cow, with a trough to put the grain in and a place to tie the cow. But the flies just loved the manure and we had to haul the waste products out of the barn every day. To control the flies, we would spray the cow and the barn with DDT.

Now it's time to milk it. Cows come in all shapes and sizes. Some have big handles, and some have small ones. I think the proper word is teats. The front ones are normally bigger than the rear ones and much easier to milk. It seemed like every time, right in the middle of milking, the cow would need to relieve itself. Now, if you ever milked a cow, you know what I'm talking about, and if you haven't, well just use your imagination. Did you ever watch a dog stand on three legs and scratch his belly with his back foot? That's what the cow does and, unless you're really fast, guess where the foot ends up when you're milking it. By this time, the pail is at least half full and you don't want to come home with an empty pail. So, you try to get most of the color out so at least the milk looks white. Oh well. We have a good strainer at home!

Chickens

I was one of the last to get married and I traveled a lot, so I didn't have my own place. The folks had a big house in Michigan, and they needed lots of help keeping it up and having wood to keep the fire going so I would stay with them in the summer when I was in Michigan.

One day I came home and there was a big box in the den with about 100 little balls of yellow fluff running around in it. I said, "Mom, what's going on?" "Oh, we're going to raise some chickens." They never did anything small.

Little chickens double in size every day and, as those 100 little chickens started to grow up, in about two days the house smelled like a chicken coup. We needed an alternative plan in a hurry. But never fear! They had it all under control with heaters and lights feeders and whatever it takes to raise 100 chickens. They had done this before. We built a coop and secured it so the fox couldn't get in and we watched the little things grow. It sure was nice to get them out of the house. We put up a chain link fence around the yard so they could run and find all the bugs and worms any chicken could want. They loved it. We still had the cow, so they had all the sour milk they could eat, and they were growing really nice.

One day, I saw a fox looking through the fence with that hungry look in his eye. We had a good fence. No problem. They even locked Tyke, our dog, in the yard to prevent any stray vermin from dining on the chickens. After carefully plugging all holes in the fence, they locked the gate. Tyke didn't like being left behind. By the time the folks got back to the house, Tyke was there to greet them.

Every night, Mom would go and chase the chickens into the coop and put them on the roost. A chicken's intellect is close to the bottom rung of the ladder. If they stayed on the floor, there wasn't enough room and they would suffocate. Then Mom would close the coop so no other animals could get in. This worked great for about four weeks. As the chickens got bigger, Mom got a little lax about closing the coop. One morning, when they went to feed the chickens, there was about 30 chickens piled up in the corner of the coop. Not eaten. Just piled up. This had the folks stumped. What would do that? They performed an autopsy and found that the craw was missing in each chicken. The next night, the same thing happened. What could it possibly be? They went through the list of possibilities but nothing fit. As was Father's habit, he talked with everyone about it and someone said, "It sounds like an owl." Father set a trap on the tallest post in the yard, knowing the owl would land on that post to look things over. Sure enough, the next morning we had an owl. Problem solved.

Raising the chickens was only half of the story. Now they need to be butchered. Today, that's easy. You just call someone, and he brings out his equipment and it takes him about one minute and he hands you a bag with a dressed chicken in it. This was the old days. Mom got the cauldron out and boiled water. Father found a piece of hay wire about four feet long and put a hook on the end so he could catch a chicken by the foot. He had a block of wood about two feet long and a sharp double-bit axe. He would sit in the middle of the chicken yard and, when one came close, he would catch it by the foot and that chicken would become history. I'm sure you heard the saying "jumped around like a chicken with his head cut off." Well, this is where it comes from. Those chickens can really move after their head has been cut off.

Then it's time to gather them up and take them to the cauldron of hot water and strip the feathers off. I usually leave somewhere around this time because I hate to butcher things and the smell is, well, not pleasant. I like to see my meat cooked and ready to eat. Mom knew what she was doing, because this was some of the best chicken I have ever eaten!

Our parents were very resourceful, self-reliant people. They knew how to raise their own food and preserve it—a lost art in this generation.

Lumberjacks

Father loved the woods. We had a nice little forest behind the lodge and Father would spend lots of time inspecting his trees. Every year, he would go out and look at each tree to see how much it grew and when it should be harvested.

One day, Father decided it was time to harvest our timber. I could tell Father had experience in the woods by the way he gathered his tools and prepared them. The saws were sharp. The ax was sharp.

Father had every tree memorized and he knew which way he wanted it to fall and which way to run if something went wrong. It was important to have an escape route. We picked up the ax, the crosscut saw, the chain saw, the gas can, bar oils, a couple wedges and a sharpening file. We were ready to go. We felt like lumberjacks, carrying all our tools out to the woods to cut the first tree. When we determined where it would fall, we picked up the crosscut and proceeded to cut the tree down.

Normally, a tree would go right where it was supposed to go. But there's always the tree that doesn't follow the rules. It's leaning the wrong way or there are other trees in the way, or we make a miscalculation. Then the challenge is to recover. That's where falling wedges come in. We seldom had a problem we couldn't work through. Once in a while, we would hang one up. But not often. When it happened, we would leave it and, the next morning, it would be on the ground.

When I was with Father, I never used a chain saw to cut a tree down. He knew how to use a crosscut saw and that's what he was comfortable with so that's the way we did it. That was about 1962. Since then, I've cut down many trees with a chainsaw. So much better!

Collecting Copper

One of Father's passions was collecting copper. Wherever he saw a piece of copper, he would put it in his pocket and take it home. He was well-known among his friends for scavenging copper. He would build a small fire in the backyard and burn the insulation off his haul. Then he would find a container for packing his loot and hide it in the attic. He would collect several hundred pounds every year. When he was in Michigan, he would call dealers in California to compare the price of copper to see where he could make the most money. When he was in California, he would call Michigan to get their price. He would haul it to wherever the price was higher. He always tried to get me to haul his copper across the country so he could pick up an extra three cents per pound. Kathy had our motorhome loaded with all things we couldn't live without. One time, I stopped in Colorado to visit John's daughter Annie and Nels. He had a big scale to weigh trucks. Our motorhome was 1300 pounds over GVW-max allowable weight, without the copper. I offered Father to buy the copper myself if I didn't have to haul it!

When he couldn't carry it to the attic, Father started storing his copper in the garage but then he would worry about someone stealing it, so he would try to hide it under some other junk. Then he would forget where he put it and, sure enough, when he came back in the spring his worst fears would have come true. He was convinced someone stole his copper. I lived this story with Father every year. When Father passed, I started cleaning out the garage and attic and found copper, battery chargers, and tools of all kinds. Mostly junk. It took three years and lots of big fires to clean up the property, but it's a beautiful place and I'm so thankful that Father had the vision to buy it.

There are many more stories I could tell, and probably will, but that's not my point. Father was a very blessed man. He raised six boys, had numerous grandkids and a number of great-grandchildren. He started several successful businesses and provided well for his family and for his retirement. He didn't have to die after climbing the ladder of success only to find his ladder leaning against the wrong wall.

Father didn't need to collect scrap copper. Father had a mindset, a world view that was burned into his thinking. He saw the value in things and didn't want them going to waste. It was a worldview that made him very successful. He also had things in his worldview he couldn't overcome. We all have those weird little quirks in our personalities. Most of us don't admit that and make fun of others or downgrade them for their little quirks.

I am totally proud of my parents. I can't imagine how God could have designed them better. I see a lot of little quirks in their lives, but I see lots of weird things in lots of people. I try not to focus on those. When I started this story, I didn't expect to end up here and I think I should stop now and start another story.

Black and White

Father never passed the 8th grade in school. However, he was very intelligent, and I thought of him as a well-educated person. He read lots of books and newspapers and talked to lots of people from all walks of life. He didn't care what color you were or your ethnicity.

He could be very opinionated. He saw most things as either black or white. There was not much room for gray in his worldview. He was especially concerned when he thought someone was misquoting the Bible. Both Father and Ernie were very confrontational with anyone they thought was trying to spin the Bible to support their agenda, especially if they were in leadership positions in the church. I remember many discussions between Father and a college professor or church official where you didn't need hearing aids—or even to be in the same room—to catch the gist of the conversation.

One time Father was invited to talk to a class at Fort Wayne Seminary. He took a Bible and a hatchet to the class and, to make a point in his talk, he took the hatchet and cut the Bible in two. He wanted to show how church leaders were misusing the Bible.

Strawberries: Don't Try This at Home!

The strawberries were real. I saw them. I ate them. I talked with many people that experienced them. We have many pictures of them. I have heard many stories about how Father raised them. It was a story in our history that has no explanation that I can find except that a miracle was performed by God. I will try to explain to the best of my ability how the story unfolded and why I came to the conclusion that I presently hold.

> **The strawberries were real. I saw them. I ate them. I talked with many people that experienced them. We have many pictures of them. I have heard many stories about how Father raised them. It was a story in our history that has no explanation that I can find except that a miracle was performed by God.**

Father was a farmer. He worked with Michigan State University all through this project and their comment was that Father didn't do anything different than what they'd already tried. I have a degree in Agriculture, and I worked for ten years alongside Father, trying to reproduce the berries that Father and Ernie had produced, and we lost ground every year until we finally gave up.

It all started when Father would walk through the neighbor's field on his way to work. He couldn't resist sampling his strawberries. They tasted so good. He finally bought a few plants from him and started his own nursery while working with Michigan State. He was warned that this strawberry had never successfully been grown commercially, but Father always said that they were just dumb enough not to know it couldn't be done. Father didn't always listen well to the experts and sometimes it paid off. This was one of those times.

Father and Ernie grew a big nursery, and with the help of Michigan State, they developed a water system that would irrigate the whole farm. They had one pump down by the lake with a 6-cylinder Chevy motor. They had another one on wheels that they could move around, powered by an 8-cylinder flathead Ford. Michigan State made a special sprinkler nozzle that would cover an acre at each setting. During harvest, they irrigated all night and picked all day. They bought a new Dodge truck and modified it with special springs to give the berries a soft ride. Late every day, Father would head for Detroit so he could be at the fruit market early the next morning to sell his berries and return home for the next load. He would get a little sleep and head for Detroit again. This lasted about 2 weeks. Meanwhile, Ernie would supervise the pickers and irrigate the berries.

When the huge harvest was over in 1948, they needed to start getting ready for the next year. They decided to make their own containers and, as a result, they started the veneer mill. They never cut veneer for their containers, but the mill took off and, as a result, they stopped farming and paid attention to the mill.

In the 1960's, Father and I decided to try to revive the strawberries. We took our plants and started working with them to see if we could bring them back to their glory days. Father searched his memory for everything he had done to grow these berries and we tried to retrace his steps. He remembered that, in the '30s, thirteen years before his success with the berries, he had dug some mud (marl) out of the lake to sell to the farmers. Michigan State professors said it was great stuff. So, he got a drag line and dug a big pile of mud up on his land and tried to sell it to the farmers. He sold $3 worth. He had this big pile of mud on his field, and he couldn't farm it and he couldn't sell it so what to do? He decided to spread it on his own field and went back to farming his oats and beans. Eventually, he found Edgerton's strawberries and decided to try growing them. By this time, he was into crop rotation, and he grew sweet clover as a cover crop and planted strawberries, and they were very successful in the '40s.

Now it was the '60s. My brothers and I got 5-gallon pails and hauled mud up to the garden. It was hard work! So, we bought an old manure spreader, found a 30-gallon barrel, welded some handles onto it and used our tractor to pull it with our own makeshift drag line. It was crude but it sure beat 5-gallon pails. We hauled tons of mud up to the garden and planted cover crops. The sweet clover grew six feet tall. It was taller than the tractor and I had an awful time trying to work it down so we could plant strawberries. Father and I thought we really had something! We felt good about it. We planted the strawberries just like Father did before. We planted a double row. Each plant got two "runners." We set the runners with a stone to start the new plant. We picked all the blossoms off the first year so the plant could put all its strength into the plant and not into fruit. We covered the berries with straw so they wouldn't freeze. We would pet each plant and name it, so it felt good about itself, and we waited until spring. Despite our efforts, every year the plants went downhill a little more until Father and I gave up. Mom carried on for several more years and finally gave up also. We tried everything Father could think of, but nothing worked.

I finally came to the conclusion that God put His blessing on our folks just because He wanted to bless them, and it had little or nothing to do with how good of farmers they were. The berries were for a time and then it was time to move on. All during this time, Father and Ernie remembered their vow and were faithful to keep it. The Bible says if you are faithful in little things, He can bless you with bigger things (Luke 16:10). The folks were faithful and now it was time to move on to the next chapter. The veneer mill.

> **I finally came to the conclusion that God put His blessing on our folks just because He wanted to bless them for their faithfulness, and it had little or nothing to do with how good of farmers they were.**

God is good. He knows what's best.

PS: About ten years ago, 2012, I came across a person that worked picking berries for Father and he saved some plants and offered to give me some. I planted them and took care of them for several years, but I couldn't revive them and finally gave up again.

Tim: (Son #4)

The Traffic Circle

In 1956, the Russians invaded Hungary, which sent a lot of people to refugee camps. So, in 1957, when I was 10 years old, my dad and mom sponsored two Hungarian refugee families to come to Huntington Beach, California. Father gave them a place to live, and he also gave them different jobs and was teaching 'em how to work. It seemed to me as a ten-year-old kid that these Hungarian men, Nick and Leslie Spurber, didn't really have a good concept of how to work. We, as kids, were all acquainted with work. By that time, I was already working in the sawmill.

Around that time, Father bought up the inventory of a lumber yard in Paramount, California. The lumber yard had gone out of business, so he bought all the windows and doors, the moldings and whatever lumber was there. We would go up with the pickup or small truck and get truckloads of this stuff and bring it down to our lumber yard in Huntington Beach.

One of the vehicles that we used was this little 1951 Dodge Pickup. It was my two older brothers' pride and joy. It was black and they had fixed it up really nice and we used it to haul lumber down from Paramount.

One day, Father collected Leslie and Nick and me and the four of us got in the little narrow cab of this 1951 Dodge Pickup and headed towards Paramount. On the way, there was this traffic circle that we had to go around in Long Beach. As we were going around the traffic circle, it was really tight in the cab with two big Hungarians and little 10-year-old me and Father. So, we're going around the traffic circle at the same time that a cement truck is going around the traffic circle. The cement truck was a tractor pulling two big trailers of dry cement. As we're going around, Father starts changing lanes and he drives right underneath the trailer. The rear dual wheels went up onto our bumper, pushing the back end of the truck down onto the pavement and pivoting us around so our nose was in the air.

Before we knew it, we were pointing towards the middle of the traffic circle while being dragged, bouncing and skidding sideways around the traffic circle. It was quite the ride! Finally, we got stopped and the cement truck driver got stopped and there we all are, he and us, standing in the middle of the traffic circle and Father is angry!

During the bumping, as we were skidding sideways around the circle, one of the lenses of Father's sunglasses got knocked out. He looks like a pirate with one sunglass lens in and one glass out. He didn't bother to take the glasses off as he starts to reprimand the truck driver. He's telling the truck driver that he needs to get more sleep, he should watch where he's going, and he really needs to drive better.

It was interesting to me because, as the 10-year-old looking at the situation with the two Hungarians, I'm thinking it was our fault. Father was saying, "No, no," it wasn't his fault. It was the truck driver's fault because he didn't get enough sleep. He looked a little sleepy. Anyway, the lesson Father was modeling is to make sure you never give up your ground. You always want to make sure that you point out the other guy's fault and never admit your own. It's the opposite of what Jesus teaches. It was the wrong lesson to teach, but it's the one that a flawed parent taught a young boy.

After a few minutes of pointing out to the truck driver where he was at fault, we got back into our pickup. It still ran. It just ran crooked. The cement truck driver got back in his truck, and we all went on with the rest of our day.

We went up to the lumber yard and picked up the lumber and, when we got home, it was a shock to Dave and John to see their pickup driving very, very crooked. But we had accomplished our goal. We got the lumber, and we got back to Huntington Beach safe and sound—schooled in how to deal with a fender-bender traffic accident.

A Lesson About CATS, ORGS and OPS

There are many ways to look at people. One way that I have found helpful to understand people and utilize employees is to think in three categories: Catalyzers (CATS), Organizers (ORGS) and Operators (OPS).

Each type works very differently. If you can appreciate the difference and not criticize your partner for being different, you can accomplish great things.

1) CATS—They are visionaries. They have ideas, see new things, and start new things (or persuade others to do it!) There are very few in the world, but the world wouldn't change much without them. Many times, they would not be successful with their vision without an ORG to put the pieces of their vision together and make it into an organization. Ted was a CAT.

2) ORGS—There are more ORGS in the world than CATS. ORGS have the ability to understand the vision and make it work. If done right, the ORG turns the vision into reality…an enterprise. Ernie was an ORG.

3) OPS—Most people in the world are OPS. OPS get up every morning and make sure the job gets done. OPS keep refining and making the operation run better, faster, and smoother. OPS are steady. They keep track of how things work. The Behling brothers were OPS.

Some people are pure CAT, ORG or OP. Other people are a combination of the three attributes.

Ted was pure CAT. He had the vision to start:

- Two veneer mills in Michigan
- One oil well in Canada
- One ready-mix concrete plant in California
- Several real estate investments in California
- One mile of lake frontage in Michigan for a family legacy.

Ernie, the ORG, turned several of Ted's visions into successful realities.

Ted and Ernie married into the Behling family of OPS, who worked for the brothers and faithfully made their enterprises run day to day.

Together they made a team! Sadly, they didn't understand and truly appreciated the importance of the other team members, which made for unnecessary friction and criticism. It limited how far they could go in their businesses. It was very hard for them to see their own weaknesses and value the other's strengths. It takes wisdom, effort, humility, and an attitude of courage and forgiveness to be grateful for, and hold in high esteem, family and business partners who are different than ourselves.

> **It takes wisdom, effort, humility, and an attitude of courage and forgiveness to be grateful for, and hold in high esteem, family and business partners who are different than ourselves.**

Grandchild Reflections on Ted and Mary

#1 Son John's Children

Becky Manthei Joy (Wife of John's #1 deceased son Stephen)

As the widow of Ted and Mary Manthei's oldest grandson, Stephen Ray Manthei (Steve) and mother of eight of their great-grandchildren, I'm writing to share the stories that Stephen shared with me and my children before Steve's passing, as well as my experiences with Grandpa and Grandma Manthei.

Steve was so proud of his grandparents and so thankful for their example of their love for the Lord and their support of missions. One of the organizations Ted and Mary supported that Steve was so impressed with was *Far East Broadcasting Radio*. I believe Steve said that Ted and Mary were some of their most generous supporters. And yet, they never boasted about that. Ted and Mary were humble about their giving, purely wanting to see the Gospel spread throughout the nations. Steve would tell me how other supporters would come to Ted and Mary's and would discuss life and missions. Ted and Mary were generous and humble, but also wise and discerning with their donations. In true practical German fashion, there was no wasted pennies in their household.

Grandpa Ted loved to tell stories and I think that is why Steve loved him so much. Steve grew to be a storyteller much like Ted, often repeating the stories his grandfather had told him to his own children. A favorite Grandpa Ted tale was the time he and Ernie were catching skunks and got too comfortable since the skunks were coming out headfirst. The last one was a clever one and came out rear-first! I'm not sure what the moral of that story was, but it was a favorite!

But while Grandpa Ted stories were oft about skunks and popping the car in neutral to coast down a hill, Grandma Mary's stories featured a woman of strength, capability, and calm.

My late husband, Steve, was Ted and Mary's oldest grandchild, a fact he both bragged about and cherished. He loved to tell stories about how calm Grandma Mary always was, even while raising six boys or just sitting in the car with Ted. Her meals were legendary: simple, wholesome, filling, served with love, and not a spec of waste.

In 1940, Ted and Mary honeymooned in Mexico City—no doubt looking for the next great idea south of the border! Grandpa Ted was never afraid to try new things. In business, real estate, travel, or missions—Ted was always looking for new opportunities, and Mary remained steadily beside him.

> **Steve was so proud of his grandparents and so thankful for their example of their love for the Lord and their support of missions. Ted and Mary were generous supporters but never boasted about that. They were generous and humble, but also wise and discerning with their donations. In true practical German fashion, there were no wasted pennies in their household.**

I first met Ted and Mary in April of 1989 when Steve took me to the park in Desert Hot Springs to meet his beloved grandparents in person—not just in stories. Ted and Mary greeted us with open arms. She made buttermilk pancakes for us in her usual, quiet, efficient way, and later asked me to stay at the park for a few months to help her. It was during that time that I got to know Ted and Mary for myself. They were always kind to me and to each other, and I loved listening to their recited prayers before each meal.

I was able to observe, first-hand, mission organization reps visiting and Ted talking with them about how he could support their ministry of spreading the Gospel. When we rode in the car, I personally observed Grandma Mary's calm disposition, even when Grandpa Ted was not in neutral, even if the car was. The stories that their eldest grandson had handed down were indeed true.

I asked my kids (eight of Ted and Mary's great grandchildren) what their memory is of their great-grandparents. While none of my children remember Ted, all the ones old enough to remember Mary replied that they remembered her endless kindness. One child remarked that Mary had sent her the entirety of her bill for a mission's trip; a gift that child will never forget.

In our household, Grandma Mary was fondly dubbed "Purple Grandma" because of an early memory of her wearing a purple dress. She never seemed to mind my kids visiting—cheerful, noisy, and plentiful as they were. At one point Grandma Mary even took a trip to Northern California where we lived and visited us, creating a cherished memory. My last memory of Mary is marked by a picture at a wedding, where Mary presided with the calm, kind demeanor befitting a matriarch.

Linnea Manthei Horst (John's #2)

What a pair they made! I rarely saw them outside of their peaceful lodge home nestled on the Michigan shores of Walloon Lake. They seemed to just be a part of the place! But then, they looked to have another side too! They had a Southern California side with a second home and people constantly stopping to talk to them. I was always fascinated by these grandparents of mine, who didn't even try to keep up with the proverbial Joneses or care a flip about what people thought of them. Dad's parents were not in any way "normal" compared to everyone else's grandparents. They were independently unique and wonderful and one-of-a-kind and down-to-earth people, but completely out of the realm of standard grandparents.

Never once did I hear Mary Manthei talk baby talk to a darling bouncy grandbaby. Never once do I remember Ted Manthei pushing me on the swing. But each taught me how to strap a small bucket on a leather belt around my waist to hold the red raspberries I helped them pick from the garden. Describing them in full would take an entire book. I am utterly thankful for the influence that they had on me!!

> **Dad's parents were not in any way "normal" compared to everyone else's grandparents. They were independently unique and wonderful and one-of-a-kind and down-to-earth people, but completely out of the realm of standard grandparents.**

I suppose it is a common thing to want to take one's grandchildren to Disneyland. And so, they got it in their heads that they would treat my older brother Stephen, my younger sister Annie, and me to an adventure. The three of us kids loaded up in their big roomy car, and with Grandpa driving and Grandma sitting in the front passenger seat, we sped fast up the hills and coasted down them in neutral until the car would almost come to a complete stop, saving a little gas in the process. Not many words were spoken along the way, but finally we saw the theme park! We parked in a vast parking lot and then all morning we enjoyed the mind-boggling rides and ran hither and thither to "see it all!" But as time wore on and lunch time arrived, we started getting hungry. All kinds of food booths were there, but Grandpa vehemently opposed buying anything, as it all was just too expensive. So finally, Grandma helped us each get a sample ice cream cone and we sat together on a bench licking up the tiny treat. We spent the rest of that hot-hot day hungrily lugging our feet around and hoping for some refreshment. When everyone had had enough of the grueling day, we headed back to the car where Grandma's promised bananas were. We smelled them before we saw them. They were still on the dashboard and they were black, dripping, melted, and hot. And Grandpa surprisingly said, "Momma, will you peel one of those for me?" We couldn't conceive of the fact that we should be thankful for this limp aromatic food too, but I distinctly remember hearing about the delicacies of "browned bananas!!" Supposedly, people all over the world held them up high as "deliciously nutritious!!" You know, I don't remember the rides that day at Disneyland nearly as much as I remember those browned bananas!! I have never forgotten it but have giggled about it ever since whenever the story comes to mind!!

Speaking of the California theme parks, I would be remiss if I did not retell what Dad (John) told me on our last trip together. It was near the beginning of 2020, and Dad wanted to attend Uncle Tom's funeral. So, he asked me to go on a road trip with him from Fort Collins, Colorado to Desert Hot Springs, California. Along the way, his mind stretched back to his boyhood days, and he reminisced about Herb and Dan and Dave and all with story after story. He told lots of work stories but not a lot of play. I asked him what memory did he have of pleasurable times? He answered with the story of the whole family going to Knott's Berry Farm after church on Sunday for a big chicken dinner served family-style. Dad spoke of mounds of mashed potatoes whipped up with real butter and cream. Beside it would be Mrs. Knott's special fried chicken recipe that started with a half a chicken that would be rolled in seasoned breading and then was pan fried to a golden crispy hue before it was put into a baking dish and covered with cream. As it baked in the oven, a tantalizing gravy would form that was then spooned over those potatoes. A colorful tangy cranberry/berry sauce was always served with this meal too. And if there was any room left, a piece of berry pie would follow. Dad said that the meal was such a hit with the family, that Mary went home and tried to duplicate the meal. She learned how to create that same chicken, only better, and dad was so proud of her plucky culinary skills. Dad spoke of his mom making that meal for his birthday several times over and he felt so loved!!

I have one more story that dogged me pretty much the whole of my life. Both Ted and Mary (dad's side) and Gladys Greer (my mom's mom) had spent much time studying the evils of communism and even preparing for the terrible day of a potential takeover. They had gone to wilderness camps in the mountains where they learned special skills of warfare and how to prep by creating barrels of provisions. I was probably five or six years old when dad brought home what seemed like hundreds of these military green metal cans that we had to help stack in an area under the house. They filled a big space and were there only for "hard times." Every once in a while, just for kicks, mom would decide to open a can (none of them were labeled for the contents) and we would find honey or wheat berries with a box of bullets in the center, or possibly even powdered milk inside.

In the summer of 1980, our family moved from California to Greenville, South Carolina. And wouldn't you know, those green cans moved with us!!! We found a suitable place to store them in Greenville and forgot about them for a short time. But the pull to move to the farm in Georgia in 1982 resurrected the memory of them, and once again I took part in moving those heavy green cans. In 2014, when mom and dad's house burned down, it was a complete loss. Nothing was saved. But I remember going to the edge of the acrid hole and looking down to see parts of some familiar army green cans that did not fully burn up! It was said that for several days after the fire, bullets were still exploding in the smoldering ashes!!!! I will never forget visiting dad in the little house he ended up buying in Rock Hill, South Carolina after that. He had given me the tour of the house and we had poked around in the little barn out back when he said, "I could have brought the remains of the only physical thing that didn't completely burn in the fire, but I just didn't want to haul another one of those green cans anywhere!!"

Annie Manthei Nelson (John's #3)

My grandparents, Ted and Mary Manthei, were nothing like the stereotypical American grandparent. They didn't love to attend swim meets and soccer games or take us camping. When me and my siblings were small, they tolerated us fairly well as long as we didn't make too much noise, but we were not the main attraction. I will never forget the time when I was around nine that they came to our home in Northern California to explore the possibility of investing in some mountain property. I stayed home from school that day because I was still recovering from a bad bout of measles, and so I found myself in the back seat next to Grandma and Grandpa while dad drove into the Sierra Nevada mountains, past Whiskeytown and through Weaverville. When we finally stopped at our destination, the lake was very blue and the scenery beyond the scope of nine-year-old words. It was determined that this would be a very fine investment indeed, and the property was bought by the grownups, but a deeper transaction took place that day. I began to take pride in being a Manthei, in being a part of a family who took risks, who "cast their bread upon the waters" (Ecclesiastes 11:1), believing by faith that God would give the increase. That day my grandparents grew and took on an aura of grandeur in my childish mind. They became living legends who did big things, a cut above the ordinary.

> **I began to take pride in being a Manthei, in being a part of a family who took risks, who "cast their bread upon the waters" (Ecclesiastes 11:1), believing by faith that God would give the increase. That day my grandparents grew and took on an aura of grandeur in my childish mind. They became living legends who did big things, a cut above the ordinary.**

Grandpa Ted was a man of great vision. He cared nothing for social norms or fitting in or keeping up with the Joneses. In fact, he reminds me of the patriarch Jacob who envisioned the flocks and herds of Laban and set to work "makin' it happen." He was cunning and immensely shrewd, having a large portion of what the oldtimers called "mother wit," which, like Jacob, he always used to his advantage. He was not polished or smooth but rather uncouth in his person, yet he was esteemed a man of consequence by those who knew him. Grandpa loved books. The lodge in Michigan was full of bookshelves covered with the oddest assortment of books, from classical literature all the way to the latest health food fads, and even tomes on the freemasons. I came into Grandpa's den on a bright morning when I was in my early teens—without so much as a "good morning," he asked: "What do you think of British Israel?" It didn't bother him at all that I had never heard of this particular theory, and several hours later when I stumbled out, I knew a great deal. From him I gained a desire to know the mysteries hidden between the covers of a humble book.

Grandma was the perfect foil for grandpa's passionate nature. I rode to church with them one Sunday and on the way there, Grandpa ran into a deer with a loud "thwump". Grandma remarked placidly: "Well forevermore! I guess it's a good day for hitting deer." Grandma wore her calm nature with perfect serenity, and I never saw her give way to overwhelming passion of any sort. Some years after Grandpa died, I asked her if she missed him much or if she enjoyed her new-found freedom. I was honestly surprised when she answered "I miss him every single day. He was my best friend, you know." I hadn't known, because theirs was no fairy-tale romance with date nights at all the hippest places in town, no glamor of youth and beauty (he called her 'Mama' and she called him 'Ted'), but they had a robust partnership that spanned more than half-a-century pulling together in harness.

Grandma told me once that they welcomed every child that God sent (six sons nicely spaced) and never tried to hinder or refuse any blessing. I remember family worship—every night they read a chapter together and prayed aloud. Sundays always found them worshiping God at the Lutheran Church in Boyne City. I don't believe the question ever was asked in that household, "What will we do this Sunday?" Because, like the law of the Medes and Persians, it was settled already.

Grandma was the ultimate Proverbs 31 woman in many ways, but especially exemplified 31:11 *"the heart of her husband trusts in her, and he will have no lack of gain."* She was a genius at managing money, and she turned every dollar to good account. This was very good because Grandpa had determined (even told the Lord) that he would never change his lifestyle if he became rich. And he didn't. He prided himself on his Goodwill finds and even "shopped" for his shoes in the missionary barrel at church.

On the one hand, I admire my grandparents for their thrifty habits and frugal management. I know that they denied themselves many pleasures to further the kingdom of God both locally and overseas, yet I often felt beaten down with their disapproval. Although I am so thankful that Grandma taught me how to really scrape the batter out of a bowl without wasting that last tablespoon, and how to eat all the food on my plate because waste is a sin, I think their incredible focus on saving money was out of balance. It is through grace we are saved—the righteous works of Jesus Christ are credited to our account as a free gift. I know Grandpa and Grandma believed this wholeheartedly, and yet the relentless guilt that was heaped upon a wayward, wasteful grandchild (who poured a glass of water down the sink) gave a different message. But I believe Grandpa and Grandma both mellowed as they aged and became more gracious—yet their blind spot was carried on into the next generation and caused (at least) my parents much grief and suffering. But human failure never has the last word, and God is graciously at work in all his children to expose our sin and to conform us into the image of his Son. Just look at the record of the Patriarchs of the Old Testament.

Trips to Disneyland are all good and well in their place, but I wouldn't trade my very un-stereotypical grandparents for anything in the world. They taught me the fear of God as motivation for my actions and they gave me a glimpse of a transcendent world, a world of risk, of real living and real dying, a world full of real people who need Christ, instead of the tiny navel-gazing world of me, myself, and I. They were great in a very real sense, and good as the salt of the earth. I am so proud to belong to these two hardy pioneers who carved out spaces to put down roots—these two who strove mightily to make this world a better place with their faithful daily choices, and in doing so, rooted and grounded their children and grandchildren in the unchangeable soil of God's truth. They have gone to their eternal reward, and their works do follow them.

Ellen Manthei Berger: (John's #5)

If it's true what they say, that there are two types of Germans—those seeking meaning through order and those seeking it through metaphysical transcendence—then Grandpa Manthei was an infinity seeker from the beginning. Not that he was high and lofty in any regard, but he sought the invisible and lived his life on a shoestring of faith swinging far over every cliff. At least that's how I saw him. For a crusty and often unkempt man of the soil, he had a lot of soul shining past his rough edges.

I first met Grandpa and Grandma when I was about five years old. Our family rolled into Sky Valley Park around sunset on Christmas Eve. I'd never seen palm trees covered in tinsel and lights, and everything felt magical. Grandma gave me a beautiful doll, and Grandpa told outrageous, unbelievable stories that evening. My sisters and I were "John's Girls" to everyone we met, which felt like an important mantle of recognition in a family long on heritage. The next morning, I saw Grandma and Aunt Louise up to their elbows in cinnamon roll dough, and when I saw the line of guests waiting to buy breakfast and pies in the park kitchen, I felt my heart would burst with pride for the sturdy women of our heritage.

Michigan was a reverent word in our home—a word dad said when his voice got husky with memories, which was often. Since we lived in Northern California, I was 11 before I made it to Michigan. Once again, I had a magical feeling the first time I walked into the Lodge at the shores of Lake Walloon. Having grown up steeped in the legends of Ted and Ernie; hearing of hard work from dawn to dusk, twilight baths in the lake, strawberries so big they would perch on the rim of a quart jar, and an undying devotion to the faith of our fathers, I felt I was walking into a living history.

When I was 13, my brother Stephen and I hauled a load of watermelons to the farmer's market in Gaylord, and we spent three weeks at the lodge with Grandpa and Grandma. The first day there I excitedly told Grandpa that I wanted to learn to fish. He wasted no time in taking me to the apple tree in the garden to dig a bucket of worms, and then he gave me a cane pole and got me set up at the end of the dock with a fresh wriggling worm on the rusty old hook. With beginner's luck, I caught fish after fish. When I presented him with about 15 lake bream, he seemed pleased and said he'd show me how to clean them. I said: "No thanks, I'll just throw them back if I'm supposed to clean them." But that was not to be. He took me out back and cleaned the first fish on an old newspaper, deftly scaling and gutting it in seconds before returning to his recliner. I cleaned the rest of the fish, earning myself a great sense of pride and joy. A few days later, when I burned my eyeball with my curling iron and had to be taken to the emergency room, Grandpa laughed and said I should try curling my eyelashes with something less dangerous.

Grandpa was intractable, ruggedly right against all odds. Once in college my sisters and I were visiting and, on the way to church, Grandpa missed the turn. Grandma gently suggested that he'd missed the turn, but he loudly said he'd decided to go the other way. A few minutes later we hit a deer. Grandma again chided that maybe we should have taken our usual route, but Grandpa insisted that: "If we'd gone the other way, we would have hit a deer too! It's just a good day for hitting deer."

I remember hearing of legendary fights between Grandpa Manthei and my mom, back when my parents were first married, with Grandpa going so far as to pound on their cabin door and say that John needed less lovemaking so he could save his energy for work. That was the old-world way, as it was explained to me, the emphasis on work and the loud clashing of wills.

Looking back now, what I understood from my visits to the lodge was that life was about pushing yourself far beyond the narrow limitations of comfort. You needed to live way beyond the petty pursuits of the lower nature and be guided by a purpose, a mission, a passion for the world far larger than self. We exist to serve an Almighty God. And although my dad had strong theological differences with his parents as far as interpretations of Scripture, he embodied and taught us the identical practical truths. He did this by family devotions, his regular preaching at the homeless shelters, by teaching welding to youth just out of detention centers, and by his devotion to using more than the tithe to bring Christian radio to those who needed it. This focus that we individuals were small, and the world was large, but reachable, is a lesson I'm eternally grateful for. Uncle Dan once expressed this intangible Manthei philosophy as: "To do the impossible, you must see the invisible."

> **Looking back now, what I understood from my visits to the lodge was that life was about pushing yourself far beyond the narrow limitations of comfort. You needed to live way beyond the petty pursuits of the lower nature and be guided by a purpose, a mission, a passion for the world far larger than self. We exist to serve an Almighty God.**

It would be incorrect to gloss over the invaluable contribution that Grandma Mary made toward taming Ted from wily skunk trapper to a hoary-headed man whose voice would tremble when speaking of the sacred. Grandma was the picture of faithful constancy. Often, I have drawn strength in the long hours and years of motherhood from this woman who was short of stature but gigantic in character. She was ceaseless in her enterprise and had mastered the tranquil art of domesticity. Grandma was a gatherer—her table always ready to feed another mouth, her panty always stocked. From baking chocolate chip cookies with chicken fat to packing the trunk of the car with canned raspberries for the long trek to California, Grandma understood the richness of life through the shelves of her pantry, the ledger of her checkbook, and the cards she always remembered to send to her grandchildren. Few of us could keep up with her, but her example is ever in my heart, and the hearts of all her family.

Rachel Manthei Cornell (John's #6)

I grew up in a family whose roots were deeply grounded in the strength of God's Word. I want to write down some of my memories to remember all the goodness of the Lord in the land of the living. *"Only take heed to yourself, and diligently keep yourself, lest you forget the things your eyes have seen, and lest they depart from your heart all the days of your life. And teach them to your children and your grandchildren"* (Deuteronomy 4:9).

When we would pull out of town in Georgia for a family vacation in northern Michigan, we knew the word "family" was a powerful force of at least one hundred or so of our closest relatives who cared about us and would be glad we came. The annual gathering of Manthei, Behling, and Stenke families would gather at the lodge for a whole weekend of catching up and soaking in the familial sense of belonging in a broader picture of life. Grandpa Ted would play The Fox Went Out on a Windy Night on the piano while Ernie sang out the words for all to follow. The brothers demonstrated unity in spite of their diverse personalities! Hearty laughter was the hallmark of their banter! After music, lots of stories would commence about real experiences that were larger than life! I would sit in awe of these hearty souls who had such courage through life's vagaries! I bore the same name as these people, so I must have what it takes to bear up under life's thunder! A courageous spirit was born!

Grandpa always had big thoughts and visions, but occasionally he would see me playing pool. As I was intent on lining up my shot, he would help me out by exclaiming that I was going to miss the pocket (I think he could see poor shots in his sleep!) He was usually right and would then take the opportunity to explain angles and how to up my game. I was thankful for his experienced wisdom and that he took the time to teach me! I was a winner for being seen!

Grandma was a manager of managers! She had buckets handy to send young children into the garden to gather the raw materials for their dinner and always produced a huge meal enough to feed every hungry mouth in the vicinity! No one was turned away! Her apple raspberry crisp was legendary and her cinnamon rolls with raisins lured in many a famished grandchild from their play. She taught me how to freeze raspberries in square boxes. My last visit to her home on Dillon Road found her sitting in her chair being served her meal, yet she apologized to me that she was not able to cook and serve me dinner. Grandma Mary always gave what she had, and I will never forget her steady spirit of service! She wrote many a check to missionaries at her roll top desk and was able to manage their finances with generosity.

> **The legacy Ted and Mary left of keeping your hands busy in the soil, loving and forgiving your family, serving others with your bounty, and never wasting your resources are still a part of me that I will never forget!**

I think a parent gives a child the tools of managing everyday life, but a grandparent provides the frame around the picture. The legacy Ted and Mary left of keeping your hands busy in the soil, loving and forgiving your family, serving others with your bounty, and never wasting your resources are still a part of me that I will never forget!

Sarah Manthei Keister (John's #7)

Memories of Grandpa Ted and Grandma Mary

As I live my life in this world so different than the one Ted and Mary lived in, I often think of the example they set, and how they lived so purposefully. As the seventh child of their second son (John), Grandpa and Grandma seemed very old to me by the time I remember them, and yet they were so vibrant. They weren't vibrant as modern people are, with expensive hair and clothes, but with a strength and inner purpose. Grandpa and Grandma always knew what their purpose in life was, and how to achieve it. Serving God by using thrift to achieve generosity was their lodestar.

They worked hard, patiently, and near constantly. When Grandma got tired, she found sitting work to do, like snapping beans or shelling peas. Even though Grandpa was never a romantic man, he and Grandma were always so very united. They hoed the garden together, planned new business ventures, and discussed where best to give their money—always carefully making sure they got the most "ministry per dollar."

They worshiped together and had countless people in for delicious meals. Grandma made the most wonderful bean soup, biscuits, homemade bread, cookies, Swedish meatballs, and always fresh raspberries; but the one food all of us hated was the moldy cheese that grandpa always loved. He always had a bit sitting around, growing green around the edges. No fear of the grandchildren making off with that! One of the things served up with every meal at their house was ideas. Both of them had questing minds that wanted to learn and grow. Grandpa was more creative, Grandma more practical, and together they came up with many useful and encouraging ideas, which they then put into practice.

> **The legacy they left is large and beautiful. Their faith, their work ethic, and their prodigious hospitality, not to mention the epic gardening, will never be forgotten.**

Grandpa and Grandma were some of the original health nuts. We were all so astonished when, in our thirties, we discovered kombucha, thinking we had cleverly found a health food that the family had never heard of before—only to be told that Grandma made and drank it for many years!

The legacy they left is large and beautiful. Their faith, their work ethic, and their prodigious hospitality, not to mention the epic gardening, will never be forgotten.

Liz Manthei (John's #8)

Memories of Grandpa Ted and Grandma Mary Manthei

I am the 8th and youngest child of John and Cheryl Manthei. A highlight of every year was piling into the 18-passenger white van in the early morning, leaving hot and sultry Georgia heading to cool and vibrant Michigan to visit Grandpa and Grandma.

I remember as a youth being impressed with grandma's huge garden. Even as a small child I would be given a pail and told to fill the pail with berries before I came in. And when I fussed, I would be reminded that "those that don't work should not eat." I remember the simple but delicious food that grandma would feed the many people at her dinner table: cherry soup, turkey divan, bean soup, large vats of pickles and sauerkraut, and bowls of raspberries. The ½ gallon jars of whole canned chickens always impressed me as a girl, as well as the masses of fish that one of the uncles or Grandpa would catch from Walloon Lake and Grandma would fry up in cornmeal and bacon grease.

Then I fondly remember the hours of running through the great north woods as I explored with my sisters. Grandma was always quick to feed a crowd, but she never liked waste. Cleaning our plate was a high priority. Having lived through the great Depression, Grandpa and Grandma knew the value of food, and repeatedly told us that any food we wasted now, some day we would wish we had that food, and if we wanted to avert hunger and starvation in the future, we needed to value and respect and not waste food now.

Sundays we would head to the old and stately Lutheran Church, a very pleasant and hilly ½-hour drive away. Grandpa would ooze his old Lincoln up and down the hills, coasting on the downhills, and seeing how far up he could get before he had to use any gasoline again. I was surprised as a child that someone would take the extra time to try to save a penny, rather than just pushing forward at full speed to save a minute. But each penny saved was given to missions, to the Gospel around the world. Grandpa had a real heart to see the nations of the world evangelized. He liked to give to the furthermost parts of the earth to see the Lord's work done.

> **But each penny saved was given to missions, to further the Gospel around the world. Grandpa had a real heart to see the nations of the world evangelized. He liked to give to the furthermost parts of the earth to see the Lord's work done.**

As I get older, I am turning toward the best parts of how my grandparents lived, and truly love living off the land. I find myself telling my own 6-year-old son the same maxims I was told as a child, as I have found them to be life-sustaining for me.

Garret Manthei (Tim's #3)

Treats—Grandpa and Grandma had a gumball machine with jellybeans in it at their home in Sky Valley. As a 5-year-old, this was irresistible. Grandpa sat in his chair by the front slider door with a perfect vantage point of the machine and he would always give a clear reminder to "just take one" when you would approach the jellybeans. Though this reminder happened each time, it was probably necessary. The temptation was huge to take more than one! At the Lodge in Michigan, the treats up for grabs were cookies. There were at least two types, blonde cookies with cream in the middle or black cookies with cream in the middle. The trick was the same, you could only take one. Every trip to the lodge came with that choice: which cookie to take?

Dinner—Grandma (and Grandpa) would frequently invite us over for dinner. After dinner was finished, we would get to play with stuffed animals and Legos. Looking back now, I wish I had a more developed pallet to remember the food more than the Legos!

Breakfast—Every once in a while, Grandma would invite us over for breakfast. Grandma's pancakes were so much different than my mom's. I didn't understand why at the time, but looking back Grandma used so much oil they were basically deep fried! Again, if only I had had a more developed pallet.

Christmas Eve—Every Christmas Eve we would go to Grandma's for dinner. This would be followed by the Chapel candlelight service. Then we would head back to Grandma's house for dessert. Finally, we would open presents. This was a time when Grandma and her sisters would exchange gifts. A highlight of the evening was rubbing our feet on the carpet and getting the tinsel from the fake miniature Christmas tree to be attracted to our fingers via static electricity.

Cherry Soup—When we arrived in Michigan after a four-day drive across the county, Grandma would always welcome us with a hot pot of cherry soup. Without cell phones, I don't know how she timed it so well.

Ernie Manthei Family

- Herbert Ernst 1944
- Paul Joseph 1945
- Judith Constance 1947
- Mark Luther 1950
- James Andrew 1951
- Baby Boy 1952
- Benjamin Robert 1955
- Ruth Christine 1956
- Foster Child Mary Sue Keeter 1968 to 1978

Margaret Caroline Schillinger 1910-1947 — Ernst Ferdinand Manthei 1909-1985 — 1943

Ernst Ferdinand Manthei 1909-1985 — Cora Pauline Behling 1922-2020 — 1948

Ernie's Family Remembers

#1 Herb

Placing my memories and impressions of my father on paper is not an easy thing for me to do. First of all, they are many and complex, and secondly, I don't have the patience to write them all down. However, I will attempt an abbreviated edition that hopefully will capture the flavor of my feelings.

I remember Father as being somewhat of a typical German in that he was a strict disciplinarian, valued hard work, and was strong-willed and rigid in his convictions. But he also had a side that was fun-loving, mischievous, charitable, and most importantly, strong in Christian faith. He most definitely imparted many of these qualities to his children. Although we may not have always agreed with his techniques, the message got through.

Here is a sampling of a few "memories of Father." From an early age, Father steeped us in Lutheran doctrine, as well as a little "fatherly" doctrine and interpretation too. Even though I disliked evening devotions that, on occasion, could last an hour, I have often recalled ideas and thoughts presented in those sessions that have served me well in my efforts to teach Bible Class and serve as a church officer. I, too, have often recalled the hymns that we sang after devotions. Father knew well that the promise made in Proverbs 22:6, "Train up a child in the way he should go, and when he is old, he will not depart from it," would be kept, and God's blessing would rest on his efforts.

> **Father knew well that the promise made in Proverbs would be kept, and God's blessing would rest on his efforts:**
>
> **"Train up a child in the way he should go, and when he is old, he will not depart from it."**
> **Proverbs 22:6**

I suppose because I was the oldest, it was necessary for me to do some "trail blazing" and I definitely did leave some "blazing trails" on occasion.

Father considered dating to be necessary for one purpose only, finding a suitable wife. Other than that, the effort was expensive and time-consuming. As a result (and since I did not subscribe to that theory) I often found myself banished to the "Mackinac Islander" whenever I felt inclined to "chase girls." Many of my most memorable experiences from my youth are caught up in this period of our "marine efforts."

Since Father headed up the effort to log the islands, there were numerous times that we were together on the boat. When you throw into the equation our colorful captain, Dick Lyons, memorable events occurred on a daily basis. I recall a few of those now.

As you may well imagine, an "old salt" like Dick Lyons was inclined to use "salty" language at times. Father, as always, was interested in demonstrating a fine Christian example in word and deed. When rebuilding the Islander and installing the sanitary system pump, Father asked Dick, "Do you think this pump will handle Ah-Ah (crap)?" Dick replied, "Ernie, this shit pump will handle almost straight Ah-Ah!" The term became a long-standing joke amongst the crew.

Father also had a sweet tooth and loved ice cream and jam. However, he had a habit of eating out of the container, which drove Dick crazy! One day, Father opened a fresh jar of strawberry jam, dipped in his spoon and began eating from the jar. Dick could take it no longer. He grabbed the jar from Father and threw it overboard, amid Father's protests. The message got through. I never saw Father eat from a jar again.

The marine activity we engaged in was always challenging, and often dangerous. There were many injuries, but fortunately, no deaths. One of Father's bad experiences was a night in July during a fierce storm. We had left the bay on Garden Island with a full load of logs destined for Charlevoix. It was beginning to get dark and foggy, and the wind and rain were picking up as we cautiously probed our way through the rock-strewn channel to open water. The entire logging crew was on board and many of them were in the pilothouse, peering out into the gloom. Father was at the radar, trying to find a buoy and not having any luck doing so. Dick loved coffee and I thought he might appreciate a cup at that time. I poured a cup and carefully made my way up to the pilothouse. As I opened the door, the wind and rain blew in and Father, being totally frustrated, bellowed out, "There are too many shit-asses in this pilot house!" At that point, all the doors flew open and the "*#**#**#**s" bailed out in every direction! This too became a favorite story of the crew.

Later that night, the storm hit in full fury. Most of us had retired to the aft cabin when we weren't hanging over the rail, feeding the fish. Some of the logging crew had prepared hot dogs for supper that night. There were disgusting puddles of barf scattered all over the boat that night, with pieces of wieners floating in the middle of them. Dick said some of those wieners didn't have a tooth mark on them!

Father, true to form, was making his rounds and checking on the equipment. While checking the generator in the fantail, he slipped in one of those puddles as the ship rolled, and he broke several ribs. He spent the rest of the night lying in the "scuppers." However, he was strong and tough and pulled through the ordeal okay.

Eventually, I escaped from the boat long enough to do a little courting. One summer, while my fiancé and her mother from California were visiting us, Father decided that 9 p.m. was bedtime and announced the same to all of us. No one paid any attention to him and we merrily continued visiting, "pinching and kinching" (being silly). Undaunted, Father walked out to the main electrical entrance on the light pole, pulled the fuses (shutting down service to both houses) and went to bed (with the fuses.) We all quickly followed suit (minus fuses).

Eventually, I married Rain and we moved into an A-frame on Crooked Lake, about 17 miles from the farm home. Every morning for the first month, Father would call about 6 a.m. with the question, "Are you up?" I finally protested and asked him not to call me anymore. He didn't. He showed up at the door the following morning!

After the mill burned, Father announced his semi-retirement and turned the mill over to "the boys." We all pitched in to rebuild it, with Father immediately coming out of "retirement" to direct the show. Many heated discussions and arguments ensued until Father fell and developed an infection in his leg. I thought that this might end the meetings, but no! He summoned us to his hospital bed!! The heated discussions continued until the nurse threw us all out of the hospital.

Shortly after this, Father decided he wasn't appreciated at the mill anymore. He bought a dump truck and backhoe for something to do and lo, Manthei Development Corporation was born!

In later years, conflict developed between Father and Uncle Ted. While they often disagreed in business, they both agreed on the Bible, moral values, and prayer, and sometimes used these values to further their arguments. One evening at a meeting in Father's house, a rather heated argument ensued in which neither Ted nor Father would back down. Each one, wishing to have the last word, would not call it a night. Finally, Father offered a closing prayer. Ted, in proper dignity, bowed his head in quiet respect. Father immediately called upon God to recognize the fact that Ted was wrong, Father was right, and asked God to help his brother understand and mend his ways. The "Amen" was hardly spoken when Ted was ready to offer his prayer in much the same vein. Two or three prayers later, one of us offered our prayer that this event would end, and we could all go home, which is exactly what we did.

While Father certainly had his faults and shortcomings, as we sinful humans do, I have always admired the foresight and intuition Father possessed and applied to his business efforts. He had a very definite talent for recognizing a business opportunity and taking advantage of it. Coupled with hard work and determination, he became quite successful. But not only was Father successful in business, he was also successful in service to the Lord. He left an excellent example for us to follow. I don't think that I could ever completely fill those big footprints or match those long strides, but I won't go wrong trying!

Respectfully submitted in loving memory of Father,
Herb

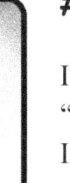

#2 Paul

I remember that Father used to say,
"If the cook's fat, the cookin's good.
If the cook's thin, the cookin' must not be too good!"

Another story I remember is when Herb and I were real young. We went down into the basement and found a wooden flat with Orange Crush soda pop in it that Dad had saved for his usage, as a special treat or to bring up when we had a party or something.

> **Father used to say,
> "If the cook's fat,
> the cookin's good.
> If the cook's thin,
> the cookin' must not
> be too good!"**

Herb and I thought, "This is great! Look at all this good stuff to drink! It was like a smorgasbord!!"

The question was how to open it? The bottles had those tight crinkled tops and you really needed a bottle opener, but we didn't want to go upstairs and maybe get caught. Well, I had just gotten a new jack knife, so we used that to pry one or two bottles open, but I wasn't too good yet at handling my new knife and the blade flipped shut and cut me real bad. I guess you could say we got caught "red-handed!"

Aunt Christel told us once that Grandma used to say: "Sis, we've worked hard today. Go down to the cellar and bring up some of that good home-made beer. We'll cool off with that."

I guess Aunt Babe liked to sit real close and lean across the table to watch whatever Grandma was doing. Once, when Grandma opened her beer, it started foaming over. She put her thumb over the top to stop it, but the pressure was too strong and it shot Babe right in the face. Aunt Babe's face was full of beer!

Apparently, Dad was carrying on his mother's tradition of keeping special beverages down in the cool cellar for treats, not to imbibe whenever, but by permission only. It was a practice passed from generation to generation.

#3 Judy

I hardly ever got to spend time alone with Father and I remember when I was about ten, Father asked me to ride downstate with him in the big semi-truck to make a delivery for the veneer mill. I was really happy that I had him all to myself and we had a good talk in the truck on the way down. He told me the story of how disappointed he was when I came out a girl instead of a boy, because Uncle Ted had three sons and Father couldn't imagine having anything but a third son. Mama Margaret had told him that one day he would be very happy to have a daughter. He told me that, as time passed, he really was happy about it! (It turned out that Uncle Ted was jealous because he didn't have a daughter.) I always loved to hear that story because it warmed my heart.

We pulled into this big company to drop off our delivery and Father had to back the trailer into the building. He was backing and backing and, all of the sudden, I heard a noise over my shoulder and looked back to see this big crease coming in behind my head. What happened was that the trailer had jack-knifed and was denting in the cab! Now Father had an embarrassing situation on his hands. He was fit to be tied and used some colorful expressions, which my memory has blanked out. He was mad!! He knew exactly who was to blame and that, when he got back, he'd have to explain that big crease in the back of the cab.

I loved it! I'd never seen him do anything wrong before and I just thought it was incredible. I thoroughly enjoyed the whole scene because, for the first time in my life, my "hero-daddy" took on human form. It was all I could do to control my laughter. The whole situation endeared him to me even more!

Ruth always calls me a "rule-follower" and, as I think about it, I feel Father instilled this into me. He used to say, "Don't be caught somewhere you shouldn't be. The roof may fall in and you'll be found in the rubble. Then people will say, 'Judy Manthei was found in the rubble of that bad place. Her poor parents are so humiliated!'"

That never left my mind. It didn't mean I didn't try to do things that were wrong. One day, my friends and I went to a "bad" movie. I was so uncomfortable. At one point, I thought I heard the roof crack! I kept praying I'd get out alive. I don't remember anything about the movie, but I was so relieved to get out of that place when the time came.

Another time, I wanted to go where "all the gang held out." It was a dance hall (condemned by Father) called "The Ponytail" in Harbor Springs. One night, not only did I go, but I picked up and took three friends. I was totally miserable the whole time. I paced from room to room, never dancing once because that was really going over the line, and I could not keep from moving through the place. I just wanted to be seen there by "the gang from school" and leave. But I brought all my friends, so I couldn't go without giving a wimpy explanation. I was so glad when the agreed-upon departure time arrived!

> **Our fathers form our earthly view of our Heavenly Father. We know His laws and when we break them, we are uncomfortable and not at peace. When we are in His precepts and principles, we are at peace in our soul.**

Our fathers form our earthly view of our Heavenly Father. We know His laws and when we break them, we are uncomfortable and not at peace. When we are in His precepts and principles, we are at peace in our soul. I like that position.

What I remember most about Father is how he always talked about the Lord to us. He quoted the Old Testament scripture verse about a father writing the Law on the child's forehead and his forearm, telling him about the Lord when you walk and talk with him, so that is what Father did with us. The Bible was in his hands a lot—when we came down the stairs for breakfast, at the supper table, in his chair at night. He talked about the Lord when we rode in the car with him and when we worked beside him. Talking about the Lord was just a plain part of his daily life.

Now, we kids got a little tired of hearing this all the time. Sometimes we closed our ears, sometimes we learned to sit at the table with our foreheads propped on our hands to hide our closed eyes while we slept. But a lot of the time, we really listened.

Father made the Bible pertinent to the times. When I look back on his training of us, I am so thankful for the God-fearing father he was. He instilled so much Biblical knowledge in us that we would have never received otherwise.

In the middle of all of it, the love he had for us was so apparent. He was truly the Greatest American Hero to me!

#4 Mark

One time, I went to Grand Rapids with Father in that Mercedes Benz. We had slick wheels on that thing and, on the way back, we got into a snowstorm and Father was trying to teach me how to drive on ice.

When we left Grand Rapids, the ground was bare, but then it started snowing and we just kept going the same speed. Pretty soon, we were passing all these guys who were slowing down, and we started seeing cars off in the ditch.

Father said, "Now, the trick of driving on ice is that you have to drive fast!" The theory was that the wind holds the car straight.

Well, we were passing and doing real good and, when we got to Boyne Falls, we pulled up behind this 4-wheel-drive Jeep outfit that was going slow. So, we went around it.

Then Father started telling me, "Now, the one thing you never want to do when you're on ice is to shift down fast." Then he said, "Here, let me show you!"

He quick-shifted down and, first thing you know, we slid sideways right into the ditch. The lesson was what not to do! So here comes this 4-wheel drive Jeep, plugging along behind us, and he stops, pulls out his rope, and pulls us back onto the road.

Here, Father had been complaining about how everyone was driving so slow! So, this guy says, "Some people just drive too fast!"

> **Father was trying to teach me how to drive on ice. He quickly shifted down and we slid sideways right into the ditch. The lesson was on what not to do!**

#5 Jim

My story about Father took place when I was a senior in high school. Father gave me that Renault R-10. Mark got one too. It was a fun little car to drive. I enjoyed it. It had a rear engine and the only problem with the car was that it had an automatic transmission. That was a miserable transmission!

I wanted to learn how to ski, so Tim and I went together and bought one season pass to share at Nubs Nob, which wasn't legal, but our names (Tim & Jim) and faces (dark hair with mustaches) were similar enough that we could get away with it. The pass only showed your face from the shoulders up, so we took turns using the pass. He'd ski one weekend and I'd ski the next weekend. It was much cheaper that way. Well, Father didn't want us to ski. He said the ski hills were where the bad people and prostitutes hung out. We looked, but we never saw one. We figured if there was a prostitute out there on the slopes, she'd freeze to death! I found out recently that Father was right. They are there, cuz I talked to Doug Kinne who operated on some of them. Father probably got that news at the coffee shop or something. So, Father said, "Don't go skiing."

Instead, Father wanted us to work. My job was to grease the equipment at the mill and do preventative maintenance. I would lube & grease all the equipment every night after school. I thought if I got all my work done at the mill, then I could take off every other Saturday to ski.

Well, each Saturday when I was getting ready to go skiing, I'd get a big lecture. "Don't go skiing."

I'd say, "I've got all the greasing done and all my work is done."

He'd still say, "Don't go. Bad people go skiing." On and on, I'd get a big chewing out all through breakfast on the evils of skiing. Anytime I went, it was against Father's blessing.

Well, this was a cold Saturday morning and when I jumped in that Renault and pushed the button into reverse, the transmission wouldn't work. I'd hit it forward…hit reverse…hit forward…hit reverse. Finally, the thing took off! It had been snowing hard all night, so we had high snowbanks in the driveway, and I hadn't taken time to scrape off the back window because I was gettin' chewed out all the way to the car. So, I'm backing out the driveway and I open the door to look out the back, and the door hits the snowbank, and HWEW, the door rips straight forward! I was driving out the driveway like mad and Father didn't see me catch the door, but I knew I was in big trouble! Deep kimchee!!

I thought, gee, now what am I going to do? I drove all the way into town with the door sticking out! I figured I'd find a place to fix that door enough so Father wouldn't notice it when I got home that night. I drove into the self-serve car wash, shut the big doors on each end to conserve heat, and started working on my car.

Well, I'm working away and about 15 minutes later, I hear a knock on the door, and here's Father, wanting change for a dollar! He needed quarters to wash his car!! He saw that car door and you know the rest of the story. It was all "downhill" after that, and not downhill skiing either!

> **The biggest thing I learned from Father is to take my calling in life seriously. I believe God has called me into the ministry of supporting missions and spreading the gospel. I work 60 hours a week at it, raising money to spread the gospel. I believe that's the real inheritance Father gave me, to win the world for Christ.**

It wasn't really that I was a rebellious kid. It was just that Father didn't want us to have any fun. The big lesson I learned from that deal was not to move unless you can see where you're going!

When I ate supper, I always sat on the left side of Father at the table, right underneath the phone. I learned two things in that position. The first was that if I didn't like my food, I could stuff it along that sliding rail on the underside of the table. The second thing I learned was to eat with the "lean factor." Anytime Father ever raised his left hand, I wasn't sure if he was going to grab the phone or hit me, so I learned to eat leaning down toward my left side in a defensive posture. That's how I gained a healthy insight into the fear of the Lord.

The biggest thing I learned from Father is to take my calling in life seriously. I believe God has called me into the ministry of supporting missions and spreading the gospel. I work 60 hours a week at it, raising money to spread the gospel. I believe that's the real inheritance Father gave me, to win the world for Christ.

#6 Ben

Father did one of those driving stories with me, too. We were on our way to Gaylord and there's a long straight stretch of road before you get to Elmira, where the road turns real sharp to go down into the little town. It was right at the start of winter, a real slushy day, and there were three of us cars driving along. We were the last car. When the first one got to that curve, it went straight ahead, right into the snowbank. Didn't turn a bit! Then the second car drove along and went in right tight beside the first guy. Father said, "Some guys just don't know how to drive in the winter!"

So, we got there and drove right tight beside the second car, with our own nose in the snowbank. Three of us, right in a row! What happened was that the slush went up around the wheels and froze and you could barely turn the wheel, just enough to get by the next guy. So here were all three of us in the snowbank, right tight in a row, in perfect condition!

> **There are three things I remember most about growing up with Father. He taught us a work ethic, he taught us a set of values, and he showed us the humor in life.**
>
> **When I think of the values he taught us, I remember Father sitting in his big chair, reading the Bible. The Bible was always there as the inspiration for a set of values, like honesty and integrity.**

There are three things I remember most about growing up with Father. He taught us a work ethic, he taught us a set of values, and he showed us the humor in life. When I think of the values he taught us,

I remember Father sitting in his big chair, reading the Bible. Well, often, he was sleeping with the Bible open. But the Bible was always there as the inspiration for a set of values, like honesty and integrity.

Father was big on the work ethic, but he also encouraged us kids to go to college. The summer after I went to Bethel, I was really burned out and wasn't sure I wanted to go back and finish college. Father said, "No problem. Let's go to work and think about it!" He went out and found two old grub hoes and we went out to some swampy ground near the railroad. Father said, "It's too wet to get equipment back in here, so we've just got to grub this swamp out. We should get it done in about a month or so." Well, we both worked real hard all day and by evening, I told Father, "You know, I've been thinking and I guess maybe I'm ready to go back to school!" Father knew exactly what he was doing!! He helped me decide right now that I needed to go back to school because I knew just what I'd be doing all fall if I stayed home!

When I think of humor, two stories come to mind.

Father used to take us out on the boat. He loved the water. He'd go out logging on Hog and Garden Islands. One time, he took us out on the Penn Yan (motorboat) to Beaver Island and, somehow or another, he was sitting on a low dock with his feet in the boat. Well, the ropes were tied loose and the boat started sliding out and there he was, with his feet in the boat and his body on the dock. All of the sudden, he fell in, so that his whole body was sagging in the water. He was straining to hang onto the dock, but he was totally soaked from his knees about to his armpits. His feet and hands were the only things out of water, and then he started laughing! He was only in 2 ½ feet of water, but he didn't know that. He could have just stood up and been up to his knees. But he was completely soaked, and you know how you can get laughing. Well, he laughed!! We were all tugging to pull him up out of the water, but we couldn't get him up. The reason he started laughing, I think, is because we probably had bean soup for supper and the bubbles were rolling up out of the water. He couldn't stop laughing! Finally, he said, "I've just got to let go." That's when he discovered the water was only 2 ½ feet deep!

The other story happened when we were building the first set of condominiums. Father was running the old Terex loader, running forward and back, forward and back. One of the electricians had a new car and he thought he'd better get it out of there because he didn't want to get it scratched up. Well, Father never saw him heading for his car to move it, so he kept backing up and all of the sudden, he felt a bump behind him. He thought it was a pile of dirt, so he hit the throttle! The big back wheel of that loader went right up on the trunk of that new car. The electrician jumped out, running and flailing his arms. He was all excited! So, Father gets out of the loader, looks at that thing and says, "Now that's a big hen to sit on that egg, isn't it!"

I remember when I was in high school, I used to like to watch Monday night NFL football. One night, I was the only guy in the living room and Father walked through just as they showed the two teams going down into their line position. The camera zoomed in for a close-up showing the handoff between the quarterback and the center. The line bends over and the quarterback reaches up to get the ball from the hike and Father says, "Ben, I don't know what you see in this. If that guy bent over like that, the only thing I'd do is kick him in the ass!" That was the extent of his appreciation of sports. He thought sports were part of the communist plot to take your mind off work and religion. Because our family was not involved in sports and extracurricular activities, we were able to have supper and devotions together as a family every night.

Father would always give us lectures. He would just be coming home from work, and I'd just be going out and he'd say, "Don't go! Now where were you going??" That was one of his favorite lines.

 **#7 Ruth**

Barely a day goes by that I don't remember some bit of wisdom from Father. He taught us continuously about life and about the Lord. What strikes me as unique in Father's approach was that, right up until he died at age 76, he maintained a child-like wonder at who God is and how He works!

I remember the first German prayer Father ever taught me when I was a toddler.

"Ich bin klein,	I am small,
Mein hertz mach rein.	My heart make clean.
Soll niemand drinn' wohnen	Let no one live there
Als Jesus allein."	But Jesus alone. Amen.

Looking back, the thing I remember most about growing up was family devotions. It didn't matter if any of us made other plans for the evening. Nobody could leave the house until devotions were over. I certainly didn't appreciate it at the time! But looking back, that's how Father taught us that God always comes first!

I think that having dinner and devotions together every day was the big thing that made our family so close. Those significant conversations around the table molded my thinking, especially on Sundays after church, when Pastor Moldstad stayed with us, and Mom served her famous Spanish Rice and Father's devotions went on for hours! The discussions got so lively that Mom had to develop a system so Father and Pastor would have to take turns talking. She handed them a spoon and the rules were: "Whoever was holding the spoon got to talk. The other person had to listen." Of course, they fought over the spoon!

Father's favorite books in the Bible were the prophets: Ezekiel, Daniel and Revelation. Devotions became very interesting when he'd read an article from that day's newspaper and then the passage in Scripture that related to that particular event. It made the Bible so alive and relevant!

Our mealtime liturgy went like this: We always prayed before eating; then we enjoyed Mom's wonderful food; then we ended with devotions, Luther's Evening Prayer, and a hymn. Father always picked one of his three favorite hymns; "The Lord's My Shepherd" or "Praise God from Whom all Blessings Flow " or "Holy, Holy, Holy." Judy told me that one Sunday they sang "Holy, Holy, Holy" in her church down in Illinois and her son, James, asked how Grandpa's song got to be in the Lutheran hymnal!

> **Looking back, the thing I remember most about growing up was family devotions. Nobody could leave the house until devotions were over. I certainly didn't appreciate it at the time! But looking back, that's how Father taught us that God always comes first!**

We always ended the time with Luther's Evening prayer. As a little girl, I used to tell Mom that the prayer was just too long and, if I tried to say the whole thing, I'd run out of breath and die! The prayer had a lot of Amens in it. When I had friends over, they'd bow their heads and then look up after every Amen. Then, we'd keep praying and they'd bow their heads again. By the last Amen, they didn't dare to look up. I felt a bit sorry for them, but I also found it to be very funny!

The prayer went like this:

> "Oh give thanks unto the Lord, for He is good,
> For His mercy endureth forever. **Amen**.
> In the name of the God the Father, Son, and Holy Ghost. **Amen**.
> We thank Thee, our heavenly Father, through Jesus Christ, Thy dear Son,
> That Thou hast graciously kept us this day from all harm and danger
> And we ask Thee that thou wouldst forgive us our sins, wherever we have done wrong,
> And graciously keep us this night,
> For into Thy hands we commend ourselves; our bodies, souls, and all things.
> Let Thy holy angel be with us, that the wicked foe may have no power over us. **Amen**.
> The Lord bless us and keep us.
> The Lord make His face to shine upon us and be gracious unto us.
> The Lord lift up his countenance upon us and give us peace. **Amen!**"

"Devotions" were a very serious thing at our house, and it was the only time I remember when laughter was not allowed. Well, you know how it is when you're not supposed to laugh. Everything is suddenly funny! Ben sat straight across from me, and he just loved to get me into trouble, so he would make faces and gestures at me, and I would hold it in as long as I could, but when suppressed laughter can no longer be contained, it's explosive! That would irk Father something terrible. "You kids are always laughing and kinching around!" he'd say. "You just can't take life seriously!" Eventually, he made me read the devotions, but then Ben would then peek over the top of the book or around the sides, and I'd explode again. I still have to be very careful not to look at Ben in a serious situation!

Something that impressed me about Father was his foresight in caring for Mom financially after he was gone through the Galster Building rental property. I also saw how he watched over his sisters. Although he was opposed to Christel's marriage and boycotted her wedding, he still gave her land to build a home and a job for her husband. When Babe had her stroke and got divorced, Father found her a little home downtown in walking distance from everything she needed. He gave property to me and Judy which enabled me to buy my home. He took good care of the women in his life!

Father was an excellent driver and I remember more of his lessons than those I learned in Drivers Ed. One time, Father was taking me back to school in Saginaw and we were cruising along peacefully when, all of the sudden, Father pulled onto the shoulder and slammed on the brakes! Immediately, a "hot" car zipped past us, did a 360 in front of us, and then kept going. Father said, "Yup, you've got to watch your rearview mirror!" He pulled back onto the road, and I thought, WHOA! When I asked how he knew what the other car was going to do, he said the guy was driving crazy and he just thought he'd better give him a little space.

Another story I remember is when Father went down to the Clothes Post to buy a new summer suit. It must have been for a family wedding. Anyway, he couldn't get over how light and flimsy the fabric felt. He told the clerk, "I'm afraid if I ever let out a 'pooh', I'll blow the back end right out of these pants!" The clerk answered, "Well, Manthei, if you've got that problem, I guess you'd better wear your handkerchief low!"

Father got such a kick out of that. Some of his favorite jokes and stories were along those lines. He always said that passing gas was "cheap entertainment" and it made him laugh harder than any expensive movie he could ever see!

One event that impacted me profoundly was Judy's wedding. For starters, Father didn't approve of the marriage because he felt that Dave valued his own fancy car more highly than he valued Judy, so Father had no desire to entrust his precious daughter into Dave's hands. Father felt so strongly about it that he offered to take Judy on a tour of Germany if she'd break it off. The wedding festivities started off with a bang the night before, when Herb nearly got arrested for throwing a cherry bomb while the groom was threatening Father with a monkey wrench. On the wedding day, the junior groomsman hid in the barn and Judy had to coax him out. During the wedding, apples fell on the heads of guests, the photographer's perch collapsed with a crash, a city-slicker groomsman got stung by a bee, and last but not least, a black cat circled the altar and crawled under Judy's dress! I decided then and there that I would never marry someone if my family didn't approve.

When I was twenty-one, I left the Lutheran Church, and that had a definite negative impact on my relationship with Father. It was one thing for his adult sons to make that choice, but his baby girl? Especially after they'd invested in three years of Lutheran high school and two years of Lutheran college and a year on a Lutheran mission field! They never expected it to backfire like that. But I think, more than anything, the folks were hurt because they felt we had rejected the faith they'd worked so diligently to teach us. The next seven years of relating to Father were stress-filled. Each Sunday when I was with them, Father challenged my choice of churches, and I didn't respond well! Finally, that last summer when he was sick, I think he came to see that I had not rejected the faith. I had simply grown in ways I would not have within that particular church. We took the time to truly listen and appreciate one other and the breach was healed, for which I am eternally grateful.

I've never met another person like Father. Dr. Preus, from Concordia Lutheran Seminary once told me, "There are only three persons your father will listen to: the Father, the Son, and the Holy Spirit!" Although that was exasperatingly true, I truly miss him. He made God so real to me! I'm very much looking forward to seeing him again in heaven, where we will all enjoy the Lord together forever!

Foster-Daughter Mary Sue

When I lived in West Virginia, we just ran the streets and, at age three, my brother burned himself while I watched. I lived a pretty rough life down there. The neighbors are the ones that must have called Welfare and my brother David to have us put into a foster home. David got in contact with Pastor Moldstad, and Pastor Moldstad got into contact with the Mantheis.

When I first came to live there, I wondered if the Man*thei's* all wore ties!

> **When I first came to live there, I wondered if the Man*thei* men all wore ties!**

Coming to their house was a totally different thing. They prayed before they ate and had devotions. That's where I learned about God. Before that, I probably never even knew there was one!

When we had devotions, if Mary didn't understand or give the right answer, Mary would get whacked in the head and everyone would laugh. I probably didn't understand too much of the devotions. You had to pay attention and I guess I didn't do that. Another time, I was doing my homework and when I didn't get it, I got whacked in the head then too. I also remember going to church one time and I slept through most of it, so the next Saturday, I had to go to bed early. I remember that!

I always had to work in the garden, which I hated, and then Ben and Ruth had to re-pick my rows.

One good thing was traveling. We went to California, to Disneyland and Knott's Berry Farm. At Mark's wedding, we went to Sturbridge Village in Massachusetts, and that was fun. I was a very good navigator, and I could see the signs before anyone else could. I remember traveling across the country to California and Mary had to sleep on the floor. Ruth and Ben got the back seat.

> **God took a father from me that I never really knew and gave me a father that I got to know well. He was a good father. I had him as a father-figure for many years and got to know what a true father was all about.**

Shortly after I came to live with the Manthei family, we got Bruno, and that was a good thing, too.

Raising me up was another good thing. If that never happened, who knows where I would be. Could be dead by now.

When Father died, I thought God should have never taken him away from me, because he already took my other dad. But God took a father from me that I never really knew and gave me a father that I got to know well. He was a good father. He was a hard man, but he meant well. I had him as a father-figure for many years, and then God took him from me, but at least I got to know what a true father was all about.

Cora

One of my best stories was when David and Lara were little and, you know how they spent weeks with us up here. This was Venetian Festival, and we were going to Charlevoix at night to watch the fireworks.

Let me back up. The Sunday before, we had gone out to dinner after church with a whole car full of people and Louise was sitting in the back seat telling Father how to drive. He finally said to her, "Louise, I know how to drive! I've driven for years. Don't say anything more. Just let me do the driving!"

Now here we were, driving down the hill into Charlevoix and I saw the red light, indicating that the bridge was about to go up, but I didn't say anything. I thought, I'm not going to be a backseat driver. Father knows how to drive, and I'll just let him do it.

Well, he slowed down and went through the light just as the gate came down on the back of the car. Then the bridge immediately started coming up! He tried to back up quick, but the gate was sitting on the trunk, so he ripped that flimsy board right off!

Across the channel, a police car was sitting, and he had watched the whole thing. As soon as the bridge came down, he crossed over and whipped around behind up, and then he came up to the window. When he looked in and saw who it was, he said, "Manthei, you rascal! Get out of here." Father knew all the cops over there.

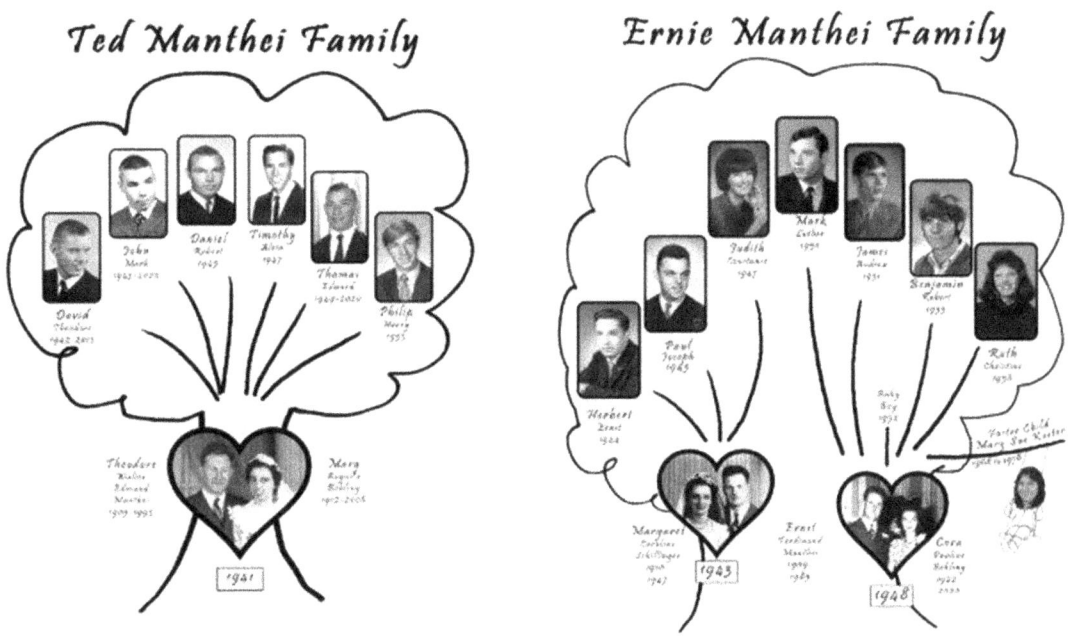

PART FIVE
Four Lives Well Lived

Ted and Mary Manthei   Ernie and Cora Manthei

Theodore Walter Edmond Manthei

Ted was born on May 2, 1905, on State Street in Petoskey, Michigan. He was baptized at Zion Lutheran Church in Petoskey. At the age of two, the family moved to a farm on Townsend Road, five miles west of Petoskey. He went to Maplewood School until the start of 8th grade, when sickness struck the family, and he was needed at home. Ted and a neighbor bought 67 acres of land on Walloon Lake and farmed together, raising oats and beans. A few years later, he and his partner John split the land. John chose the upper half, which was already cleared for farming, and Ted took the lower half by the lake.

Ted started a strawberry patch of four acres. Ernie joined him. In 1940, Mary Behling assisted in harvesting strawberries in the summer, so Ted and Mary got better acquainted and were engaged in August. Mary finished the fall semester teaching at the Lutheran School in Mount Clemens while Ted built them a home. Ted and Mary were married at Wilson Township Lutheran Church on January 25, 1941. They honeymooned in California and Mexico.

Returning to Michigan, Ted planted more berries and more beans. That fall, Ted and Ernie started a veneer mill to make berry boxes and crates. Berries were out with the war and veneer took over. Due to lung problems, Ted and Mary moved to California for the winter months while Ernie carried on with the mill. While there, Ted and Mary got into real estate and clearing land titles. They spent many winters at their home in Huntington Beach, California.

In the early '60s, Ted and Ernie acquired land near Desert Hot Springs with a clubhouse and five motel rooms. They invited Mary's sister Lorraine and Al Sonnenberg to live there and start a retreat ministry until the land was developed. In 1970, Tim Manthei finished college and began building a mobile home park. The Sonnenbergs managed the park for a few months until land was given to them for a retreat center a mile away. In 1971, Sky Valley Mobile Home Park opened and, soon after, Mary and Ted moved to the park and assisted in many ways.

Ted loved to study the Bible and witnessed to everyone he met. He loved to collect scrap iron and copper to reprocess and sell in order to give the money to missions, part of the great heart Ted always had for mission outreach. Ted passed away on May 15, 1993, of heart and kidney failure. He was buried at Greenwood Cemetery in Petoskey, Michigan.

Ted's Timeline

1905 Ted is born
1914 Ted starts trap line
1922 Ted and John work a deal with Frank X Schluttenhofer to buy 80 acres
1923 Ted & John cut 355 cord of firewood in 55 days during summer
1923 Ted and John trap by Wilderness State Park in the fall
1924 Pick rocks of land, start farming, get counsel from MSU
1925 January, Deed recorded in John K name in morning. Half to Ted in afternoon. Paid $1500
1933 June, Ted and John buy south half of farm from Frank B Schluttenhofer for $1200 with loan from John Brill
1936 Ted and John pay off mortgage
1936 Ted and John split, Ted and Ernie partner and start farming together
1937 Ted experiments with strawberries
1940 Quit claim deed from different people with interest in farm, including Constance
1940 Ted gets engaged to Mary and builds their home
1941 Ted marries Mary (1-25-41) Honeymoon in Mexico and California. Big berry crop
1941 Bought veneer lathe (Dec 11, 1941, America joins WWII)
1942 (Dave is born 2-12-42)
1943 Ted and Mary winter in CA (John is born 10-23-43)
1944 T&E start Manthei Brothers Veneer Mill in Petoskey, Tithing
1945 Ted and Mary move to Lynwood, CA 3310 Alma Street. (Dan is born 6-20-45)
1947 Ted buys 20 acres in Huntington Beach (Tim is born 9-9-47)
1948 Ernie drills oil well in Canada
1949 (Tom is born 12-3-49)
1951 T&E build Soo Veneer Mill
1953 Ted builds Kruger and Peters Redi-Mix Plant (Phil is born 2-18-53)
      Meets Japanese war pilot
1954 Ted buys 40 acre tract of land in Huntington Beach with Ernie and Browns
1955 Ted gets MI people to buy CA land
1960 Soo Veneer Mill partners buy 80 acres in Sky Valley
1961 Ted gets group of MI and CA people to invest in 50 acres
1962 Ted buys 2000 acres in N. CA after three other partners back out
1966 Ted buys out Soo Veneer Mill partners in Sky Valley 80 acres
1967 Petoskey mill burns. Sell Manthei Brothers to Manthei Inc
1970 Tim builds RV park in Sky Valley
1973 Ted starts selling CA property
1974 Ted and Mary start wintering in Sky Valley
1980 All CA property is sold

Mary Augusta Behling Manthei

I thank God every day that He placed me in a Christian family that loved the Lord.

I was born on April 12, 1912, at home on our family farm. We lived in a rural community on Behling Road in Wilson Township near Boyne City, Michigan. My parents were Harry and Gertrude Behling, both new immigrants from Germany. I was named after my grandmothers, Marie Stenke and Augusta Behling. My name is Mary Augusta Behling Manthei.

We went to a one-room country school one mile from home for eight grades. We walked unless it was too stormy. Then dad took us in the sleigh with horses or we stayed at Grandma's overnight as she lived right near the school. Later I went to Boyne City High School and graduated in 1930.

I worked as a domestic for a year before studying for one year at Charlevoix Country Normal School where I trained to be a teacher. After that I taught one year at a little one-room country school in Advance, Michigan.

I found out I liked teaching, but I wanted to teach in a Christian school, so I enrolled at Concordia Teachers College in Seward Nebraska and studied there for a year. I was then given a "call" to teach at a Lutheran school in Annandale, Minnesota. After a year in that cold country, I accepted another "call" to teach in a Lutheran school in Mount Clemens, Michigan, where it was much warmer and closer to home.

When I was twenty-nine, during summer vacation I came home and worked in the strawberry harvest on the Manthei farm near Petoskey. I had known the Manthei brothers for many years through the Walther League church group and activities, but we became better acquainted in the strawberry fields and a romance developed. I liked Ted because he was an enterprising person.

We got engaged in August. I went back to Mount Clemens that fall to teach for one more semester. Ted started building the house in October. We were married on January 25, 1941. For our honeymoon he took me to the warm climates of Texas, Mexico, and California.

After we were married, Ted and I raised strawberries during the summer and helped develop a little mill to make berry boxes that fall. We came up with the idea of the mill so we could employ more of the family. This grew into the Manthei Brothers Veneer Mill and then we added the Soo Veneer Mill. Our businesses were dedicated to the Lord, and we were blessed!

Ted and I didn't enjoy the cold winters in Michigan so we decided to go to California and see what we could develop there. We started out in Lynwood, then bought a farm in Huntington Beach. We ran a sawmill there for many years.

I was a busy mother, raising six sons and helping Ted with land investments and developments. Eventually we sold our land in Huntington Beach and helped our boys develop Sky Valley Mobile Home Park in the desert. As it grew, I spent many hours in "Grandma's Kitchen" making soup, bread, pies—also making wonderful friends!

Our children are:

David Theodore	02-12-42
John Mark	10-23-44
Daniel Robert	06-20-45
Timothy Alvin	09-07-47
Thomas Edward	12-03-49
Phillip Harry	02-18-53

Ernst Ferdinand Manthei

Ernie Manthei was born in his family home on July 10, 1909, to German immigrant parents, Ferdinand and Constance Manthei. They owned a 40-acre farm on Townsend Road, Resort Township, Emmet County, Michigan. He had two older brothers, Herbert (Herbie) and Theodore (Ted), and two younger sisters, Christel and Matilda (Babe). He was baptized as an infant and confirmed as a teenager at Zion Lutheran Church in Petoskey.

Starting at age five, Ernie attended Maplewood School in Resort Township. He spoke only German on the first day of school but soon learned English. When he was nine years old, he contracted Scarlet Fever which developed into Bright's Disease, and he nearly died. His brother Herbie was sick at the same time and did die from the disease.

It took three years for Ernie to complete 8th grade. He lost one year due to his illness and another when his teacher left mid-year. After that he worked on the family farm with his parents. In his late teens, he worked winters cutting ice for the City of Petoskey. He sold Super Maid Aluminum Cookware door to door. He also took a short course in ice cream making at Michigan State College and worked for the Freeman Dairy in Petoskey.

As a young man, Ernie farmed with his brother Ted. They raised navy beans and then strawberries. Getting enough berry boxes and crates became a problem so they bought a lathe to make their own crates, which launched them into the veneer business. They built the Manthei Brothers Veneer Mill on Ted's property at the end of Manthei Road on Walloon Lake in the early 1940s.

On January 6, 1943, Ernie married Margaret Schillinger at Immanuel Lutheran Church in Grand Rapids, Michigan. They had three children: Herb, Paul and Judy. November 1947, Margaret died after being ill for less than a week. Diagnosis was viral encephalitis, later understood to be Guillain-Barre Syndrome. Her body slowly paralyzed from the feet up until she could no longer breathe. Judy was 9 months old. Paul and Herb were 2 and 3 years old.

On July 21, 1948, Ernie married Cora Behling at St. John's Lutheran Church in Orange, CA. They honeymooned from California to Canada where Ernie drilled an oil well in Alberta, the proceeds of which would go to spreading the Gospel. Four children were born to them: Mark, Jim, Ben, and Ruth.

In 1953 Ernie built a second veneer mill in Sault Ste. Marie (Soo) Michigan. About that time, they bought the White Swan so they could harvest logs from the islands. It sank in 1956 and they replaced it with the Mackinac Islander. They sold the Soo Mill and Mackinac Islander shortly after the Petoskey mill burned in 1967. Ted and Ernie then dissolved their partnership. In retirement, Ernie helped his sons and nephews rebuild the mill as Manthei Inc. He also helped his sons launch Manthei Development Corporation in Charlevoix and build the Pine Bluff condominium complex. He enjoyed running errands for the boys and purchasing machinery. He also greatly enjoyed giving slide shows in Petoskey and Sky Valley Park. His pictures weren't the best, but the audience always loved his stories.

After the children left the nest, Ernie and Cora spent their winters in Sky Valley Park. They also visited Peru, where Ruth was serving on the mission field. He and Cora traveled to Germany and took a cruise to Alaska. In his later years, Ernie's greatest passion was reading his Bible and discussing Biblical truths with anyone who would listen. Supporting missions was always a top family priority.

Ernie went to his heavenly home on October 10, 1985, at the age of 76, just six weeks after being diagnosed with liver cancer.

Ernie's Timeline

1909   Ernie born

1912   Christel born
1919   Scarlet Fever, Herbie dies

1920   House rebuilt. Oct 13 Certificate of Naturalization
1921   Babe born
1922   Oswald dies, cement plant
1923   Chicken dinners and Northview Farm. Asters
1924   Ernie confirmed. Ernie completes 8th grade, June 15
1927   Jailbird
1928   Super Maid Cookware, Oct/Nov
1929   Chicago, couldn't find jobs, then to Oldsmobile, Lansing

1930   Trucking for Emmet County
1931   March, Ice Cream Makers Short Course at MSU in Lansing
1932   Selling Super Maid Cookware in Belding
1933   Ernie partners with Ted
1934   Ferdinand dies
1936   T&J pay off mortgage, split, T&E partnership begins
1937   Ted experiments with strawberries, winters in FL with Goebel
1938   Bad bean year
1939   Good bean year

1940   Strawberries, irrigation and water cannon
1941   Big berry crop, bought veneer lathe, raising pigs for war effort (Dec 11, 1941)
1942   Ernie meets Margaret, gets engaged
1943   Ernie marries Margaret 1-31-43   US send troops to Europe Sept '43
1944   T&E start Manthei Brothers Veneer Mill in Petoskey (Herb is born 1-22-44)
1945   (Paul is born 1-19-45) WWII ends, May in Europe (Herman), August in Pacific (Bob)
1947   (Judy is born 2-26-47) Margaret dies (Nov '47)
1948   Ernie marries Cora (7-21-48)
1948   Ernie drills oil well in Canada
1949   Back to Canada, June, oil comes in, Chester and the union

1950   (Mark is born 4-6-50)
1951   T&E build Soo Veneer Mill (Jim is born 11-17-51)
1952   Constance dies (Jan.) Broadcast to Japan. Bought White Swan
1952   Notestine is manager, Ted story
1953   Dedicate Soo Mill
1954   Don Dunkel family
1955   (Ben is born 2-25-55)
1956   White Swan sinks, (Ruth is born 12-25-56)
1957   Convert Islander, hire Dick

1961 Islander collision
1965 Judy graduates
1967 Petoskey mill burns, Sell Manthei Brothers to Manthei Inc
1968 Mackinac Islander is sold
1969 Soo Veneer Mill is sold

1970 Manthei Development Corporation
1971 Condos
1973 Stone and gravel
1974 Family Christmas in CA
1976 Start wintering in CA
1977 Mission trip to Peru
1979 Help John Shep launch Thoughts of Faith radio ministry to Ukraine

1980 Slide shows at Petoskey Rotary Club and Sky Valley Park
1981 To Alaska to find Islander/BelAir
1983 To Germany to celebrate 35th anniversary
1985 Ernie dies

Cora Behling Manthei

I am Cora Behling Manthei, #7 in the Harry Behling family lineup of twelve. I was born on October 1, 1922, in our home in Wilson Township near Boyne City, Michigan. I was baptized on October 29, 1922, by Rev. William Opitz, and my godparents were Uncle William and Aunt Gustie Stenke. On August 30, 1936, I was confirmed at Christ Lutheran Church in Wilson Township by Rev. Victor Felten.

My elementary education from Chart Class through eighth grade was at Knop School in Wilson Township, and I graduated from Boyne City High School in 1940. In high school I studied home economics and took typing and shorthand classes. Right after high school graduation, I traveled with my graduating class to the World's Fair in New York City.

After graduating I had two temporary office jobs in Boyne City, one in the office of the National Youth Administration and one at the Federal Land Bank. The next year I moved to Grand Rapids, Michigan, to live with my sister Bessie and Aunt Harriett Stone. I worked several years there at the Michigan Trust Company.

In 1944 I traveled to California with my sister Mary, her two small sons David and John, and her husband Ted Manthei. We settled in Lynwood, CA. While there I worked at Western Gear Corporation for several years as a secretary. Then I returned home to Michigan to keep house for my brothers Bob, Henry, and Ed while Mama and Papa and brother Jim took a trip to California to stay with Mary and Ted for the winter. The next fall, my brothers and I went back to Huntington Beach, CA, where Mary and Ted had moved.

That same fall of 1947, Ernie Manthei's wife Margaret passed away, and several months later he traveled with his three small children and his mother to visit Mary and Ted in California. I had known Ernie for many years, but that winter we became reacquainted and by summer we were engaged. We were married on July 21, 1948, at St. John's Lutheran Church in Orange, California. By that time Ernie and Ted were involved in drilling an oil well in Canada. Our honeymoon was spent traveling to Blackfoot, Alberta, Canada where he was working on the oil well project.

In the late fall we returned to Petoskey and I became mother to Herb, Paul and Judy. They had been in the care of Grandma Manthei all summer. Herbie was three, Paul was two and Judy was only 9 months old when their mother died.

During the following years Mark, James, Benjamin, and Ruth were born, so for many years I was a full-time wife, mother, and homemaker for our family of seven children.

In 1960 I had a complete thyroidectomy for thyroid cancer. In 2001 I had a triple-bypass surgery.

Sadly, Ernie died in 1985 of liver cancer. We had been married for thirty-seven action-packed happy years.

We bought our mobile home in Sky Valley Park, Desert Hot Springs, CA in 1977. It remains my winter home. In 1989 my son Ben and his wife Nancy took over the homestead on Townsend Road where we had raised our family and where Ernie had been born and died. At that time, I moved to Pine Bluff Estates, a condominium complex built by Manthei Development Corporation on the edge of Petoskey city limits.

Our children are:

Herbert Ernst	1-21-44
Paul Joseph	1-19-45
Judith Constance`	2-26-47
Mark Luther	4-6-50
James Andrew	11-17-51
Benjamin Robert	2-25-55
Ruth Christine	12-25-56

We were foster parents for Mary Sue Keeder Eaton for ten years between the ages of 8-18.

Written October 25, 2003

APPENDIX

Manthei Family Timeline

1800s: The German Empire

1800		Karl Püschel is born	(Dittersbach, Schlesien)
1809		Susanna (Yung) Püschel is born	(Dittersbach, Schlesien)
1845	May 8	Oswald Menzel is born	(Waldenburg, Schlesien)
1849		Christiana Püschel is born	(Dittersbach, Schlesien)
1874		Oswald marries Christiana	(Dittersbach, Schlesien)
1878	Apr 17	Ferdinand Manthei is born	(Oblatzkowo, Posen)
1884	May 21	Constance Menzel is born	(Oblatzkowo, Posen)
1890	Jul 14	Mama Christiana Menzel dies	(Oblatzkowo, Posen)
1892		Oswald remarries and moves	(Wotostwo, Posen)
1893	Dec	Fred Menzel comes to America	(Petersburg, MI)
1895	Feb	Ferdinand comes to America	(Palatine, IL)
1898		Oswald returns to homeland	(Frieburg, Schlesien)
		Walter Menzel comes to America	(Gladwin, MI)
1899	Apr 17	Ferdinand is granted Naturalization	(Joliet, IL)

1900s: Coming to America!

1900	Sep 17	Ferdinand begins working for American Bridge Co, (Chicago)
1901	Jan-Oct	Ferdinand works for American Bridge Co.
	Feb 18	Ferdinand loans Fred Menzel $150 for trip to Germany
	Mar 24	Constance boards SS Pretoria in Hamburg, Germany
	Apr 6	Constance arrives in New York City, USA
		Constance nannies for a professor in Chicago
		Ferdinand's journal, "A Declaration of Love at First Sight"
	Oct-Dec	Ferdinand works for A.I. Bragg in Petersburg, MI
1902	Jan-Nov	Ferdinand works all year for A.I. Bragg in Petersburg, MI
	Aug 8	Ferdinand and Constance wed in Petersburg, MI
1903	Jan 12	Ferdinand and Constance move to Tigerton, WI
	Feb 26	Ferdinand works for Tigerton/Badger Lumber Companies
	Summer	Ferdinand works for G.N.W. Railway Co and Schwanke
	Fall	Ferdinand works for Brockmann Lumber, Arndt Lumber
	Nov 15	Herbert Oswald (Herbie) Manthei is born
	Dec 6	Herbie is baptized
1904	Jan-Apr	Ferdinand works for Tigerton & Badger Lumber Co, Am Bridge
	Feb	Edmund Menzel comes to America (Petersburg, Petoskey)
	Apr	Oswald and Christel Menzel come to America
	Jun 4	Ferdinand withdraws savings, Tigerton, WI $253.22
	Jun 6	Ferdinand starts savings account in Petoskey, MI $253.22
	Jun 7	Ferdinand starts working for P.M. Ry, then G.R. & I. Ry
1905	May 2	Theodore (Ted) Manthei is born
	Jun 19	Ferdinand purchases the farm on Townsend Road from Fochtman
	Aug 22	Bought a white cow and a red cow
1906	Year-round	Farming!
		Ferdinand buys horse, sleigh, harness, pigs, chickens, cow
		Sells wood, oats, potatoes, corn, apples, meat, eggs, butter
1909	Jul 10	Ernst (Ernie) Manthei is born

1910s: Growin' Up in the Olden Days

1910	Aug	Ferdinand shingled the granary, bought a buggy
	Sept	Ted starts school
1912	Jun 13	Christel is born
1914		Ernie starts school
		Ted starts trap line
		Billeau barn goes up
1915		Constance becomes an entrepreneur:

- Hosting chicken dinners at Northview Farm
- Shipping asters to Chicago

First telephone and car
Sport dies

1917	Apr 6	America goes to war with the German Empire
		German-Americans are rendered "undesirable."
		Ferdinand is warned to "Stay out of town!"
1918		Herbie and Ted are confirmed at Zion Lutheran Church
1919	Jan	Scarlet Fever!
	Apr 2	Herbie dies
		Ernie nearly dies, miracle story
		Ferdinand drills for water
	Sep 28	Uncle Edmond Menzel dies, cement plant accident

1920s: Finding Our Way in the World

1920	Oct 13	Manthei family receives USA Certificate of Naturalization
	Winter	Ferdinand remodels the house
1921	Apr 27	Mathilda (Babe) Manthei is born
		Ted and Ernie start building a motor boat, first creative enterprise
		Ted works at Petoskey Portland Cement Company
1922		Ted partners with John Kopenkoskey
		Ted and John buy 80 acres from Frank X Schluttenhofer
	Aug 9	Grandpa Oswald Menzel dies downstate
1923	Summer	Ted & John cut 355 cord of firewood in 55 days
	Fall	Ted and John trap near Wilderness State Park
1924	Spring	Ted picks rocks off land
	Summer	Ted starts farming with counsel from MSU
	Sep 28	Ernie is confirmed at Zion Lutheran Church
		First family car
1925	January	Deed recorded in John K name in morning.
		(Half to Ted in afternoon. Paid $1500)
	Jun 15	Ernie receives his 8th grade diploma from Maplewood School
		Ernie's works as water boy at Petoskey Portland Cement Company
1926		The flowers fade (asters develop sickness)
		Ted pays off his farm from sale of bean crop
1927		Ted and Ernie finish building their speedboat
		Christel graduates and wins canning competition
		Ernie cuts ice in Gladwin to avoid landing in jail
1928	Oct/Nov	Ted and Ernie sell Super Maid Cookware, Ted lands in jail
1929	Winter	No jobs in Petoskey or Chicago.
		Ted and Ernie work for Oldsmobile in Lansing, MI.
		Stock Market crash!

1930s: Farming Our Own Land

1930	Winter	Constance and Ted go to a clinic in Missouri for health issues
1931	Winter	Ernie attends Michigan State College, Ice Cream Makers Course Ernie works at Freeman Dairy Christel meets Chet
1932		Ernie buys a truck and hauls gravel for Emmet County Ferdinand develops a heart disease Ernie takes over farming at the homestead
	Winter	Ernie works in Belding, MI. Christel gets engaged
1933	June	Ted and John buy south half of farm from Frank B Schluttenhofer; Ernie farms with Ted and John
1934	Spring	Ted and John pay off mortgage and split property
	Jun 13	Christel marries Chet
	Summer	Ted and Ernie partner and start farming certified seed beans
	Sep 1	Death of Ferdinand, age 56, from chronic myocarditis
1936		First indoor bathroom
	Winter	Ted and Ernie pick oranges in Florida
1937		Ted takes Bible seriously and teaches Ernie in the fields Ted sees future office in a dream Ted experiments with strawberries Ted and Ernie buy a Maytag washing machine for Constance Ernie gives Christel land to build a home Ted experiments with strawberries, winters in FL with Goebel
1938		Dave Fero helps Ernie on the farm Bad bean year! Electricity comes to Resort Twp, radio story Hitler invasions begin in Europe
1939		Big bean year! Dave Fero leaves in August Ernie researches irrigation with Michigan Dept of Agriculture

1940s: From Agriculture to Industry

1940		Babe marries Bob Notestine
		Ted get quit claim deed from investors in his farm, including Constance
		Ted and Ernie develop irrigation system with oil lines and boiler flues
		Big berry year! Water cannon
		Ted and Mary get engaged
	Sep	Manthei Brothers buy a "crate factory"
	Fall	Ted builds home on edge of strawberry field
1941	Jan 25	Ted and Mary get married, honeymoon in Mexico California Canada
		Failed attempts at building crates
		Herb Trier moves to Petoskey, helps with berries and crates
	Dec 7	Americans join WWII after bombing of Pearl Harbor, Dave Fero drafted
1942	Feb 12	Dave born to Ted and Mary
	Summer	Ernie meets Margaret
	Fall	Ernie and Margaret get engaged
1943	Jan 31	Ernie marries Margaret in Grand Rapids, MI. No honeymoon (WWII)
	Oct 23	John born to Ted and Mary
1944	Jan 22	Herb is born to Ernie and Margaret
		Malachi 3:10 Tithing dispute
1945	Jan 19	Paul is born to Ernie and Margaret
	March	Ted starts wintering in CA, builds home at 3310 Alma St, Lynwood
		Manthei Bros Veneer Mill is launched! (Lloyd Dorenberg)
	May 8	WWII ends in Europe
	Jun 20	Dan is born to Ted and Mary
	Summer	Manthei Bros ship berries to Mackinaw Island for Governor's Convention
	Sep 2	WWII ends in Japan
1947	Feb 26	Judy is born to Ernie and Margaret
		Veneer mill turns a profit! Shingles go up, Ted's dream fulfilled
	Sep 9	Tim is born to Ted and Mary
	Nov	Ted buys 20 acres in Huntington Beach, CA
	Nov 27	Margaret dies at age 37, leaving behind Ernie, Herb, Paul, and Jud
1948	Summer	Ernie begins oil venture in Blackfoot, Alberta
	Jul 21	Ernie marries Cora Behling in Orange, CA
		Problems with union, Al Behling hired to run the veneer mill
1949	June	Ernie returns to Canada, oil comes in! Problem with Chester
	Dec 3	Tom is born to Ted and Mary

1950s: Growing Families and Enterprises

1950	Apr 6	Mark is born to Ernie and Cora
1951		Ted and Ernie begin to build the Soo Veneer Mill
	Nov 17	Jim is born to Ernie and Cora
1952	Jan 15	Constance dies
		First broadcast to Japan
	Oct 28	Stillborn baby Peter is born to Cora and Ernie
		Purchased White Swan freighter to haul logs
1953	Feb 18	Phil is born to Ted and Mary
	Aug 2	Dedicate Soo Veneer Mill
		Ted builds Krueger & Peters Ready Mix
1954		Ernie sponsors Dunkel family from Canada to work at the mill
		Ted finds investors to buy 40-acre tract of land in Huntington Beach
1955	Feb 25	Ben is born to Ernie and Cora
		Ted finds MI investors to buy more CA land
		Chet Cone graduates as Reverend
		Babe has a stroke
1956	Nov 28	White Swan sinks
	Dec 25	Ruth is born to Ernie and Cora
1957		Ernie sponsors Wally Dunkel from Canada
		Ernie buys and converts the Mackinac Islander, hires Dick Lyons

1960s: Land, Logging and Loss

1960   Soo Veneer Mill partners buy 80 acres in Sky Valley

1961   Ted gets group of MI and CA people to invest in 50 acres in Sky Valley
               Ernie buys and renovates the Galster Building in Petoskey
               Mackinac Islander collision with a Greek ship

1962   Communist scare and Dallas Roquemore
               Ted buys 2000 acres in Cohasset, CA after three other partners back out

1966   Ernie starts logging on Hog Island
               Ted buys out Soo Veneer Mill partners in Sky Valley 80 acres

1967   Veneer mill burns in September
               Manthei Brothers partnership is dissolved

1968   Ted and Ernie help sons rebuild the veneer mill as Manthei Inc.
               Mackinac Islander is sold to King Crab Corporation

1969   Soo Veneer Mill is sold
               Ernie and Cora acquire foster children, Jack and Mary Sue

1970s: Retirement Projects

1970   Ted's son, Tim begins building RV park in Sky Valley, CA
              Ernie helps sons launch Manthei Development Corporation

1971   Ernie and sons build Pine Bluff Condominiums

1973   Ernie and sons crush stone and gravel on Charlevoix property
              Ted starts selling CA properties

1974   Ted and Mary start wintering in Sky Valley, joint family Christmas in Sky Valley

1976   Ernie and Cora start wintering in Sky Valley

1977   Ernie and Cora visit Ruth in Peru, family conflicts with the Lutheran church

1979   Ernie helps John Shep launch radio ministry into Ukraine

1980s: The Last Days

1980		All CA properties are sold except Sky Valley
		Ernie begins slideshow presentations at Sky Valley and Rotary Clubs
	Oct 8	Babe dies
1981		Ernie and Cora visit Alaska to track down the Mackinac Islander
1983		Ernie and Cora celebrate 35th anniversary with a trip to Germany
1985	Oct 11	Ernie dies

1990s: Ted's Journey Home to Heaven

1993		Ted's talks to an angel
	May 25	Ted dies

THREE GENERATIONS

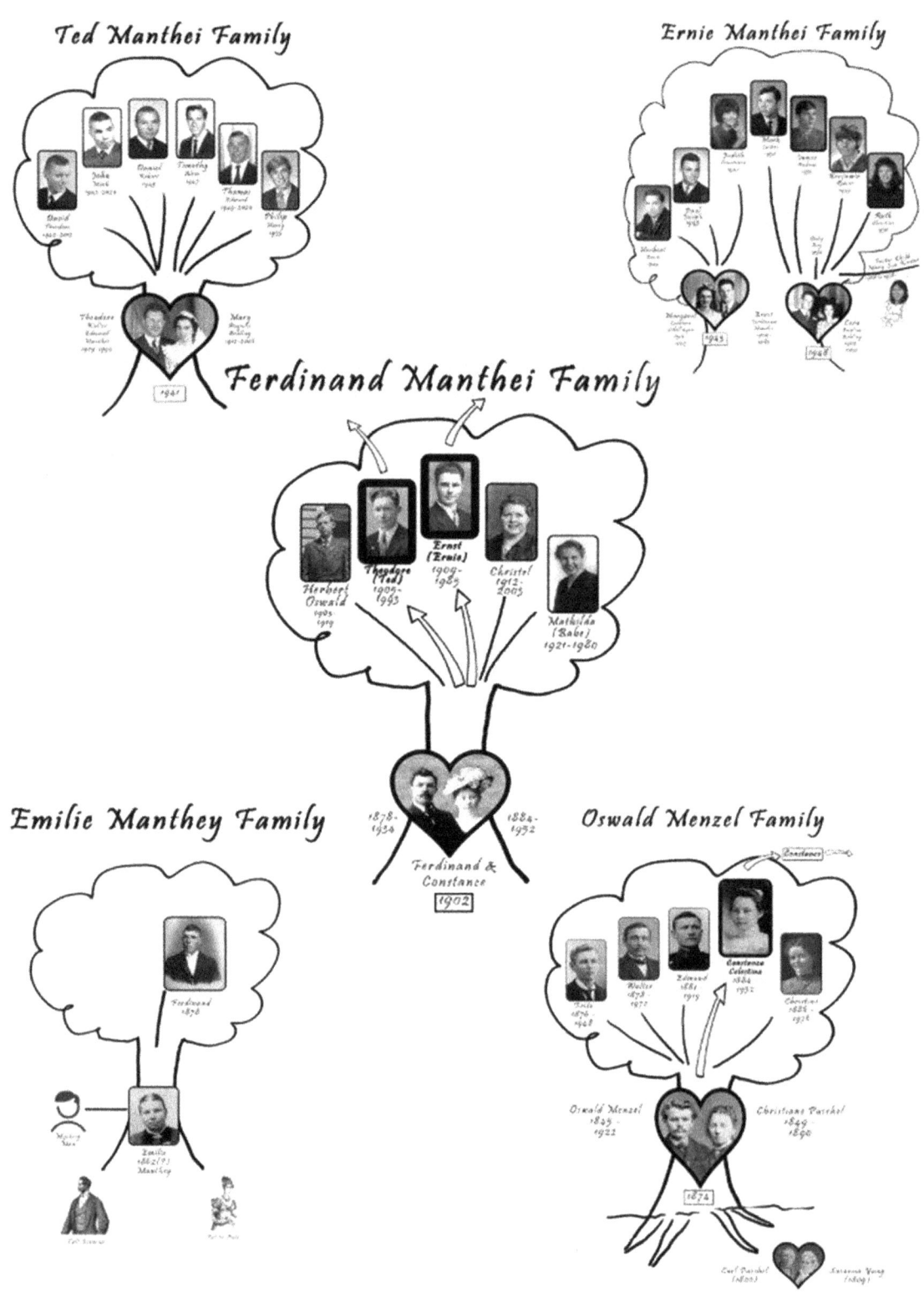

The Lord has been good. He has been faithful to all generations.

The Immigrants: Ferdinand Manthei & Constance Menzel

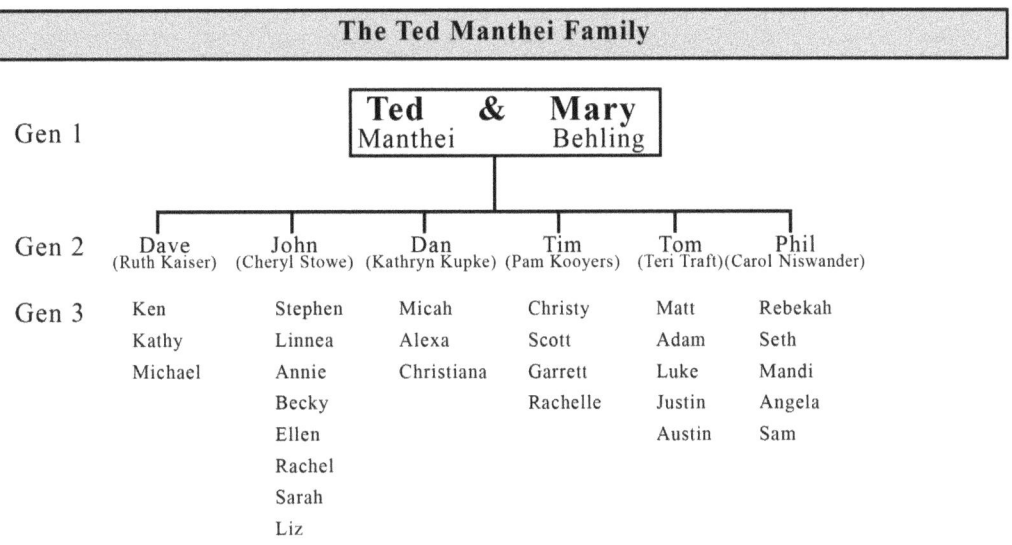

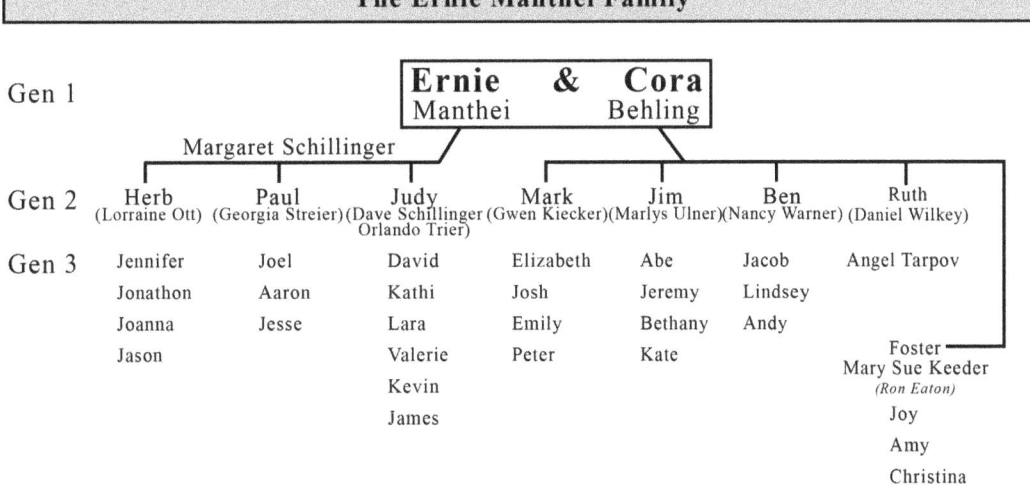

AUTHOR'S FAREWELL

"Thus I will end the story here. If I have written well and made my point in the narrative, this is what I myself desired. But if it was done poorly and is just average, this is the best I could do. This then shall be the end."
2 Maccabees 15:38, 39

Joyfully,

Ruth Manthei Wilkey

www.ingramcontent.com/pod-product-compliance
Lightning Source LLC
Chambersburg PA
CBHW042351070526
44585CB00028B/2889